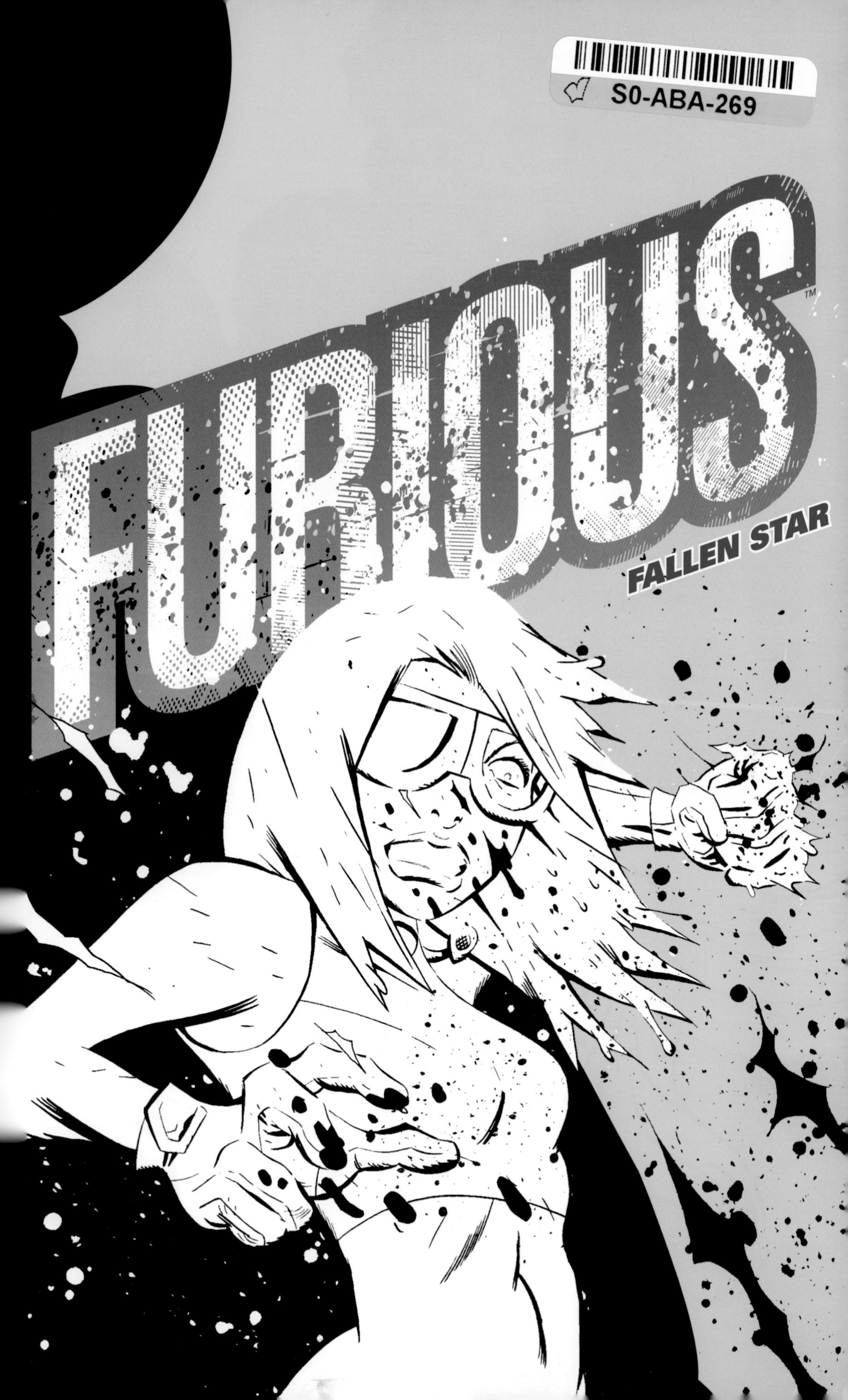
FURIOUS™
FALLEN STAR

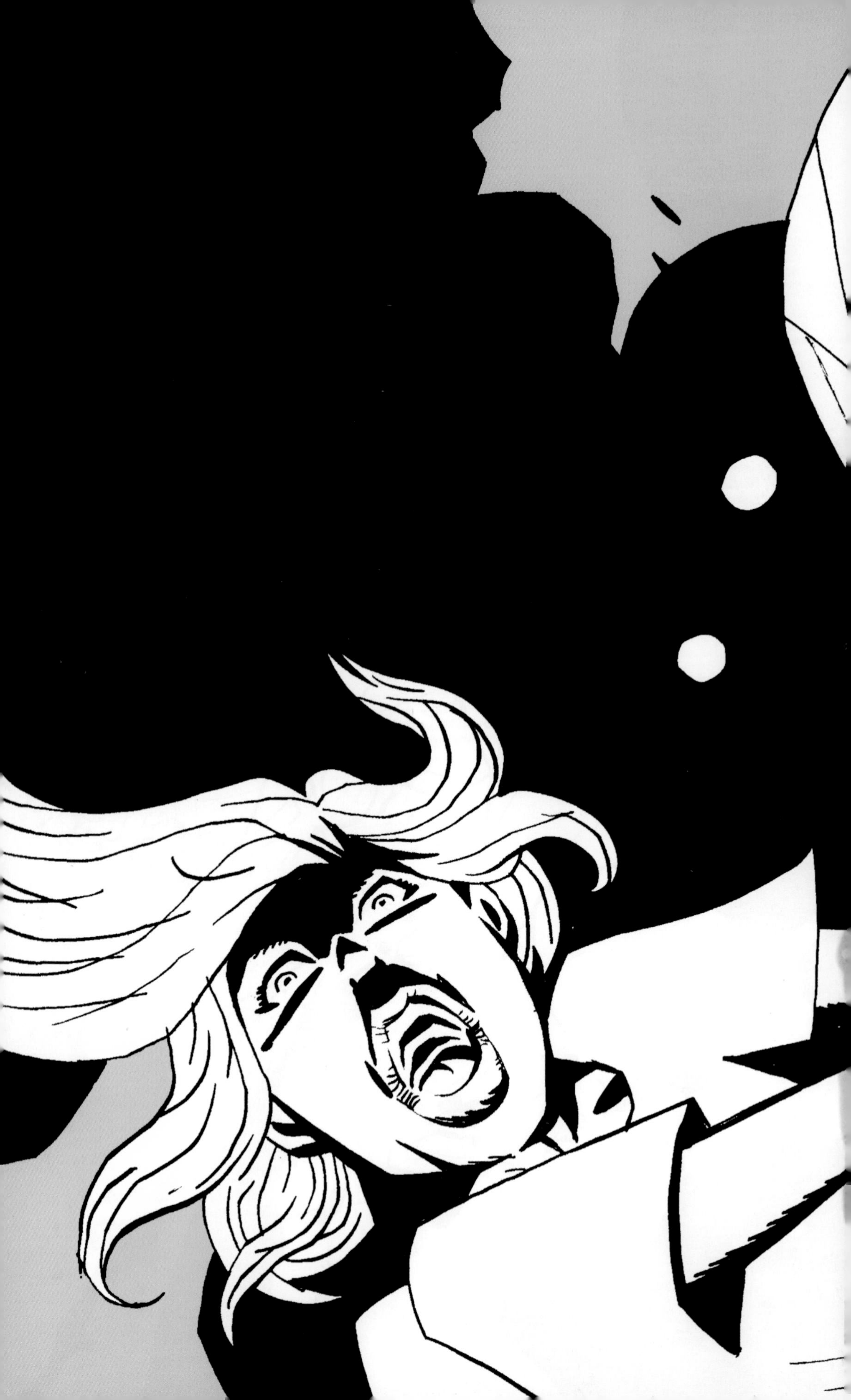

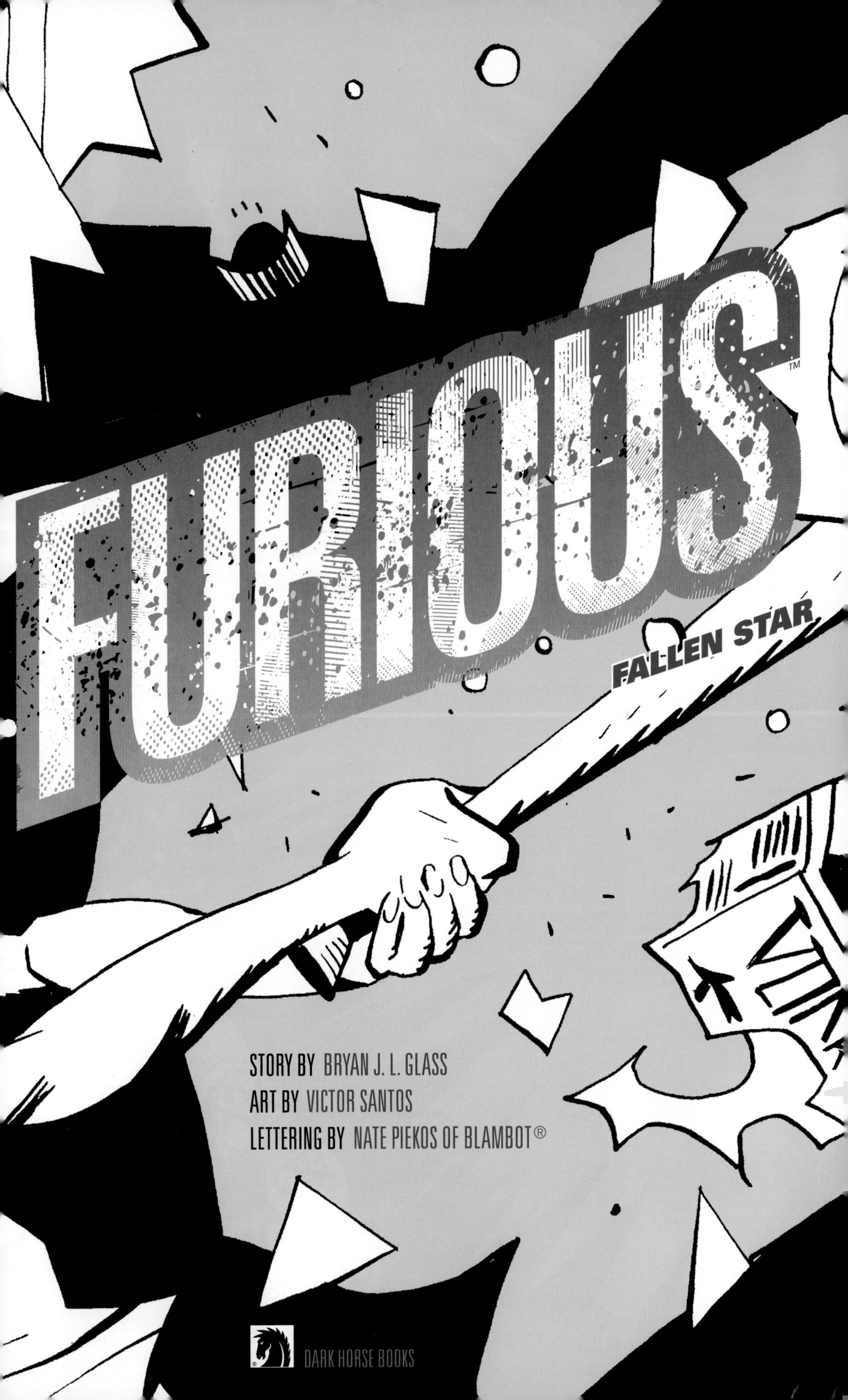

FURIOUS™

FALLEN STAR

STORY BY BRYAN J. L. GLASS

ART BY VICTOR SANTOS

LETTERING BY NATE PIEKOS OF BLAMBOT®

DARK HORSE BOOKS

PRESIDENT & PUBLISHER MIKE RICHARDSON

EDITOR JIM GIBBONS

ASSISTANT EDITOR SPENCER CUSHING

DIGITAL PRODUCTION CHRISTINA McKENZIE

COLLECTION DESIGNER DAVID NESTELLE

Special thanks to Mark Waid, Tim Seeley, Nathan Edmondson, Michael Avon Oeming, Mark Buckingham, and Adam Hughes.

Neil Hankerson Executive Vice President • Tom Weddle Chief Financial Officer • Randy Stradley Vice President of Publishing • Michael Martens Vice President of Book Trade Sales • Anita Nelson Vice President of Business Affairs • Scott Allie Editor in Chief • Matt Parkinson Vice President of Marketing • David Scroggy Vice President of Product Development • Dale LaFountain Vice President of Information Technology • Darlene Vogel Senior Director of Print, Design, and Production • Ken Lizzi General Counsel • Davey Estrada Editorial Director • Chris Warner Senior Books Editor • Diana Schutz Executive Editor • Cary Grazzini Director of Print and Development • Lia Ribacchi Art Director • Cara Niece Director of Scheduling • Tim Wiesch Director of International Licensing • Mark Bernardi Director of Digital Publishing

Published by Dark Horse Books
A division of Dark Horse Comics, Inc.
10956 SE Main Street
Milwaukie, OR 97222

First edition: September 2014
ISBN 978-1-61655-468-2

10 9 8 7 6 5 4 3 2 1
Printed in China

International Licensing: (503) 905-2377
Comic Shop Locator Service: (888) 266-4226

This volume collects the comic book series Furious #1–#5 and the Dark Horse Presents story "Role Model," all from Dark Horse Comics.

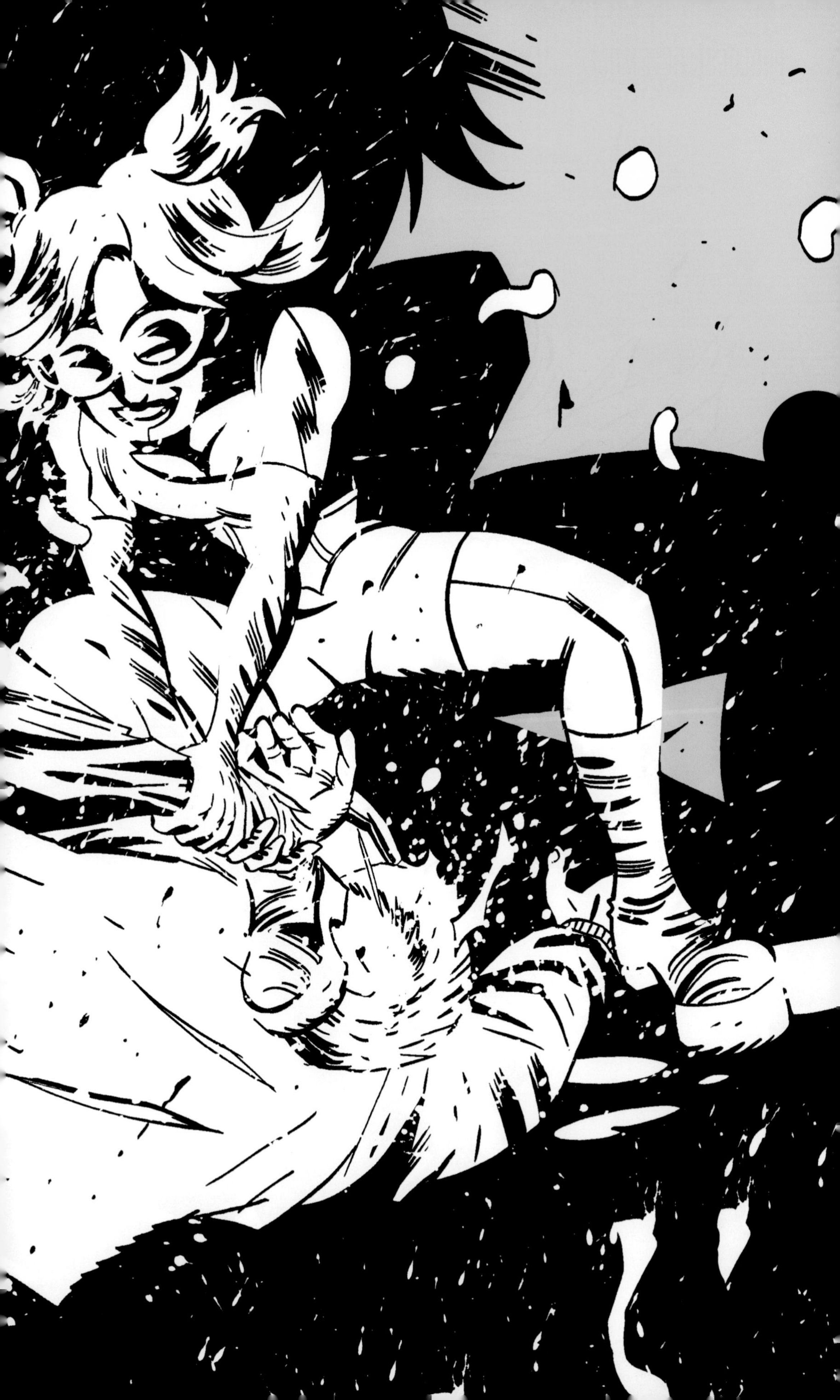

PROLOGUE: ROLE MODEL

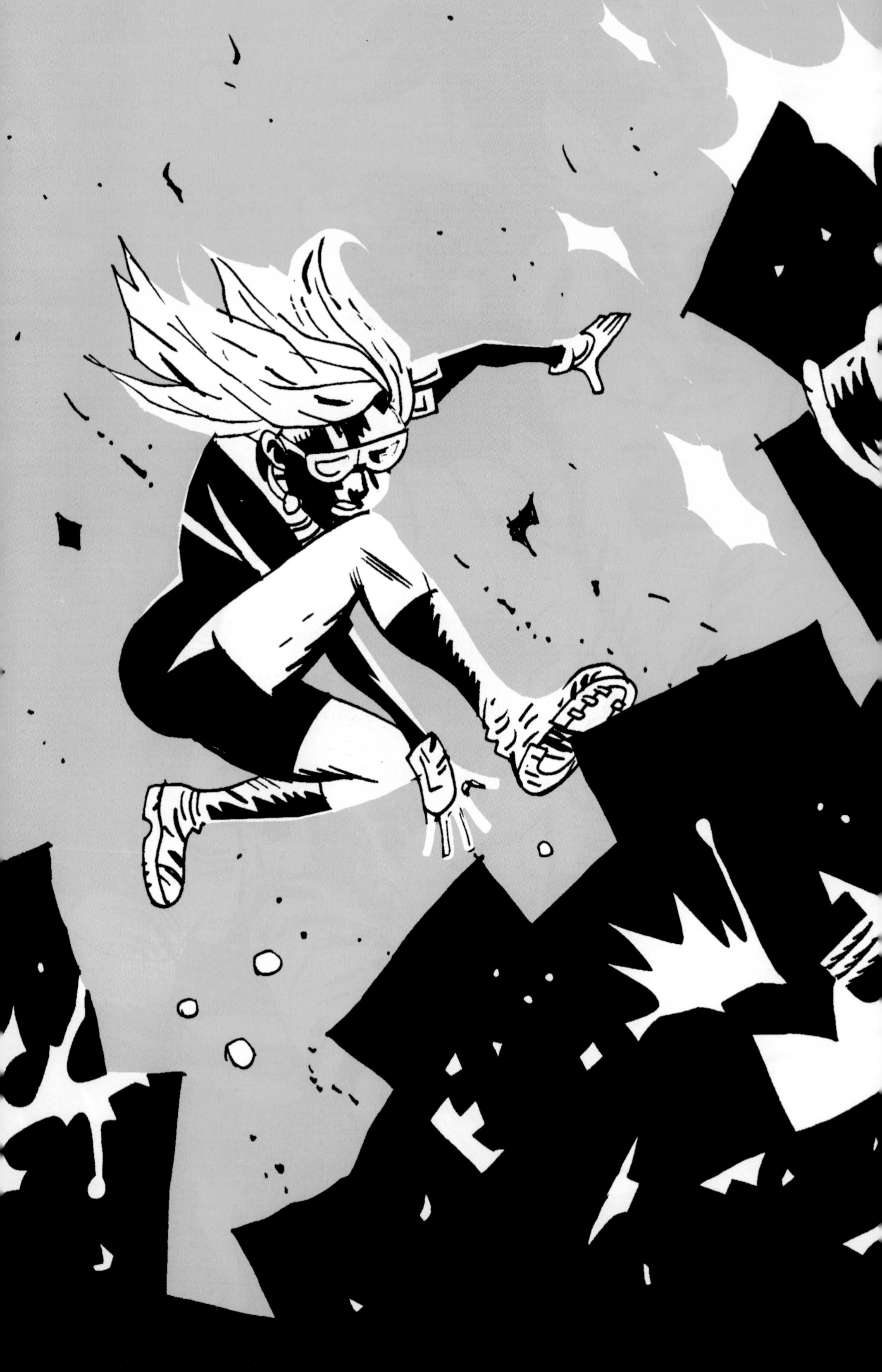

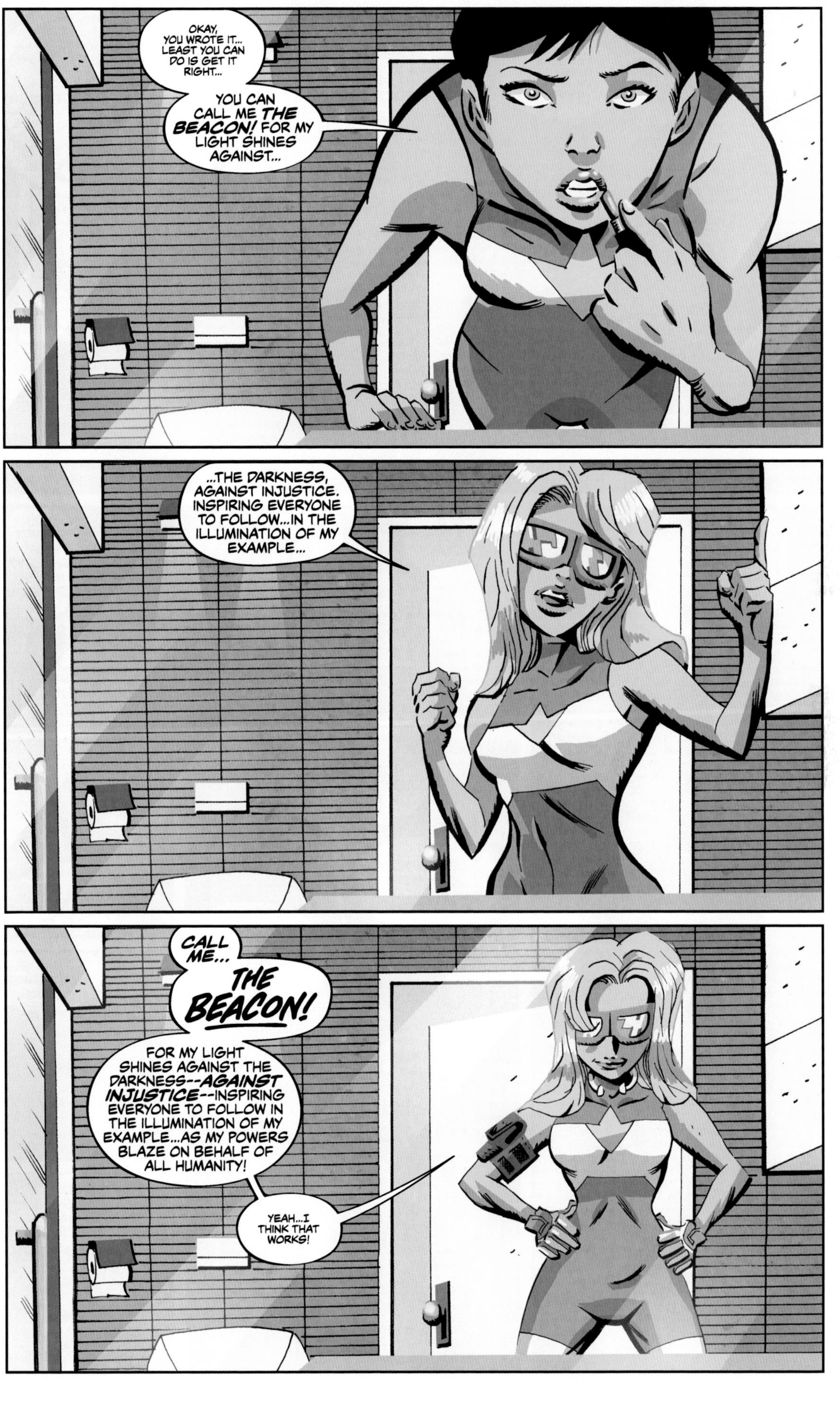

OKAY, YOU WROTE IT... LEAST YOU CAN DO IS GET IT RIGHT...
YOU CAN CALL ME THE BEACON! FOR MY LIGHT SHINES AGAINST...
...THE DARKNESS, AGAINST INJUSTICE. INSPIRING EVERYONE TO FOLLOW...IN THE ILLUMINATION OF MY EXAMPLE...
CALL ME...
THE BEACON!
FOR MY LIGHT SHINES AGAINST THE DARKNESS--AGAINST INJUSTICE--INSPIRING EVERYONE TO FOLLOW IN THE ILLUMINATION OF MY EXAMPLE...AS MY POWERS BLAZE ON BEHALF OF ALL HUMANITY!
YEAH...I THINK THAT WORKS!

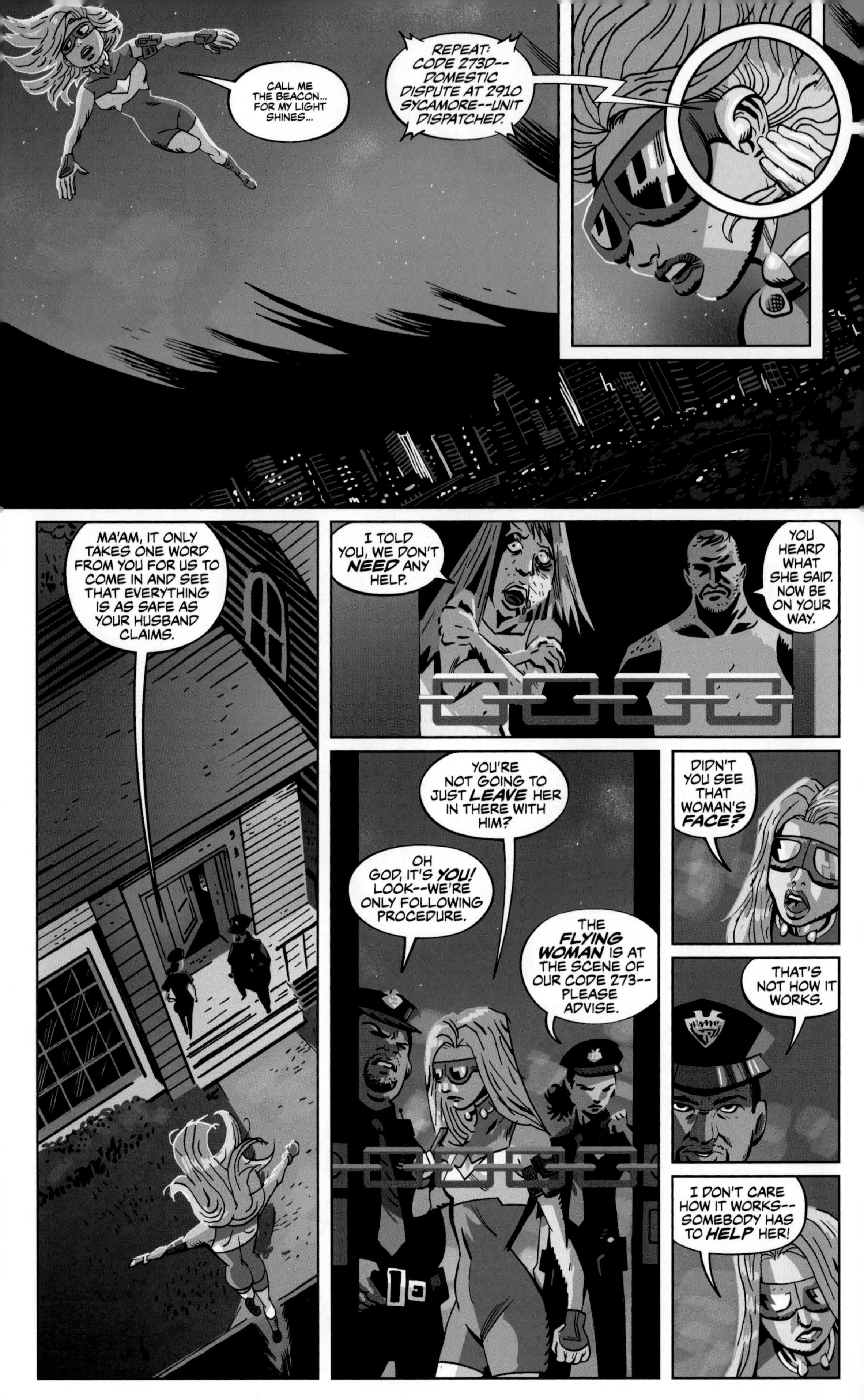
CALL ME THE BEACON... FOR MY LIGHT SHINES...
REPEAT: CODE 273D--DOMESTIC DISPUTE AT 2910 SYCAMORE--UNIT DISPATCHED.
MA'AM, IT ONLY TAKES ONE WORD FROM YOU FOR US TO COME IN AND SEE THAT EVERYTHING IS AS SAFE AS YOUR HUSBAND CLAIMS.
I TOLD YOU, WE DON'T NEED ANY HELP.
YOU HEARD WHAT SHE SAID. NOW BE ON YOUR WAY.
YOU'RE NOT GOING TO JUST LEAVE HER IN THERE WITH HIM?
OH GOD, IT'S YOU! LOOK--WE'RE ONLY FOLLOWING PROCEDURE.
THE FLYING WOMAN IS AT THE SCENE OF OUR CODE 273--PLEASE ADVISE.
DIDN'T YOU SEE THAT WOMAN'S FACE?
THAT'S NOT HOW IT WORKS.
I DON'T CARE HOW IT WORKS--SOMEBODY HAS TO HELP HER!

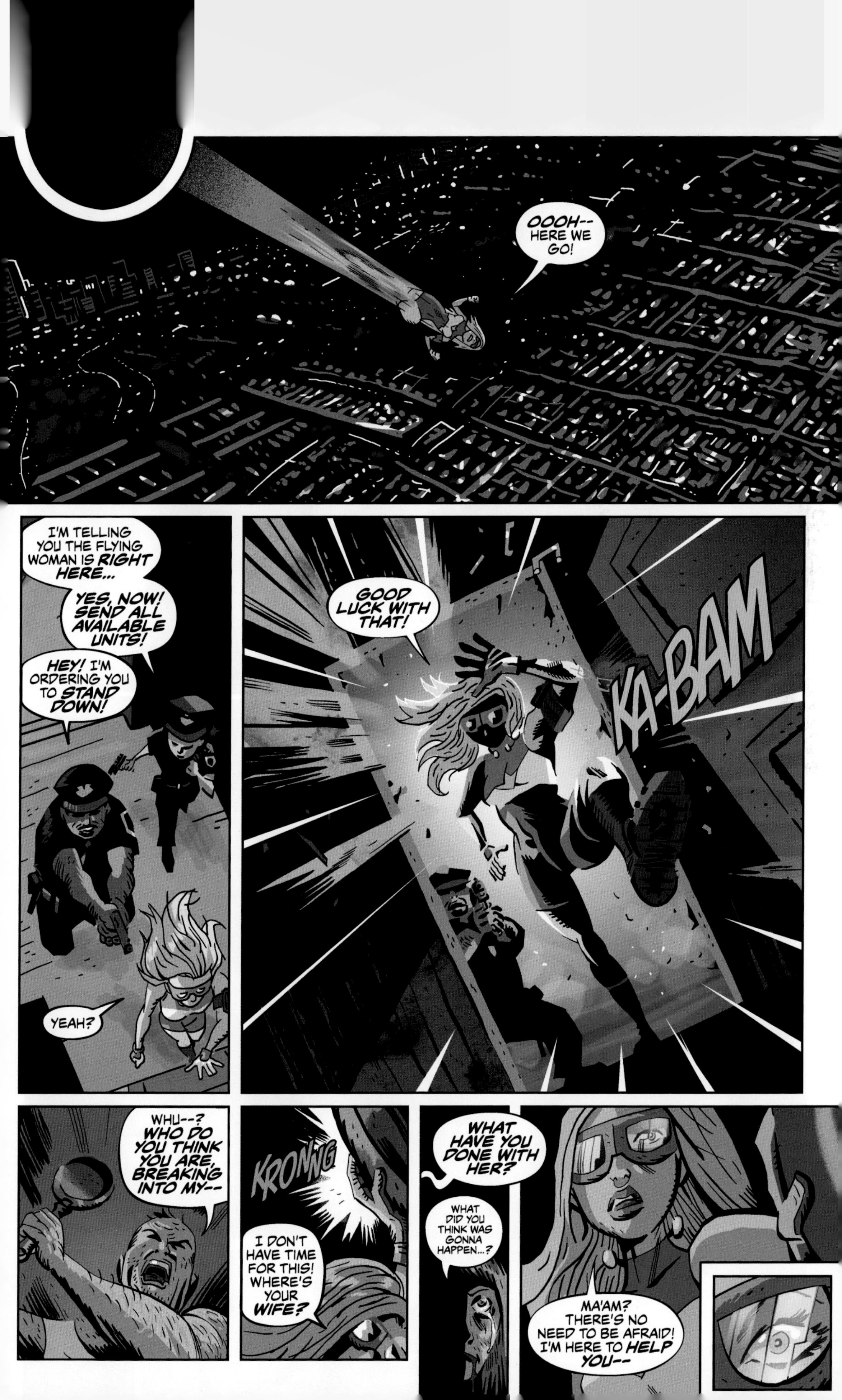

OOOH-- HERE WE GO!
I'M TELLING YOU THE FLYING WOMAN IS RIGHT HERE...
YES, NOW! SEND ALL AVAILABLE UNITS!
HEY! I'M ORDERING YOU TO STAND DOWN!
YEAH?
GOOD LUCK WITH THAT!
KA-BAM
WHU--? WHO DO YOU THINK YOU ARE, BREAKING INTO MY--
KRONNG
I DON'T HAVE TIME FOR THIS! WHERE'S YOUR WIFE?
WHAT HAVE YOU DONE WITH HER?
WHAT DID YOU THINK WAS GONNA HAPPEN...?
MA'AM? THERE'S NO NEED TO BE AFRAID! I'M HERE TO HELP YOU--

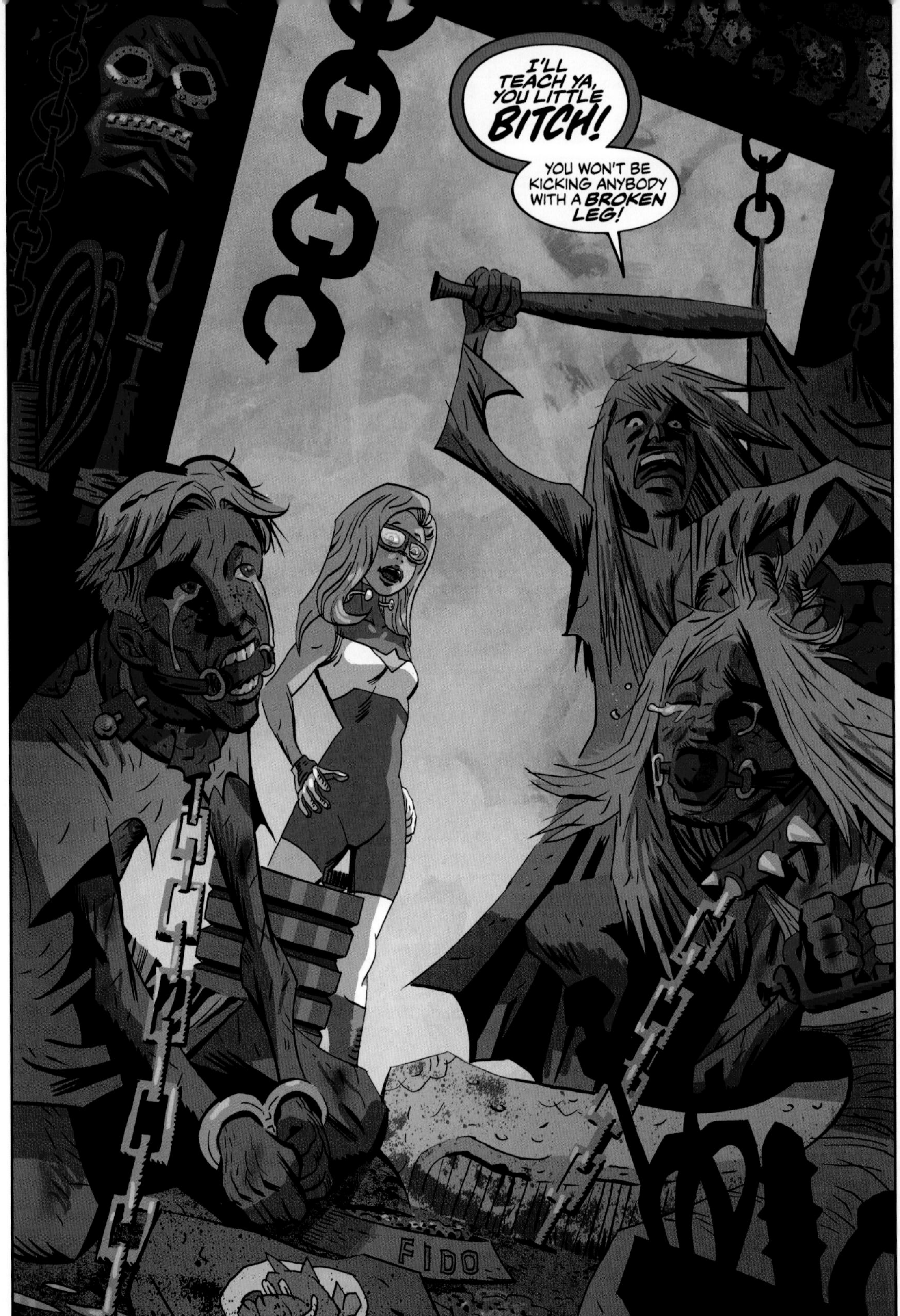
I'LL TEACH YA, YOU LITTLE BITCH!
YOU WON'T BE KICKING ANYBODY WITH A BROKEN LEG!
FIDO

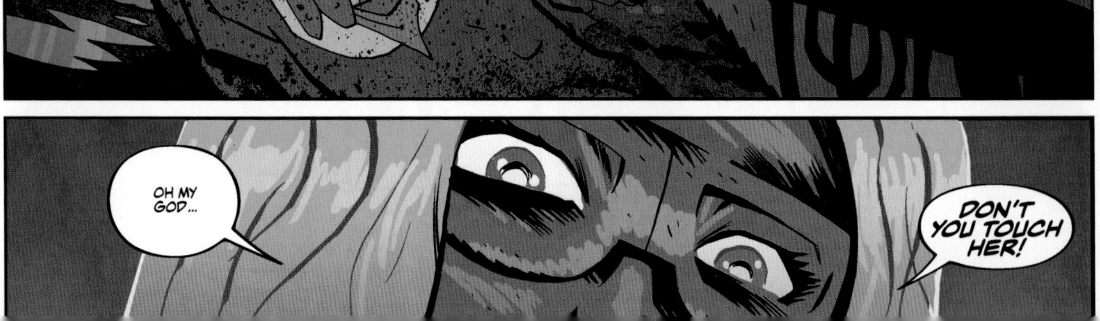
OH MY GOD...
DON'T YOU TOUCH HER!

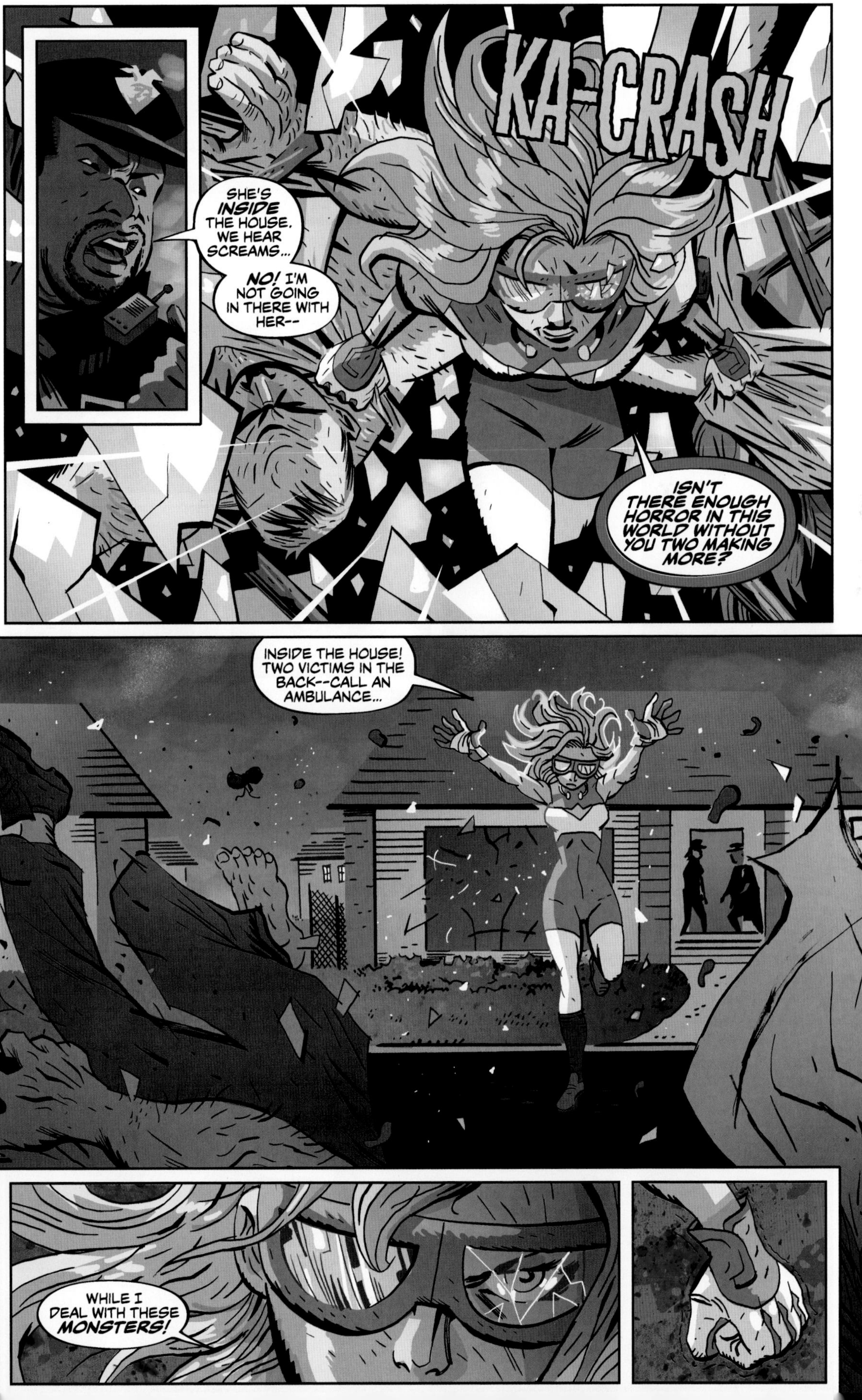
KA-CRASH
SHE'S INSIDE THE HOUSE. WE HEAR SCREAMS...
NO! I'M NOT GOING IN THERE WITH HER--
ISN'T THERE ENOUGH HORROR IN THIS WORLD WITHOUT YOU TWO MAKING MORE?
INSIDE THE HOUSE! TWO VICTIMS IN THE BACK--CALL AN AMBULANCE...
WHILE I DEAL WITH THESE MONSTERS!

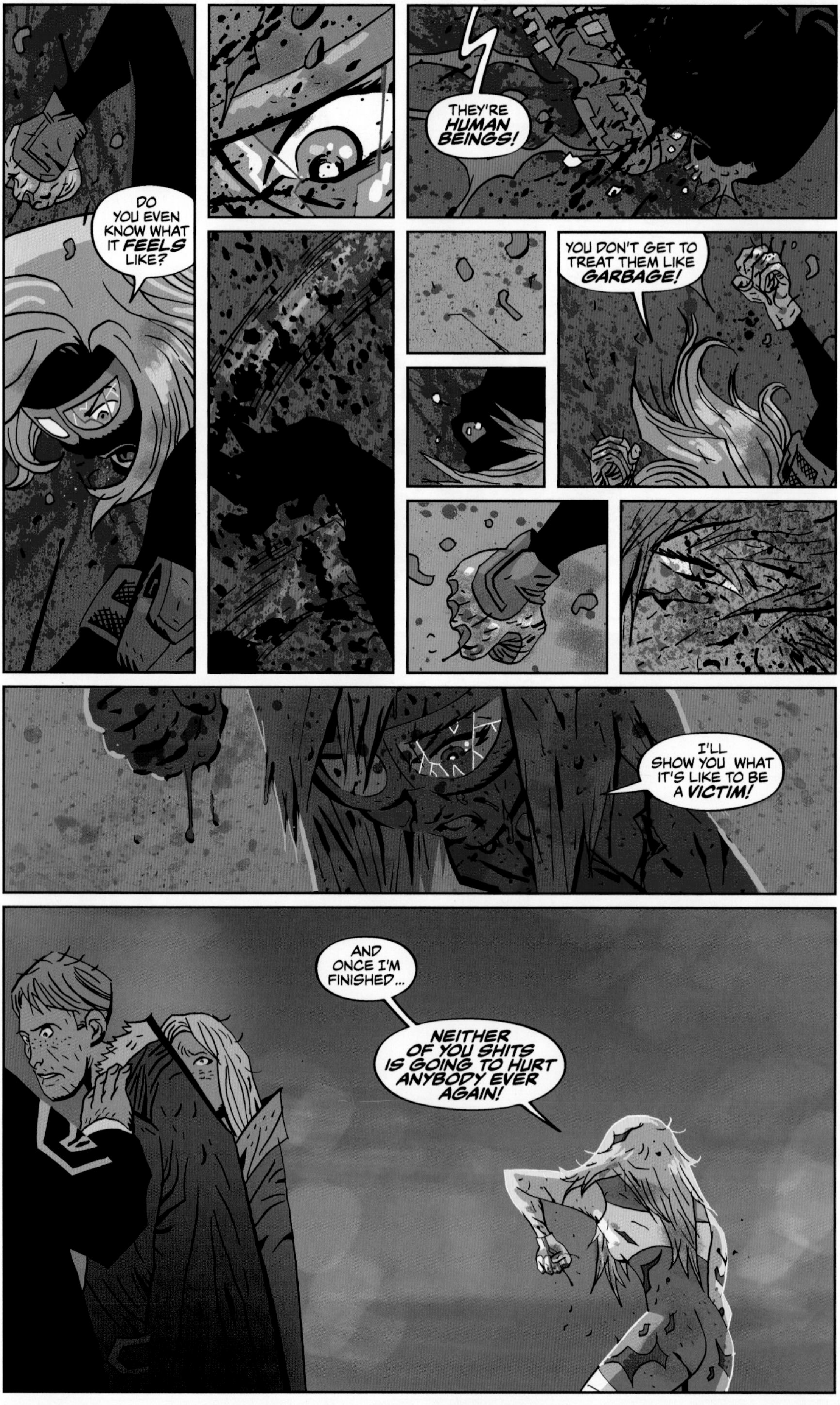
DO YOU EVEN KNOW WHAT IT **FEELS** LIKE?
THEY'RE **HUMAN BEINGS!**
YOU DON'T GET TO TREAT THEM LIKE **GARBAGE!**
I'LL SHOW YOU WHAT IT'S LIKE TO BE A **VICTIM!**
AND ONCE I'M FINISHED...
NEITHER OF YOU SHITS IS GOING TO HURT ANYBODY EVER AGAIN!

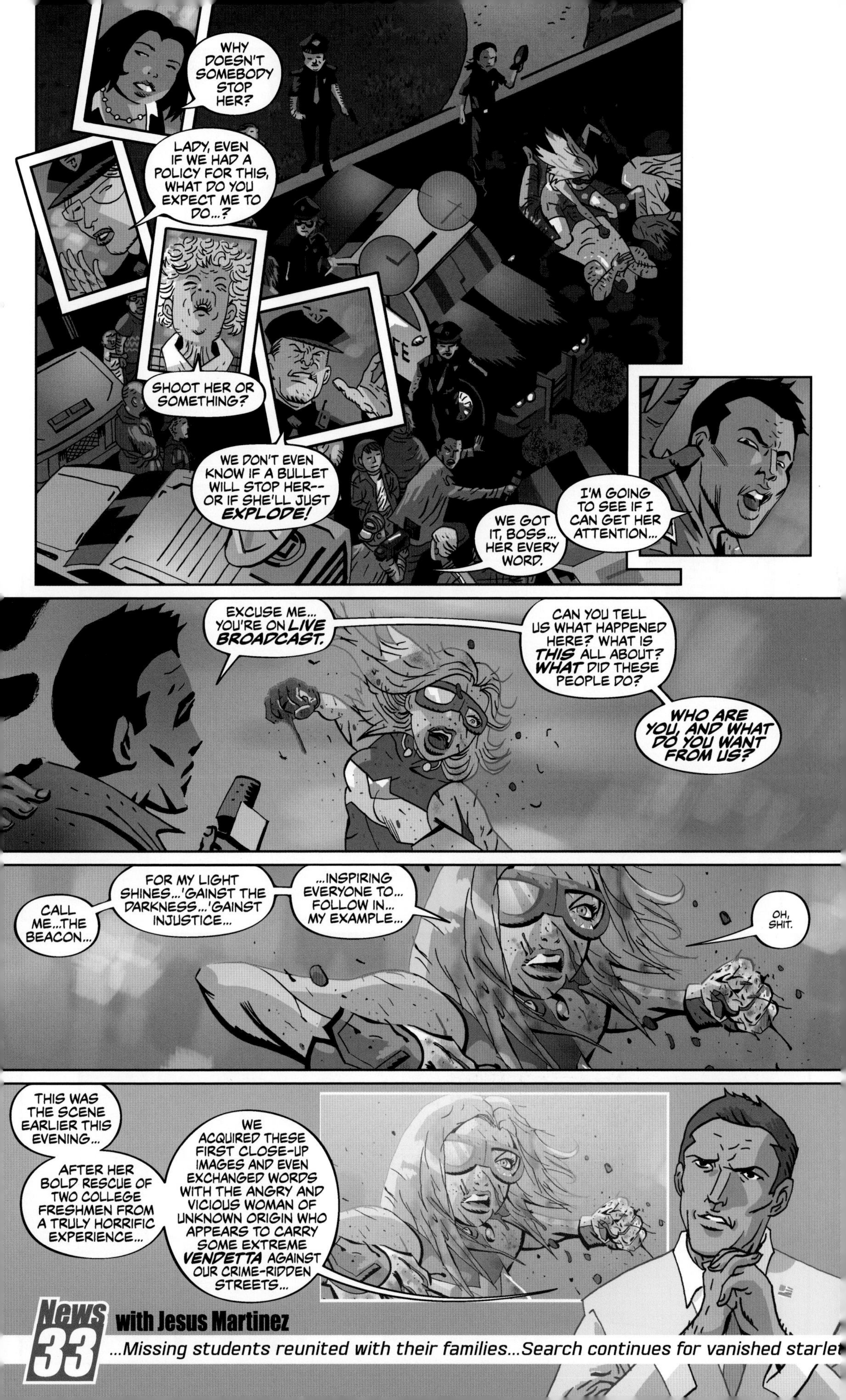

WHY DOESN'T SOMEBODY STOP HER?
LADY, EVEN IF WE HAD A POLICY FOR THIS, WHAT DO YOU EXPECT ME TO DO...?
SHOOT HER OR SOMETHING?
WE DON'T EVEN KNOW IF A BULLET WILL STOP HER--OR IF SHE'LL JUST EXPLODE!
WE GOT IT, BOSS... HER EVERY WORD.
I'M GOING TO SEE IF I CAN GET HER ATTENTION...
EXCUSE ME... YOU'RE ON LIVE BROADCAST.
CAN YOU TELL US WHAT HAPPENED HERE? WHAT IS THIS ALL ABOUT? WHAT DID THESE PEOPLE DO?
WHO ARE YOU, AND WHAT DO YOU WANT FROM US?
CALL ME...THE BEACON...
FOR MY LIGHT SHINES...'GAINST THE DARKNESS...'GAINST INJUSTICE...
...INSPIRING EVERYONE TO... FOLLOW IN... MY EXAMPLE...
OH, SHIT.
THIS WAS THE SCENE EARLIER THIS EVENING...
AFTER HER BOLD RESCUE OF TWO COLLEGE FRESHMEN FROM A TRULY HORRIFIC EXPERIENCE...
WE ACQUIRED THESE FIRST CLOSE-UP IMAGES AND EVEN EXCHANGED WORDS WITH THE ANGRY AND VICIOUS WOMAN OF UNKNOWN ORIGIN WHO APPEARS TO CARRY SOME EXTREME VENDETTA AGAINST OUR CRIME-RIDDEN STREETS...
News 33 with Jesus Martinez
...Missing students reunited with their families...Search continues for vanished starlet

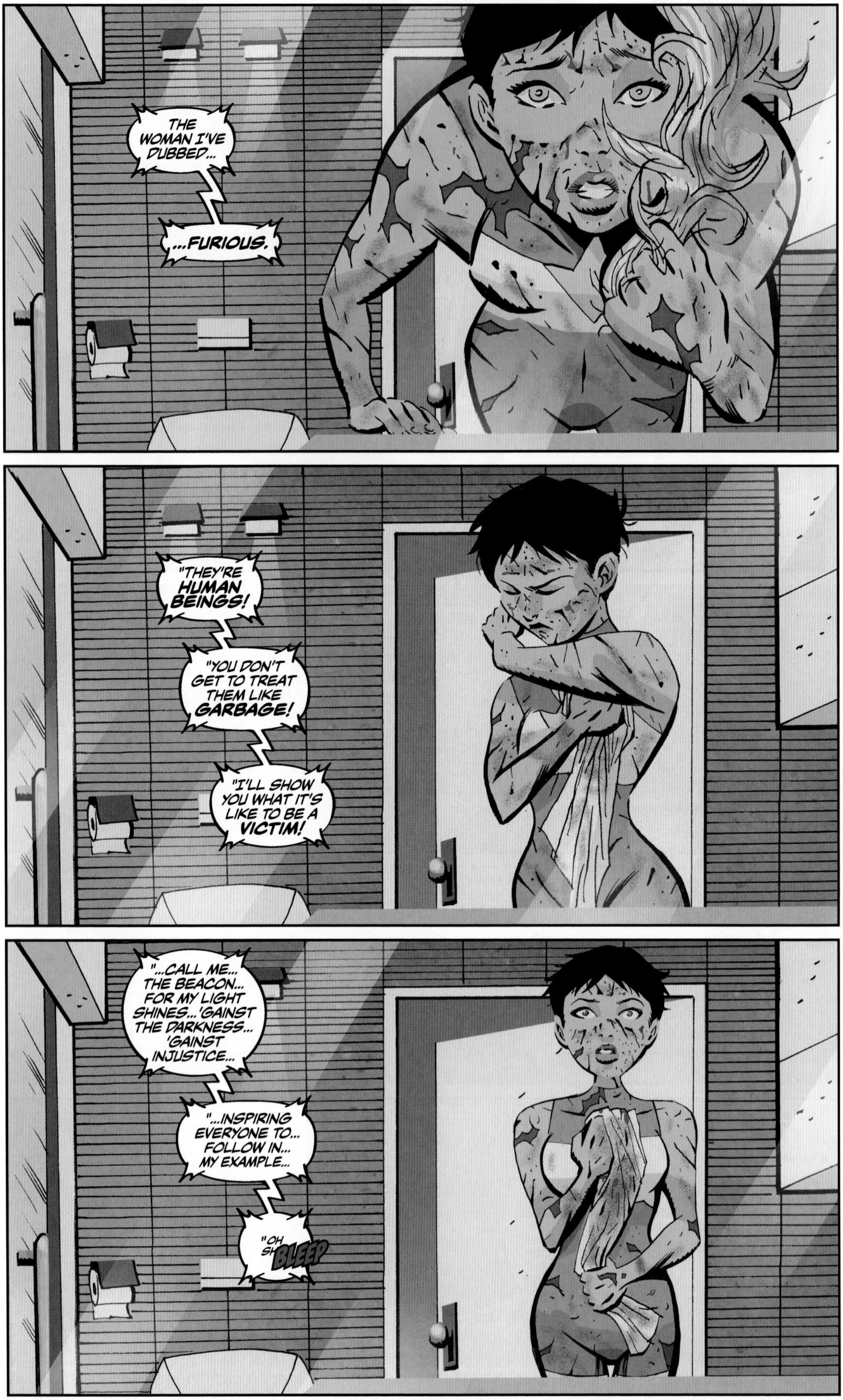
THE WOMAN I'VE DUBBED...
...FURIOUS.
"THEY'RE HUMAN BEINGS!
"YOU DON'T GET TO TREAT THEM LIKE GARBAGE!
"I'LL SHOW YOU WHAT IT'S LIKE TO BE A VICTIM!
"...CALL ME... THE BEACON... FOR MY LIGHT SHINES...'GAINST THE DARKNESS... 'GAINST INJUSTICE...
"...INSPIRING EVERYONE TO... FOLLOW IN... MY EXAMPLE...
"OH SH-BLEEP

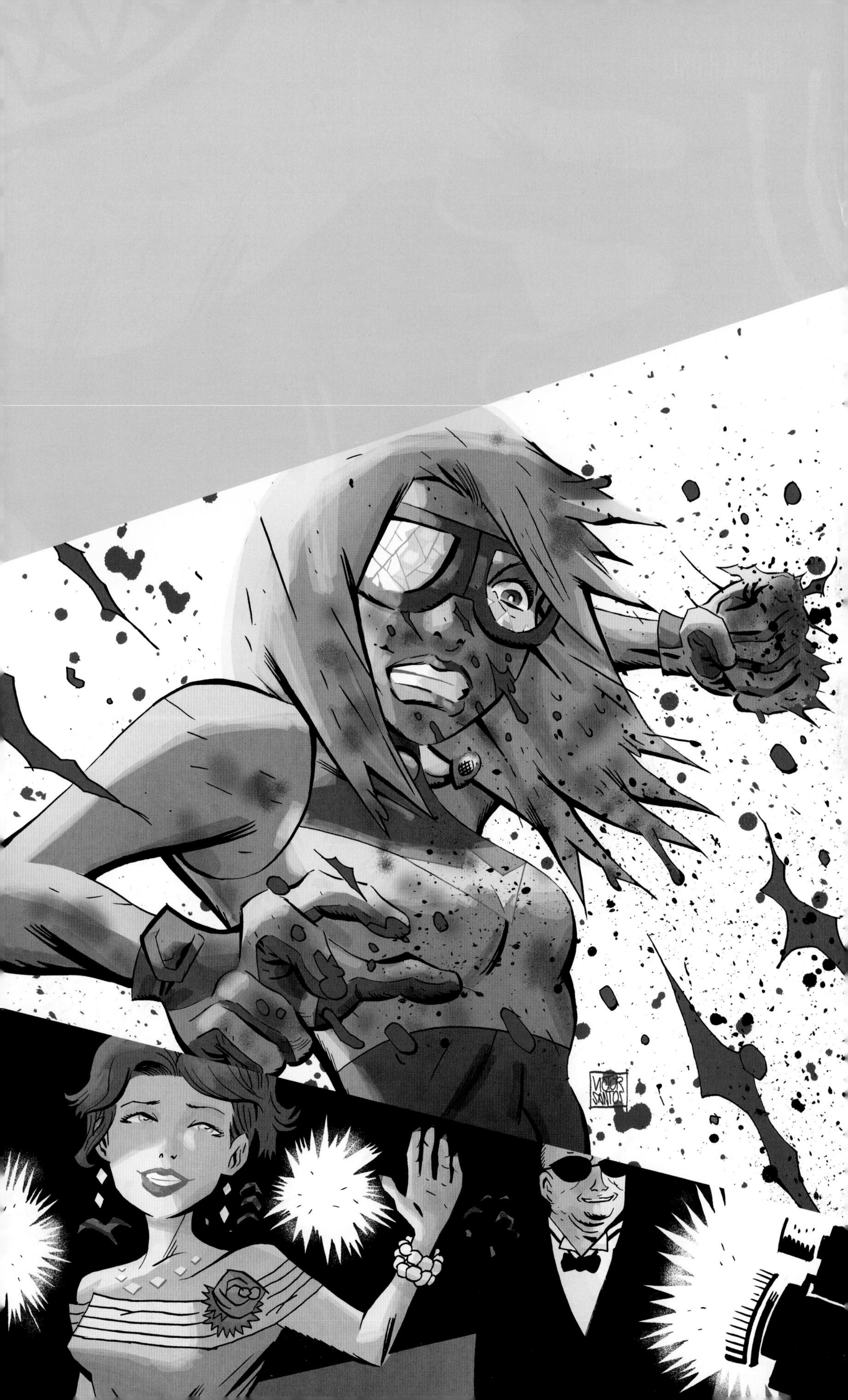
VICTOR SANTOS

CHAPTER ONE: LIFE'S A BITCH

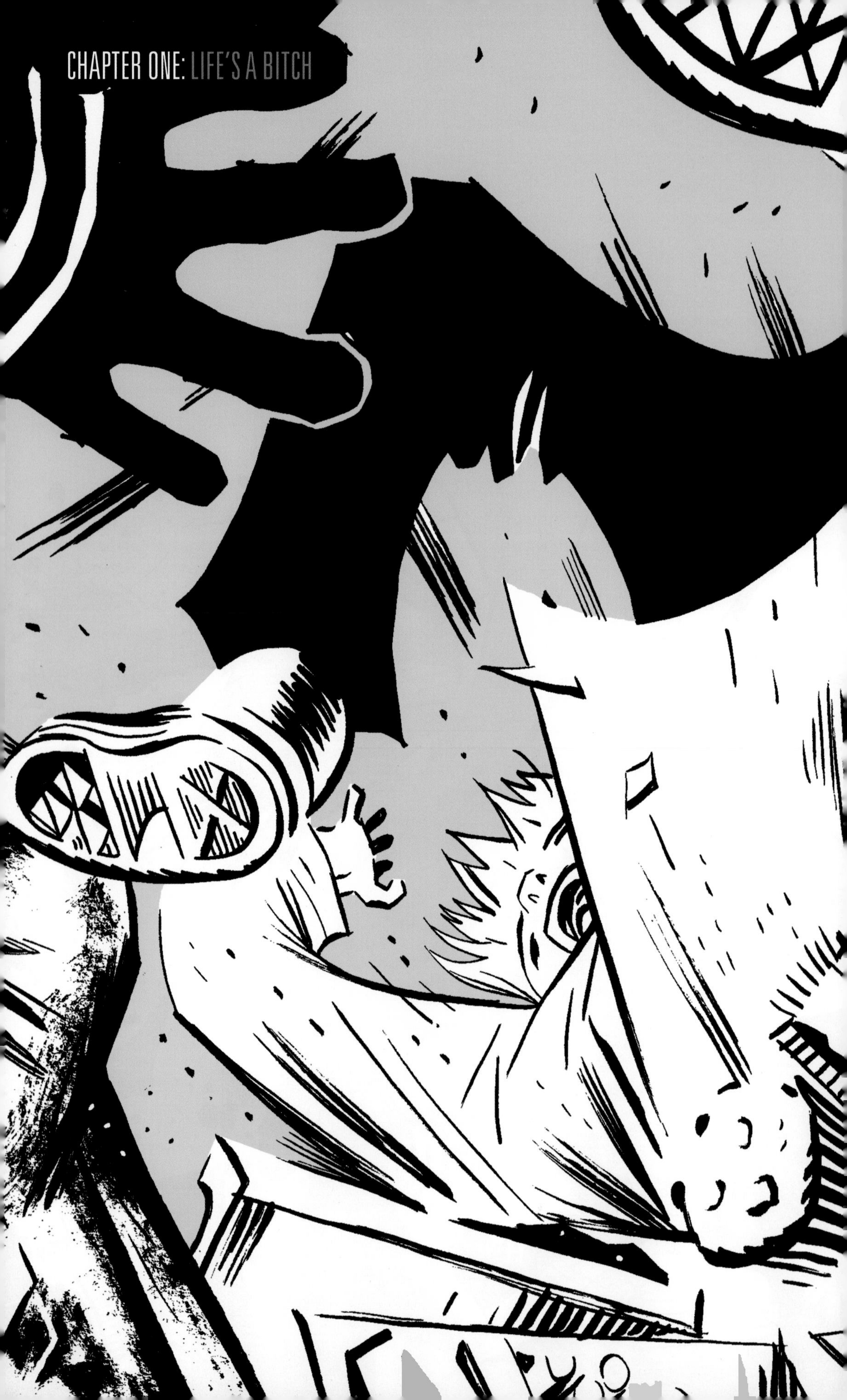

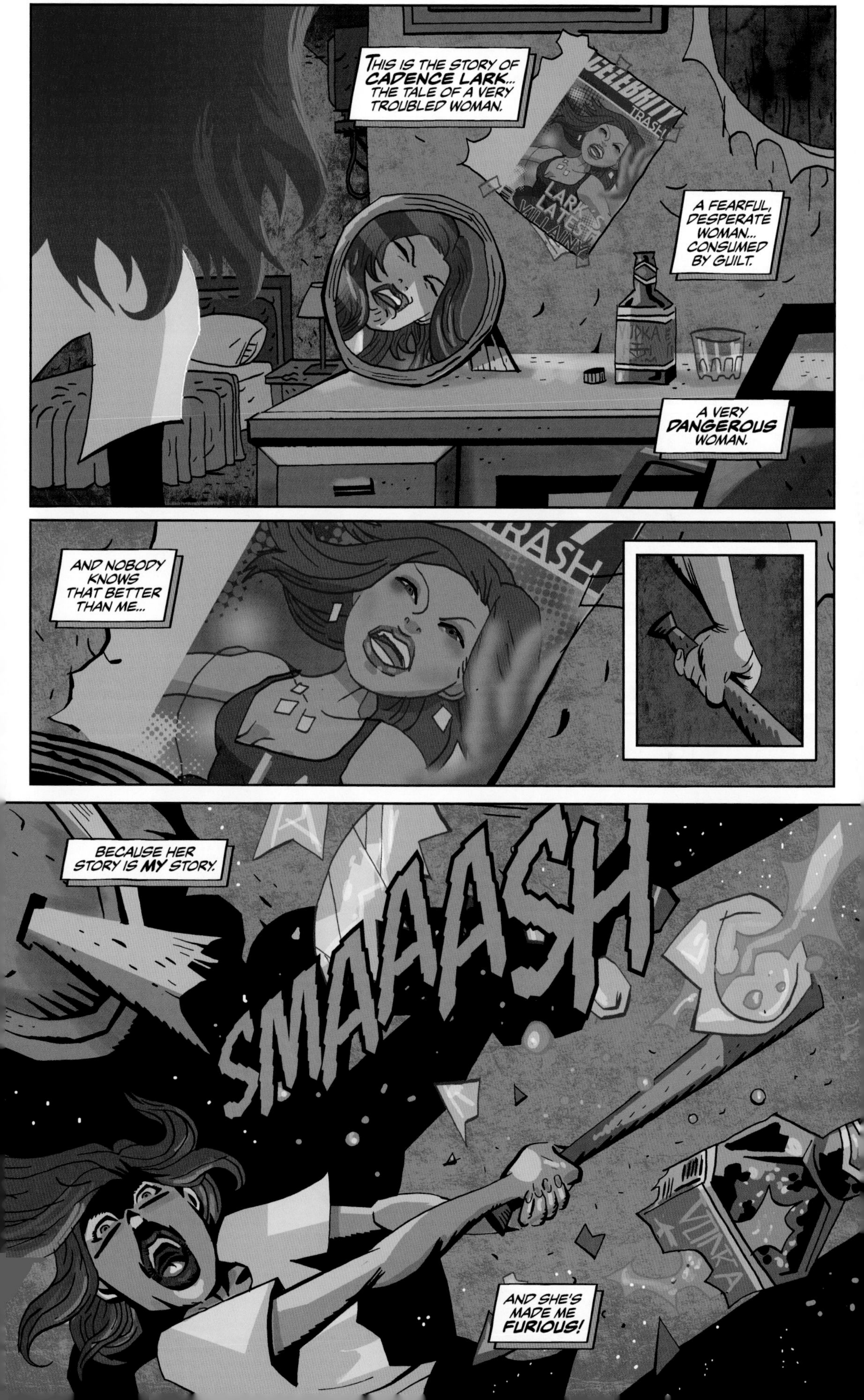
THIS IS THE STORY OF CADENCE LARK... THE TALE OF A VERY TROUBLED WOMAN.
CELEBRITY TRASH
LARK'S LATEST VILLAINY
A FEARFUL, DESPERATE WOMAN... CONSUMED BY GUILT.
VODKA
A VERY DANGEROUS WOMAN.
AND NOBODY KNOWS THAT BETTER THAN ME...
TRASH
BECAUSE HER STORY IS MY STORY.
SMAAASH
VODKA
AND SHE'S MADE ME FURIOUS!

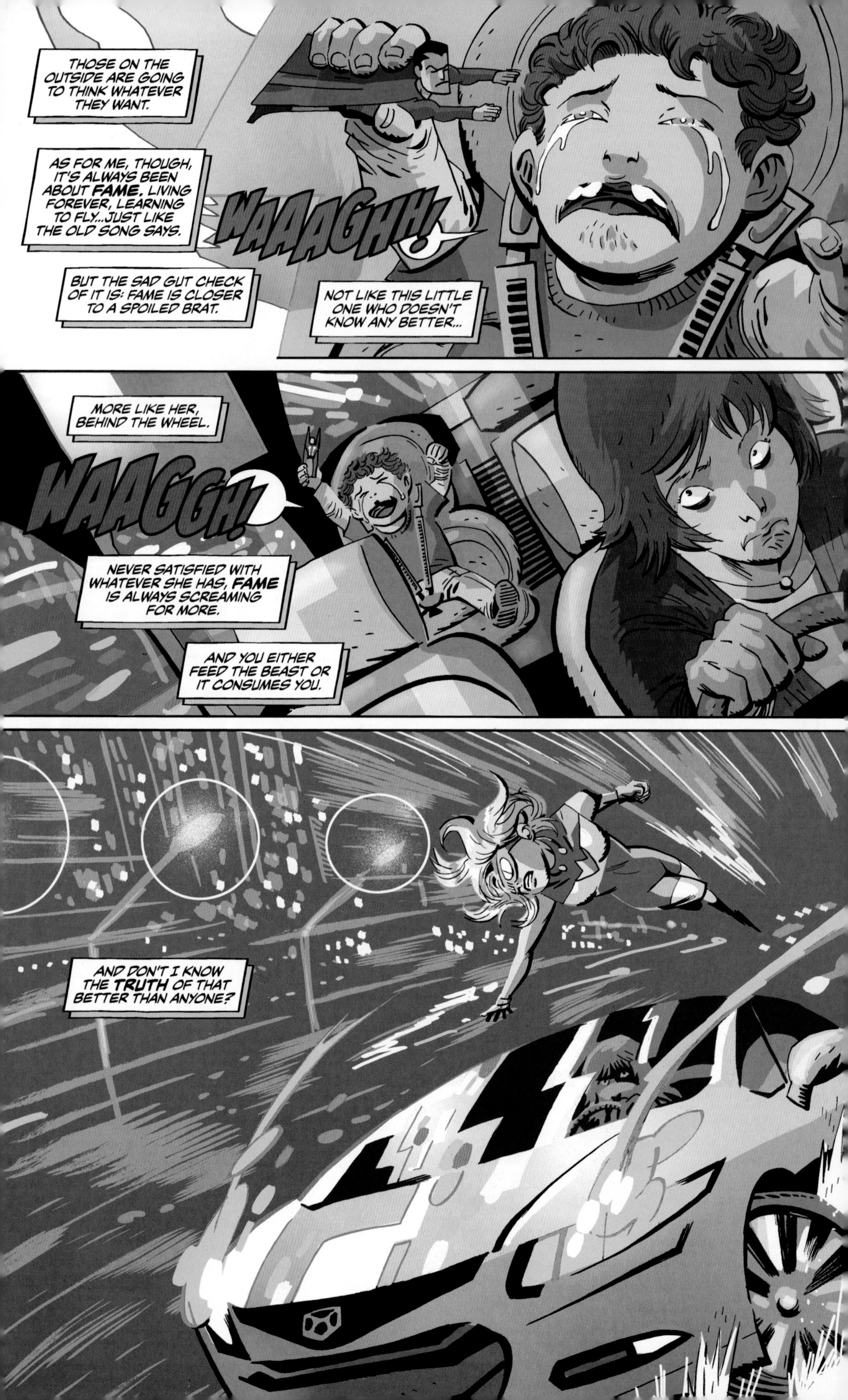
THOSE ON THE OUTSIDE ARE GOING TO THINK WHATEVER THEY WANT.
AS FOR ME, THOUGH, IT'S ALWAYS BEEN ABOUT **FAME.** LIVING FOREVER, LEARNING TO FLY...JUST LIKE THE OLD SONG SAYS.
WAAAGHH!
BUT THE SAD GUT CHECK OF IT IS: FAME IS CLOSER TO A SPOILED BRAT.
NOT LIKE THIS LITTLE ONE WHO DOESN'T KNOW ANY BETTER...
MORE LIKE HER, BEHIND THE WHEEL.
WAAGGH!
NEVER SATISFIED WITH WHATEVER SHE HAS, **FAME** IS ALWAYS SCREAMING FOR MORE.
AND YOU EITHER FEED THE BEAST OR IT CONSUMES YOU.
AND DON'T I KNOW THE **TRUTH** OF THAT BETTER THAN ANYONE?

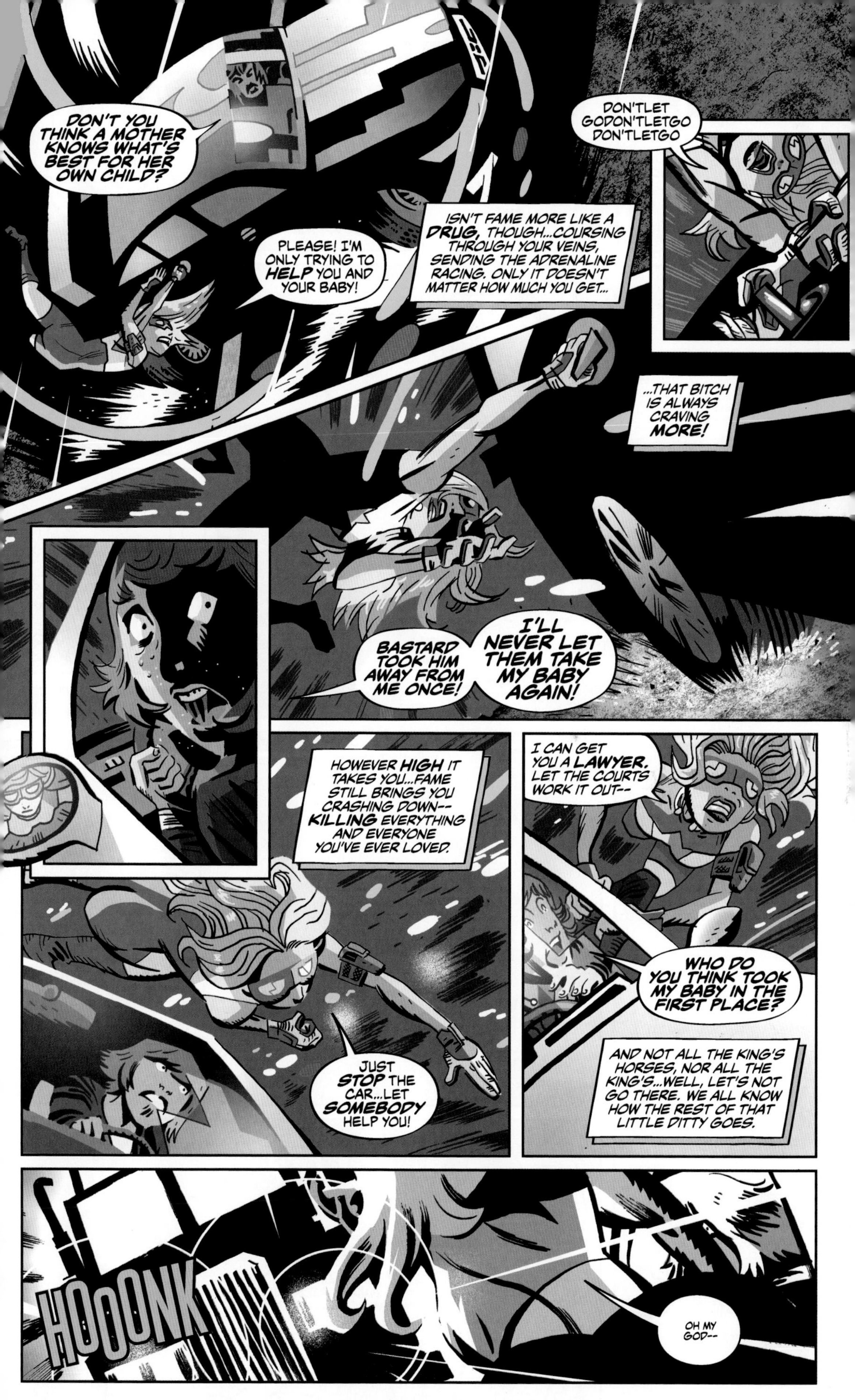
DON'T YOU THINK A MOTHER KNOWS WHAT'S BEST FOR HER OWN CHILD?
PLEASE! I'M ONLY TRYING TO HELP YOU AND YOUR BABY!
ISN'T FAME MORE LIKE A DRUG, THOUGH...COURSING THROUGH YOUR VEINS, SENDING THE ADRENALINE RACING. ONLY IT DOESN'T MATTER HOW MUCH YOU GET...
DON'TLET GODON'TLETGO DON'TLETGO
...THAT BITCH IS ALWAYS CRAVING MORE!
BASTARD TOOK HIM AWAY FROM ME ONCE!
I'LL NEVER LET THEM TAKE MY BABY AGAIN!
HOWEVER HIGH IT TAKES YOU...FAME STILL BRINGS YOU CRASHING DOWN--KILLING EVERYTHING AND EVERYONE YOU'VE EVER LOVED.
JUST STOP THE CAR...LET SOMEBODY HELP YOU!
I CAN GET YOU A LAWYER. LET THE COURTS WORK IT OUT--
WHO DO YOU THINK TOOK MY BABY IN THE FIRST PLACE?
AND NOT ALL THE KING'S HORSES, NOR ALL THE KING'S...WELL, LET'S NOT GO THERE. WE ALL KNOW HOW THE REST OF THAT LITTLE DITTY GOES.
HOOONK
OH MY GOD--

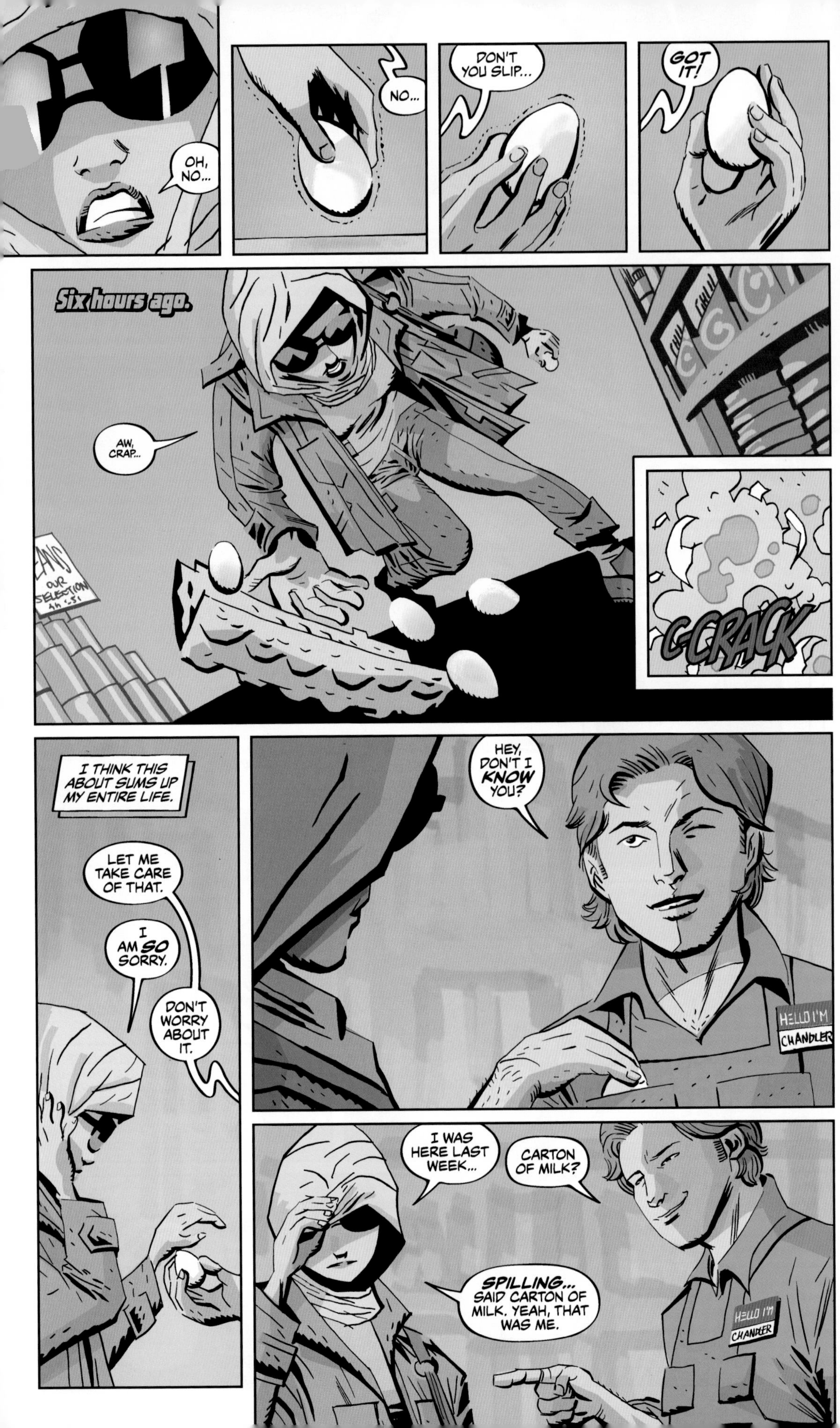
OH, NO...
NO...
DON'T YOU SLIP...
GOT IT!
Six hours ago.
AW, CRAP...
OUR SELECTION
C-CRACK
I THINK THIS ABOUT SUMS UP MY ENTIRE LIFE.
LET ME TAKE CARE OF THAT.
I AM SO SORRY.
DON'T WORRY ABOUT IT.
HEY, DON'T I KNOW YOU?
HELLO I'M CHANDLER
I WAS HERE LAST WEEK...
CARTON OF MILK?
SPILLING... SAID CARTON OF MILK. YEAH, THAT WAS ME.
HELLO I'M CHANDLER

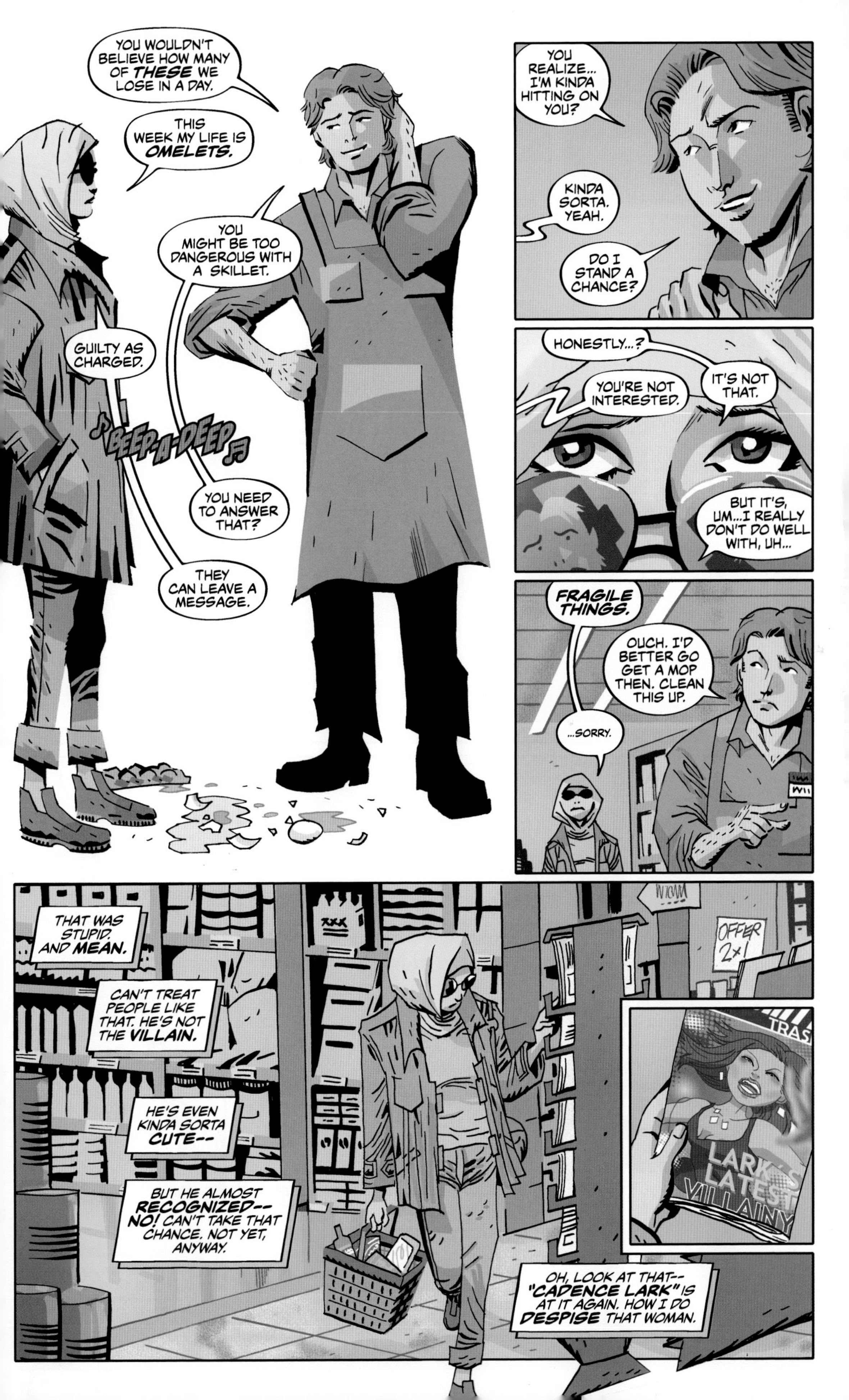
YOU WOULDN'T BELIEVE HOW MANY OF *THESE* WE LOSE IN A DAY.
THIS WEEK MY LIFE IS *OMELETS.*
YOU MIGHT BE TOO DANGEROUS WITH A SKILLET.
GUILTY AS CHARGED.
BEEP-A-DEEP
YOU NEED TO ANSWER THAT?
THEY CAN LEAVE A MESSAGE.
YOU REALIZE... I'M KINDA HITTING ON YOU?
KINDA SORTA. YEAH.
DO I STAND A CHANCE?
HONESTLY...?
YOU'RE NOT INTERESTED.
IT'S NOT THAT.
BUT IT'S, UM...I REALLY DON'T DO WELL WITH, UH...
FRAGILE THINGS.
OUCH. I'D BETTER GO GET A MOP THEN. CLEAN THIS UP.
...SORRY.
THAT WAS STUPID. AND *MEAN.*
CAN'T TREAT PEOPLE LIKE THAT. HE'S NOT THE *VILLAIN.*
HE'S EVEN KINDA SORTA *CUTE--*
BUT HE ALMOST *RECOGNIZED--* *NO!* CAN'T TAKE THAT CHANCE. NOT YET, ANYWAY.
OFFER 2x1
LARK'S LATEST VILLAINY
OH, LOOK AT THAT-- *"CADENCE LARK"* IS AT IT AGAIN. HOW I DO *DESPISE* THAT WOMAN.

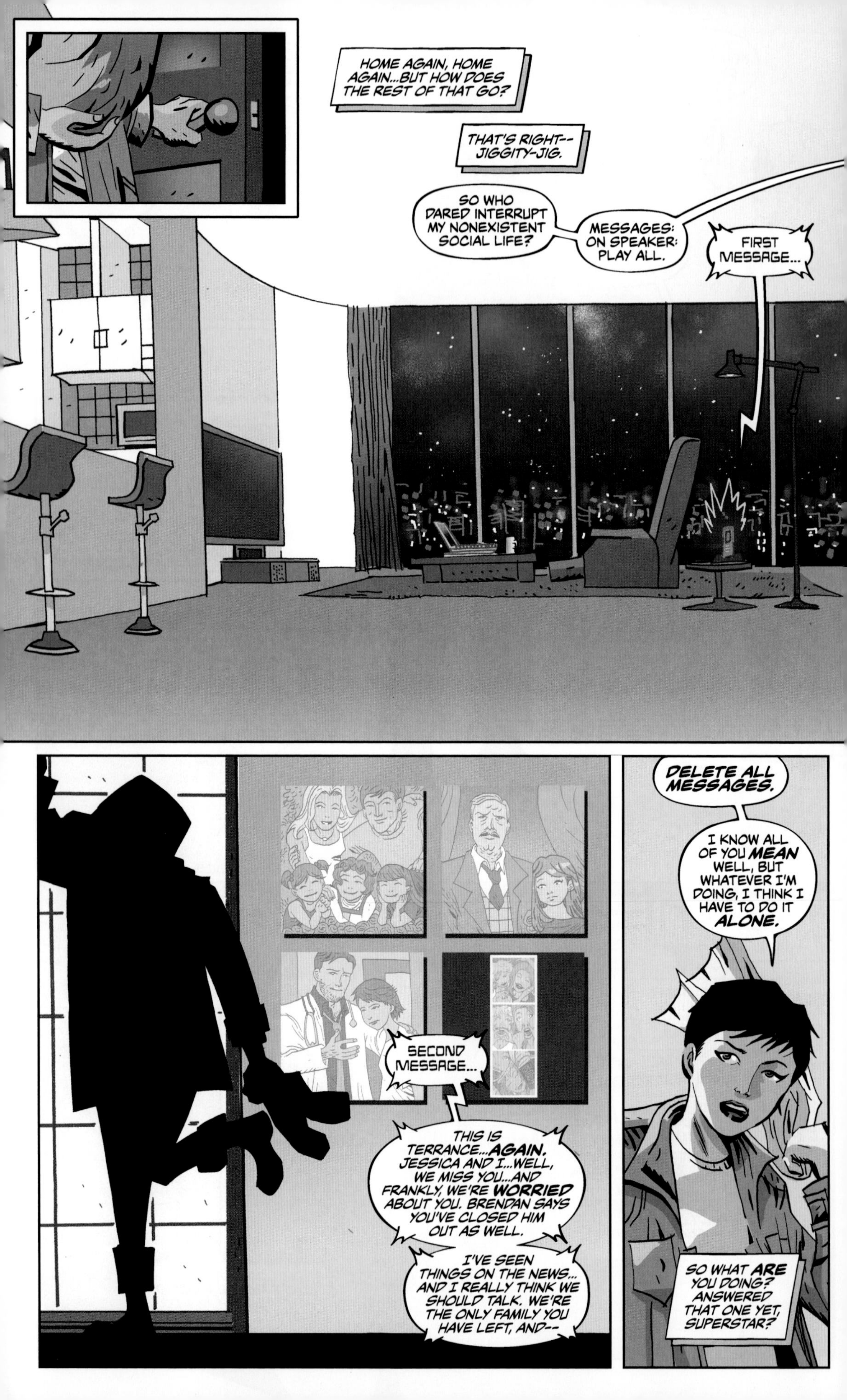
HOME AGAIN, HOME AGAIN...BUT HOW DOES THE REST OF THAT GO?
THAT'S RIGHT-- JIGGITY-JIG.
SO WHO DARED INTERRUPT MY NONEXISTENT SOCIAL LIFE?
MESSAGES: ON SPEAKER: PLAY ALL.
FIRST MESSAGE...
SECOND MESSAGE...
THIS IS TERRANCE...AGAIN. JESSICA AND I...WELL, WE MISS YOU...AND FRANKLY, WE'RE WORRIED ABOUT YOU. BRENDAN SAYS YOU'VE CLOSED HIM OUT AS WELL.
I'VE SEEN THINGS ON THE NEWS... AND I REALLY THINK WE SHOULD TALK. WE'RE THE ONLY FAMILY YOU HAVE LEFT, AND--
DELETE ALL MESSAGES.
I KNOW ALL OF YOU MEAN WELL, BUT WHATEVER I'M DOING, I THINK I HAVE TO DO IT ALONE.
SO WHAT ARE YOU DOING? ANSWERED THAT ONE YET, SUPERSTAR?

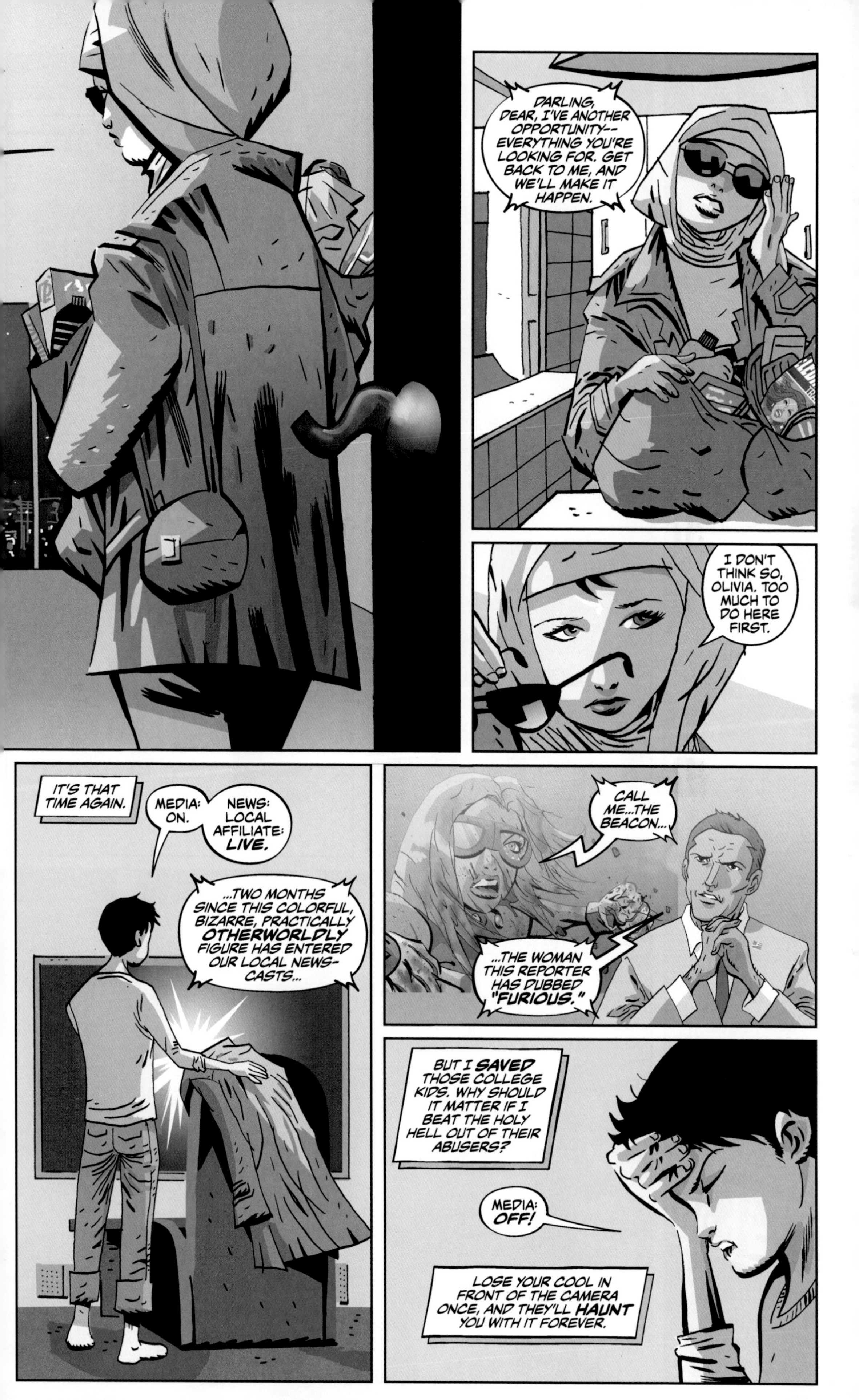
DARLING, DEAR, I'VE ANOTHER OPPORTUNITY-- EVERYTHING YOU'RE LOOKING FOR. GET BACK TO ME, AND WE'LL MAKE IT HAPPEN.
I DON'T THINK SO, OLIVIA. TOO MUCH TO DO HERE FIRST.
IT'S THAT TIME AGAIN.
MEDIA: ON.
NEWS: LOCAL AFFILIATE: LIVE.
...TWO MONTHS SINCE THIS COLORFUL, BIZARRE, PRACTICALLY OTHERWORLDLY FIGURE HAS ENTERED OUR LOCAL NEWS-CASTS...
CALL ME...THE BEACON...
...THE WOMAN THIS REPORTER HAS DUBBED "FURIOUS."
BUT I SAVED THOSE COLLEGE KIDS. WHY SHOULD IT MATTER IF I BEAT THE HOLY HELL OUT OF THEIR ABUSERS?
MEDIA: OFF!
LOSE YOUR COOL IN FRONT OF THE CAMERA ONCE, AND THEY'LL HAUNT YOU WITH IT FOREVER.

SO HERE I AM ON MY SELF-APPOINTED ROUNDS. AND ANOTHER CHANCE TO TRY TO GET IT RIGHT.

IT HELPS IF YOU THINK OF IT LIKE A **DATE**: ME, THE MOODY, SELF-ABSORBED ONE--

HE, THE DASHING YOUNG SUPER-MARKET CLERK, IGNORANT OF THE IMPACT HE'S MADE WITH HIS DARK, PIERCING EYES, PERFECT HAIR, AND THAT LONG, HARD... **JANITORIAL MOP.**

STOP BEING SO MEAN. JUST TAKE IT ONE STEP AT A TIME, AND TRY NOT TO DO ANYTHING STUPID FOR A CHANGE.

ANOTHER SATURDAY NIGHT, AND I AIN'T GOT NOBODY... ♪

I STILL REMEMBER HOW MUCH MOM ADORED **SAM COOKE.** I WAS ONLY FIVE OR SIX, BUT...IF SHE ONLY KNEW **THEN** HOW I'D BE SPENDING MY NIGHTS NOW.

24 h STO

COLD DRINKS

YOU CAN FIND PRACTICALLY ANYTHING ONLINE. SO IF YOU'VE DECIDED YOUR ROAD TO **REDEMPTION** IS SPANDEX AND A REALLY UNHEALTHY DESIRE TO WANT TO STOP THE BAD GUYS...

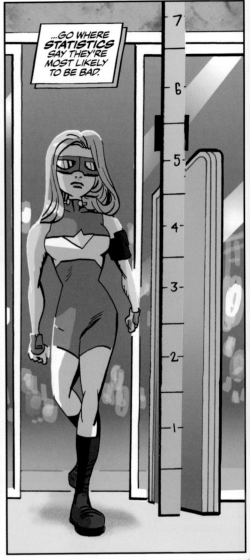

...GO WHERE **STATISTICS** SAY THEY'RE MOST LIKELY TO BE BAD.

WHOA...IT'S THE **COMIC BOOK CHICK!**

HEY! I DON'T WANT **TROUBLE** IN MY STORE!

SO TURN ROUND. TAKE YOUR **FURIOUS** SOMEPLACE ELSE!

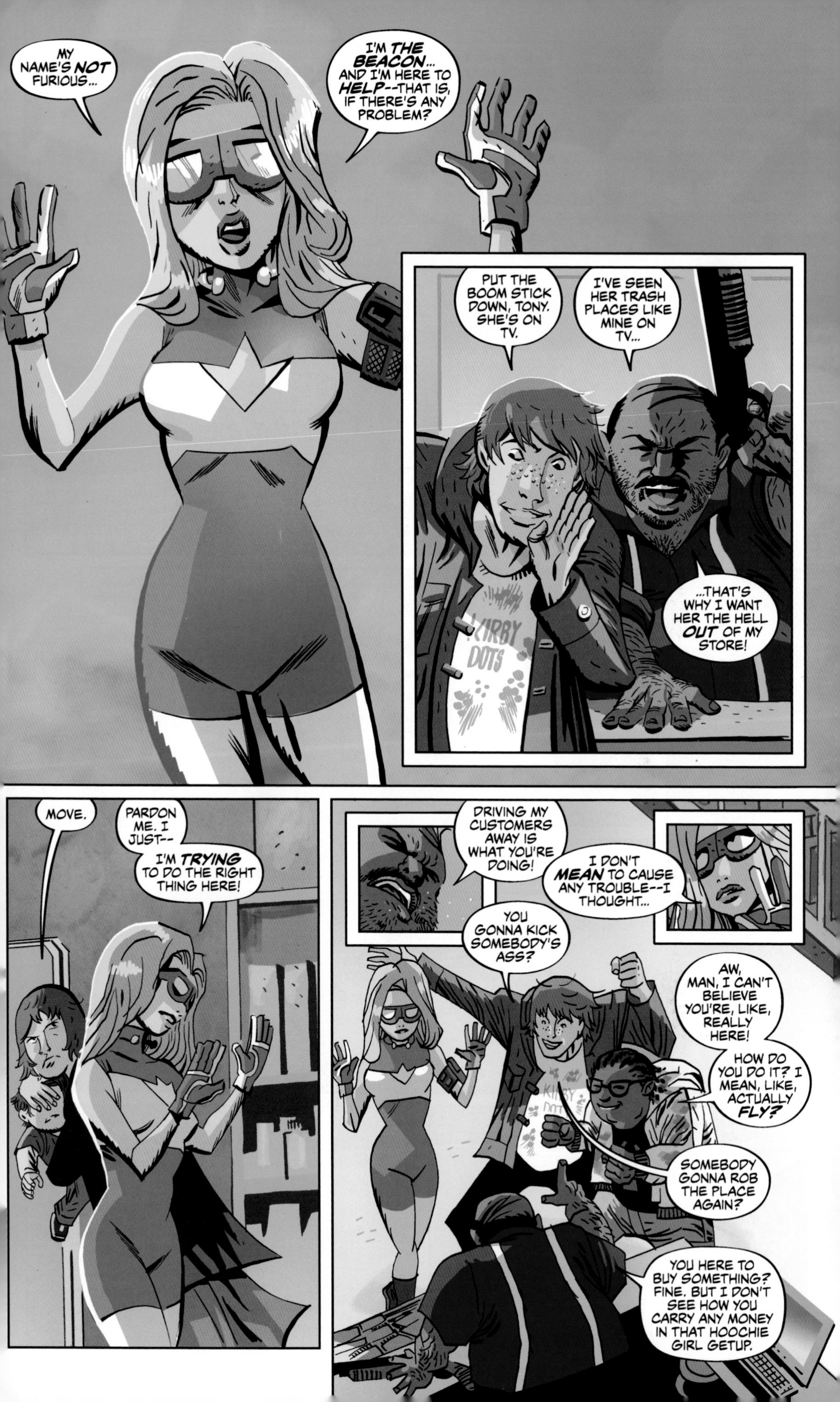
MY NAME'S NOT FURIOUS...
I'M THE BEACON... AND I'M HERE TO HELP--THAT IS, IF THERE'S ANY PROBLEM?
PUT THE BOOM STICK DOWN, TONY. SHE'S ON TV.
I'VE SEEN HER TRASH PLACES LIKE MINE ON TV...
...THAT'S WHY I WANT HER THE HELL OUT OF MY STORE!
KIRBY DOTS
MOVE.
PARDON ME. I JUST--
I'M TRYING TO DO THE RIGHT THING HERE!
DRIVING MY CUSTOMERS AWAY IS WHAT YOU'RE DOING!
I DON'T MEAN TO CAUSE ANY TROUBLE--I THOUGHT...
YOU GONNA KICK SOMEBODY'S ASS?
AW, MAN, I CAN'T BELIEVE YOU'RE, LIKE, REALLY HERE!
HOW DO YOU DO IT? I MEAN, LIKE, ACTUALLY FLY?
SOMEBODY GONNA ROB THE PLACE AGAIN?
YOU HERE TO BUY SOMETHING? FINE. BUT I DON'T SEE HOW YOU CARRY ANY MONEY IN THAT HOOCHIE GIRL GETUP.

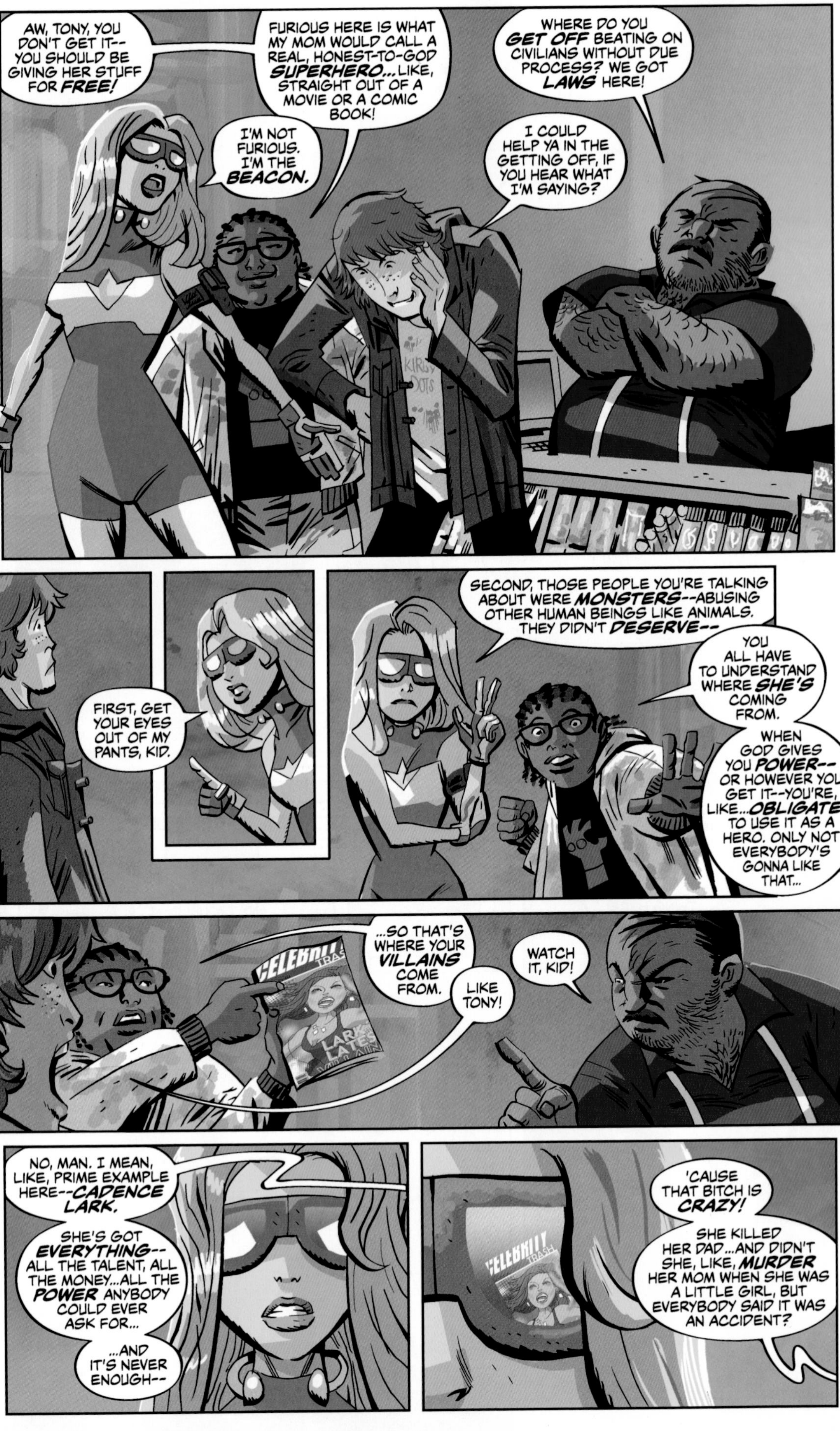
AW, TONY, YOU DON'T GET IT-- YOU SHOULD BE GIVING HER STUFF FOR FREE!
FURIOUS HERE IS WHAT MY MOM WOULD CALL A REAL, HONEST-TO-GOD SUPERHERO... LIKE, STRAIGHT OUT OF A MOVIE OR A COMIC BOOK!
I'M NOT FURIOUS. I'M THE BEACON.
WHERE DO YOU GET OFF BEATING ON CIVILIANS WITHOUT DUE PROCESS? WE GOT LAWS HERE!
I COULD HELP YA IN THE GETTING OFF, IF YOU HEAR WHAT I'M SAYING?
FIRST, GET YOUR EYES OUT OF MY PANTS, KID.
SECOND, THOSE PEOPLE YOU'RE TALKING ABOUT WERE MONSTERS--ABUSING OTHER HUMAN BEINGS LIKE ANIMALS. THEY DIDN'T DESERVE--
YOU ALL HAVE TO UNDERSTAND WHERE SHE'S COMING FROM.
WHEN GOD GIVES YOU POWER-- OR HOWEVER YOU GET IT--YOU'RE, LIKE...OBLIGATED TO USE IT AS A HERO. ONLY NOT EVERYBODY'S GONNA LIKE THAT...
...SO THAT'S WHERE YOUR VILLAINS COME FROM.
LIKE TONY!
WATCH IT, KID!
NO, MAN. I MEAN, LIKE, PRIME EXAMPLE HERE--CADENCE LARK.
SHE'S GOT EVERYTHING-- ALL THE TALENT, ALL THE MONEY...ALL THE POWER ANYBODY COULD EVER ASK FOR...
...AND IT'S NEVER ENOUGH--
'CAUSE THAT BITCH IS CRAZY!
SHE KILLED HER DAD...AND DIDN'T SHE, LIKE, MURDER HER MOM WHEN SHE WAS A LITTLE GIRL, BUT EVERYBODY SAID IT WAS AN ACCIDENT?

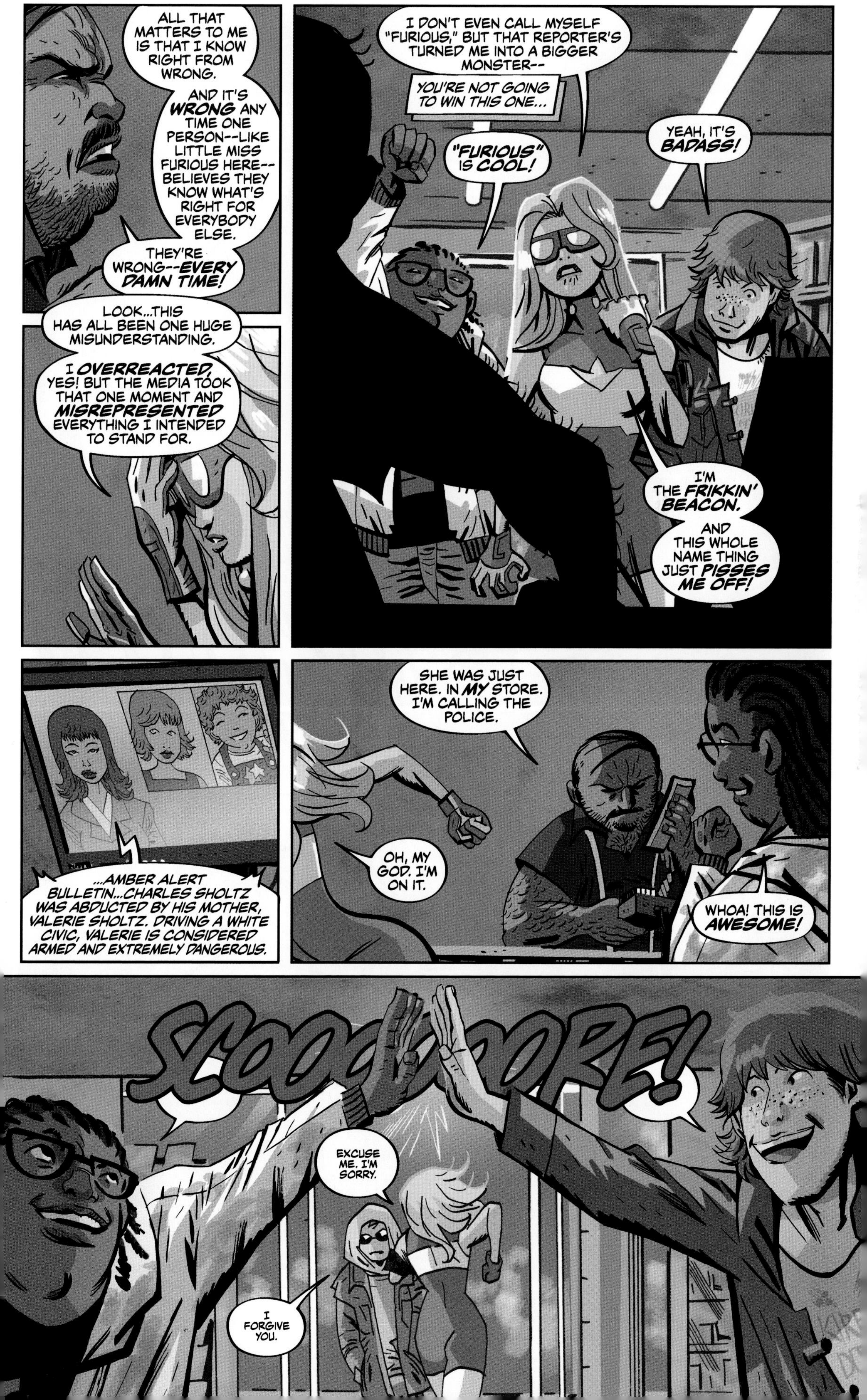
ALL THAT MATTERS TO ME IS THAT I KNOW RIGHT FROM WRONG.
AND IT'S **WRONG** ANY TIME ONE PERSON--LIKE LITTLE MISS FURIOUS HERE--BELIEVES THEY KNOW WHAT'S RIGHT FOR EVERYBODY ELSE.
THEY'RE WRONG--**EVERY DAMN TIME!**
LOOK...THIS HAS ALL BEEN ONE HUGE MISUNDERSTANDING.
I **OVERREACTED**, YES! BUT THE MEDIA TOOK THAT ONE MOMENT AND **MISREPRESENTED** EVERYTHING I INTENDED TO STAND FOR.
I DON'T EVEN CALL MYSELF "FURIOUS," BUT THAT REPORTER'S TURNED ME INTO A BIGGER MONSTER--
YOU'RE NOT GOING TO WIN THIS ONE...
"FURIOUS" IS **COOL!**
YEAH, IT'S **BADASS!**
I'M THE **FRIKKIN' BEACON.**
AND THIS WHOLE NAME THING JUST **PISSES ME OFF!**
...AMBER ALERT BULLETIN...CHARLES SHOLTZ WAS ABDUCTED BY HIS MOTHER, VALERIE SHOLTZ. DRIVING A WHITE CIVIC, VALERIE IS CONSIDERED ARMED AND EXTREMELY DANGEROUS.
SHE WAS JUST HERE. IN **MY** STORE. I'M CALLING THE POLICE.
OH, MY GOD. I'M ON IT.
WHOA! THIS IS **AWESOME!**
SCOO ORE!
EXCUSE ME. I'M SORRY.
I FORGIVE YOU.

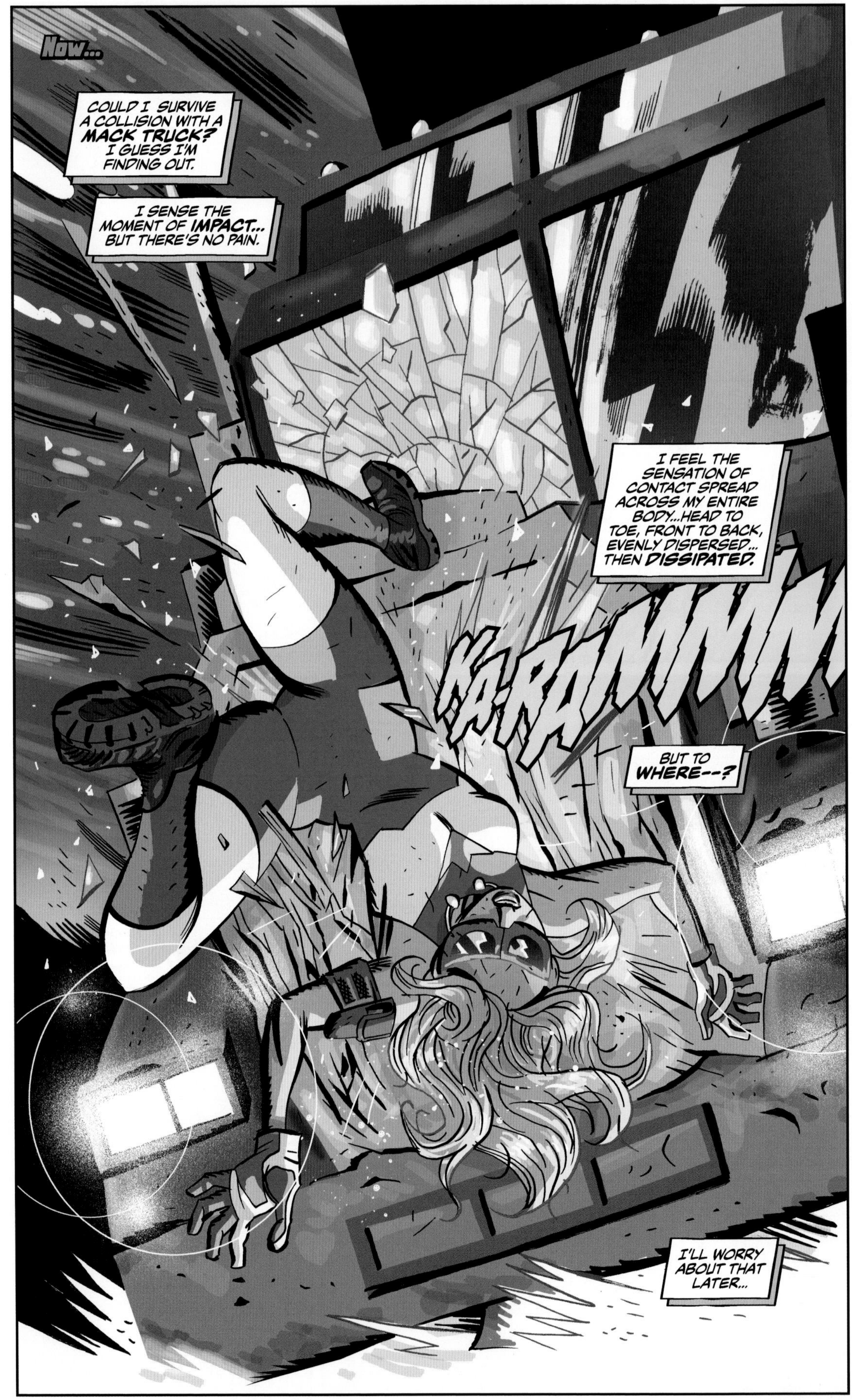
Now...
COULD I SURVIVE A COLLISION WITH A MACK TRUCK? I GUESS I'M FINDING OUT.
I SENSE THE MOMENT OF IMPACT... BUT THERE'S NO PAIN.
I FEEL THE SENSATION OF CONTACT SPREAD ACROSS MY ENTIRE BODY...HEAD TO TOE, FRONT TO BACK, EVENLY DISPERSED... THEN DISSIPATED.
KA-RAMMMM
BUT TO WHERE--?
I'LL WORRY ABOUT THAT LATER...

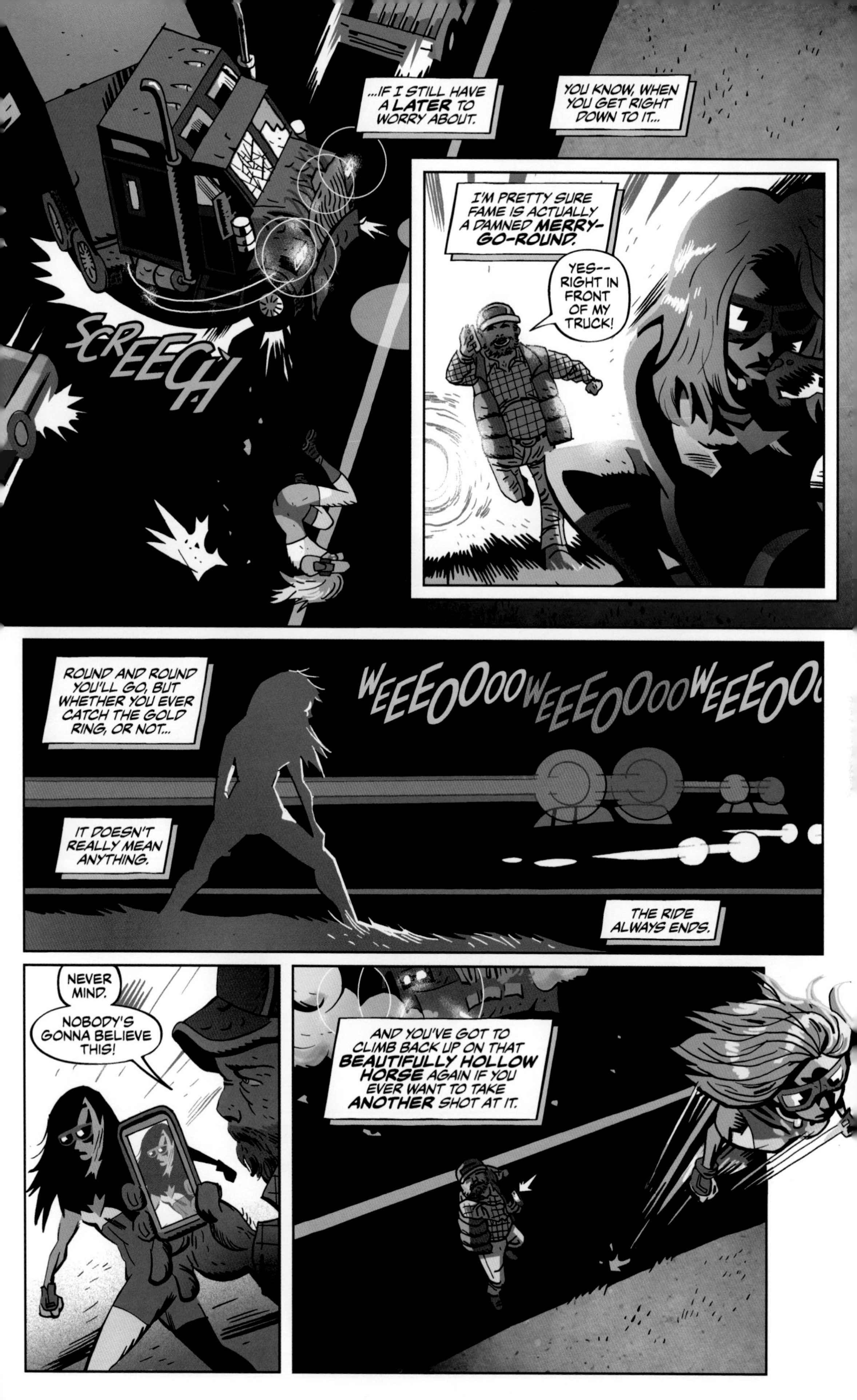
...IF I STILL HAVE A LATER TO WORRY ABOUT.
YOU KNOW, WHEN YOU GET RIGHT DOWN TO IT...
SCREECH
I'M PRETTY SURE FAME IS ACTUALLY A DAMNED MERRY-GO-ROUND.
YES-- RIGHT IN FRONT OF MY TRUCK!
ROUND AND ROUND YOU'LL GO, BUT WHETHER YOU EVER CATCH THE GOLD RING, OR NOT...
WEEEOOOOWEEEOOOOWEEEOO
IT DOESN'T REALLY MEAN ANYTHING.
THE RIDE ALWAYS ENDS.
NEVER MIND.
NOBODY'S GONNA BELIEVE THIS!
AND YOU'VE GOT TO CLIMB BACK UP ON THAT BEAUTIFULLY HOLLOW HORSE AGAIN IF YOU EVER WANT TO TAKE ANOTHER SHOT AT IT.

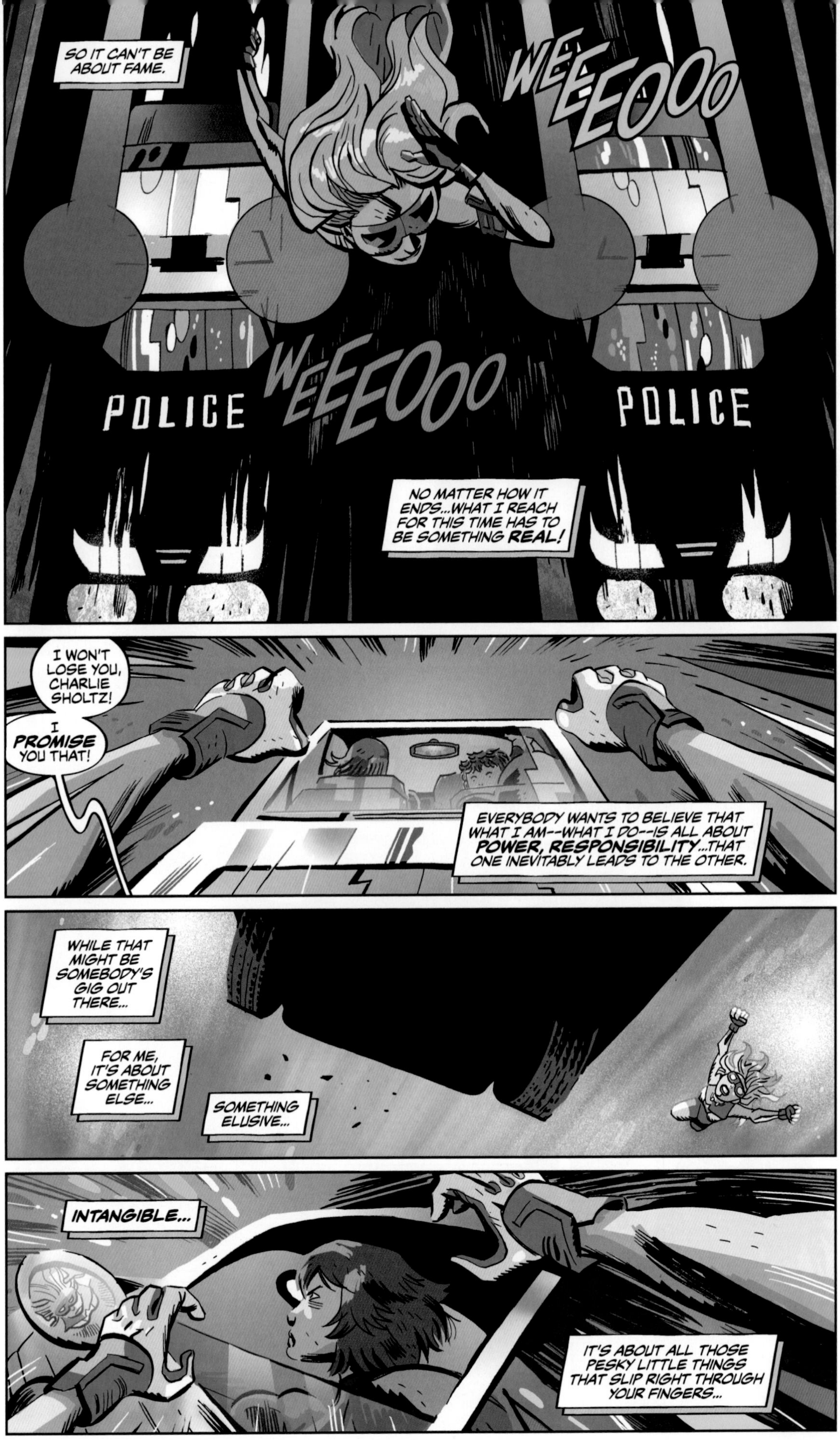
SO IT CAN'T BE ABOUT FAME.
WEEEOOO
POLICE
WEEEOOO
POLICE
NO MATTER HOW IT ENDS...WHAT I REACH FOR THIS TIME HAS TO BE SOMETHING REAL!
I WON'T LOSE YOU, CHARLIE SHOLTZ!
I PROMISE YOU THAT!
EVERYBODY WANTS TO BELIEVE THAT WHAT I AM--WHAT I DO--IS ALL ABOUT POWER, RESPONSIBILITY...THAT ONE INEVITABLY LEADS TO THE OTHER.
WHILE THAT MIGHT BE SOMEBODY'S GIG OUT THERE...
FOR ME, IT'S ABOUT SOMETHING ELSE...
SOMETHING ELUSIVE...
INTANGIBLE...
IT'S ABOUT ALL THOSE PESKY LITTLE THINGS THAT SLIP RIGHT THROUGH YOUR FINGERS...

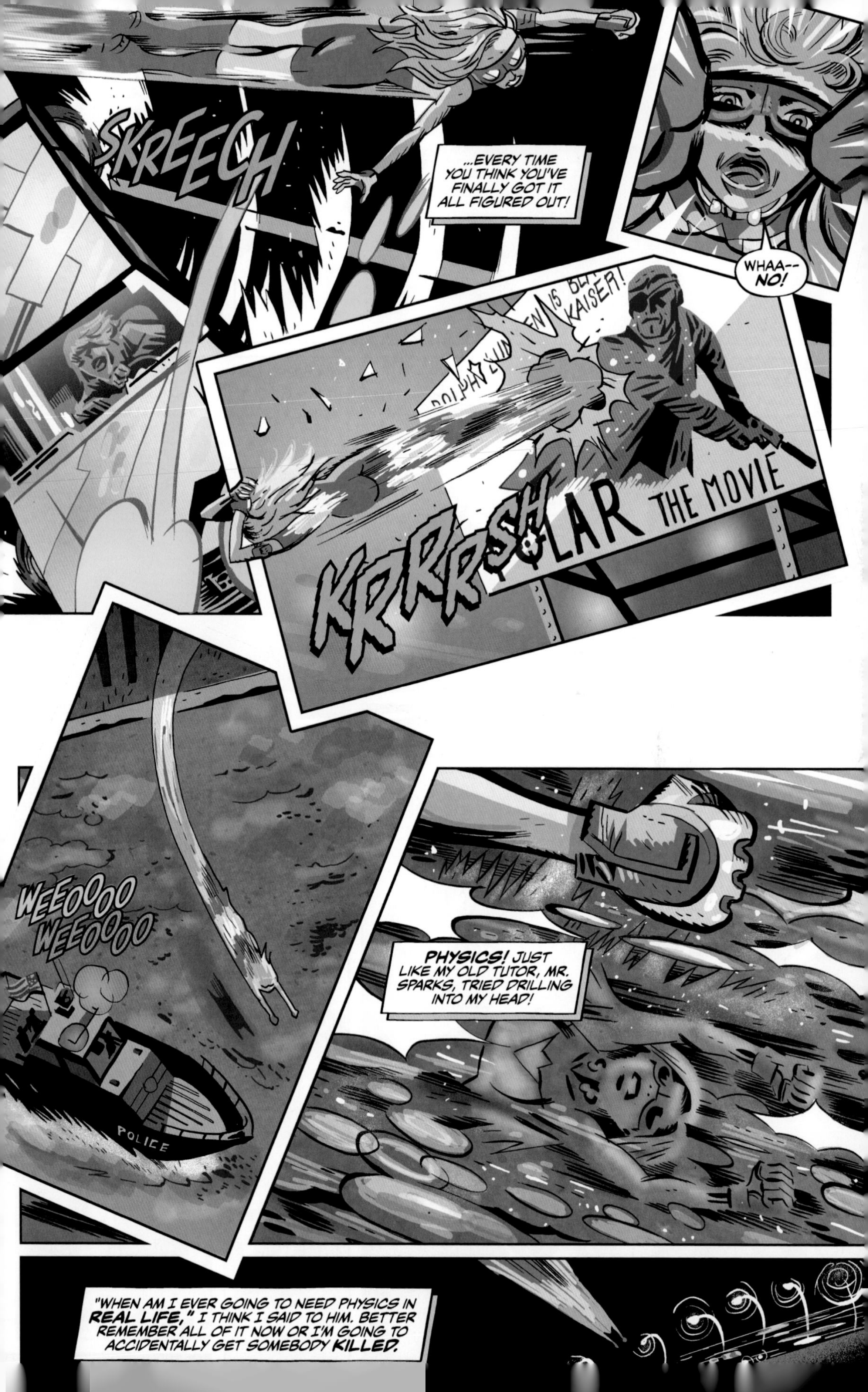
SKREECH
...EVERY TIME YOU THINK YOU'VE FINALLY GOT IT ALL FIGURED OUT!
WHAA-- NO!
KRRRSH
THE MOVIE
WEEOOOO
WEEOOOO
POLICE
PHYSICS! JUST LIKE MY OLD TUTOR, MR. SPARKS, TRIED DRILLING INTO MY HEAD!
"WHEN AM I EVER GOING TO NEED PHYSICS IN REAL LIFE," I THINK I SAID TO HIM. BETTER REMEMBER ALL OF IT NOW OR I'M GOING TO ACCIDENTALLY GET SOMEBODY KILLED.

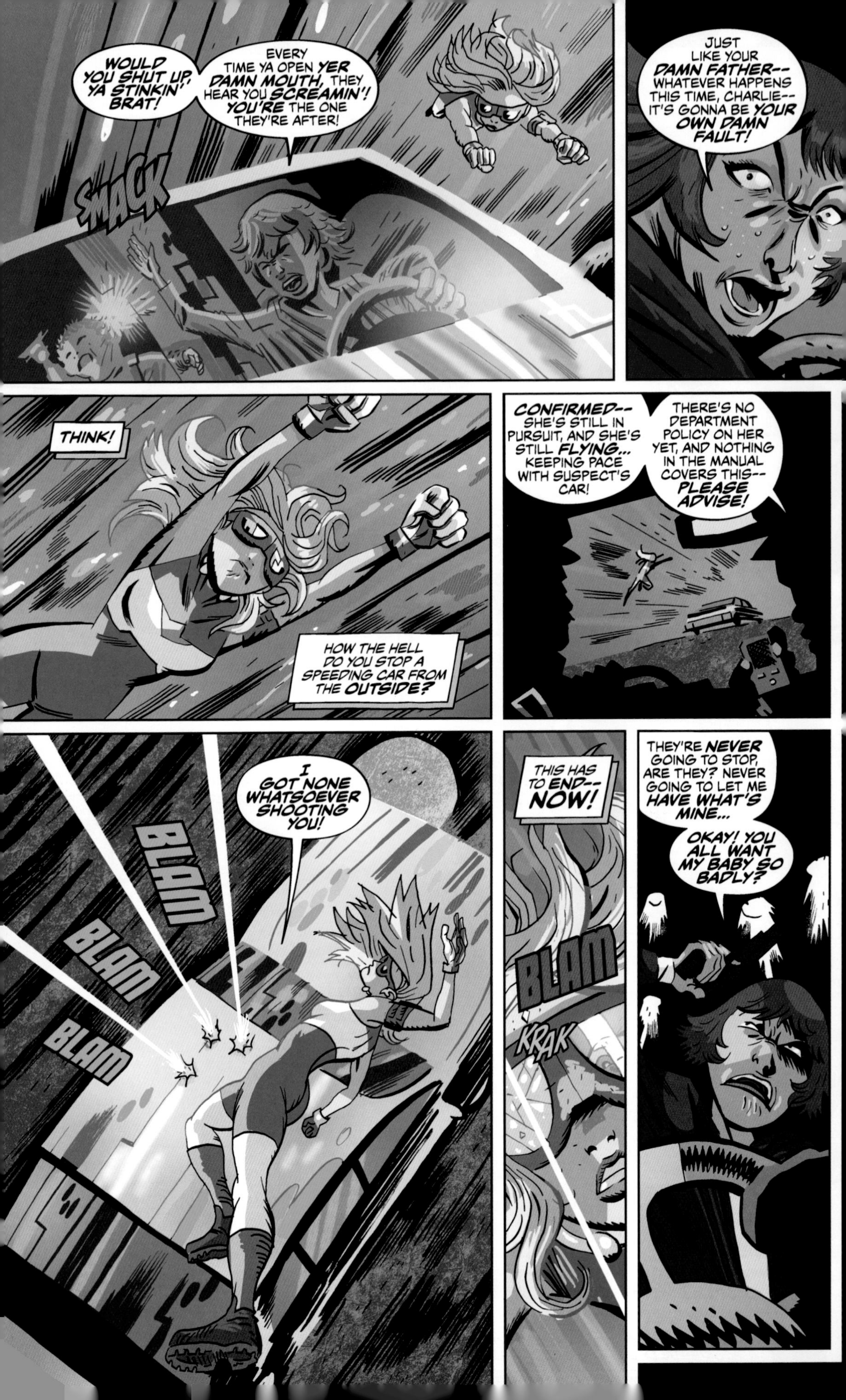
WOULD YOU SHUT UP, YA STINKIN' BRAT!
EVERY TIME YA OPEN YER DAMN MOUTH, THEY HEAR YOU SCREAMIN'! YOU'RE THE ONE THEY'RE AFTER!
SMACK
JUST LIKE YOUR DAMN FATHER-- WHATEVER HAPPENS THIS TIME, CHARLIE-- IT'S GONNA BE YOUR OWN DAMN FAULT!
THINK!
HOW THE HELL DO YOU STOP A SPEEDING CAR FROM THE OUTSIDE?
CONFIRMED-- SHE'S STILL IN PURSUIT, AND SHE'S STILL FLYING... KEEPING PACE WITH SUSPECT'S CAR!
THERE'S NO DEPARTMENT POLICY ON HER YET, AND NOTHING IN THE MANUAL COVERS THIS-- PLEASE ADVISE!
I GOT NONE WHATSOEVER SHOOTING YOU!
BLAM
BLAM
BLAM
THIS HAS TO END-- NOW!
BLAM
KRAK
THEY'RE NEVER GOING TO STOP, ARE THEY? NEVER GOING TO LET ME HAVE WHAT'S MINE...
OKAY! YOU ALL WANT MY BABY SO BADLY?

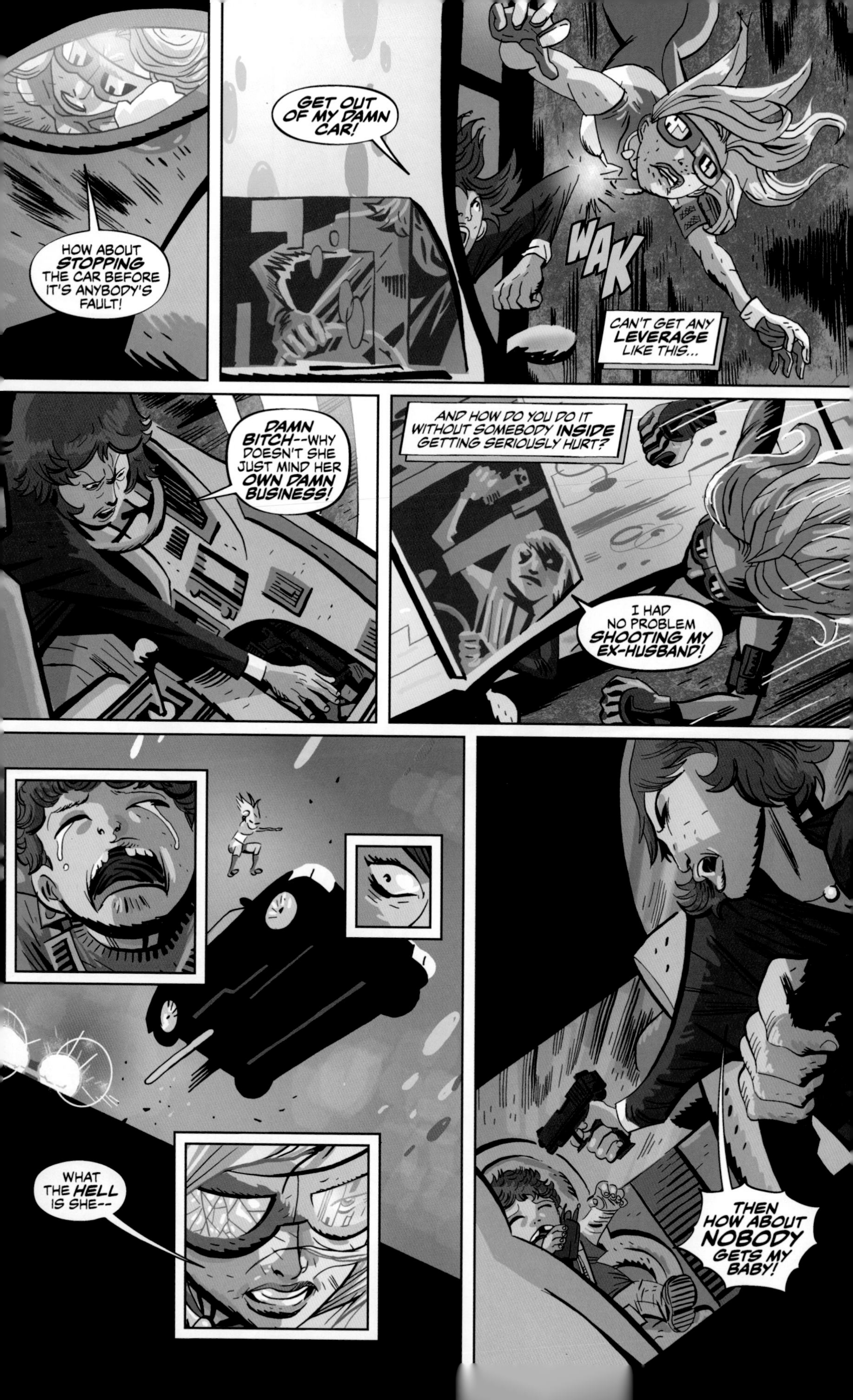
HOW ABOUT STOPPING THE CAR BEFORE IT'S ANYBODY'S FAULT!
GET OUT OF MY DAMN CAR!
WAK
CAN'T GET ANY LEVERAGE LIKE THIS...
DAMN BITCH--WHY DOESN'T SHE JUST MIND HER OWN DAMN BUSINESS!
AND HOW DO YOU DO IT WITHOUT SOMEBODY INSIDE GETTING SERIOUSLY HURT?
I HAD NO PROBLEM SHOOTING MY EX-HUSBAND!
WHAT THE HELL IS SHE--
THEN HOW ABOUT NOBODY GETS MY BABY!

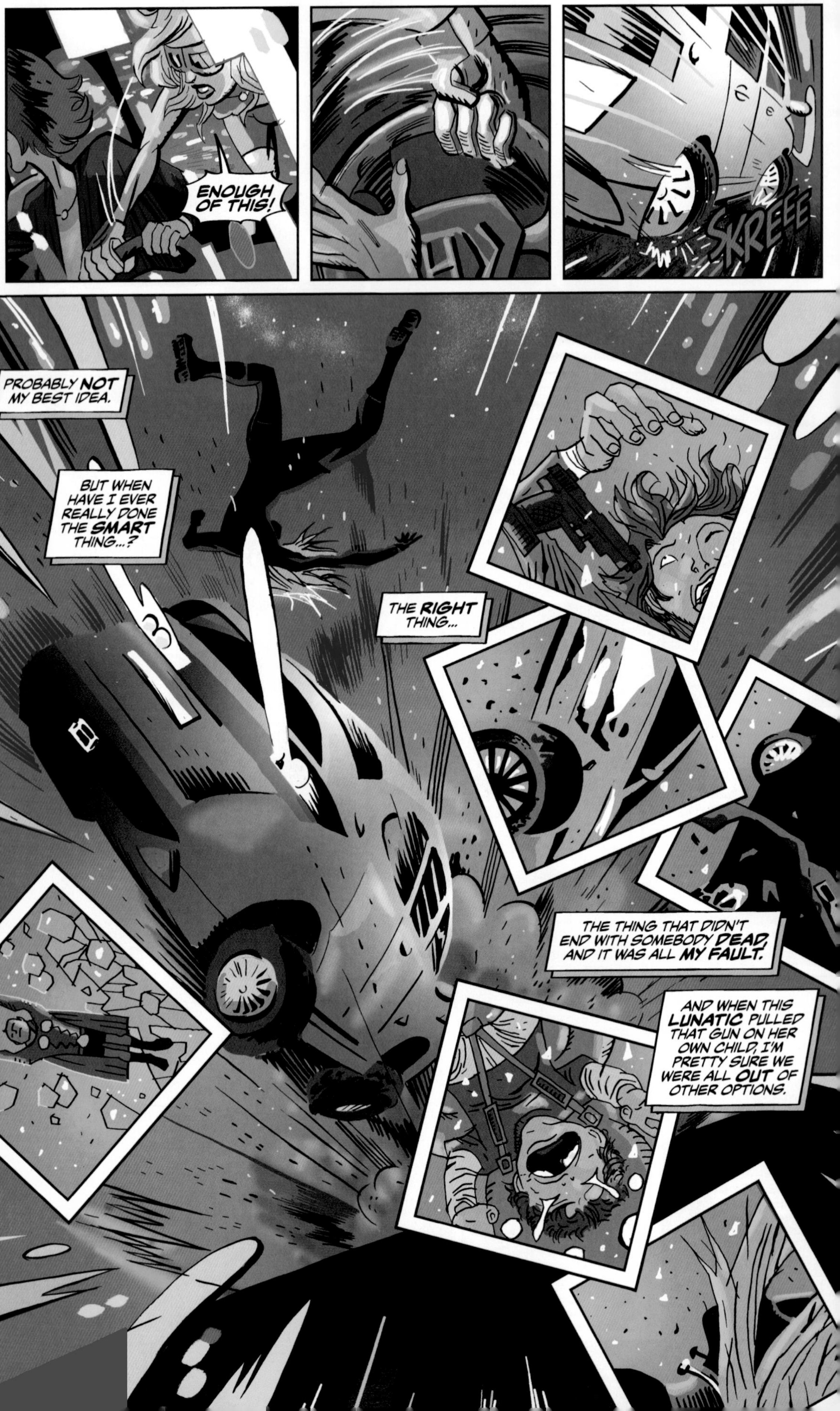
ENOUGH OF THIS!
SKREEE
PROBABLY NOT MY BEST IDEA.
BUT WHEN HAVE I EVER REALLY DONE THE SMART THING...?
THE RIGHT THING...
THE THING THAT DIDN'T END WITH SOMEBODY DEAD, AND IT WAS ALL MY FAULT.
AND WHEN THIS LUNATIC PULLED THAT GUN ON HER OWN CHILD, I'M PRETTY SURE WE WERE ALL OUT OF OTHER OPTIONS.

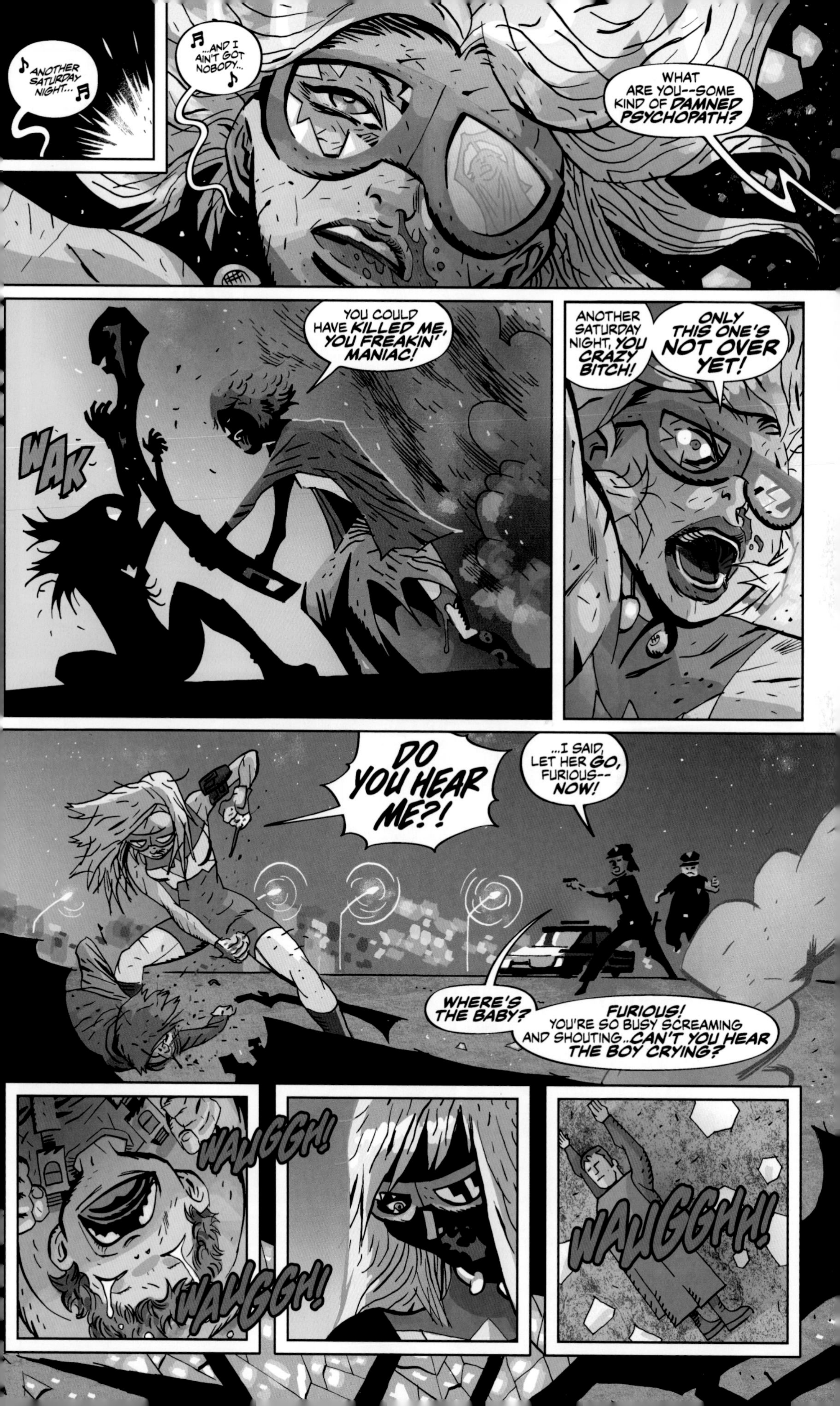
♪ ANOTHER SATURDAY NIGHT... ♫
♫ ...AND I AIN'T GOT NOBODY... ♪
WHAT ARE YOU--SOME KIND OF DAMNED PSYCHOPATH?
YOU COULD HAVE KILLED ME, YOU FREAKIN' MANIAC!
WAK
ANOTHER SATURDAY NIGHT, YOU CRAZY BITCH!
ONLY THIS ONE'S NOT OVER YET!
DO YOU HEAR ME?!
...I SAID, LET HER GO, FURIOUS-- NOW!
WHERE'S THE BABY?
FURIOUS! YOU'RE SO BUSY SCREAMING AND SHOUTING...CAN'T YOU HEAR THE BOY CRYING?
WAUGGH!
WAUGGH!
WAUGGHH!

I CAN STILL FEEL IT, CHURNING UP MY GUTS...ANGER...**RAGE!** OR MAYBE GETTING HIT BY THAT TRUCK IS GOING TO **KILL** ME AFTER ALL!

BUT I'VE GOT TO DO **SOMETHING**...DO SOMETHING RIGHT BEFORE I **EXPLODE** ON THE WRONG PERSON!

YOU'VE STILL GOT A LONG WAY TO GO CRAWLING OUT OF THIS **DAMNED HOLE** YOU DUG FOR YOURSELF.

...YEAH, IT'S A MESS. OWNER WAS BLUDGEONED ON THE BACK OF THE HEAD WITH A **BASEBALL BAT**...

WITH ANY LUCK, MAYBE SOME IDIOT WILL STILL TRY TO HOLD UP THIS STORE TONIGHT AFTER ALL...

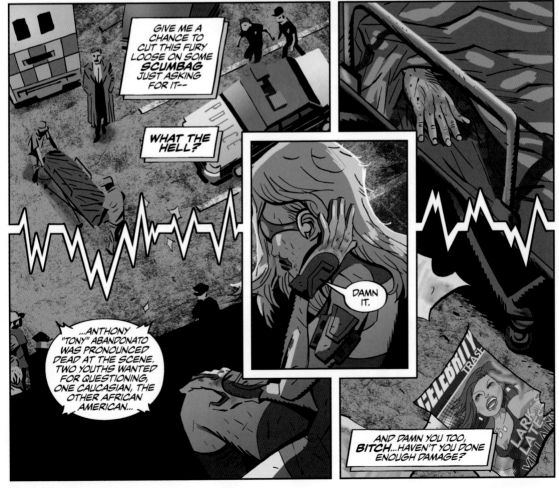

GIVE ME A CHANCE TO CUT THIS FURY LOOSE ON SOME **SCUMBAG** JUST ASKING FOR IT--

WHAT THE **HELL?**

DAMN IT.

...ANTHONY "TONY" ABANDONATO WAS PRONOUNCED DEAD AT THE SCENE. TWO YOUTHS WANTED FOR QUESTIONING, ONE CAUCASIAN, THE OTHER AFRICAN AMERICAN...

AND DAMN YOU TOO, **BITCH**...HAVEN'T YOU DONE ENOUGH DAMAGE?

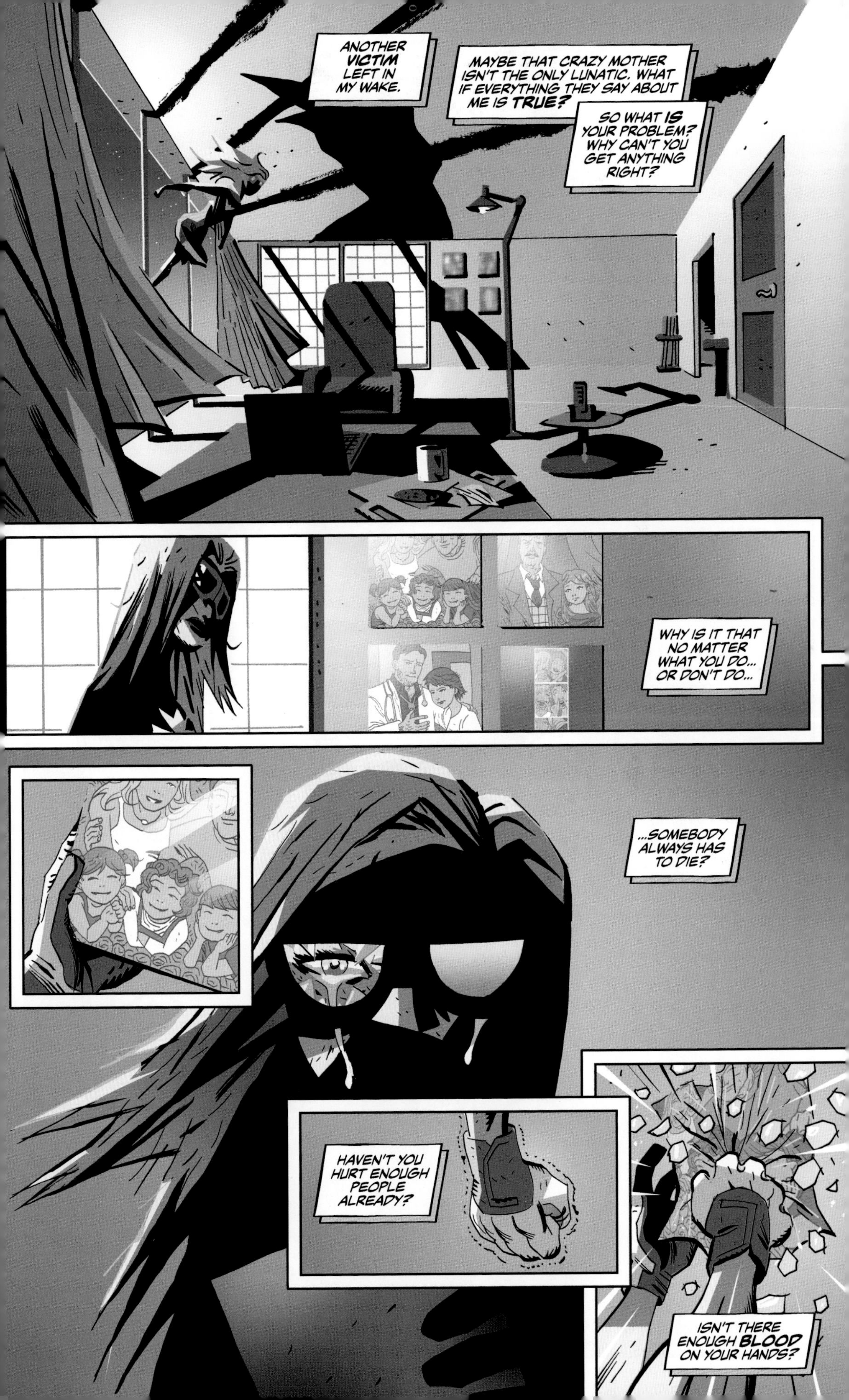
ANOTHER VICTIM LEFT IN MY WAKE.
MAYBE THAT CRAZY MOTHER ISN'T THE ONLY LUNATIC. WHAT IF EVERYTHING THEY SAY ABOUT ME IS TRUE?
SO WHAT IS YOUR PROBLEM? WHY CAN'T YOU GET ANYTHING RIGHT?
WHY IS IT THAT NO MATTER WHAT YOU DO... OR DON'T DO...
...SOMEBODY ALWAYS HAS TO DIE?
HAVEN'T YOU HURT ENOUGH PEOPLE ALREADY?
ISN'T THERE ENOUGH BLOOD ON YOUR HANDS?

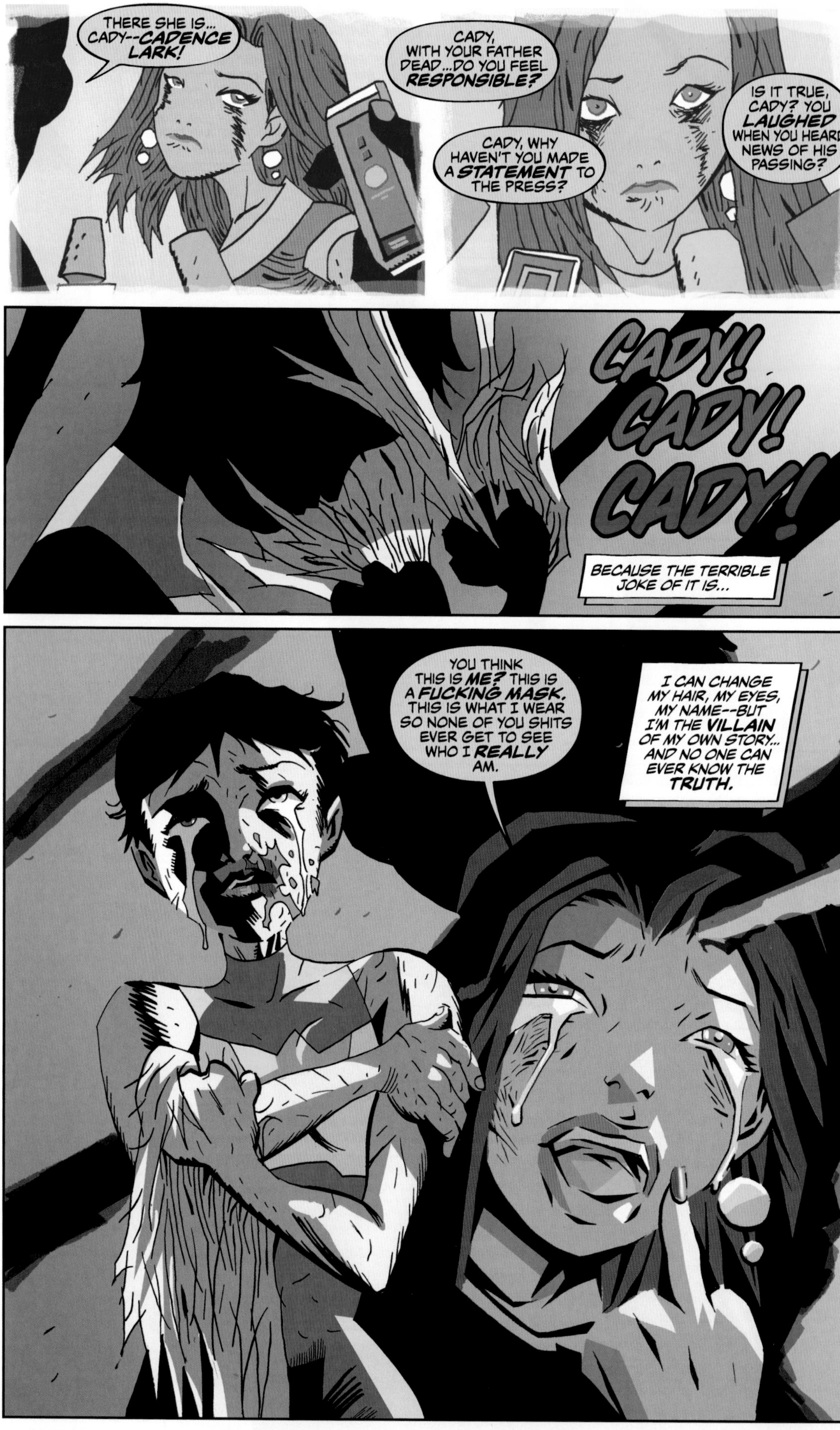
THERE SHE IS... CADY--CADENCE LARK!
CADY, WITH YOUR FATHER DEAD...DO YOU FEEL RESPONSIBLE?
CADY, WHY HAVEN'T YOU MADE A STATEMENT TO THE PRESS?
IS IT TRUE, CADY? YOU LAUGHED WHEN YOU HEARD NEWS OF HIS PASSING?
CADY! CADY! CADY!
BECAUSE THE TERRIBLE JOKE OF IT IS...
YOU THINK THIS IS ME? THIS IS A FUCKING MASK. THIS IS WHAT I WEAR SO NONE OF YOU SHITS EVER GET TO SEE WHO I REALLY AM.
I CAN CHANGE MY HAIR, MY EYES, MY NAME--BUT I'M THE VILLAIN OF MY OWN STORY... AND NO ONE CAN EVER KNOW THE TRUTH.

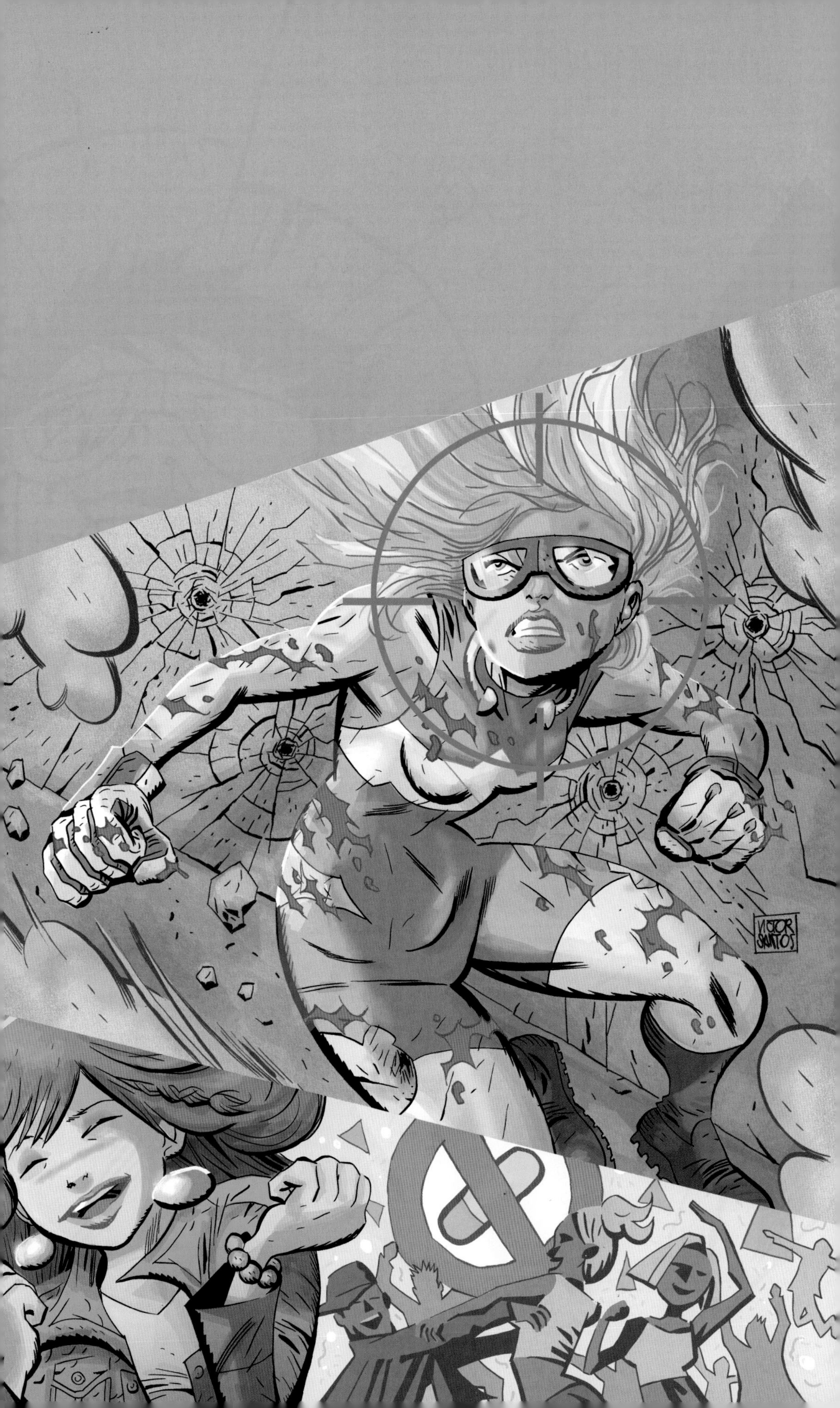
VICTOR SANTOS

CHAPTER TWO: A DREAM OF FLYING

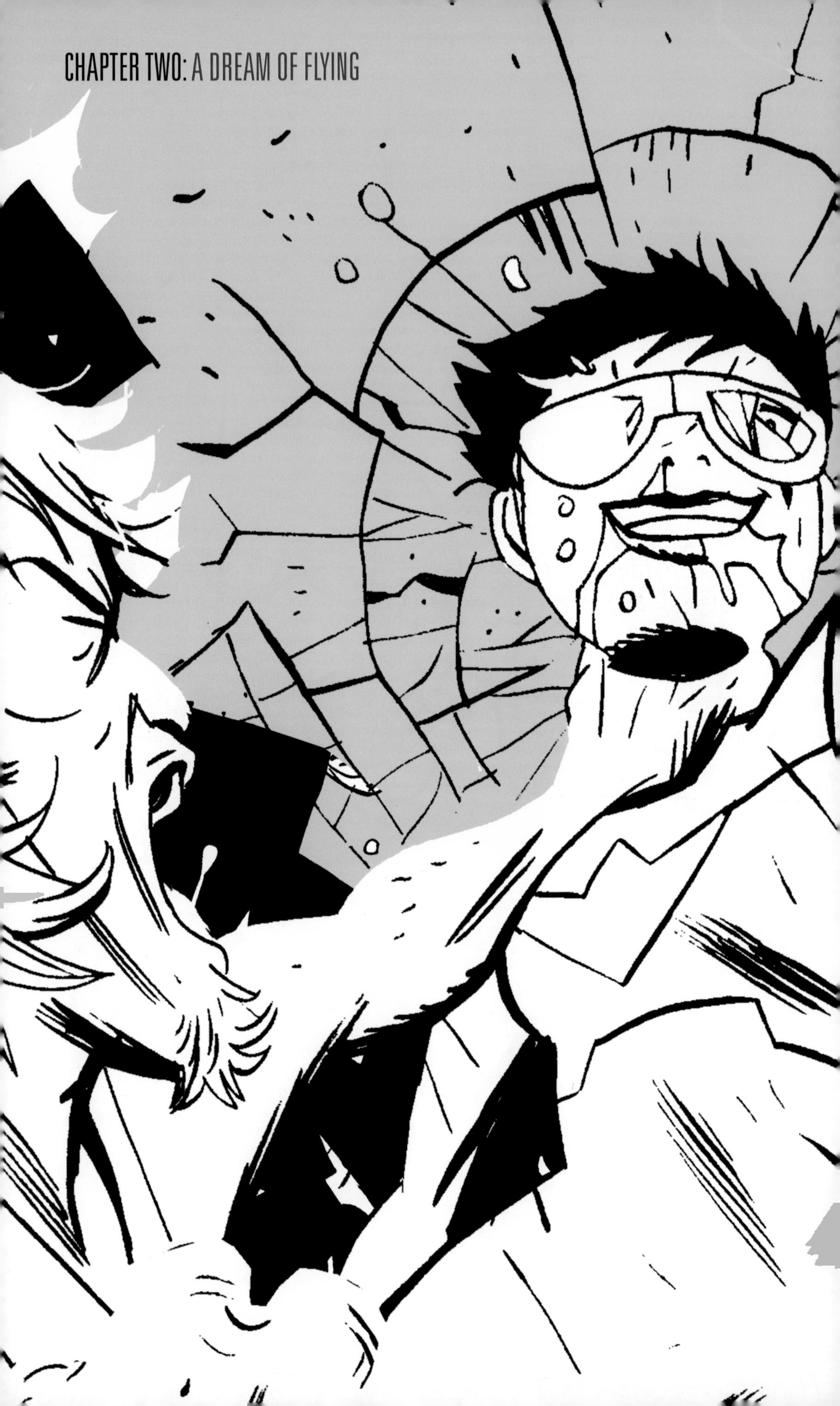

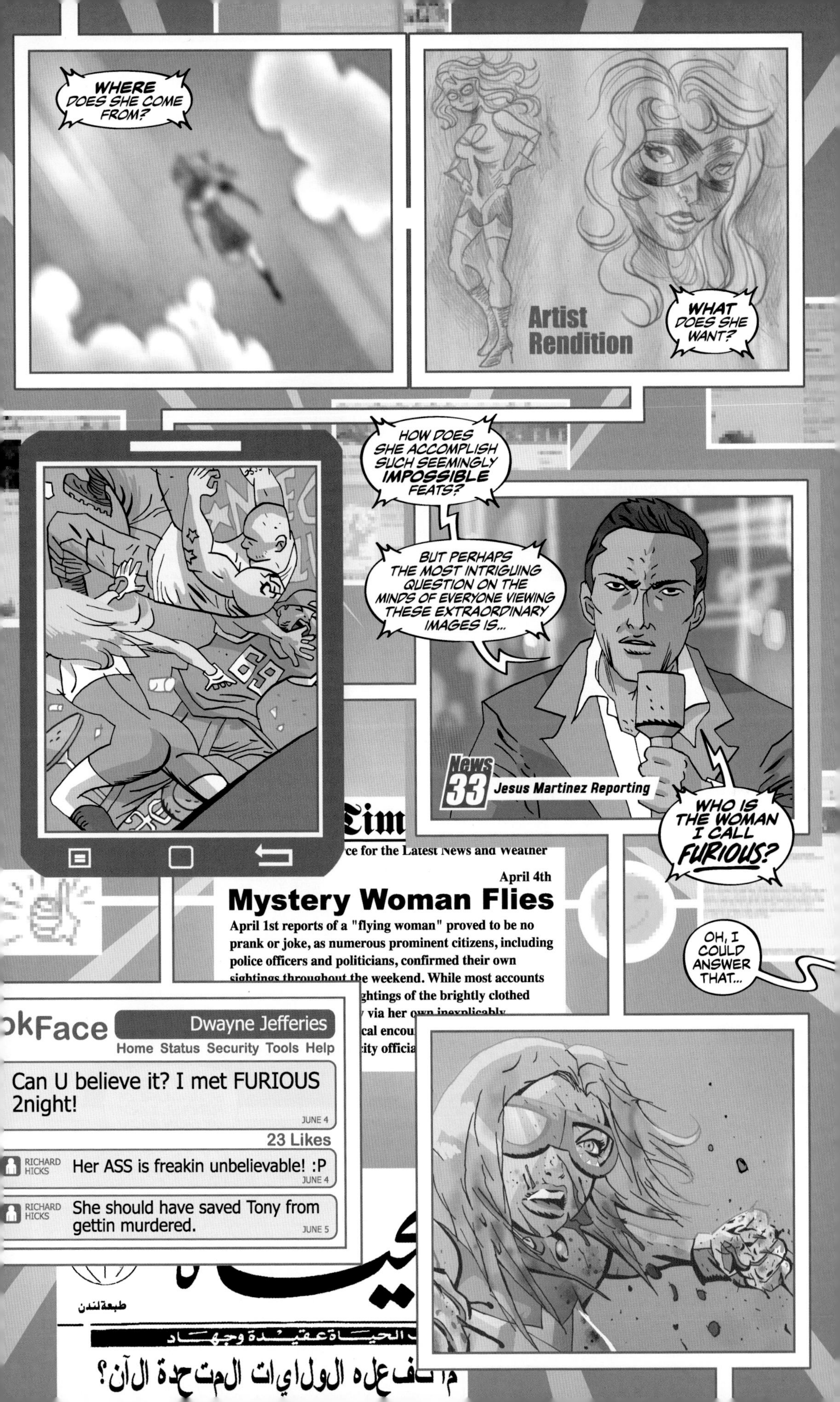

WHERE DOES SHE COME FROM?
Artist Rendition
WHAT DOES SHE WANT?
HOW DOES SHE ACCOMPLISH SUCH SEEMINGLY IMPOSSIBLE FEATS?
BUT PERHAPS THE MOST INTRIGUING QUESTION ON THE MINDS OF EVERYONE VIEWING THESE EXTRAORDINARY IMAGES IS...
News 33 Jesus Martinez Reporting
WHO IS THE WOMAN I CALL FURIOUS?
rce for the Latest News and Weather
April 4th
Mystery Woman Flies
April 1st reports of a "flying woman" proved to be no prank or joke, as numerous prominent citizens, including police officers and politicians, confirmed their own sightings throughout the weekend. While most accounts
ghtings of the brightly clothed
y via her own inexplicably
cal encou
ity officia
OH, I COULD ANSWER THAT...
okFace
Dwayne Jefferies
Home Status Security Tools Help
Can U believe it? I met FURIOUS 2night!
JUNE 4
23 Likes
RICHARD HICKS Her ASS is freakin unbelievable! :P
JUNE 4
RICHARD HICKS She should have saved Tony from gettin murdered.
JUNE 5
طبعة لندن

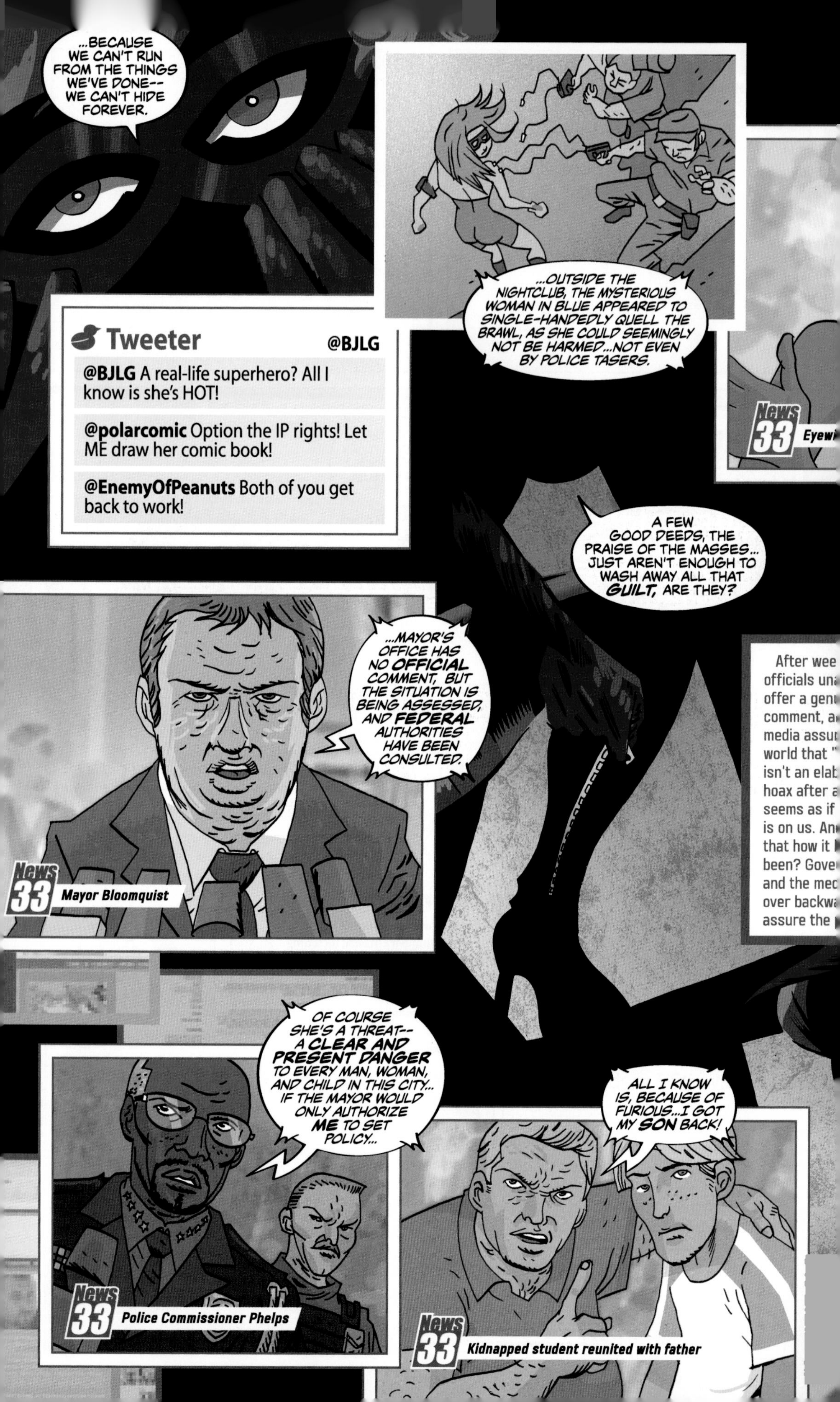

...BECAUSE WE CAN'T RUN FROM THE THINGS WE'VE DONE-- WE CAN'T HIDE FOREVER.
...OUTSIDE THE NIGHTCLUB, THE MYSTERIOUS WOMAN IN BLUE APPEARED TO SINGLE-HANDEDLY QUELL THE BRAWL, AS SHE COULD SEEMINGLY NOT BE HARMED...NOT EVEN BY POLICE TASERS.
News 33 Eyewi
Tweeter @BJLG
@BJLG A real-life superhero? All I know is she's HOT!
@polarcomic Option the IP rights! Let ME draw her comic book!
@EnemyOfPeanuts Both of you get back to work!
A FEW GOOD DEEDS, THE PRAISE OF THE MASSES... JUST AREN'T ENOUGH TO WASH AWAY ALL THAT GUILT, ARE THEY?
...MAYOR'S OFFICE HAS NO OFFICIAL COMMENT, BUT THE SITUATION IS BEING ASSESSED, AND FEDERAL AUTHORITIES HAVE BEEN CONSULTED.
News 33 Mayor Bloomquist
After wee officials una offer a gen comment, a media assu world that " isn't an elab hoax after a seems as if is on us. An that how it been? Gove and the med over backwa assure the
OF COURSE SHE'S A THREAT-- A CLEAR AND PRESENT DANGER TO EVERY MAN, WOMAN, AND CHILD IN THIS CITY... IF THE MAYOR WOULD ONLY AUTHORIZE ME TO SET POLICY...
News 33 Police Commissioner Phelps
ALL I KNOW IS, BECAUSE OF FURIOUS...I GOT MY SON BACK!
News 33 Kidnapped student reunited with father

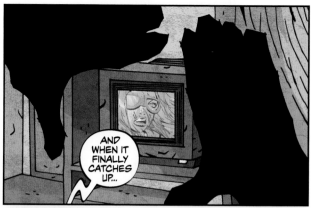

...AND IT'S LIKE SHE CAME OUT OF NOWHERE-- SWOOPING OUT OF THE SKY...AND SHE *SAVED MY LIFE!*

AND WHEN IT FINALLY CATCHES UP...

mony

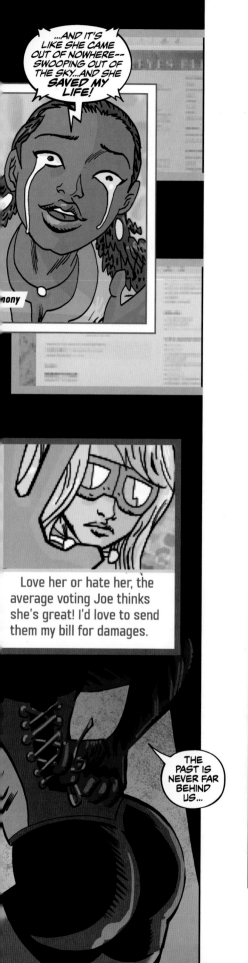

Love her or hate her, the average voting Joe thinks she's great! I'd love to send them my bill for damages.

THE PAST IS NEVER FAR BEHIND US...

WELL, WE CAN'T ESCAPE WHO WE *REALLY* ARE--*I WON'T LET US!*

KISS, *KISS...*

BANG, BANG!

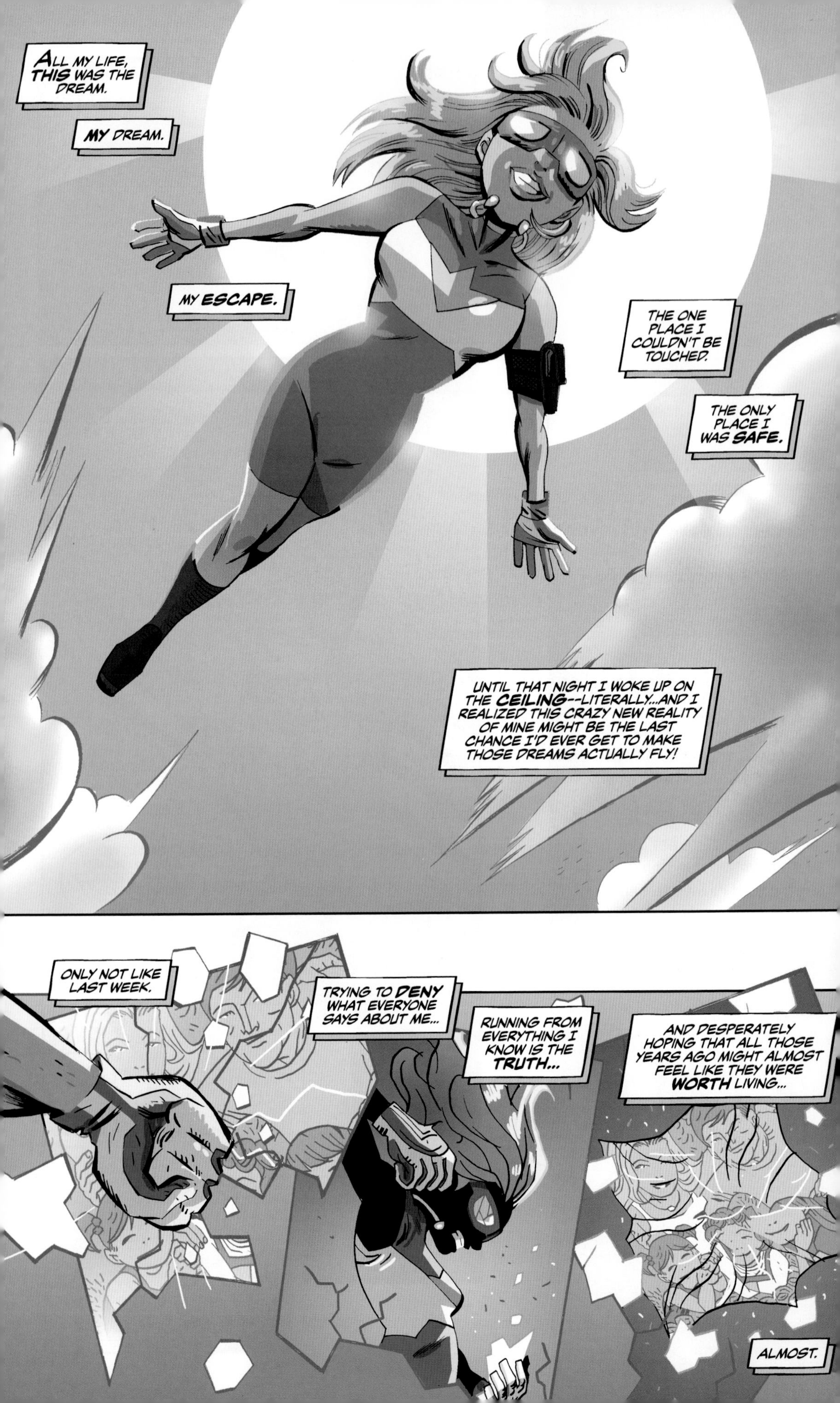

ALL MY LIFE, THIS WAS THE DREAM.
MY DREAM.
MY ESCAPE.
THE ONE PLACE I COULDN'T BE TOUCHED.
THE ONLY PLACE I WAS SAFE.
UNTIL THAT NIGHT I WOKE UP ON THE CEILING--LITERALLY...AND I REALIZED THIS CRAZY NEW REALITY OF MINE MIGHT BE THE LAST CHANCE I'D EVER GET TO MAKE THOSE DREAMS ACTUALLY FLY!
ONLY NOT LIKE LAST WEEK.
TRYING TO DENY WHAT EVERYONE SAYS ABOUT ME...
RUNNING FROM EVERYTHING I KNOW IS THE TRUTH...
AND DESPERATELY HOPING THAT ALL THOSE YEARS AGO MIGHT ALMOST FEEL LIKE THEY WERE WORTH LIVING...
ALMOST.

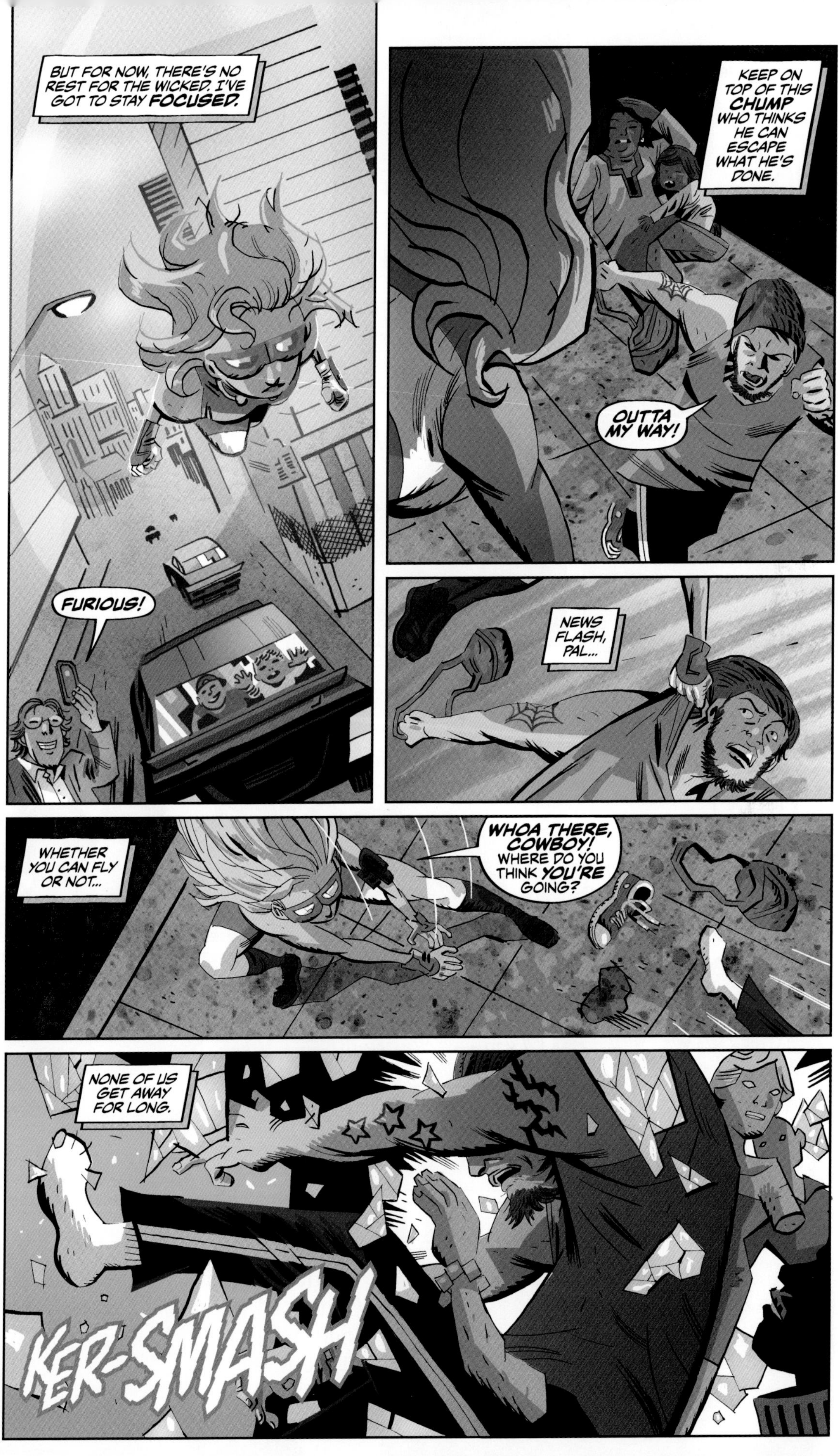
BUT FOR NOW, THERE'S NO REST FOR THE WICKED. I'VE GOT TO STAY FOCUSED.
FURIOUS!
KEEP ON TOP OF THIS CHUMP WHO THINKS HE CAN ESCAPE WHAT HE'S DONE.
OUTTA MY WAY!
NEWS FLASH, PAL...
WHETHER YOU CAN FLY OR NOT...
WHOA THERE, COWBOY! WHERE DO YOU THINK YOU'RE GOING?
NONE OF US GET AWAY FOR LONG.
KER-SMASH

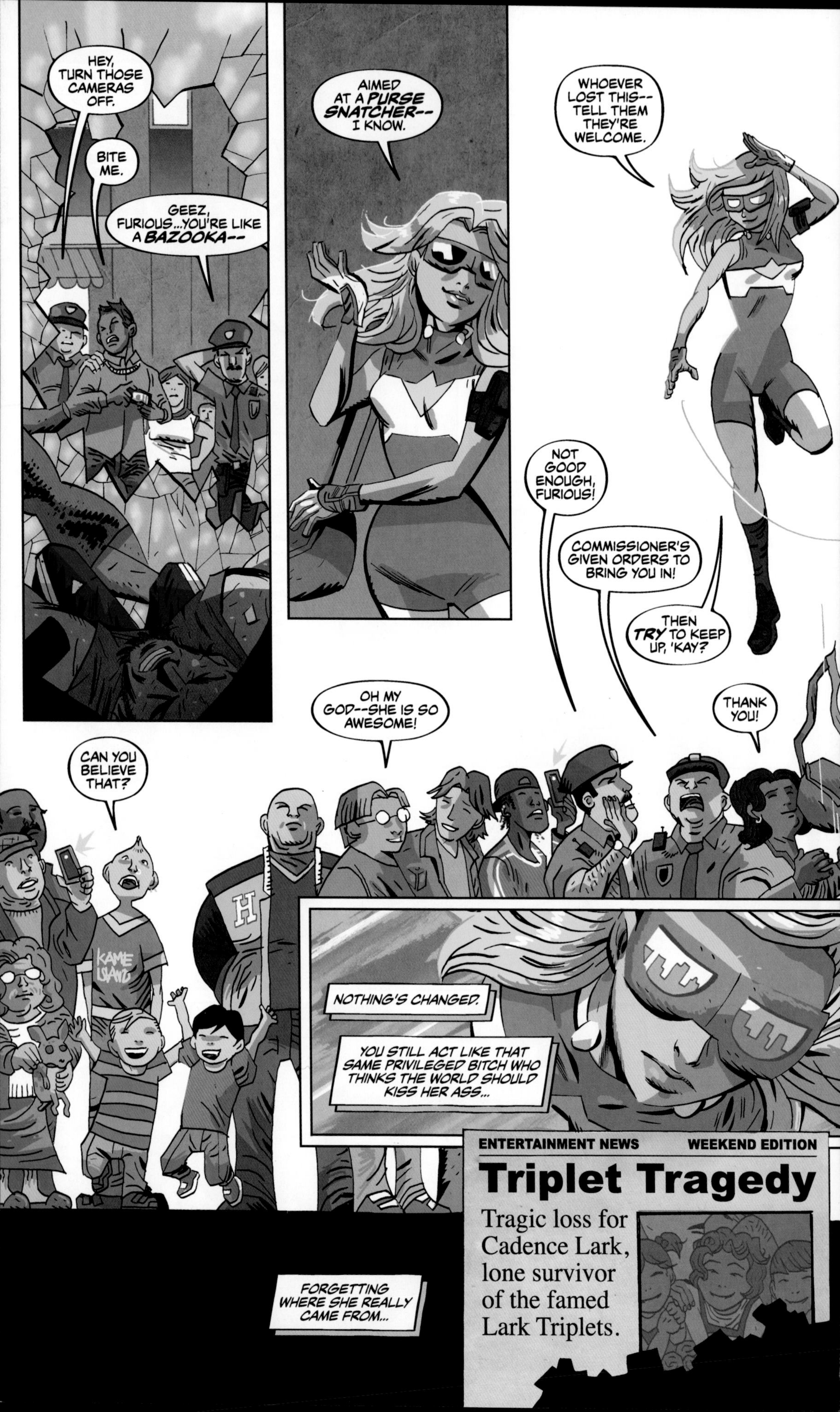
HEY, TURN THOSE CAMERAS OFF.
BITE ME.
GEEZ, FURIOUS...YOU'RE LIKE A BAZOOKA--
AIMED AT A PURSE SNATCHER-- I KNOW.
WHOEVER LOST THIS-- TELL THEM THEY'RE WELCOME.
NOT GOOD ENOUGH, FURIOUS!
COMMISSIONER'S GIVEN ORDERS TO BRING YOU IN!
THEN TRY TO KEEP UP, 'KAY?
CAN YOU BELIEVE THAT?
OH MY GOD--SHE IS SO AWESOME!
THANK YOU!
KAME LAND
H
NOTHING'S CHANGED.
YOU STILL ACT LIKE THAT SAME PRIVILEGED BITCH WHO THINKS THE WORLD SHOULD KISS HER ASS...
ENTERTAINMENT NEWS
WEEKEND EDITION
Triplet Tragedy
Tragic loss for Cadence Lark, lone survivor of the famed Lark Triplets.
FORGETTING WHERE SHE REALLY CAME FROM...

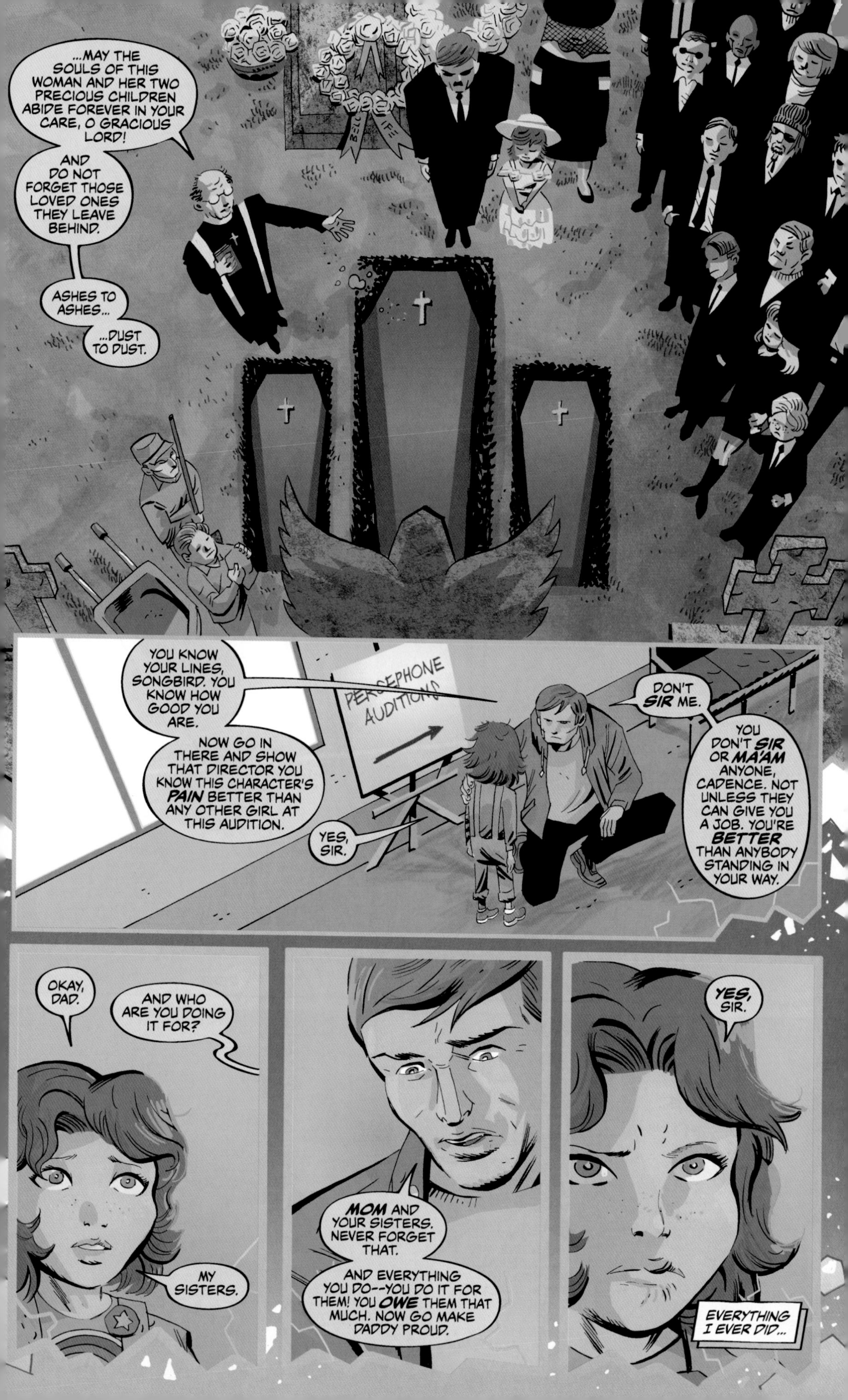
...MAY THE SOULS OF THIS WOMAN AND HER TWO PRECIOUS CHILDREN ABIDE FOREVER IN YOUR CARE, O GRACIOUS LORD!
AND DO NOT FORGET THOSE LOVED ONES THEY LEAVE BEHIND.
ASHES TO ASHES...
...DUST TO DUST.
YOU KNOW YOUR LINES, SONGBIRD. YOU KNOW HOW GOOD YOU ARE.
NOW GO IN THERE AND SHOW THAT DIRECTOR YOU KNOW THIS CHARACTER'S PAIN BETTER THAN ANY OTHER GIRL AT THIS AUDITION.
PERSEPHONE AUDITIONS
YES, SIR.
DON'T SIR ME.
YOU DON'T SIR OR MA'AM ANYONE, CADENCE. NOT UNLESS THEY CAN GIVE YOU A JOB. YOU'RE BETTER THAN ANYBODY STANDING IN YOUR WAY.
OKAY, DAD.
AND WHO ARE YOU DOING IT FOR?
MY SISTERS.
MOM AND YOUR SISTERS. NEVER FORGET THAT.
AND EVERYTHING YOU DO--YOU DO IT FOR THEM! YOU OWE THEM THAT MUCH. NOW GO MAKE DADDY PROUD.
YES, SIR.
EVERYTHING I EVER DID...

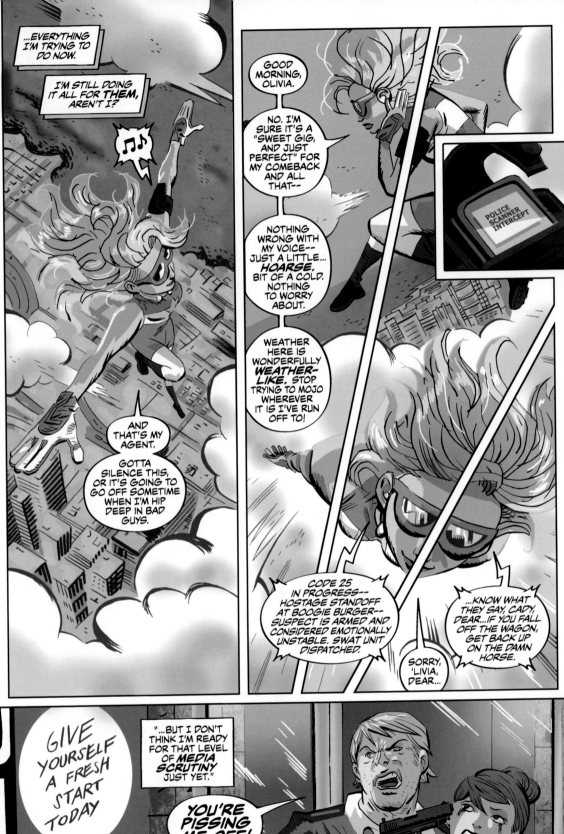

...EVERYTHING I'M TRYING TO DO NOW.

I'M STILL DOING IT ALL FOR *THEM*, AREN'T I?

♪♪

AND THAT'S MY AGENT.

GOTTA SILENCE THIS, OR IT'S GOING TO GO OFF SOMETIME WHEN I'M HIP DEEP IN BAD GUYS.

GOOD MORNING, OLIVIA.

NO. I'M SURE IT'S A "SWEET GIG, AND JUST PERFECT" FOR MY COMEBACK AND ALL THAT--

NOTHING WRONG WITH MY VOICE-- JUST A LITTLE... *HOARSE.* BIT OF A COLD. NOTHING TO WORRY ABOUT.

WEATHER HERE IS WONDERFULLY *WEATHER- LIKE.* STOP TRYING TO MOJO WHEREVER IT IS I'VE RUN OFF TO!

POLICE SCANNER INTERCEPT

CODE 25 IN PROGRESS-- HOSTAGE STANDOFF AT BOOGIE BURGER-- SUSPECT IS ARMED AND CONSIDERED EMOTIONALLY UNSTABLE. SWAT UNIT DISPATCHED.

...KNOW WHAT THEY SAY, CADY, DEAR...IF YOU FALL OFF THE WAGON, GET BACK UP ON THE DAMN HORSE.

SORRY, 'LIVIA, DEAR...

GIVE YOURSELF A FRESH START TODAY

"...BUT I DON'T THINK I'M READY FOR THAT LEVEL OF *MEDIA SCRUTINY* JUST YET."

YOU'RE PISSING ME OFF!

AND BELIEVE ME, *YOU DO NOT WANT* TO PISS ME OFF! NOT *TODAY!* NOT *EVER!* OR THE BLOOD OF ALL THESE PEOPLE IS GONNA BE ON *YOUR HANDS!*

CLAIRE

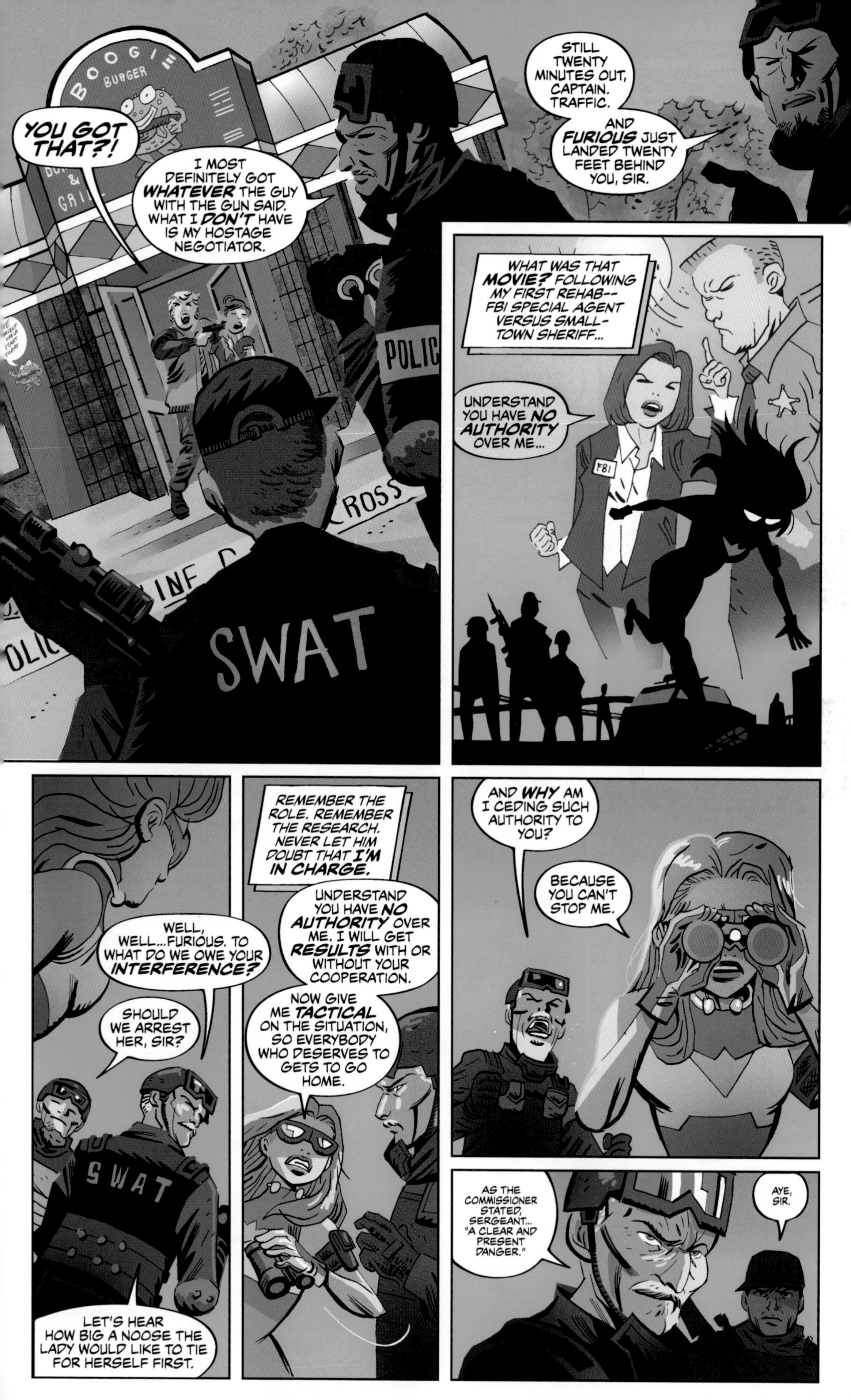

BOOGIE BURGER
YOU GOT THAT?!
I MOST DEFINITELY GOT WHATEVER THE GUY WITH THE GUN SAID. WHAT I DON'T HAVE IS MY HOSTAGE NEGOTIATOR.
STILL TWENTY MINUTES OUT, CAPTAIN. TRAFFIC.
AND FURIOUS JUST LANDED TWENTY FEET BEHIND YOU, SIR.
POLIC
SWAT
WHAT WAS THAT MOVIE? FOLLOWING MY FIRST REHAB-- FBI SPECIAL AGENT VERSUS SMALL-TOWN SHERIFF...
UNDERSTAND YOU HAVE NO AUTHORITY OVER ME...
FBI
WELL, WELL...FURIOUS. TO WHAT DO WE OWE YOUR INTERFERENCE?
SHOULD WE ARREST HER, SIR?
LET'S HEAR HOW BIG A NOOSE THE LADY WOULD LIKE TO TIE FOR HERSELF FIRST.
SWAT
REMEMBER THE ROLE. REMEMBER THE RESEARCH. NEVER LET HIM DOUBT THAT I'M IN CHARGE.
UNDERSTAND YOU HAVE NO AUTHORITY OVER ME. I WILL GET RESULTS WITH OR WITHOUT YOUR COOPERATION.
NOW GIVE ME TACTICAL ON THE SITUATION, SO EVERYBODY WHO DESERVES TO GETS TO GO HOME.
AND WHY AM I CEDING SUCH AUTHORITY TO YOU?
BECAUSE YOU CAN'T STOP ME.
AS THE COMMISSIONER STATED, SERGEANT... "A CLEAR AND PRESENT DANGER."
AYE, SIR.

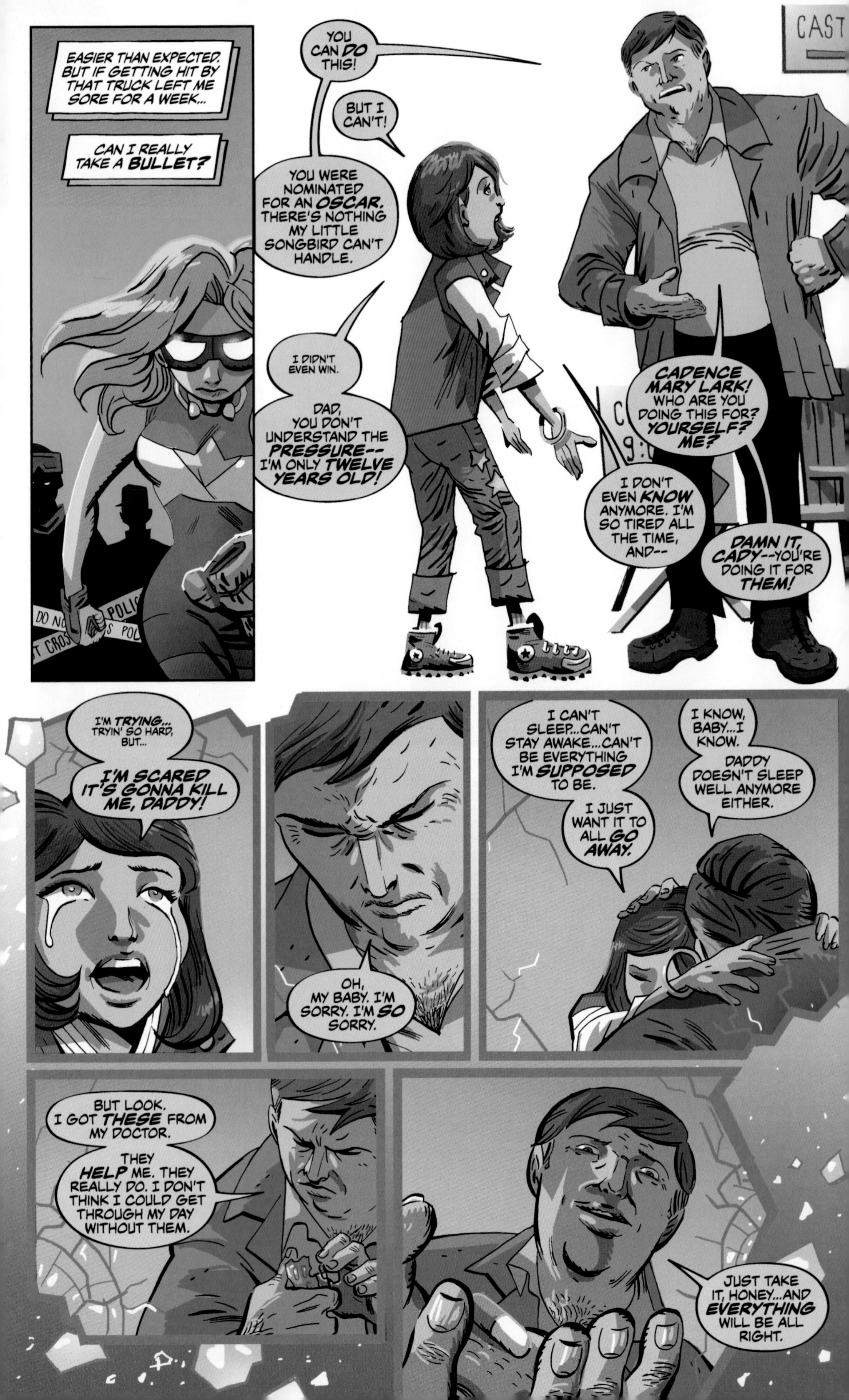
EASIER THAN EXPECTED. BUT IF GETTING HIT BY THAT TRUCK LEFT ME SORE FOR A WEEK...
CAN I REALLY TAKE A BULLET?
YOU CAN DO THIS!
BUT I CAN'T!
YOU WERE NOMINATED FOR AN OSCAR. THERE'S NOTHING MY LITTLE SONGBIRD CAN'T HANDLE.
I DIDN'T EVEN WIN.
DAD, YOU DON'T UNDERSTAND THE PRESSURE-- I'M ONLY TWELVE YEARS OLD!
CADENCE MARY LARK! WHO ARE YOU DOING THIS FOR? YOURSELF? ME?
I DON'T EVEN KNOW ANYMORE. I'M SO TIRED ALL THE TIME, AND--
DAMN IT, CADY--YOU'RE DOING IT FOR THEM!
CAST
DO NO
POLIC
T CROS
S POL
I'M TRYING... TRYIN' SO HARD, BUT...
I'M SCARED IT'S GONNA KILL ME, DADDY!
OH, MY BABY. I'M SORRY. I'M SO SORRY.
I CAN'T SLEEP...CAN'T STAY AWAKE...CAN'T BE EVERYTHING I'M SUPPOSED TO BE.
I JUST WANT IT TO ALL GO AWAY.
I KNOW, BABY...I KNOW.
DADDY DOESN'T SLEEP WELL ANYMORE EITHER.
BUT LOOK. I GOT THESE FROM MY DOCTOR.
THEY HELP ME. THEY REALLY DO. I DON'T THINK I COULD GET THROUGH MY DAY WITHOUT THEM.
JUST TAKE IT, HONEY...AND EVERYTHING WILL BE ALL RIGHT.

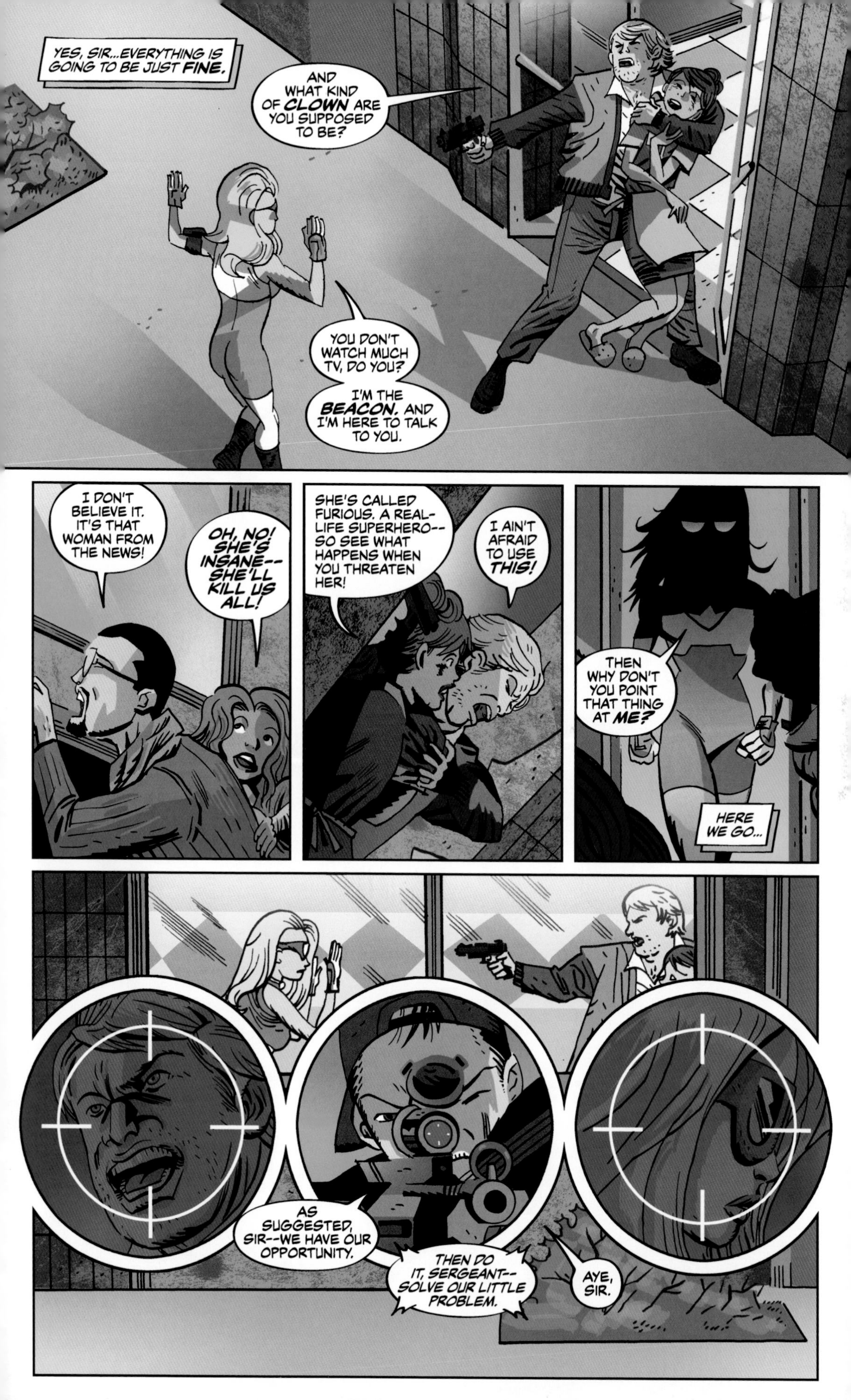
YES, SIR...EVERYTHING IS GOING TO BE JUST FINE.
AND WHAT KIND OF CLOWN ARE YOU SUPPOSED TO BE?
YOU DON'T WATCH MUCH TV, DO YOU?
I'M THE BEACON. AND I'M HERE TO TALK TO YOU.
I DON'T BELIEVE IT. IT'S THAT WOMAN FROM THE NEWS!
OH, NO! SHE'S INSANE--SHE'LL KILL US ALL!
SHE'S CALLED FURIOUS. A REAL-LIFE SUPERHERO--SO SEE WHAT HAPPENS WHEN YOU THREATEN HER!
I AIN'T AFRAID TO USE THIS!
THEN WHY DON'T YOU POINT THAT THING AT ME?
HERE WE GO...
AS SUGGESTED, SIR--WE HAVE OUR OPPORTUNITY.
THEN DO IT, SERGEANT--SOLVE OUR LITTLE PROBLEM.
AYE, SIR.

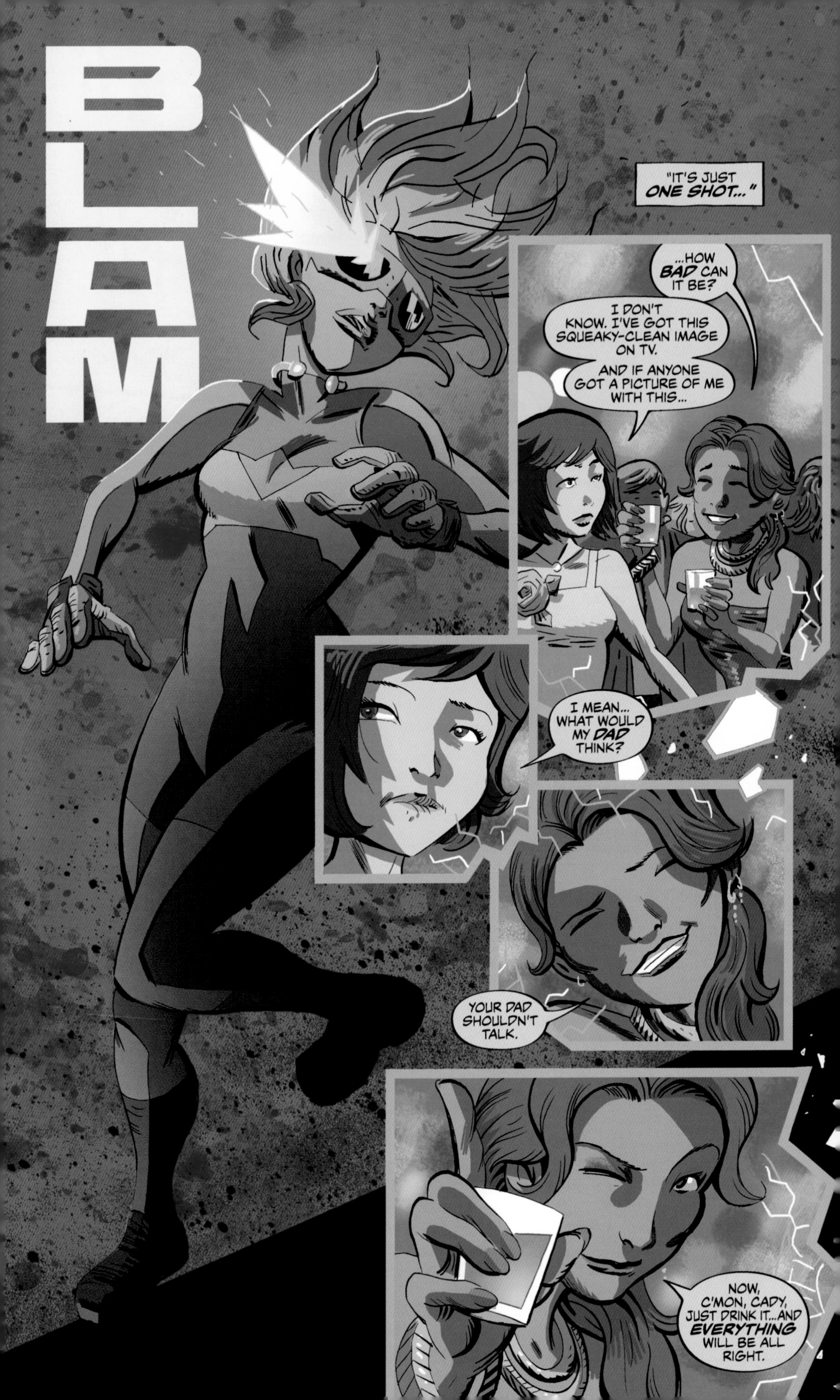
BLAM
"IT'S JUST ONE SHOT..."
...HOW BAD CAN IT BE?
I DON'T KNOW. I'VE GOT THIS SQUEAKY-CLEAN IMAGE ON TV.
AND IF ANYONE GOT A PICTURE OF ME WITH THIS...
I MEAN... WHAT WOULD MY DAD THINK?
YOUR DAD SHOULDN'T TALK.
NOW, C'MON, CADY, JUST DRINK IT...AND EVERYTHING WILL BE ALL RIGHT.

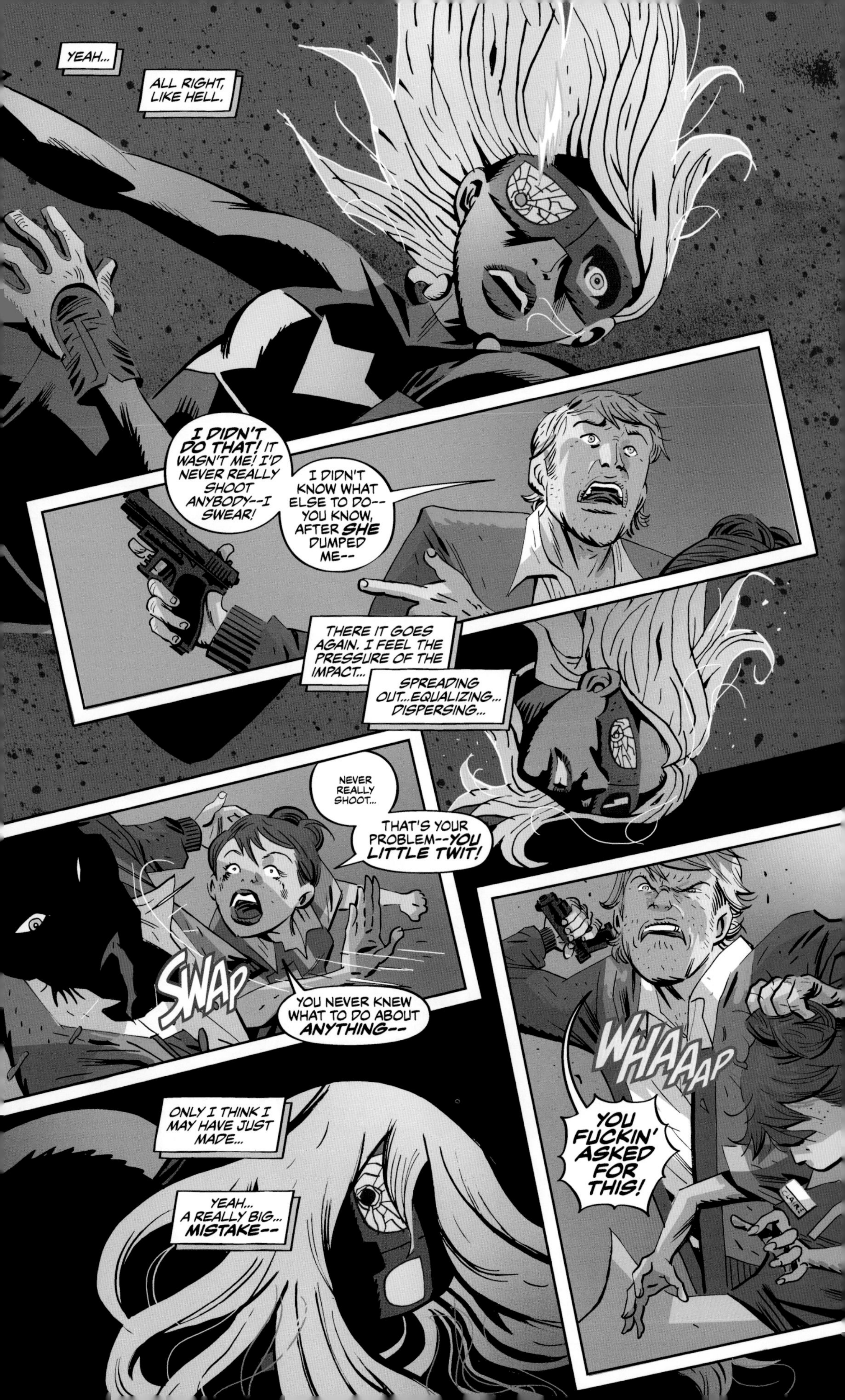
YEAH...
ALL RIGHT, LIKE HELL.
I DIDN'T DO THAT! IT WASN'T ME! I'D NEVER REALLY SHOOT ANYBODY--I SWEAR!
I DIDN'T KNOW WHAT ELSE TO DO-- YOU KNOW, AFTER SHE DUMPED ME--
THERE IT GOES AGAIN. I FEEL THE PRESSURE OF THE IMPACT...
SPREADING OUT...EQUALIZING... DISPERSING...
NEVER REALLY SHOOT...
THAT'S YOUR PROBLEM--YOU LITTLE TWIT!
SWAP
YOU NEVER KNEW WHAT TO DO ABOUT ANYTHING--
WHHAAAP
YOU FUCKIN' ASKED FOR THIS!
ONLY I THINK I MAY HAVE JUST MADE...
YEAH... A REALLY BIG... MISTAKE--

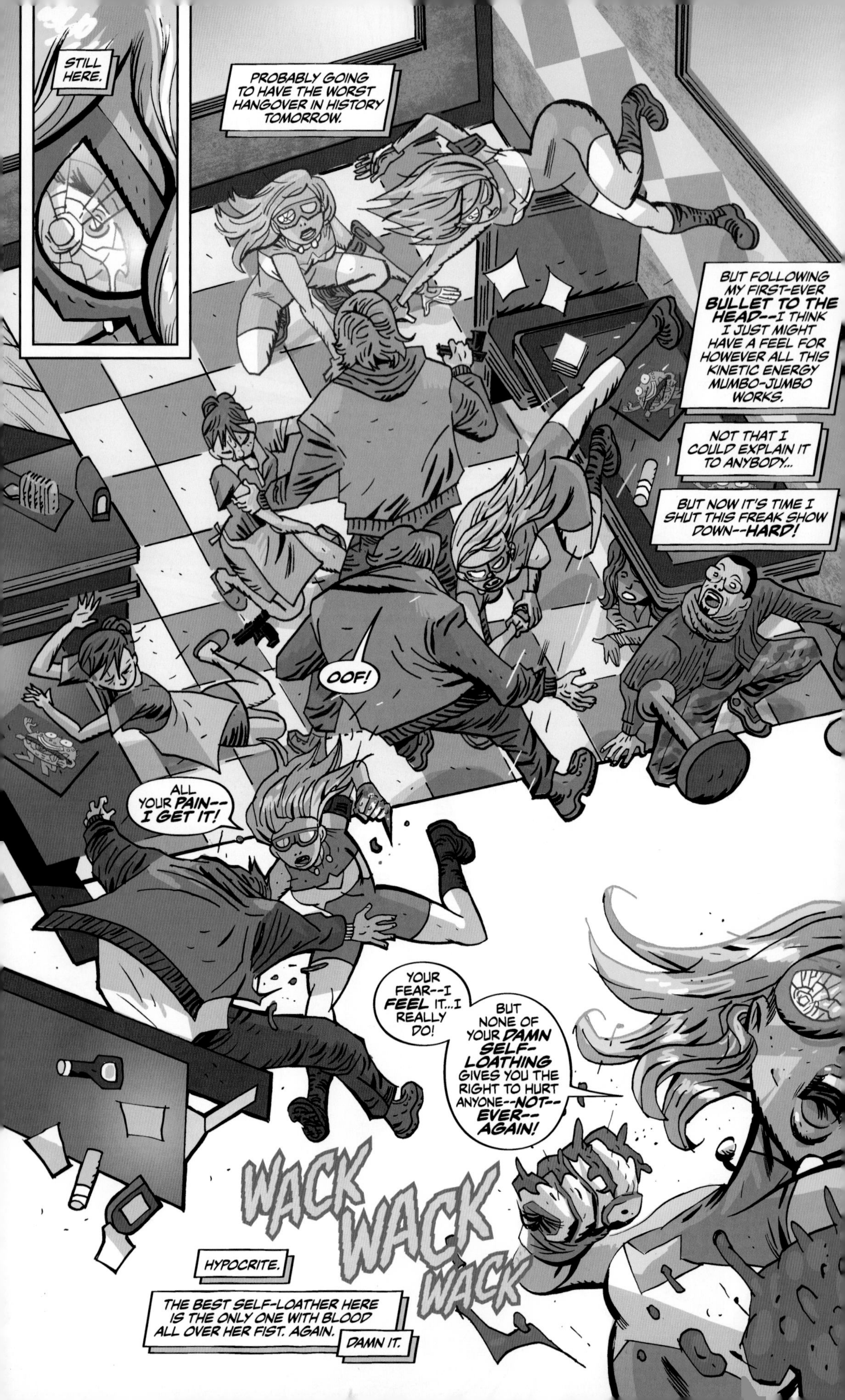

STILL HERE.
PROBABLY GOING TO HAVE THE WORST HANGOVER IN HISTORY TOMORROW.
BUT FOLLOWING MY FIRST-EVER BULLET TO THE HEAD--I THINK I JUST MIGHT HAVE A FEEL FOR HOWEVER ALL THIS KINETIC ENERGY MUMBO-JUMBO WORKS.
NOT THAT I COULD EXPLAIN IT TO ANYBODY...
BUT NOW IT'S TIME I SHUT THIS FREAK SHOW DOWN--HARD!
OOF!
ALL YOUR PAIN--I GET IT!
YOUR FEAR--I FEEL IT...I REALLY DO!
BUT NONE OF YOUR DAMN SELF-LOATHING GIVES YOU THE RIGHT TO HURT ANYONE--NOT--EVER--AGAIN!
WACK WACK WACK
HYPOCRITE.
THE BEST SELF-LOATHER HERE IS THE ONLY ONE WITH BLOOD ALL OVER HER FIST. AGAIN.
DAMN IT.

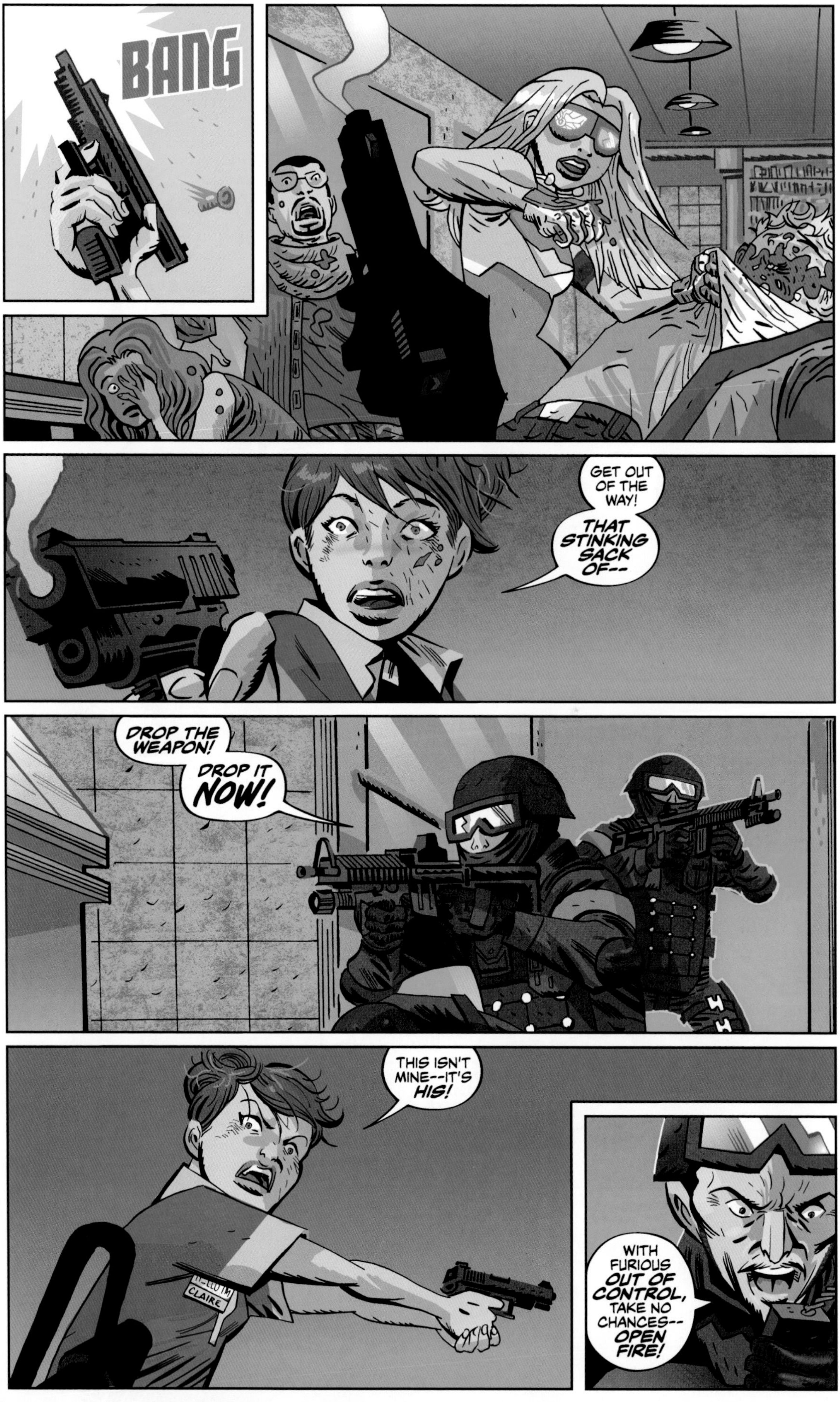
BANG
GET OUT OF THE WAY!
THAT STINKING SACK OF--
DROP THE WEAPON!
DROP IT NOW!
THIS ISN'T MINE--IT'S HIS!
CLAIRE
WITH FURIOUS OUT OF CONTROL, TAKE NO CHANCES-- OPEN FIRE!

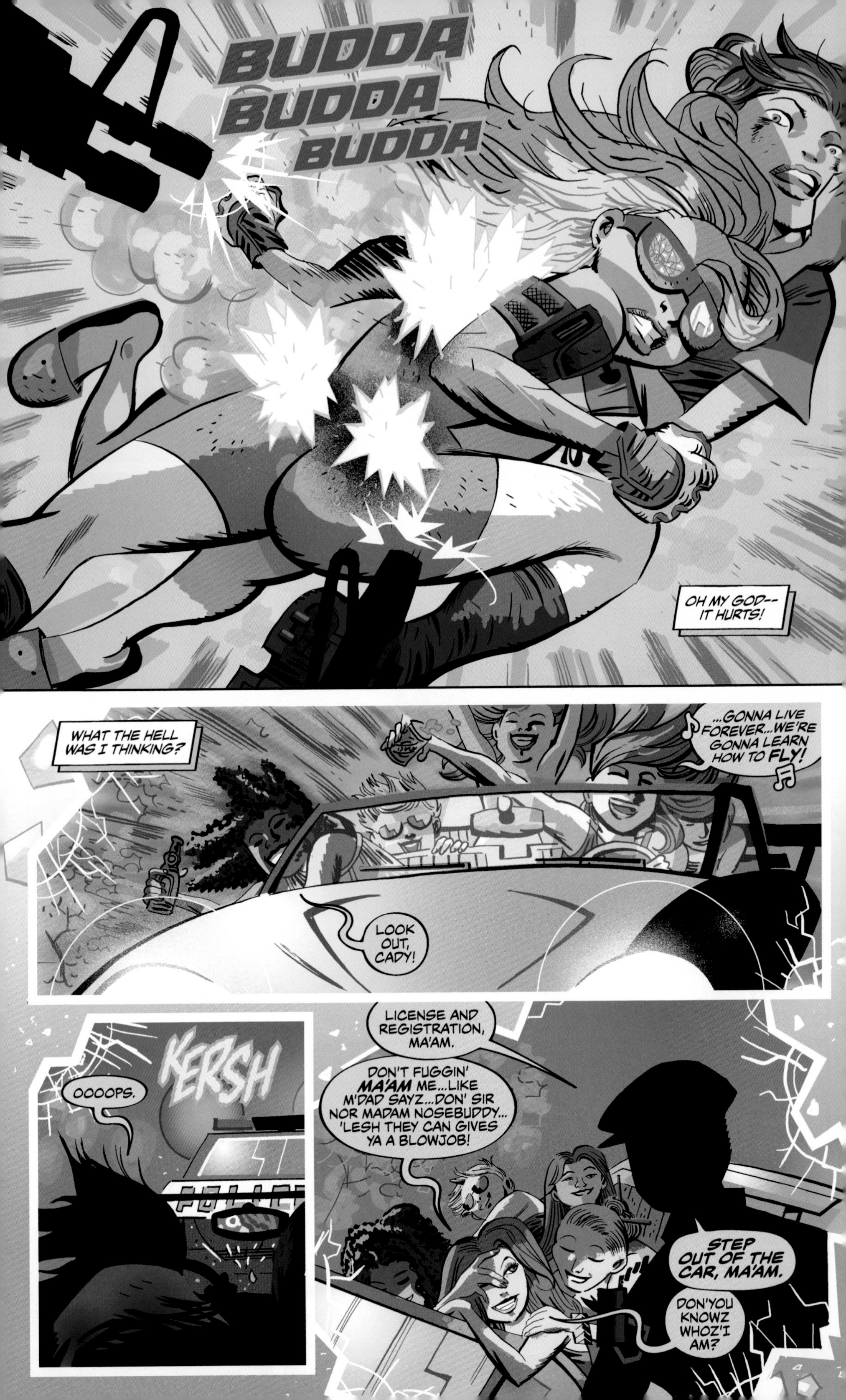
BUDDA
BUDDA
BUDDA
OH MY GOD-- IT HURTS!
WHAT THE HELL WAS I THINKING?
...GONNA LIVE FOREVER...WE'RE GONNA LEARN HOW TO FLY!
LOOK OUT, CADY!
KERSH
OOOOPS.
LICENSE AND REGISTRATION, MA'AM.
DON'T FUGGIN' MA'AM ME...LIKE M'DAD SAYZ...DON' SIR NOR MADAM NOSEBUDDY... 'LESH THEY CAN GIVES YA A BLOWJOB!
STEP OUT OF THE CAR, MA'AM.
DON'YOU KNOWZ WHOZ'I AM?

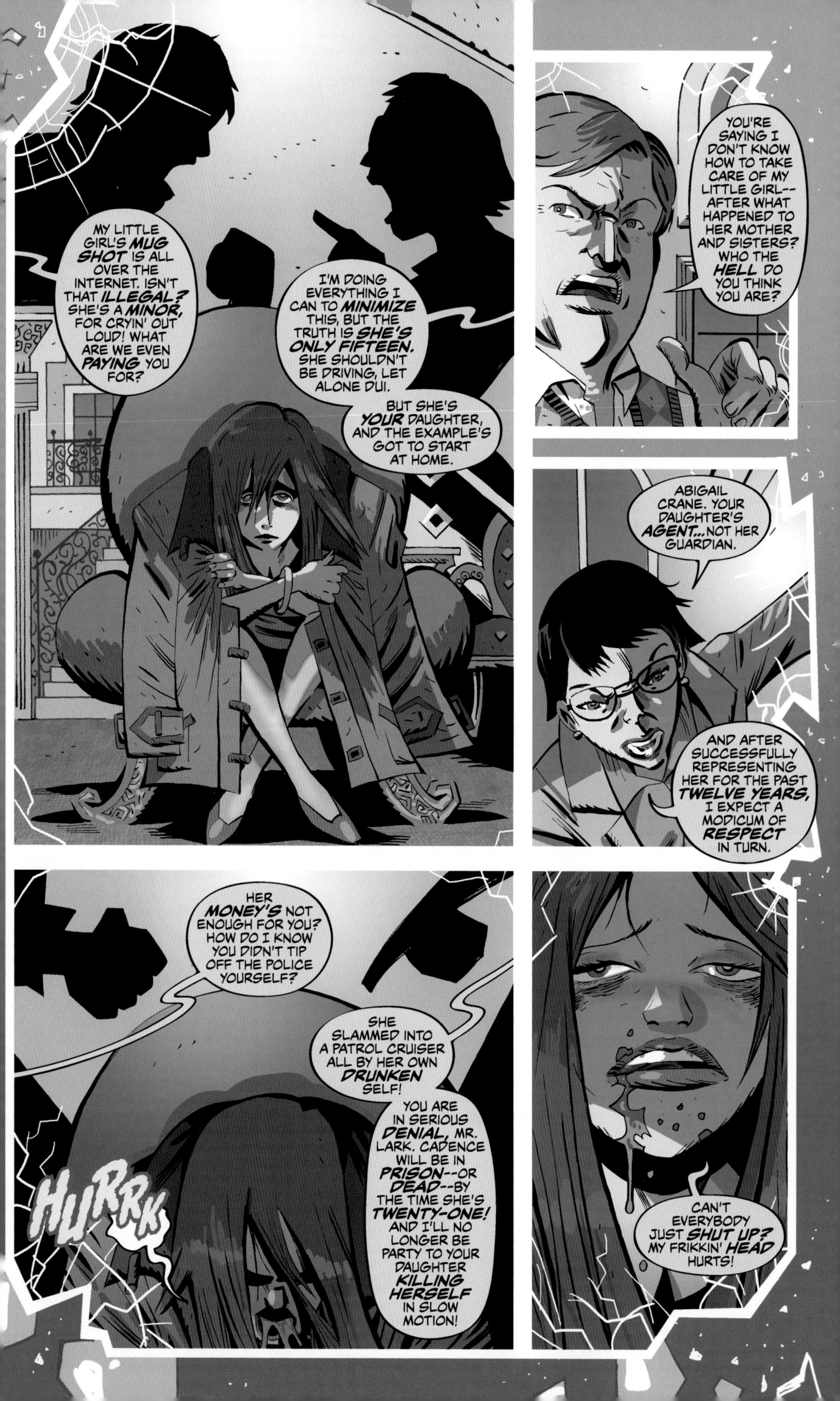

MY LITTLE GIRL'S MUG SHOT IS ALL OVER THE INTERNET. ISN'T THAT ILLEGAL? SHE'S A MINOR, FOR CRYIN' OUT LOUD! WHAT ARE WE EVEN PAYING YOU FOR?
I'M DOING EVERYTHING I CAN TO MINIMIZE THIS, BUT THE TRUTH IS SHE'S ONLY FIFTEEN. SHE SHOULDN'T BE DRIVING, LET ALONE DUI.
BUT SHE'S YOUR DAUGHTER, AND THE EXAMPLE'S GOT TO START AT HOME.
YOU'RE SAYING I DON'T KNOW HOW TO TAKE CARE OF MY LITTLE GIRL-- AFTER WHAT HAPPENED TO HER MOTHER AND SISTERS? WHO THE HELL DO YOU THINK YOU ARE?
ABIGAIL CRANE. YOUR DAUGHTER'S AGENT...NOT HER GUARDIAN.
AND AFTER SUCCESSFULLY REPRESENTING HER FOR THE PAST TWELVE YEARS, I EXPECT A MODICUM OF RESPECT IN TURN.
HER MONEY'S NOT ENOUGH FOR YOU? HOW DO I KNOW YOU DIDN'T TIP OFF THE POLICE YOURSELF?
SHE SLAMMED INTO A PATROL CRUISER ALL BY HER OWN DRUNKEN SELF!
YOU ARE IN SERIOUS DENIAL, MR. LARK. CADENCE WILL BE IN PRISON--OR DEAD--BY THE TIME SHE'S TWENTY-ONE! AND I'LL NO LONGER BE PARTY TO YOUR DAUGHTER KILLING HERSELF IN SLOW MOTION!
HURRK
CAN'T EVERYBODY JUST SHUT UP? MY FRIKKIN' HEAD HURTS!

HEAD STILL HURTS...BUZZING LIKE A SWARM OF BEES TRAPPED INSIDE A HORNETS' NEST.

SO MUCH STINGING RAGE INSIDE ME... WITH NOWHERE TO ESCAPE.

BUT AT LEAST I'M STILL STANDING.

I ORDERED A .223 ROUND TO YOUR HEAD, BUT YOU'RE STILL... **WHAT ARE YOU?**

FURY SWIRLING THROUGH MY BRAIN NOW... LIKE **STATIC.**

THAT... WAS **YOU.**

CAN FEEL IT...

ALL THAT KINETIC ENERGY-- STILL CRAWLING UNDER MY SKIN.

A CLEAR AND PRESENT DANGER TO EVERY MAN, WOMAN, AND CHILD...

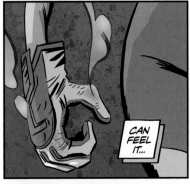

COULD HOLD IT IN...LET MYSELF BE BEDRIDDEN FOR ANOTHER WEEK OR MORE UNTIL THE PAIN FADES.

YOU ORDERED A **KILL SHOT** ON ME!

OR CHANNEL ALL THAT POWER--ALL THAT **RAGE**...

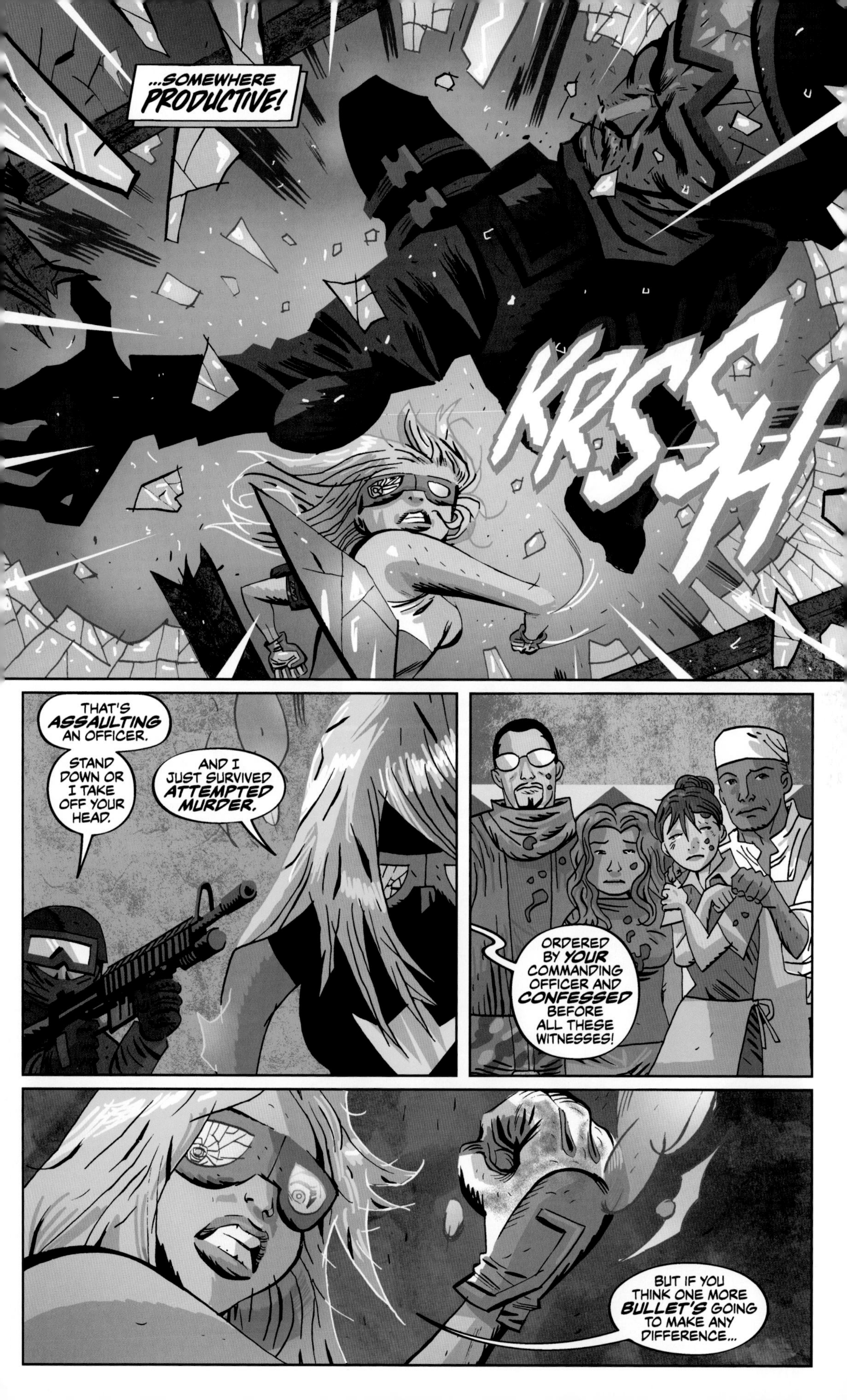

...SOMEWHERE PRODUCTIVE!
KRSSH
THAT'S ASSAULTING AN OFFICER.
STAND DOWN OR I TAKE OFF YOUR HEAD.
AND I JUST SURVIVED ATTEMPTED MURDER.
ORDERED BY YOUR COMMANDING OFFICER AND CONFESSED BEFORE ALL THESE WITNESSES!
BUT IF YOU THINK ONE MORE BULLET'S GOING TO MAKE ANY DIFFERENCE...

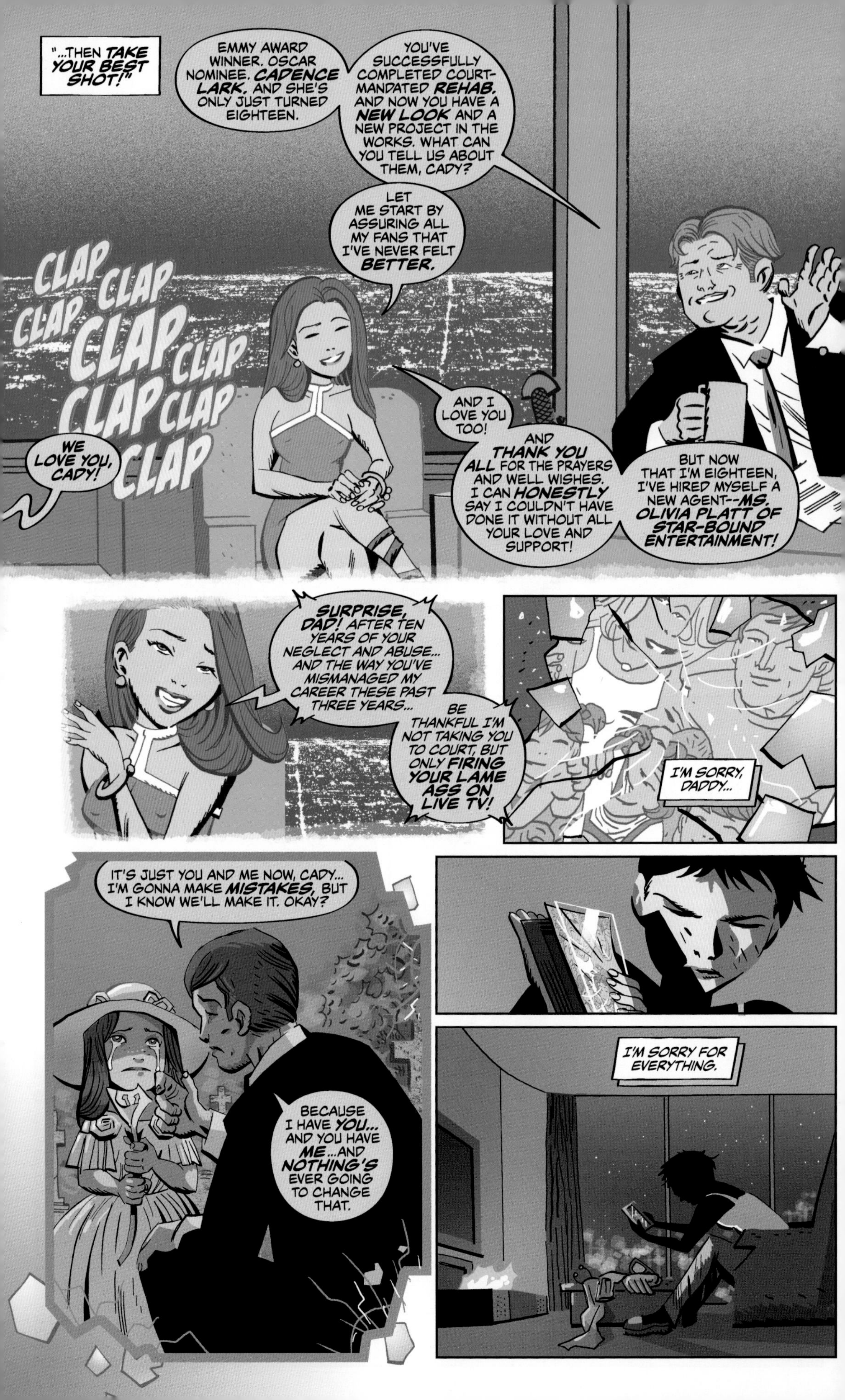
"...THEN TAKE YOUR BEST SHOT!"
EMMY AWARD WINNER. OSCAR NOMINEE. CADENCE LARK. AND SHE'S ONLY JUST TURNED EIGHTEEN.
YOU'VE SUCCESSFULLY COMPLETED COURT-MANDATED REHAB. AND NOW YOU HAVE A NEW LOOK AND A NEW PROJECT IN THE WORKS. WHAT CAN YOU TELL US ABOUT THEM, CADY?
LET ME START BY ASSURING ALL MY FANS THAT I'VE NEVER FELT BETTER.
CLAP CLAP CLAP CLAP CLAP CLAP CLAP CLAP
WE LOVE YOU, CADY!
AND I LOVE YOU TOO!
AND THANK YOU ALL FOR THE PRAYERS AND WELL WISHES. I CAN HONESTLY SAY I COULDN'T HAVE DONE IT WITHOUT ALL YOUR LOVE AND SUPPORT!
BUT NOW THAT I'M EIGHTEEN, I'VE HIRED MYSELF A NEW AGENT--MS. OLIVIA PLATT OF STAR-BOUND ENTERTAINMENT!
SURPRISE, DAD! AFTER TEN YEARS OF YOUR NEGLECT AND ABUSE... AND THE WAY YOU'VE MISMANAGED MY CAREER THESE PAST THREE YEARS...
BE THANKFUL I'M NOT TAKING YOU TO COURT, BUT ONLY FIRING YOUR LAME ASS ON LIVE TV!
I'M SORRY, DADDY...
IT'S JUST YOU AND ME NOW, CADY... I'M GONNA MAKE MISTAKES, BUT I KNOW WE'LL MAKE IT. OKAY?
BECAUSE I HAVE YOU... AND YOU HAVE ME...AND NOTHING'S EVER GOING TO CHANGE THAT.
I'M SORRY FOR EVERYTHING.

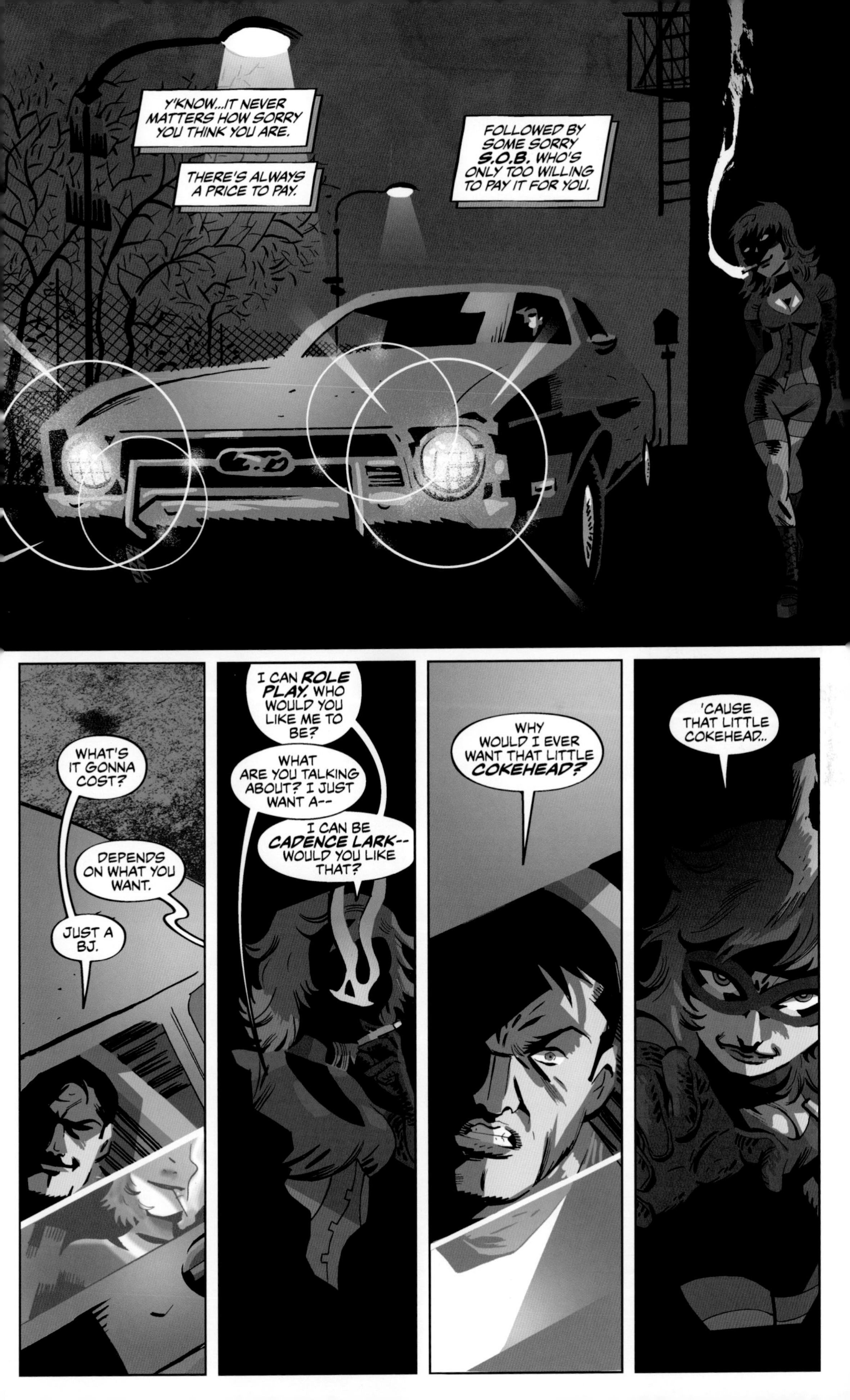
Y'KNOW...IT NEVER MATTERS HOW SORRY YOU THINK YOU ARE.
THERE'S ALWAYS A PRICE TO PAY.
FOLLOWED BY SOME SORRY S.O.B. WHO'S ONLY TOO WILLING TO PAY IT FOR YOU.
WHAT'S IT GONNA COST?
DEPENDS ON WHAT YOU WANT.
JUST A BJ.
I CAN ROLE PLAY. WHO WOULD YOU LIKE ME TO BE?
WHAT ARE YOU TALKING ABOUT? I JUST WANT A--
I CAN BE CADENCE LARK-- WOULD YOU LIKE THAT?
WHY WOULD I EVER WANT THAT LITTLE COKEHEAD?
'CAUSE THAT LITTLE COKEHEAD...

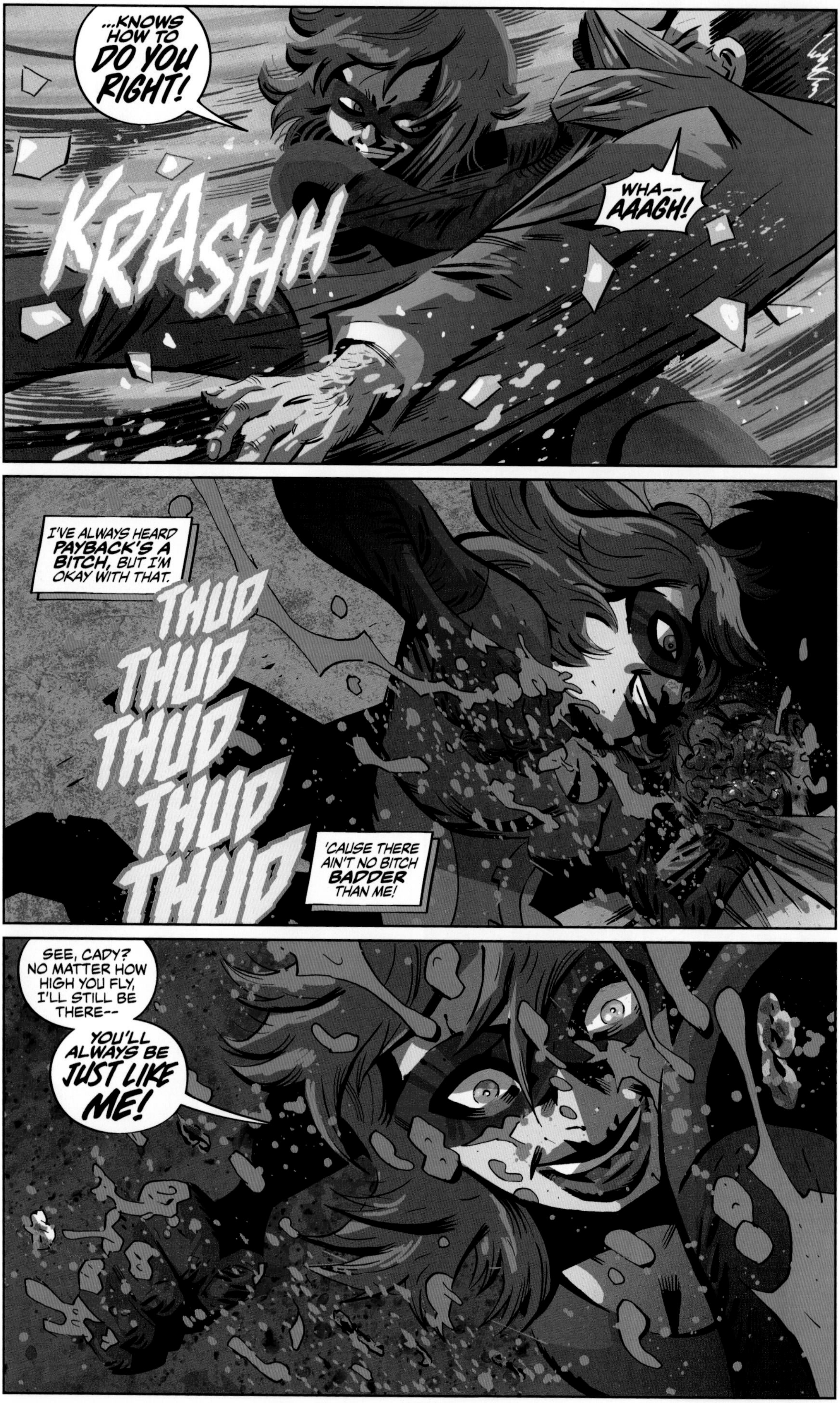
...KNOWS HOW TO DO YOU RIGHT!
KRASHH
WHA-- AAAGH!
I'VE ALWAYS HEARD PAYBACK'S A BITCH, BUT I'M OKAY WITH THAT.
THUD THUD THUD THUD THUD
'CAUSE THERE AIN'T NO BITCH BADDER THAN ME!
SEE, CADY? NO MATTER HOW HIGH YOU FLY, I'LL STILL BE THERE--
YOU'LL ALWAYS BE JUST LIKE ME!

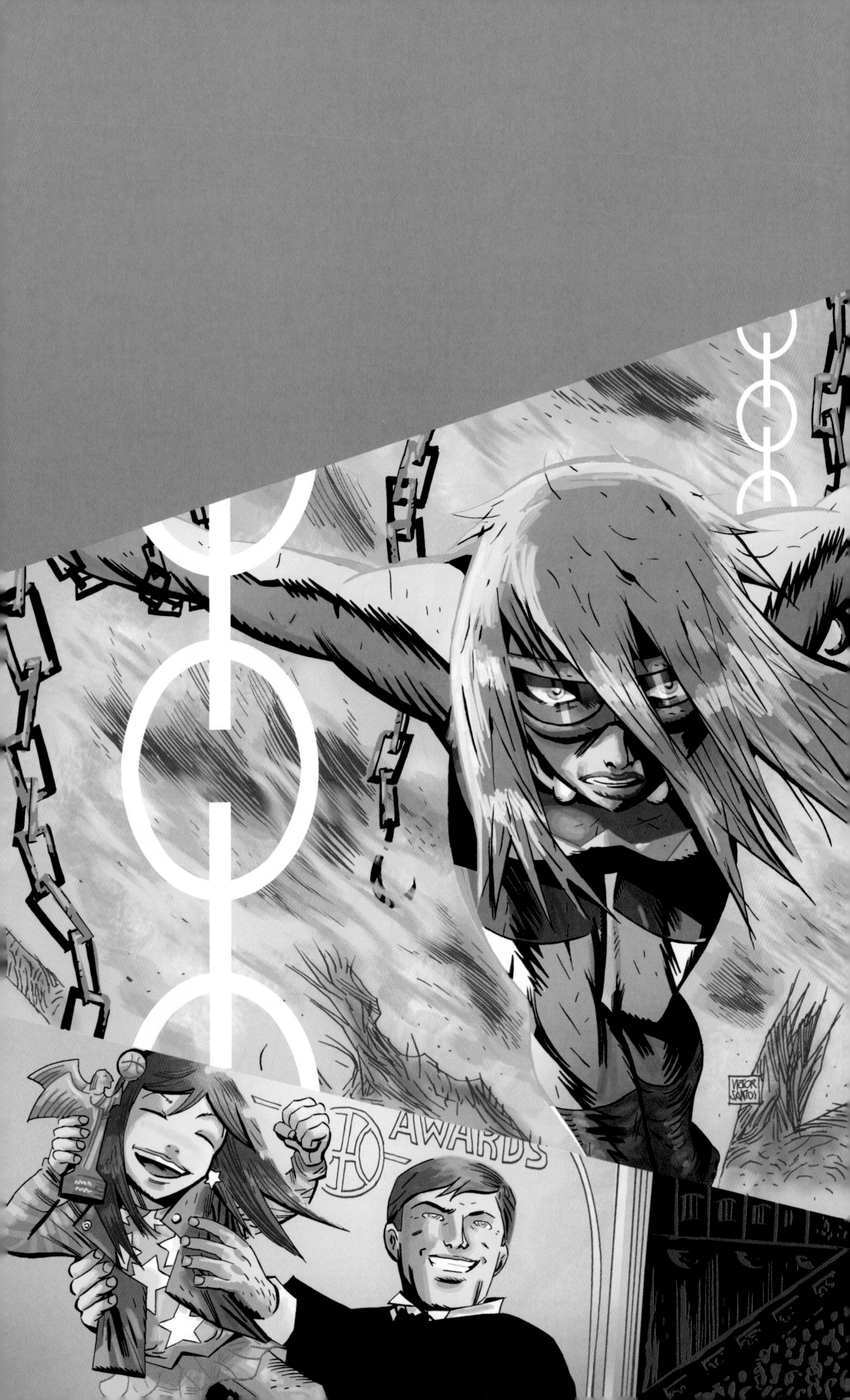
AWARDS

CHAPTER THREE: BLAZE OF GLORY

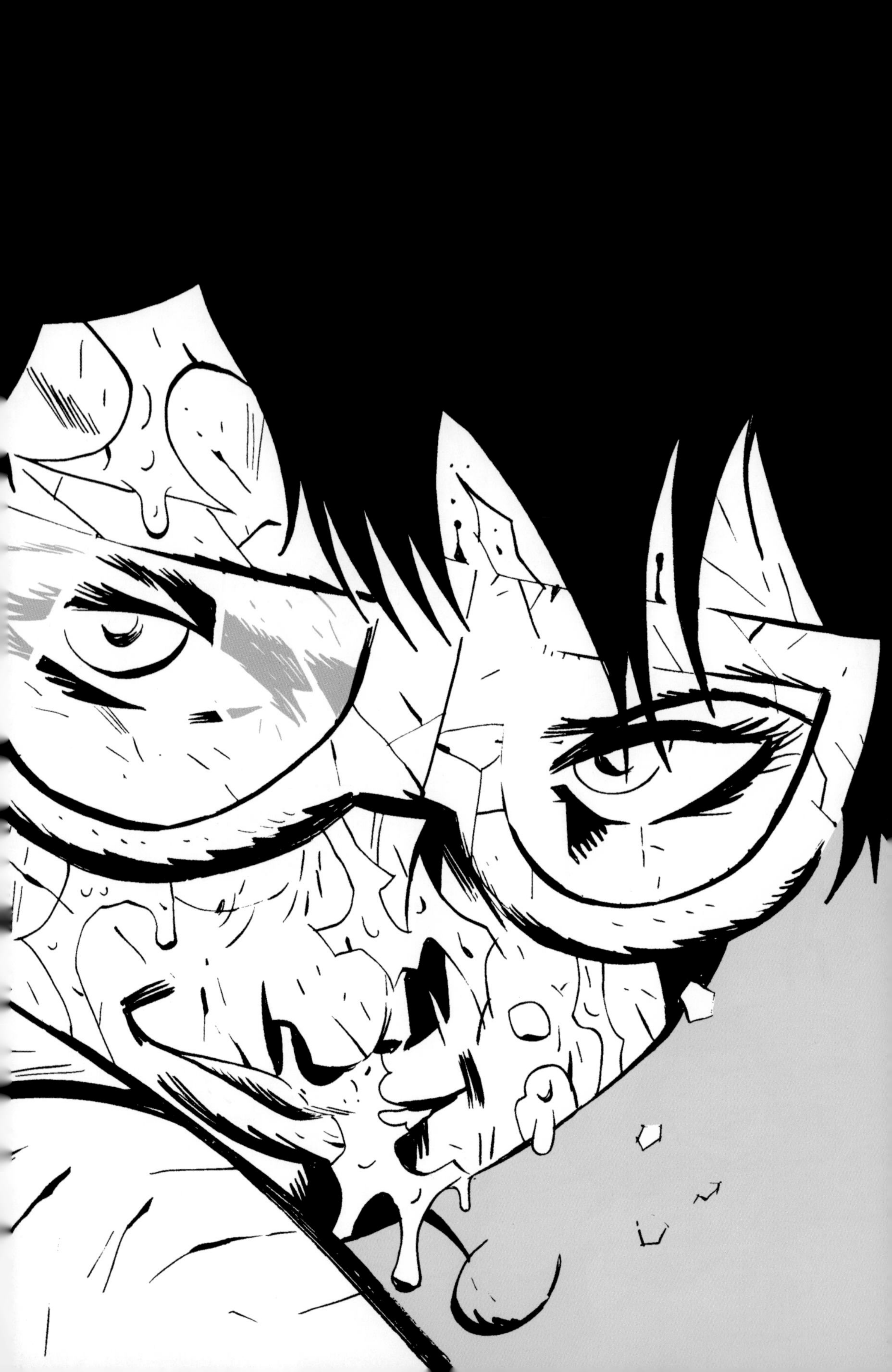

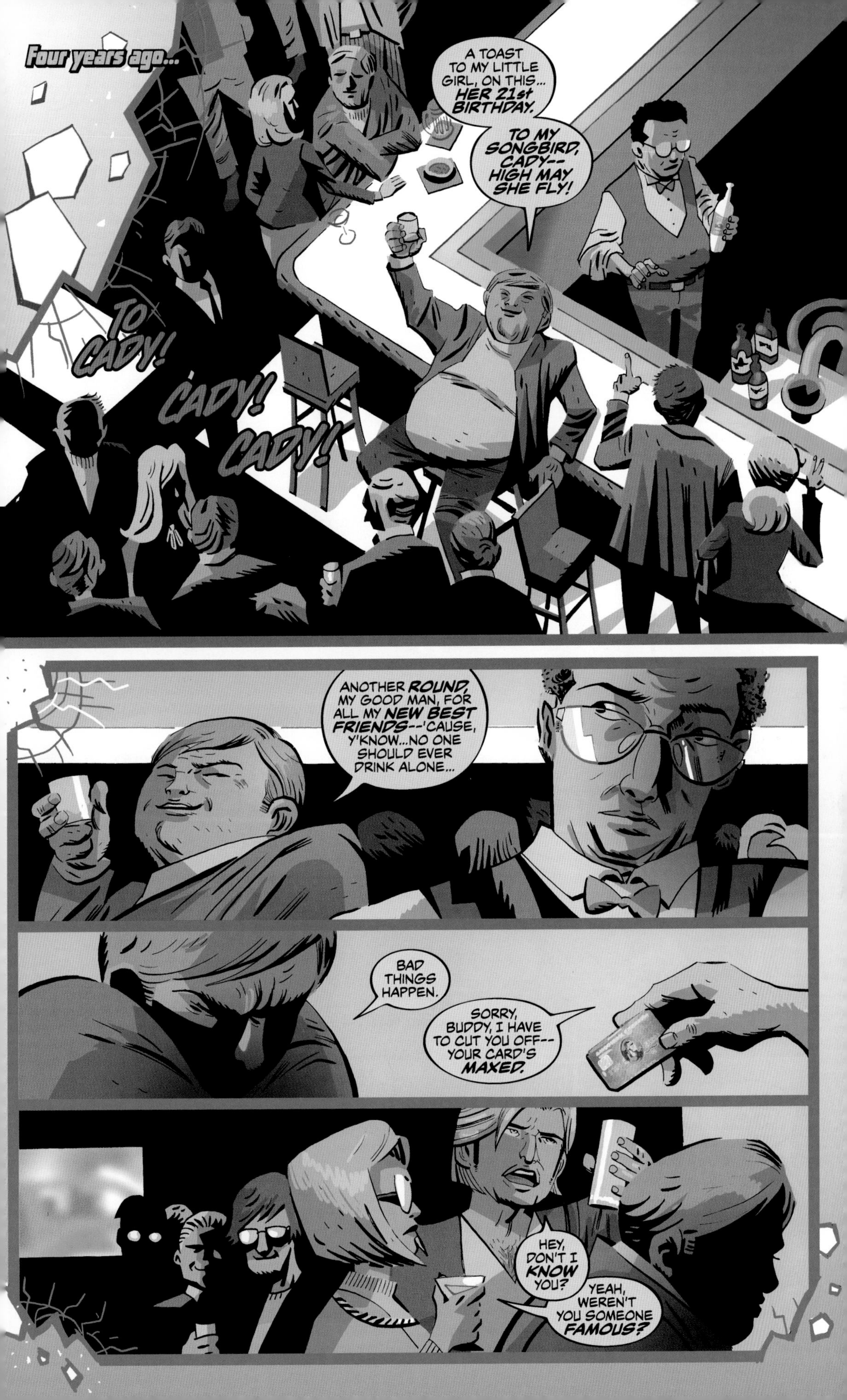
Four years ago...
A TOAST TO MY LITTLE GIRL, ON THIS... HER 21st BIRTHDAY.
TO MY SONGBIRD, CADY-- HIGH MAY SHE FLY!
TO CADY!
CADY!
CADY!
ANOTHER ROUND, MY GOOD MAN, FOR ALL MY NEW BEST FRIENDS--'CAUSE, Y'KNOW...NO ONE SHOULD EVER DRINK ALONE...
BAD THINGS HAPPEN.
SORRY, BUDDY, I HAVE TO CUT YOU OFF-- YOUR CARD'S MAXED.
HEY, DON'T I KNOW YOU?
YEAH, WEREN'T YOU SOMEONE FAMOUS?

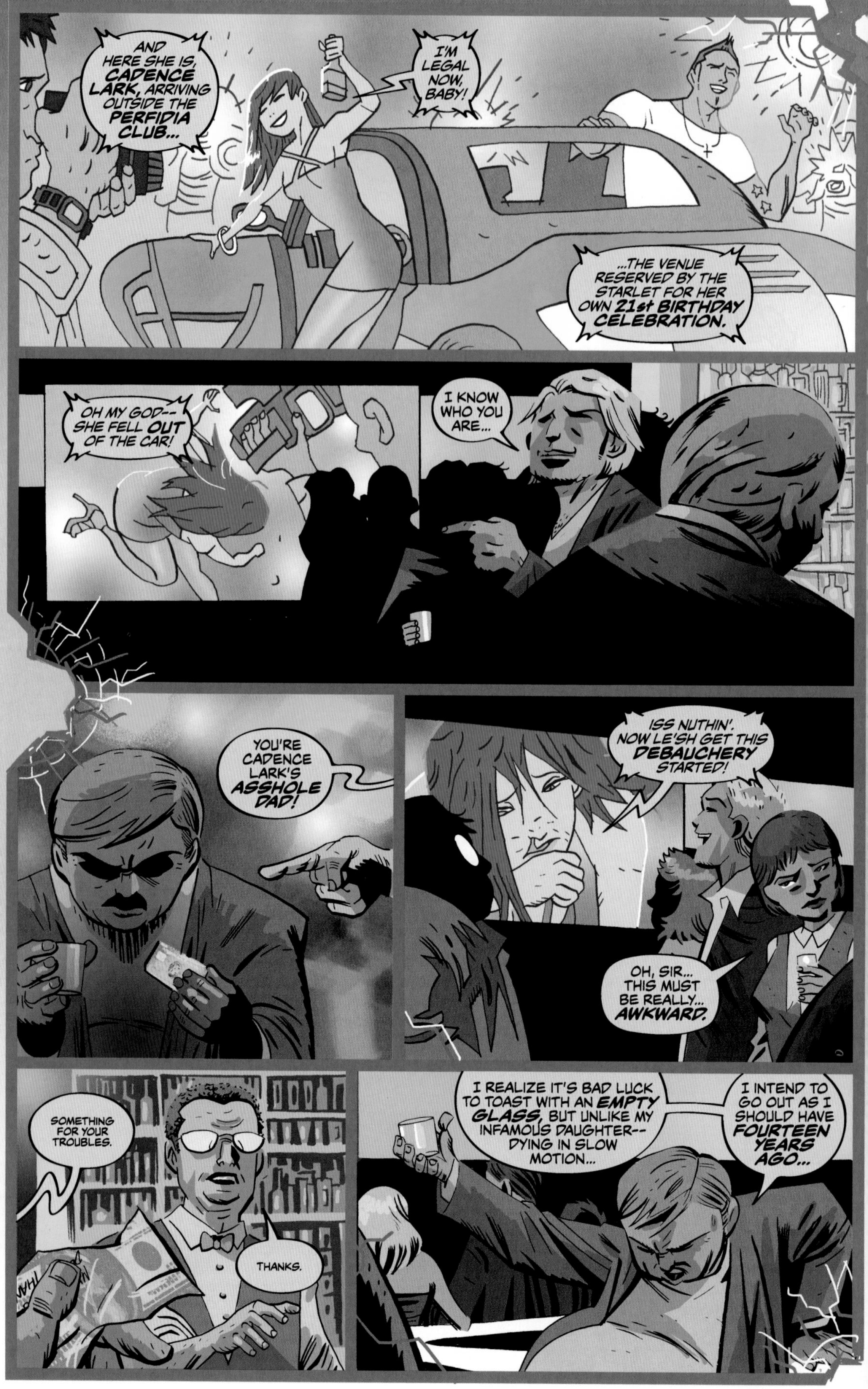
AND HERE SHE IS, CADENCE LARK, ARRIVING OUTSIDE THE PERFIDIA CLUB...
I'M LEGAL NOW, BABY!
...THE VENUE RESERVED BY THE STARLET FOR HER OWN 21st BIRTHDAY CELEBRATION.
OH MY GOD-- SHE FELL OUT OF THE CAR!
I KNOW WHO YOU ARE...
YOU'RE CADENCE LARK'S ASSHOLE DAD!
ISS NUTHIN'. NOW LE'SH GET THIS DEBAUCHERY STARTED!
OH, SIR... THIS MUST BE REALLY... AWKWARD.
SOMETHING FOR YOUR TROUBLES.
THANKS.
I REALIZE IT'S BAD LUCK TO TOAST WITH AN EMPTY GLASS, BUT UNLIKE MY INFAMOUS DAUGHTER-- DYING IN SLOW MOTION...
I INTEND TO GO OUT AS I SHOULD HAVE FOURTEEN YEARS AGO...

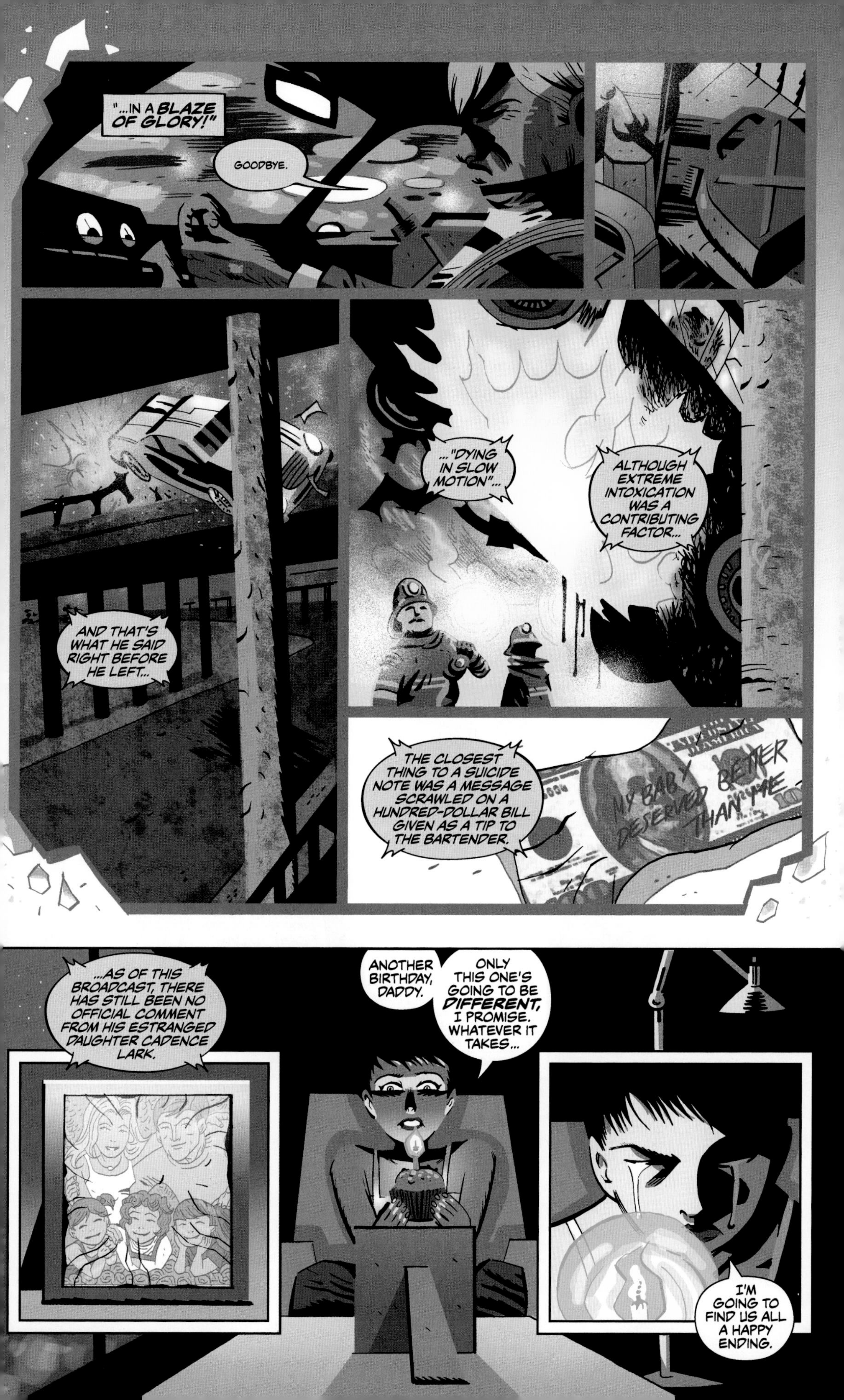
"...IN A BLAZE OF GLORY!"
GOODBYE.
AND THAT'S WHAT HE SAID RIGHT BEFORE HE LEFT...
..."DYING IN SLOW MOTION"...
ALTHOUGH EXTREME INTOXICATION WAS A CONTRIBUTING FACTOR...
THE CLOSEST THING TO A SUICIDE NOTE WAS A MESSAGE SCRAWLED ON A HUNDRED-DOLLAR BILL GIVEN AS A TIP TO THE BARTENDER.
MY BABY DESERVED BETTER THAN ME
...AS OF THIS BROADCAST, THERE HAS STILL BEEN NO OFFICIAL COMMENT FROM HIS ESTRANGED DAUGHTER CADENCE LARK.
ANOTHER BIRTHDAY, DADDY.
ONLY THIS ONE'S GOING TO BE DIFFERENT, I PROMISE. WHATEVER IT TAKES...
I'M GOING TO FIND US ALL A HAPPY ENDING.

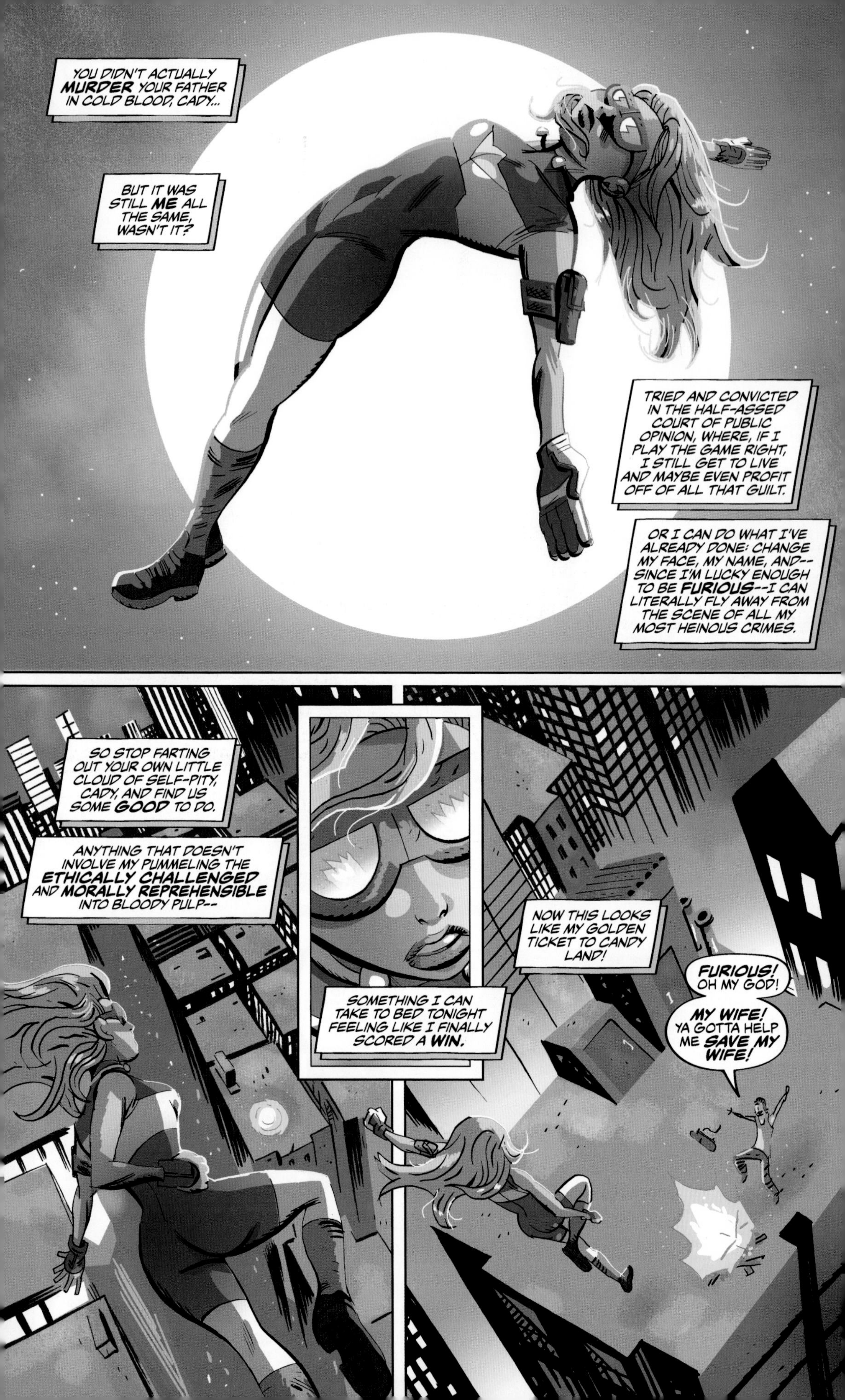

YOU DIDN'T ACTUALLY MURDER YOUR FATHER IN COLD BLOOD, CADY...
BUT IT WAS STILL ME ALL THE SAME, WASN'T IT?
TRIED AND CONVICTED IN THE HALF-ASSED COURT OF PUBLIC OPINION, WHERE, IF I PLAY THE GAME RIGHT, I STILL GET TO LIVE AND MAYBE EVEN PROFIT OFF OF ALL THAT GUILT.
OR I CAN DO WHAT I'VE ALREADY DONE: CHANGE MY FACE, MY NAME, AND--SINCE I'M LUCKY ENOUGH TO BE FURIOUS--I CAN LITERALLY FLY AWAY FROM THE SCENE OF ALL MY MOST HEINOUS CRIMES.
SO STOP FARTING OUT YOUR OWN LITTLE CLOUD OF SELF-PITY, CADY, AND FIND US SOME GOOD TO DO.
ANYTHING THAT DOESN'T INVOLVE MY PUMMELING THE ETHICALLY CHALLENGED AND MORALLY REPREHENSIBLE INTO BLOODY PULP--
SOMETHING I CAN TAKE TO BED TONIGHT FEELING LIKE I FINALLY SCORED A WIN.
NOW THIS LOOKS LIKE MY GOLDEN TICKET TO CANDY LAND!
FURIOUS! OH MY GOD!
MY WIFE! YA GOTTA HELP ME SAVE MY WIFE!

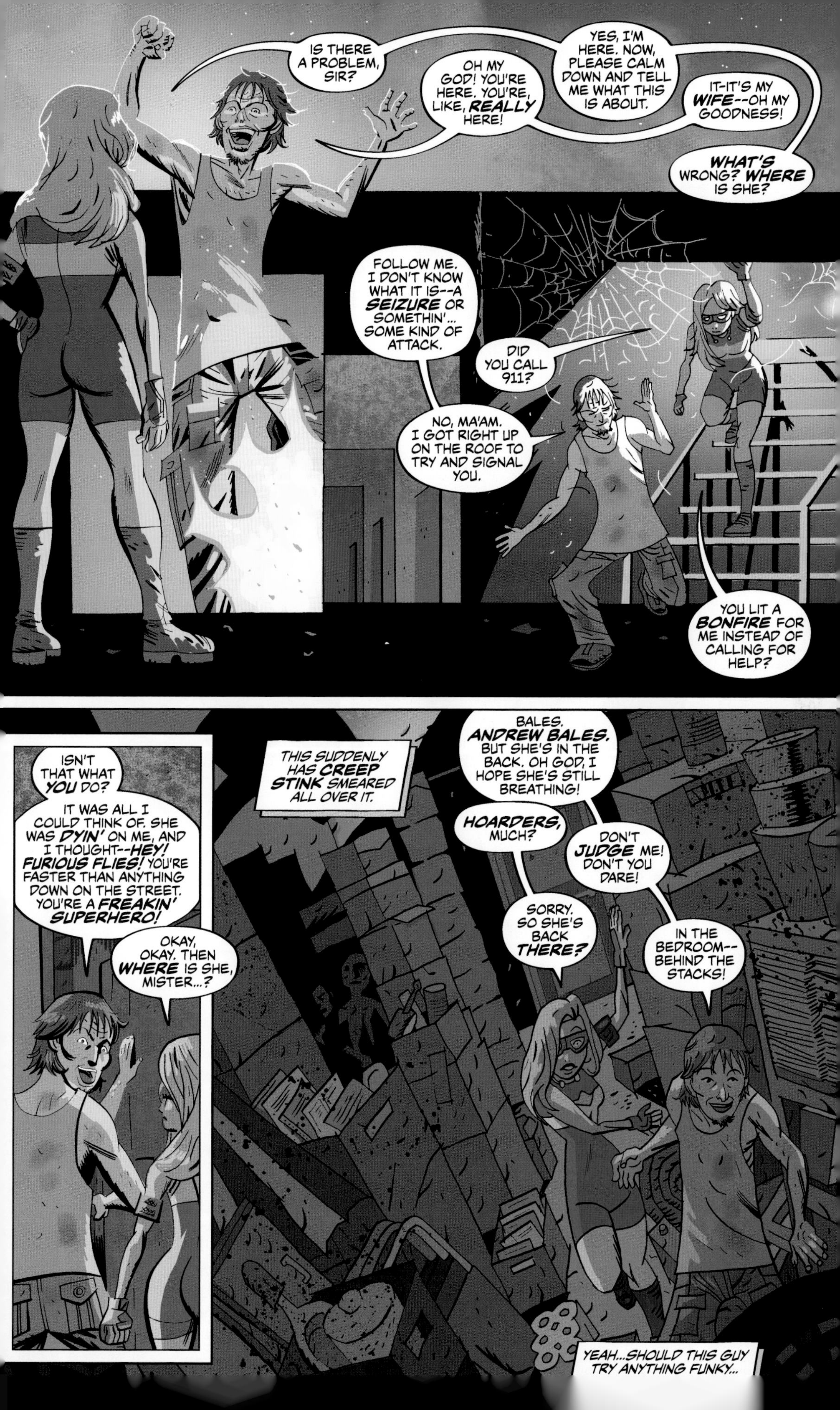

IS THERE A PROBLEM, SIR?
OH MY GOD! YOU'RE HERE. YOU'RE, LIKE, REALLY HERE!
YES, I'M HERE. NOW, PLEASE CALM DOWN AND TELL ME WHAT THIS IS ABOUT.
IT-IT'S MY WIFE--OH MY GOODNESS!
WHAT'S WRONG? WHERE IS SHE?
FOLLOW ME. I DON'T KNOW WHAT IT IS--A SEIZURE OR SOMETHIN'... SOME KIND OF ATTACK.
DID YOU CALL 911?
NO, MA'AM. I GOT RIGHT UP ON THE ROOF TO TRY AND SIGNAL YOU.
YOU LIT A BONFIRE FOR ME INSTEAD OF CALLING FOR HELP?
ISN'T THAT WHAT YOU DO?
IT WAS ALL I COULD THINK OF. SHE WAS DYIN' ON ME, AND I THOUGHT--HEY! FURIOUS FLIES! YOU'RE FASTER THAN ANYTHING DOWN ON THE STREET. YOU'RE A FREAKIN' SUPERHERO!
OKAY, OKAY. THEN WHERE IS SHE, MISTER...?
THIS SUDDENLY HAS CREEP STINK SMEARED ALL OVER IT.
BALES. ANDREW BALES. BUT SHE'S IN THE BACK. OH GOD, I HOPE SHE'S STILL BREATHING!
HOARDERS, MUCH?
DON'T JUDGE ME! DON'T YOU DARE!
SORRY. SO SHE'S BACK THERE?
IN THE BEDROOM--BEHIND THE STACKS!
YEAH...SHOULD THIS GUY TRY ANYTHING FUNKY...

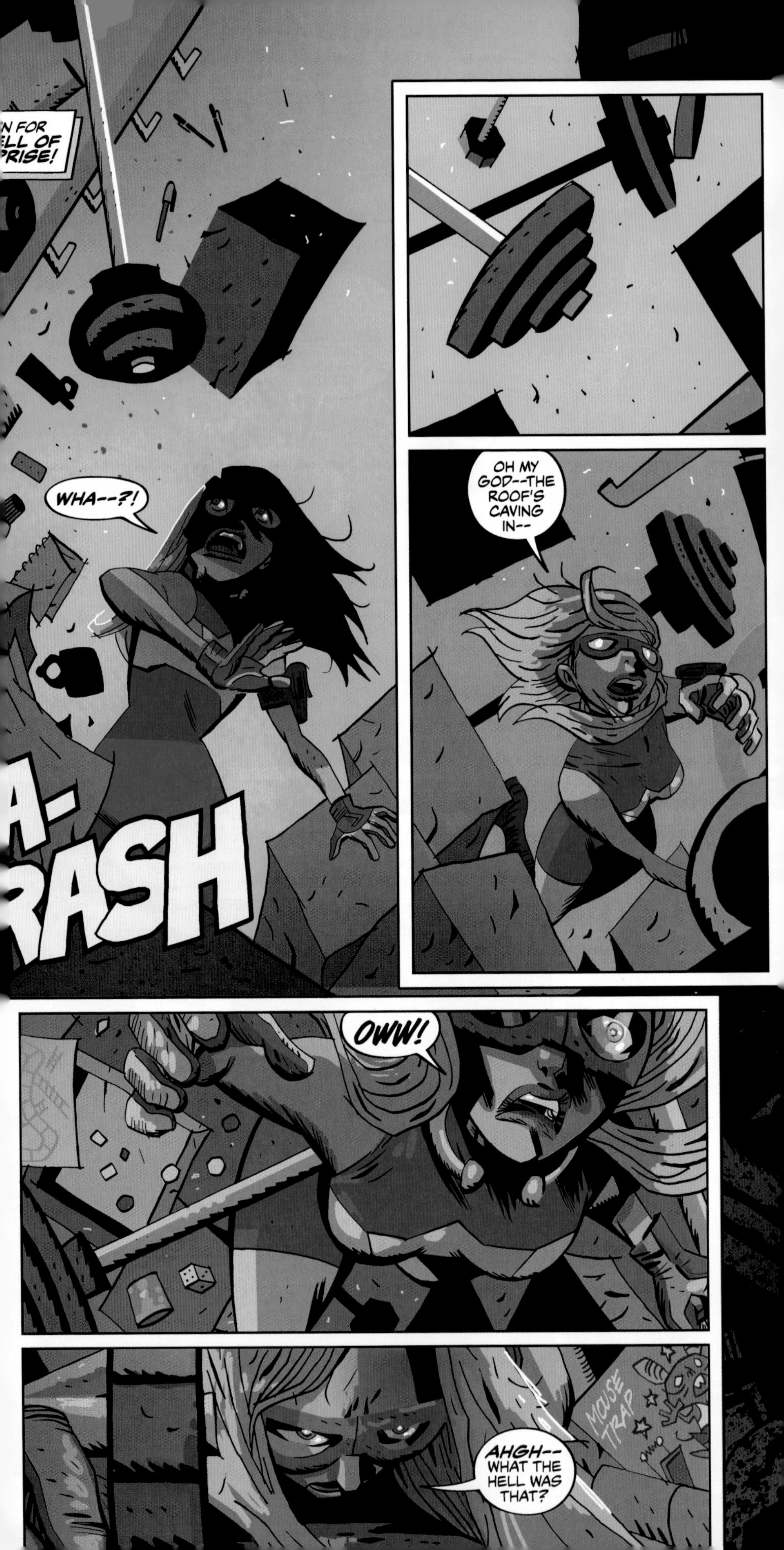
N FOR
ELL OF
PRISE!
WHA--?!
A-
RASH
OH MY GOD--THE ROOF'S CAVING IN--
OWW!
MOUSE TRAP
AHGH-- WHAT THE HELL WAS THAT?

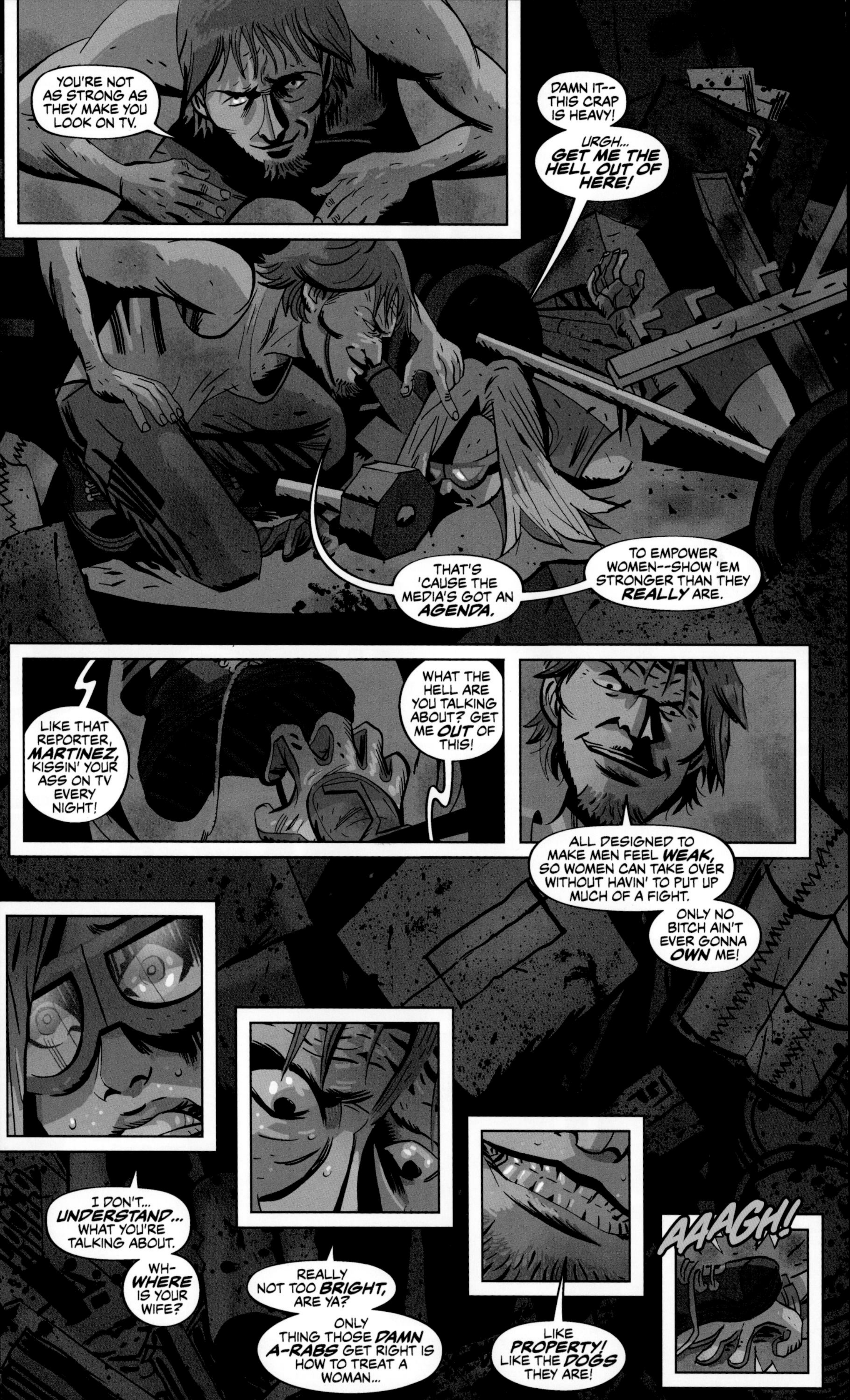

YOU'RE NOT AS STRONG AS THEY MAKE YOU LOOK ON TV.
DAMN IT-- THIS CRAP IS HEAVY!
URGH... GET ME THE HELL OUT OF HERE!
THAT'S 'CAUSE THE MEDIA'S GOT AN AGENDA.
TO EMPOWER WOMEN--SHOW 'EM STRONGER THAN THEY REALLY ARE.
LIKE THAT REPORTER, MARTINEZ, KISSIN' YOUR ASS ON TV EVERY NIGHT!
WHAT THE HELL ARE YOU TALKING ABOUT? GET ME OUT OF THIS!
ALL DESIGNED TO MAKE MEN FEEL WEAK, SO WOMEN CAN TAKE OVER WITHOUT HAVIN' TO PUT UP MUCH OF A FIGHT.
ONLY NO BITCH AIN'T EVER GONNA OWN ME!
I DON'T... UNDERSTAND... WHAT YOU'RE TALKING ABOUT.
WH- WHERE IS YOUR WIFE?
REALLY NOT TOO BRIGHT, ARE YA?
ONLY THING THOSE DAMN A-RABS GET RIGHT IS HOW TO TREAT A WOMAN...
LIKE PROPERTY! LIKE THE DOGS THEY ARE!
AAAGH!

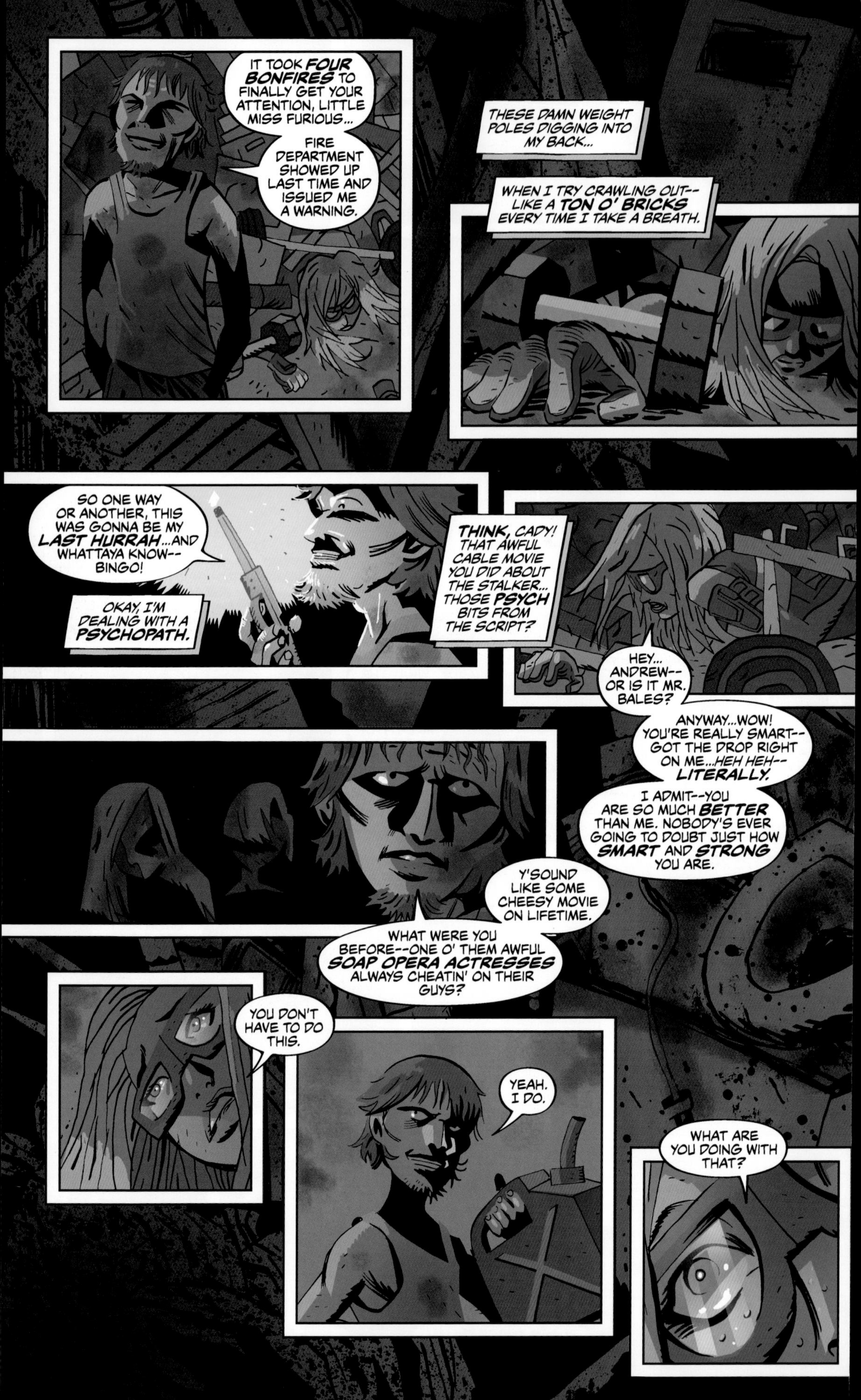
IT TOOK FOUR BONFIRES TO FINALLY GET YOUR ATTENTION, LITTLE MISS FURIOUS...
FIRE DEPARTMENT SHOWED UP LAST TIME AND ISSUED ME A WARNING.
THESE DAMN WEIGHT POLES DIGGING INTO MY BACK...
WHEN I TRY CRAWLING OUT--LIKE A TON O' BRICKS EVERY TIME I TAKE A BREATH.
SO ONE WAY OR ANOTHER, THIS WAS GONNA BE MY LAST HURRAH...AND WHATTAYA KNOW--BINGO!
OKAY, I'M DEALING WITH A PSYCHOPATH.
THINK, CADY! THAT AWFUL CABLE MOVIE YOU DID ABOUT THE STALKER... THOSE PSYCH BITS FROM THE SCRIPT?
HEY... ANDREW--OR IS IT MR. BALES?
ANYWAY...WOW! YOU'RE REALLY SMART--GOT THE DROP RIGHT ON ME...HEH HEH--LITERALLY.
I ADMIT--YOU ARE SO MUCH BETTER THAN ME. NOBODY'S EVER GOING TO DOUBT JUST HOW SMART AND STRONG YOU ARE.
Y'SOUND LIKE SOME CHEESY MOVIE ON LIFETIME.
WHAT WERE YOU BEFORE--ONE O' THEM AWFUL SOAP OPERA ACTRESSES ALWAYS CHEATIN' ON THEIR GUYS?
YOU DON'T HAVE TO DO THIS.
YEAH. I DO.
WHAT ARE YOU DOING WITH THAT?

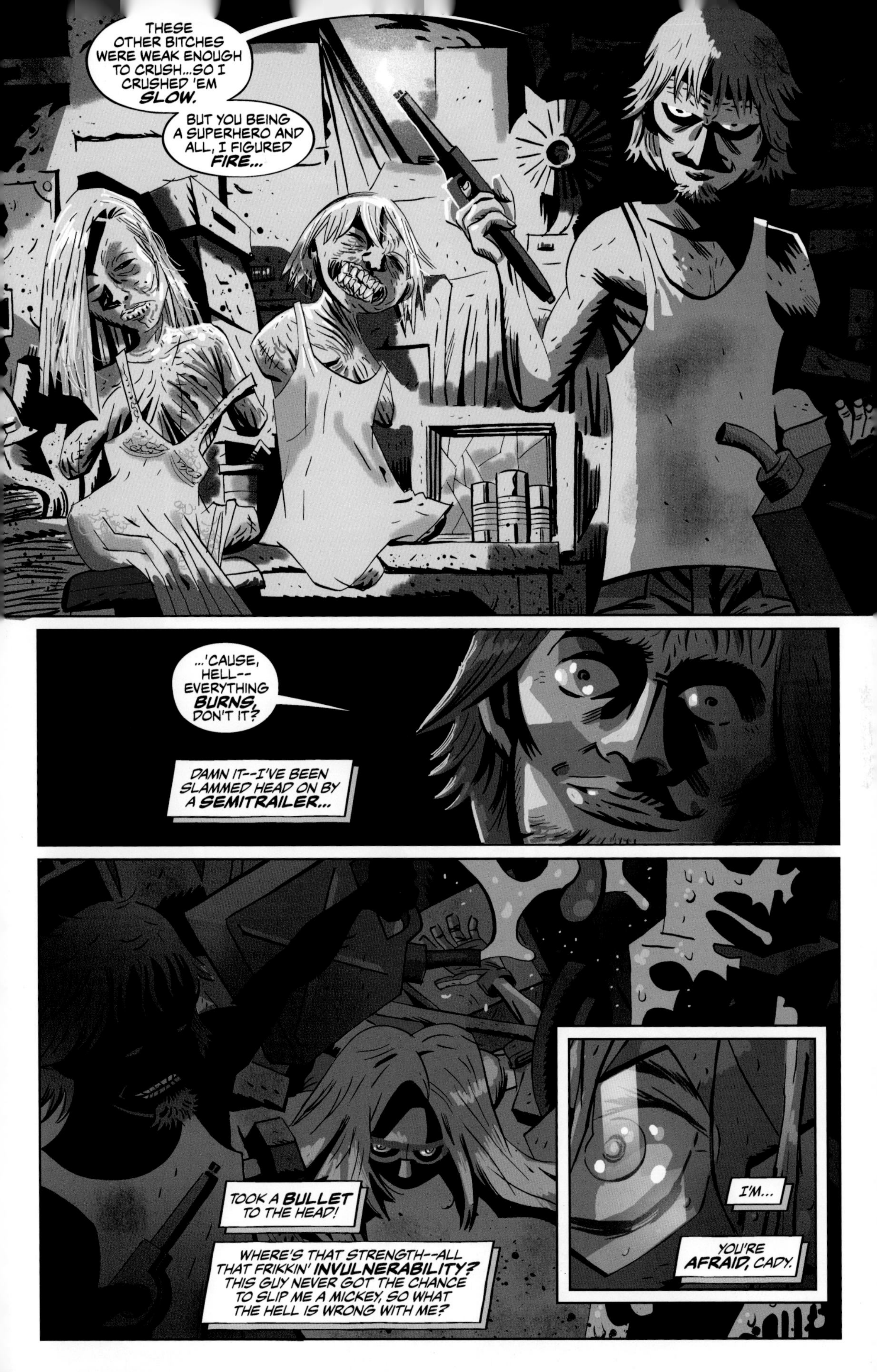
THESE OTHER BITCHES WERE WEAK ENOUGH TO CRUSH...SO I CRUSHED 'EM SLOW.
BUT YOU BEING A SUPERHERO AND ALL, I FIGURED FIRE...
...'CAUSE, HELL-- EVERYTHING BURNS, DON'T IT?
DAMN IT--I'VE BEEN SLAMMED HEAD ON BY A SEMITRAILER...
TOOK A BULLET TO THE HEAD!
WHERE'S THAT STRENGTH--ALL THAT FRIKKIN' INVULNERABILITY? THIS GUY NEVER GOT THE CHANCE TO SLIP ME A MICKEY, SO WHAT THE HELL IS WRONG WITH ME?
I'M...
YOU'RE AFRAID, CADY.

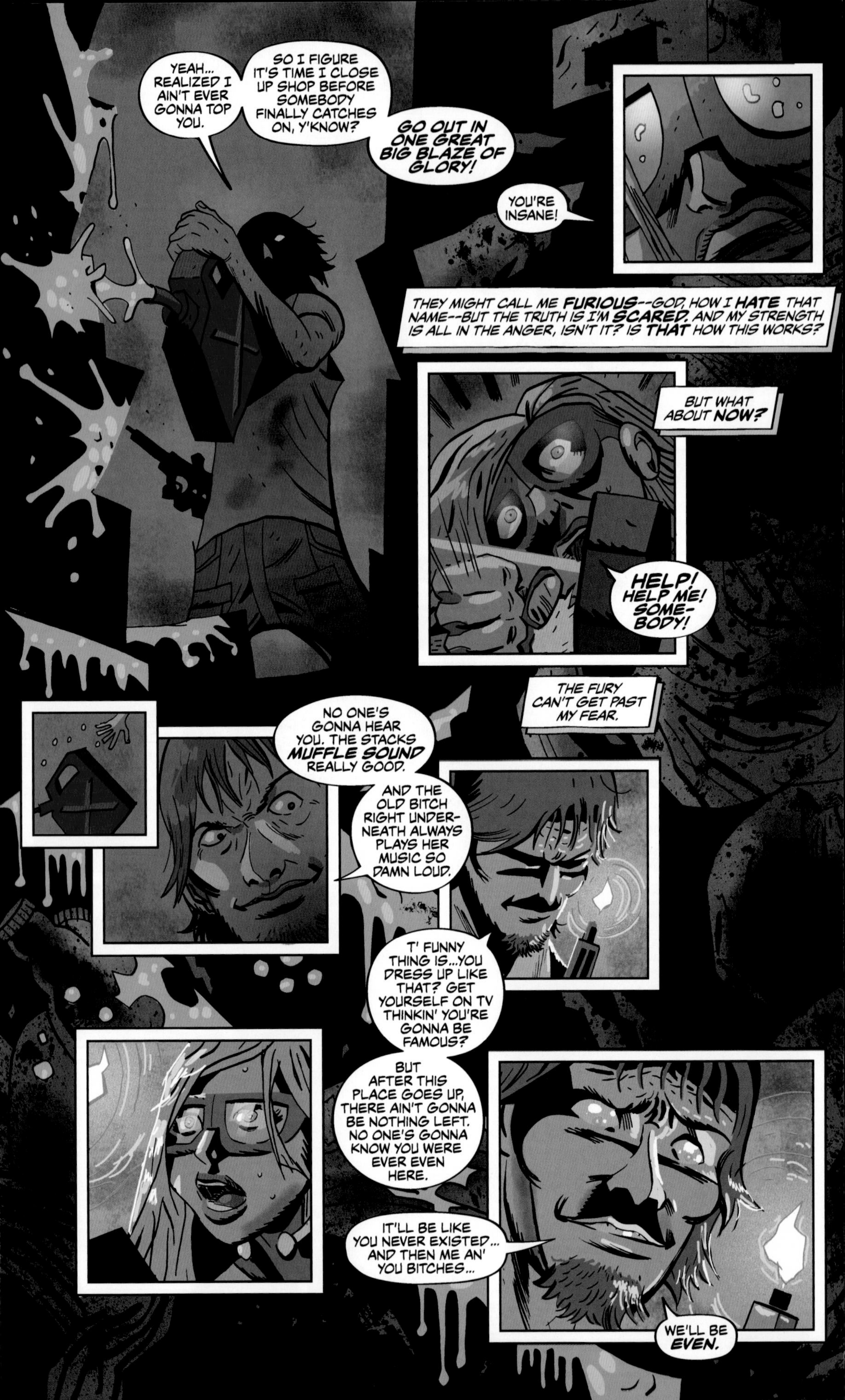
YEAH... REALIZED I AIN'T EVER GONNA TOP YOU.
SO I FIGURE IT'S TIME I CLOSE UP SHOP BEFORE SOMEBODY FINALLY CATCHES ON, Y'KNOW?
GO OUT IN ONE GREAT BIG BLAZE OF GLORY!
YOU'RE INSANE!
THEY MIGHT CALL ME FURIOUS--GOD, HOW I HATE THAT NAME--BUT THE TRUTH IS I'M SCARED. AND MY STRENGTH IS ALL IN THE ANGER, ISN'T IT? IS THAT HOW THIS WORKS?
BUT WHAT ABOUT NOW?
HELP! HELP ME! SOME-BODY!
THE FURY CAN'T GET PAST MY FEAR.
NO ONE'S GONNA HEAR YOU. THE STACKS MUFFLE SOUND REALLY GOOD.
AND THE OLD BITCH RIGHT UNDER-NEATH ALWAYS PLAYS HER MUSIC SO DAMN LOUD.
T' FUNNY THING IS...YOU DRESS UP LIKE THAT? GET YOURSELF ON TV THINKIN' YOU'RE GONNA BE FAMOUS?
BUT AFTER THIS PLACE GOES UP, THERE AIN'T GONNA BE NOTHING LEFT. NO ONE'S GONNA KNOW YOU WERE EVER EVEN HERE.
IT'LL BE LIKE YOU NEVER EXISTED... AND THEN ME AN' YOU BITCHES...
WE'LL BE EVEN.

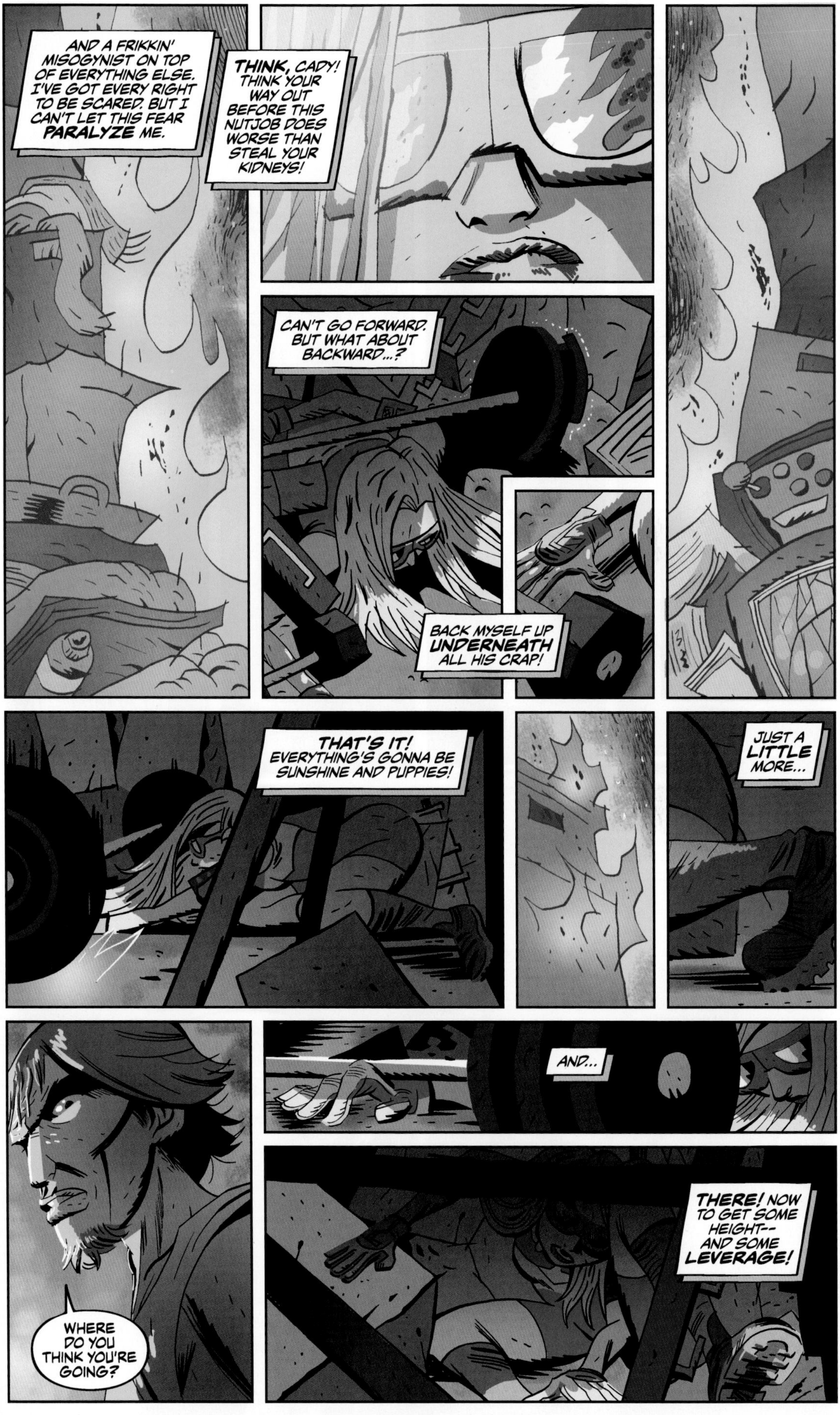

AND A FRIKKIN' MISOGYNIST ON TOP OF EVERYTHING ELSE. I'VE GOT EVERY RIGHT TO BE SCARED. BUT I CAN'T LET THIS FEAR PARALYZE ME.
THINK, CADY! THINK YOUR WAY OUT BEFORE THIS NUTJOB DOES WORSE THAN STEAL YOUR KIDNEYS!
CAN'T GO FORWARD. BUT WHAT ABOUT BACKWARD...?
BACK MYSELF UP UNDERNEATH ALL HIS CRAP!
THAT'S IT! EVERYTHING'S GONNA BE SUNSHINE AND PUPPIES!
JUST A LITTLE MORE...
WHERE DO YOU THINK YOU'RE GOING?
AND...
THERE! NOW TO GET SOME HEIGHT-- AND SOME LEVERAGE!

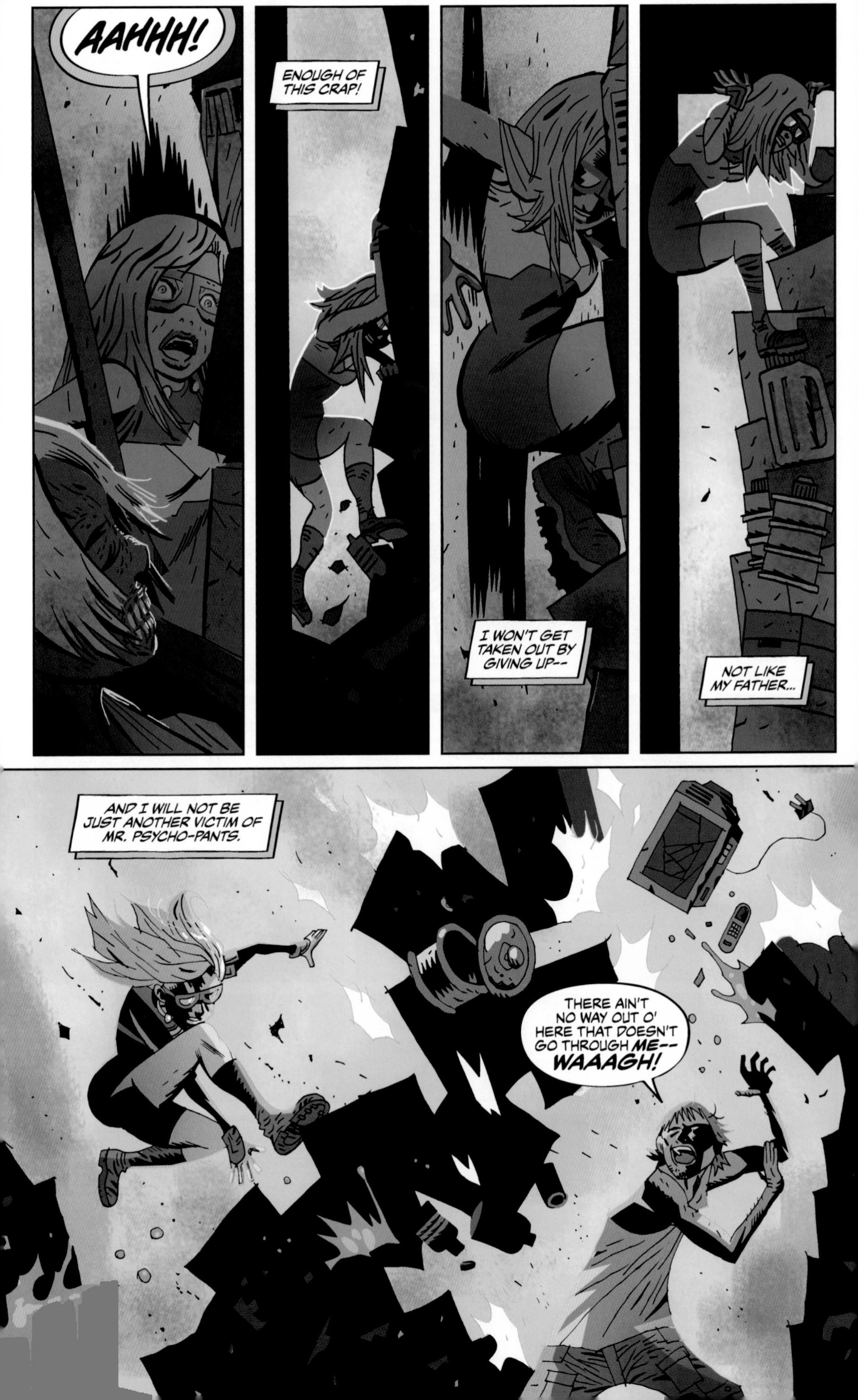
AAHHH!
ENOUGH OF THIS CRAP!
I WON'T GET TAKEN OUT BY GIVING UP--
NOT LIKE MY FATHER...
AND I WILL NOT BE JUST ANOTHER VICTIM OF MR. PSYCHO-PANTS.
THERE AIN'T NO WAY OUT O' HERE THAT DOESN'T GO THROUGH ME-- WAAAGH!

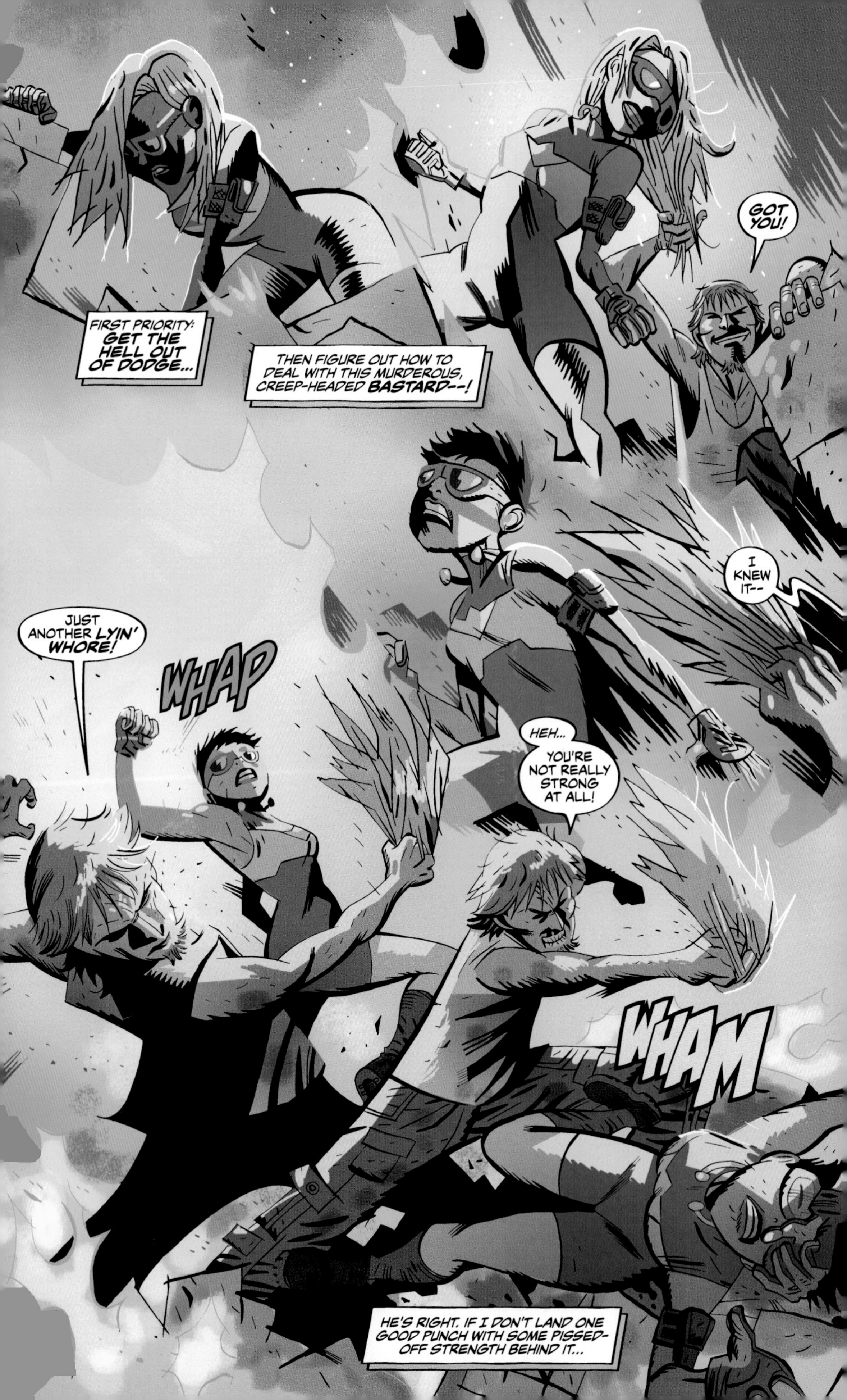
FIRST PRIORITY: GET THE HELL OUT OF DODGE...
THEN FIGURE OUT HOW TO DEAL WITH THIS MURDEROUS, CREEP-HEADED BASTARD--!
GOT YOU!
I KNEW IT--
JUST ANOTHER LYIN' WHORE!
WHAP
HEH... YOU'RE NOT REALLY STRONG AT ALL!
WHAM
HE'S RIGHT. IF I DON'T LAND ONE GOOD PUNCH WITH SOME PISSED-OFF STRENGTH BEHIND IT...

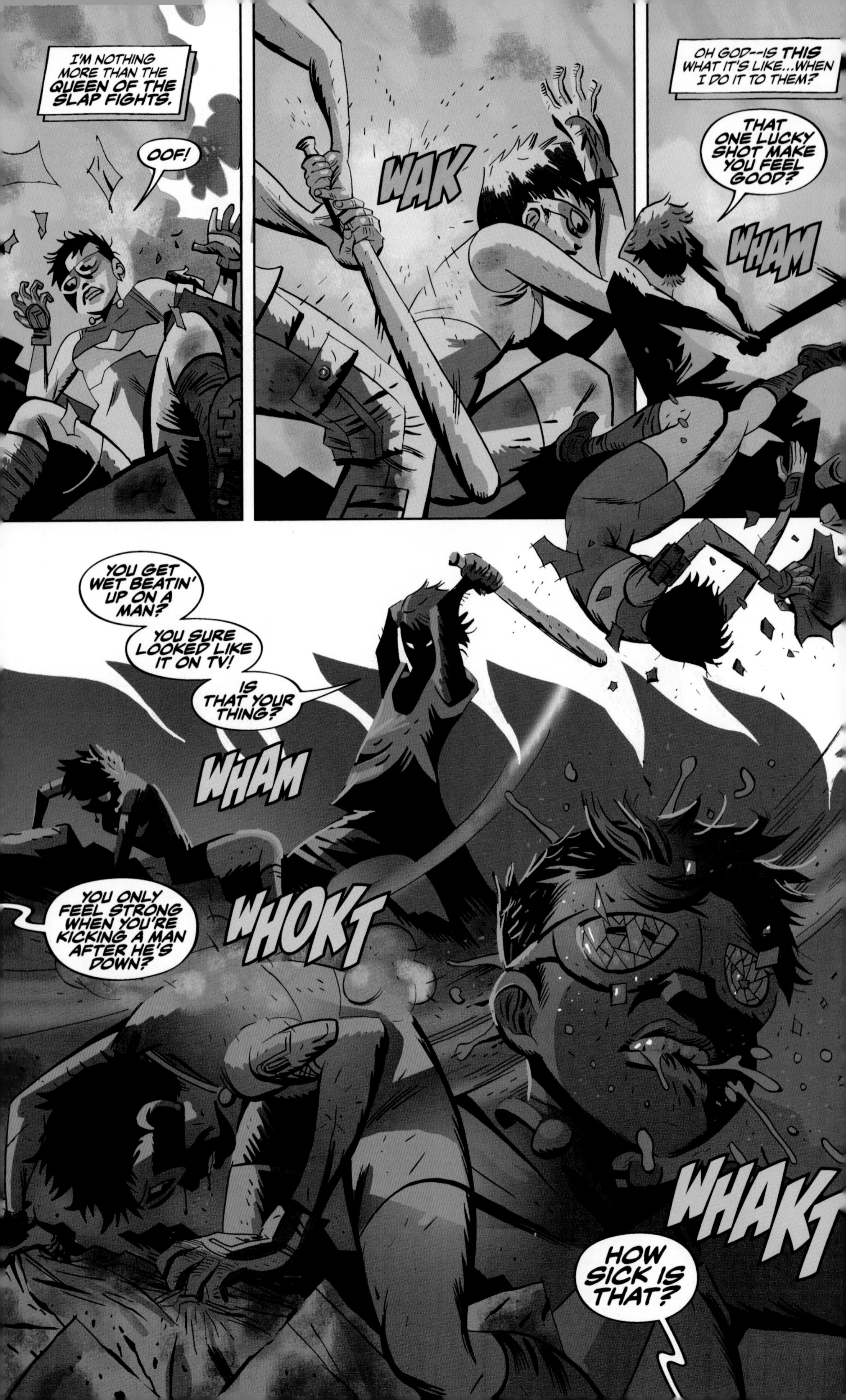

I'M NOTHING MORE THAN THE QUEEN OF THE SLAP FIGHTS.
OOF!
WAK
OH GOD--IS THIS WHAT IT'S LIKE...WHEN I DO IT TO THEM?
THAT ONE LUCKY SHOT MAKE YOU FEEL GOOD?
WHAM
YOU GET WET BEATIN' UP ON A MAN?
YOU SURE LOOKED LIKE IT ON TV!
IS THAT YOUR THING?
WHAM
YOU ONLY FEEL STRONG WHEN YOU'RE KICKING A MAN AFTER HE'S DOWN?
WHOKT
WHAKT
HOW SICK IS THAT?

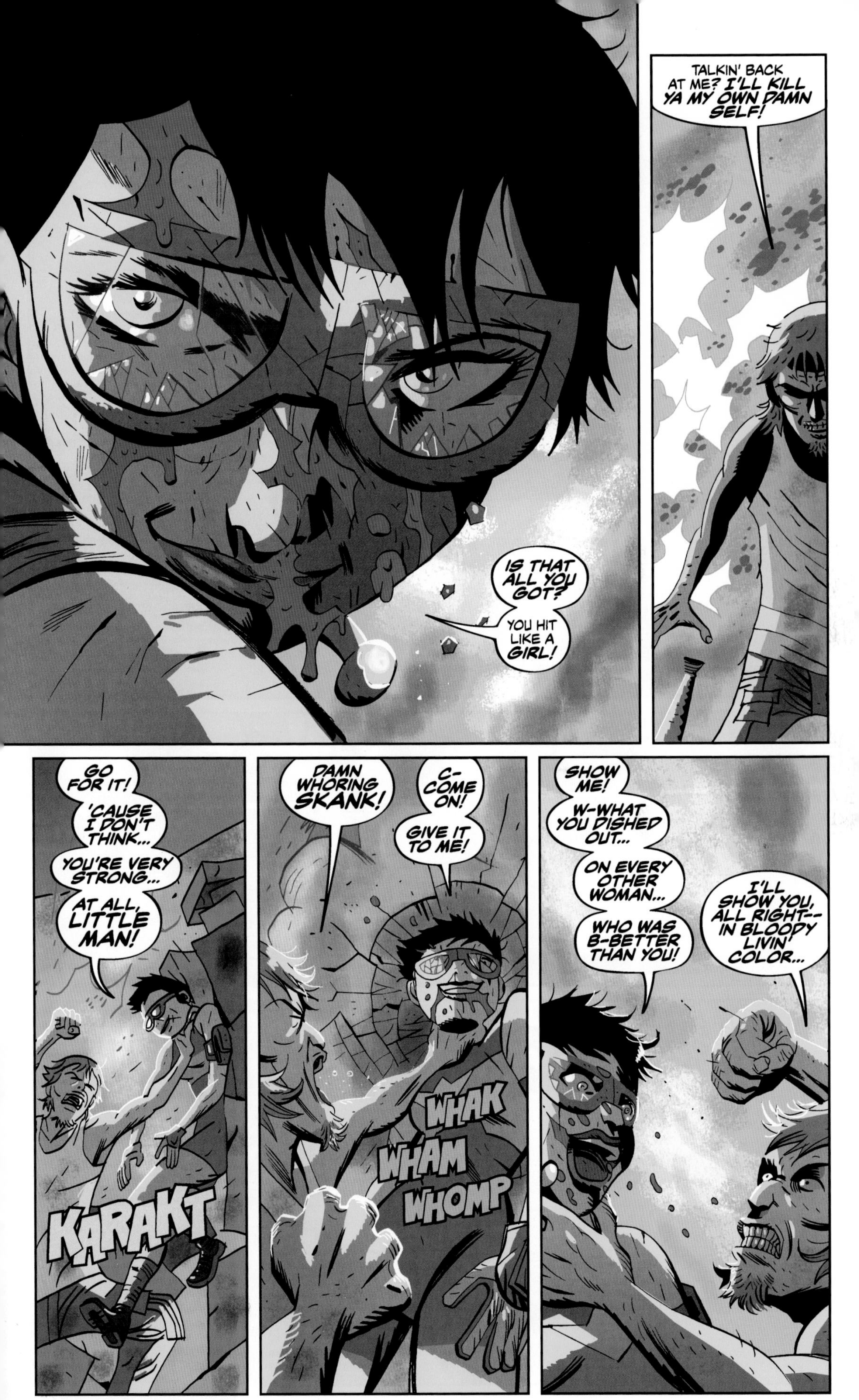
IS THAT ALL YOU GOT?
YOU HIT LIKE A GIRL!
TALKIN' BACK AT ME? I'LL KILL YA MY OWN DAMN SELF!
GO FOR IT!
'CAUSE I DON'T THINK...
YOU'RE VERY STRONG...
AT ALL, LITTLE MAN!
KARAKT
DAMN WHORING SKANK!
C-COME ON!
GIVE IT TO ME!
WHAK
WHAM
WHOMP
SHOW ME!
W-WHAT YOU DISHED OUT...
ON EVERY OTHER WOMAN...
WHO WAS B-BETTER THAN YOU!
I'LL SHOW YOU, ALL RIGHT--IN BLOODY LIVIN' COLOR...

THAT NO DAMNED BITCH IS EVER GONNA--

GONNA WHAT?

MAKE YOU FEEL *WEAK*? TAKE YOU DOWN *WITHOUT A FIGHT*?

CRAK

WHAP

HE COULDN'T HURT ME.

BUT ALL THAT KINETIC ENERGY HE THREW DOWN CHARGED ME RIGHT BACK UP.

WHAT WAS THAT?

NO BITCH IS EVER GONNA *OWN YOUR PATHETIC DAMN ASS*?!

CRAAK

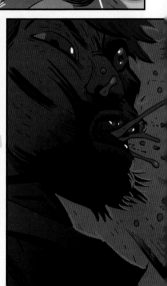

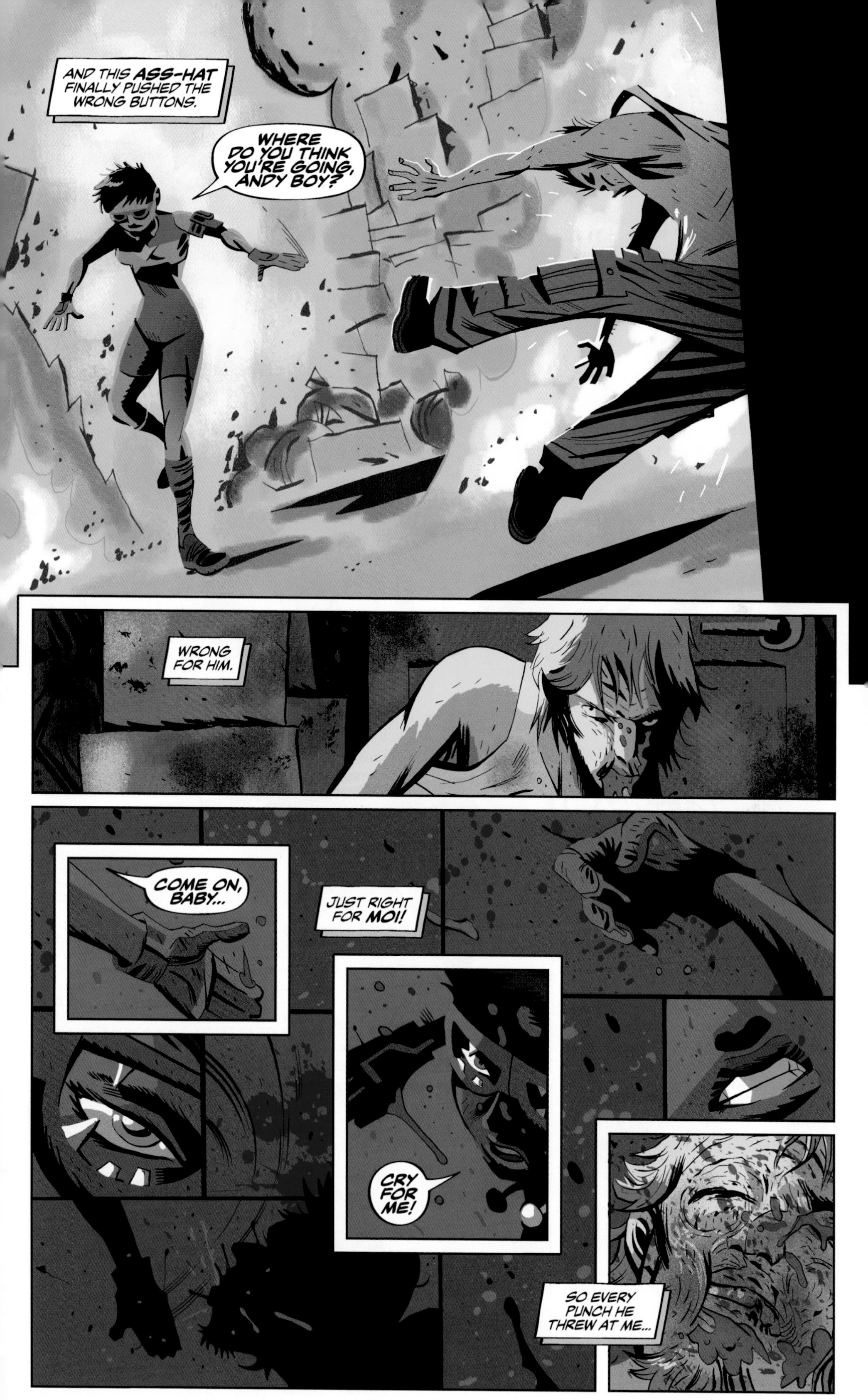

AND THIS ASS-HAT FINALLY PUSHED THE WRONG BUTTONS.
WHERE DO YOU THINK YOU'RE GOING, ANDY BOY?
WRONG FOR HIM.
COME ON, BABY...
JUST RIGHT FOR MOI!
CRY FOR ME!
SO EVERY PUNCH HE THREW AT ME...

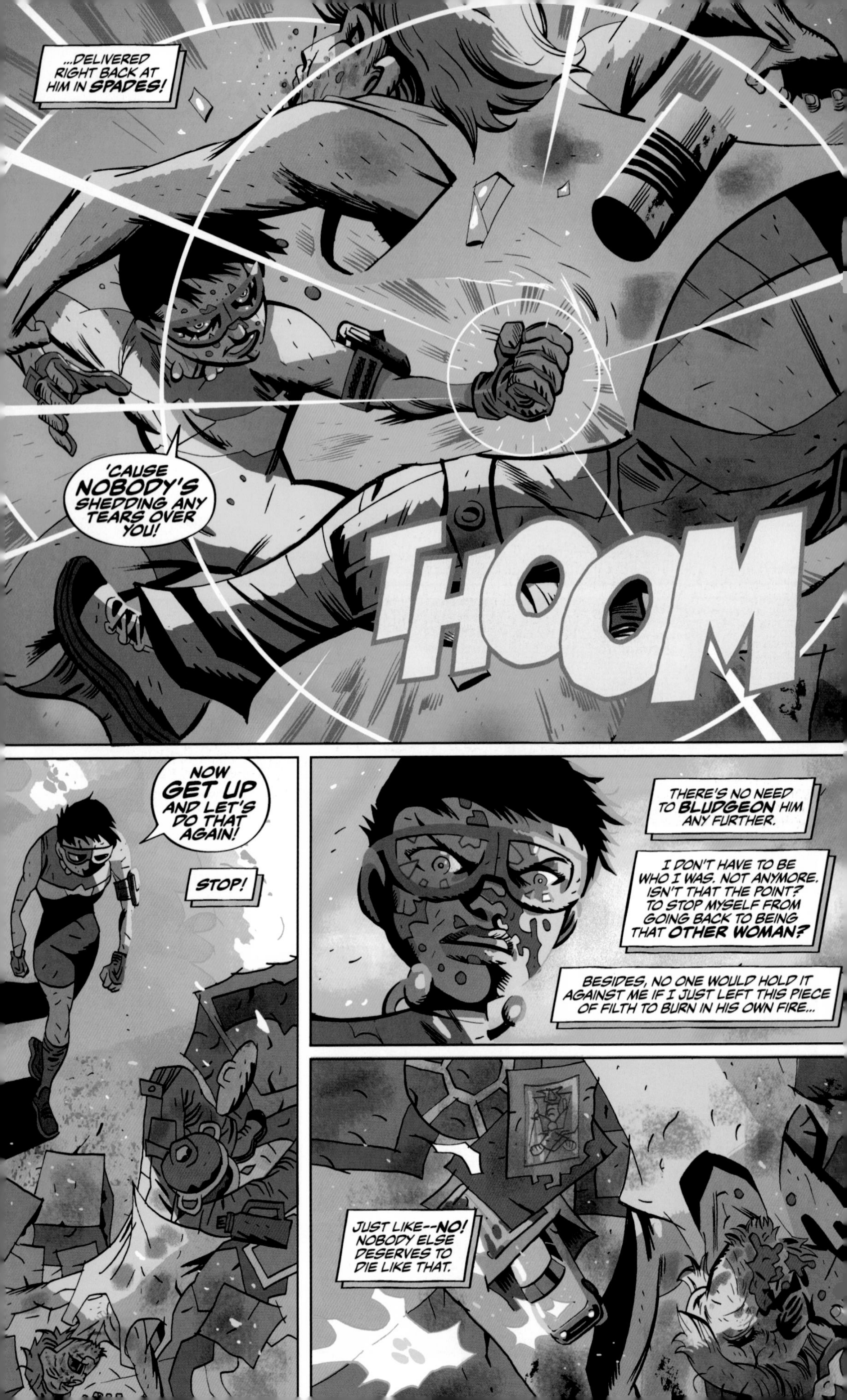
...DELIVERED RIGHT BACK AT HIM IN SPADES!
'CAUSE NOBODY'S SHEDDING ANY TEARS OVER YOU!
THOOM
NOW GET UP AND LET'S DO THAT AGAIN!
STOP!
THERE'S NO NEED TO BLUDGEON HIM ANY FURTHER.
I DON'T HAVE TO BE WHO I WAS. NOT ANYMORE. ISN'T THAT THE POINT? TO STOP MYSELF FROM GOING BACK TO BEING THAT OTHER WOMAN?
BESIDES, NO ONE WOULD HOLD IT AGAINST ME IF I JUST LEFT THIS PIECE OF FILTH TO BURN IN HIS OWN FIRE...
JUST LIKE--NO! NOBODY ELSE DESERVES TO DIE LIKE THAT.

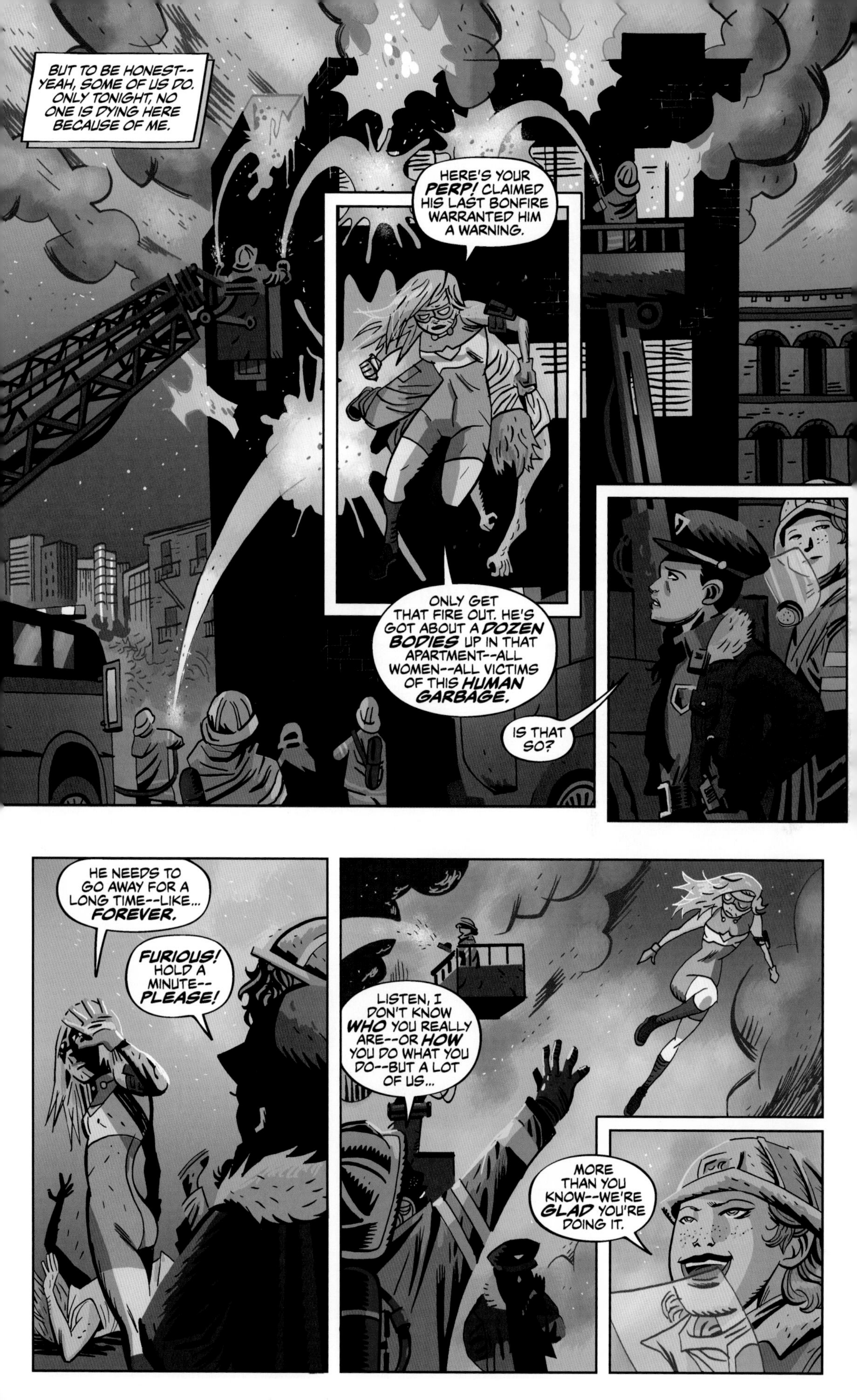
BUT TO BE HONEST--YEAH, SOME OF US DO. ONLY TONIGHT, NO ONE IS DYING HERE BECAUSE OF ME.
HERE'S YOUR PERP! CLAIMED HIS LAST BONFIRE WARRANTED HIM A WARNING.
ONLY GET THAT FIRE OUT. HE'S GOT ABOUT A DOZEN BODIES UP IN THAT APARTMENT--ALL WOMEN--ALL VICTIMS OF THIS HUMAN GARBAGE.
IS THAT SO?
HE NEEDS TO GO AWAY FOR A LONG TIME--LIKE... FOREVER.
FURIOUS! HOLD A MINUTE-- PLEASE!
LISTEN, I DON'T KNOW WHO YOU REALLY ARE--OR HOW YOU DO WHAT YOU DO--BUT A LOT OF US...
MORE THAN YOU KNOW--WE'RE GLAD YOU'RE DOING IT.

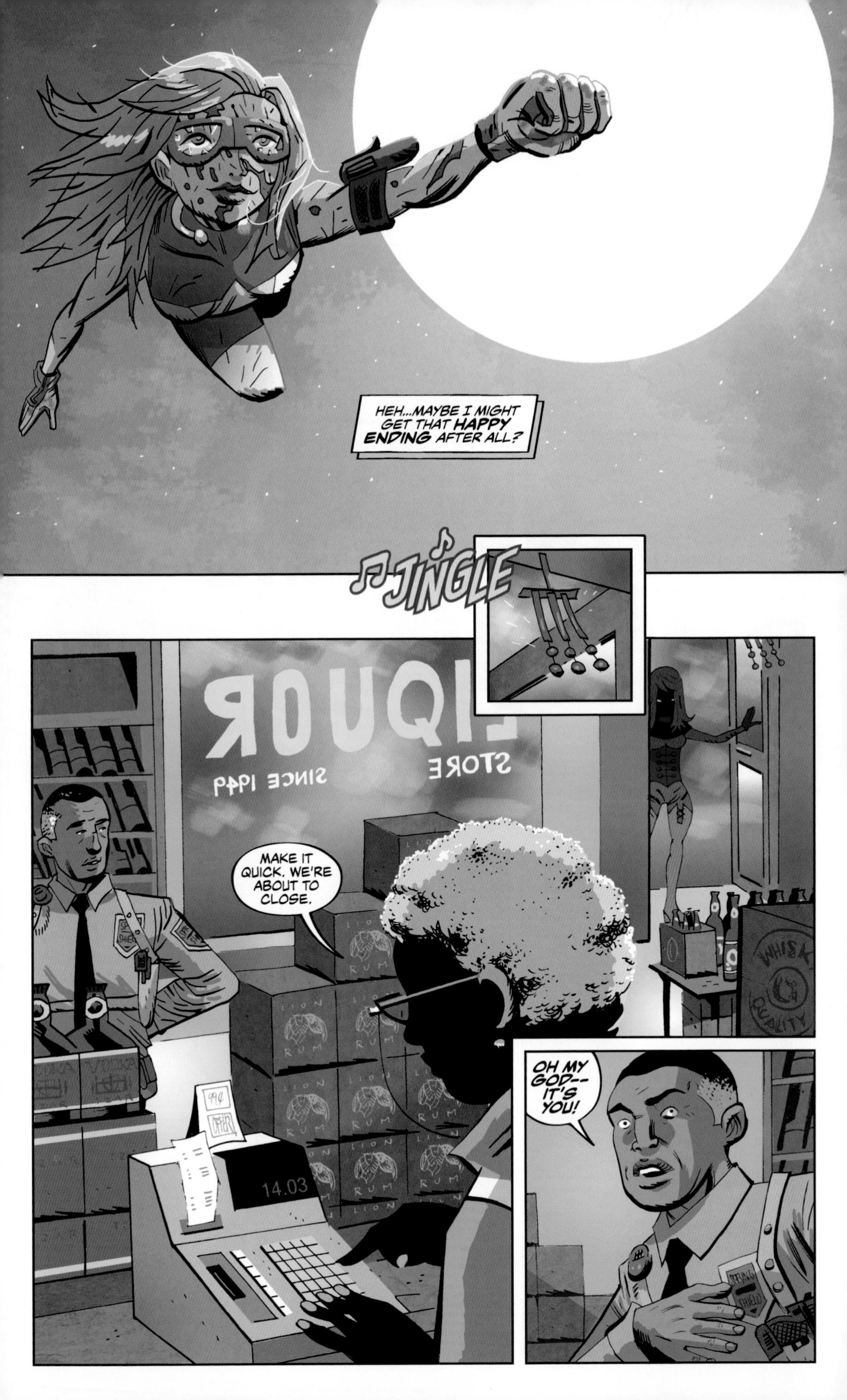
HEH...MAYBE I MIGHT GET THAT HAPPY ENDING AFTER ALL?
JINGLE
MAKE IT QUICK. WE'RE ABOUT TO CLOSE.
14.03
LION RUM
OH MY GOD-- IT'S YOU!

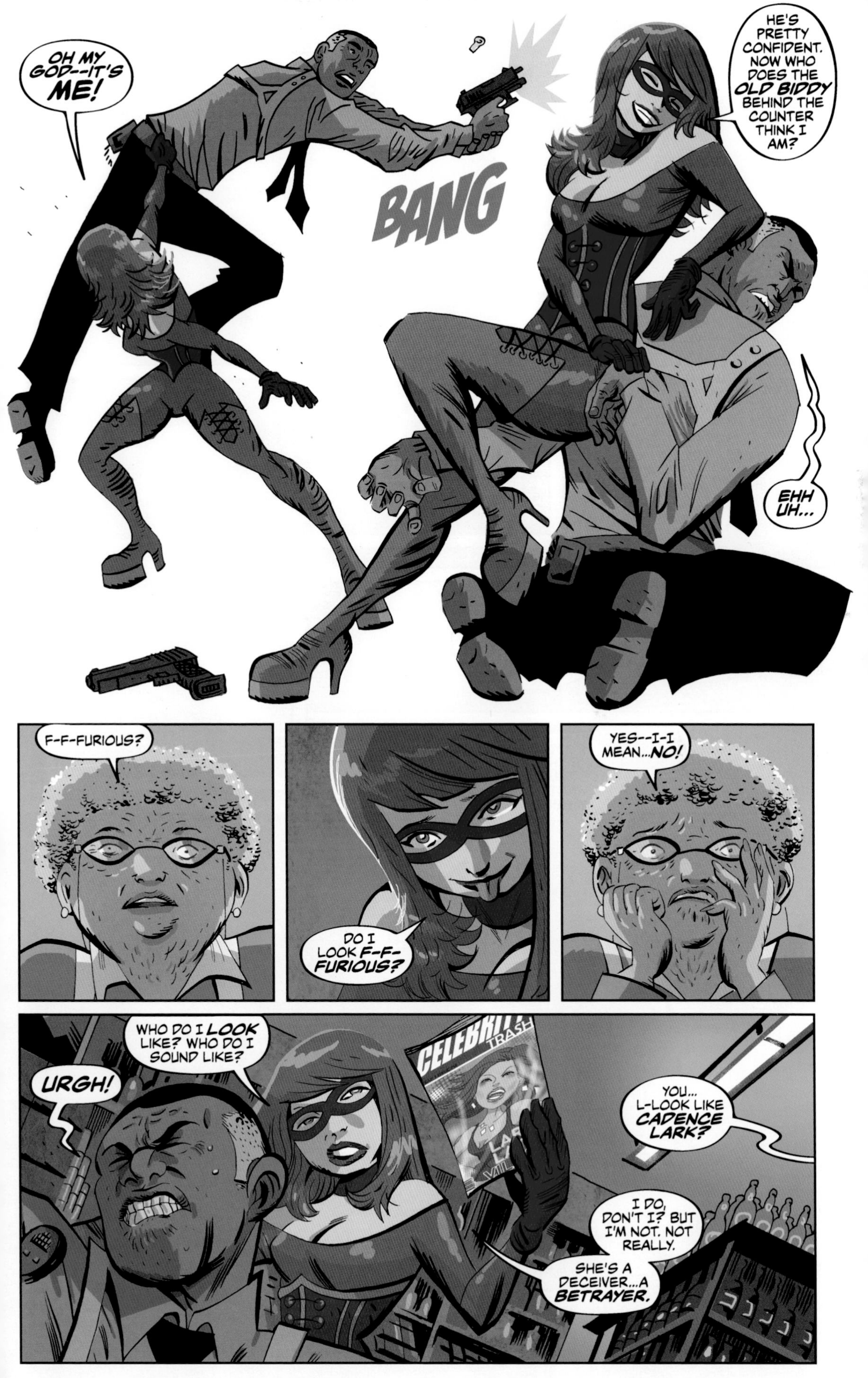

OH MY GOD--IT'S ME!
HE'S PRETTY CONFIDENT. NOW WHO DOES THE OLD BIDDY BEHIND THE COUNTER THINK I AM?
BANG
EHH UH...
F-F-FURIOUS?
DO I LOOK F-F-FURIOUS?
YES--I-I MEAN...NO!
WHO DO I LOOK LIKE? WHO DO I SOUND LIKE?
URGH!
CELEBRITY TRASH
YOU... L-LOOK LIKE CADENCE LARK?
I DO, DON'T I? BUT I'M NOT. NOT REALLY.
SHE'S A DECEIVER...A BETRAYER.

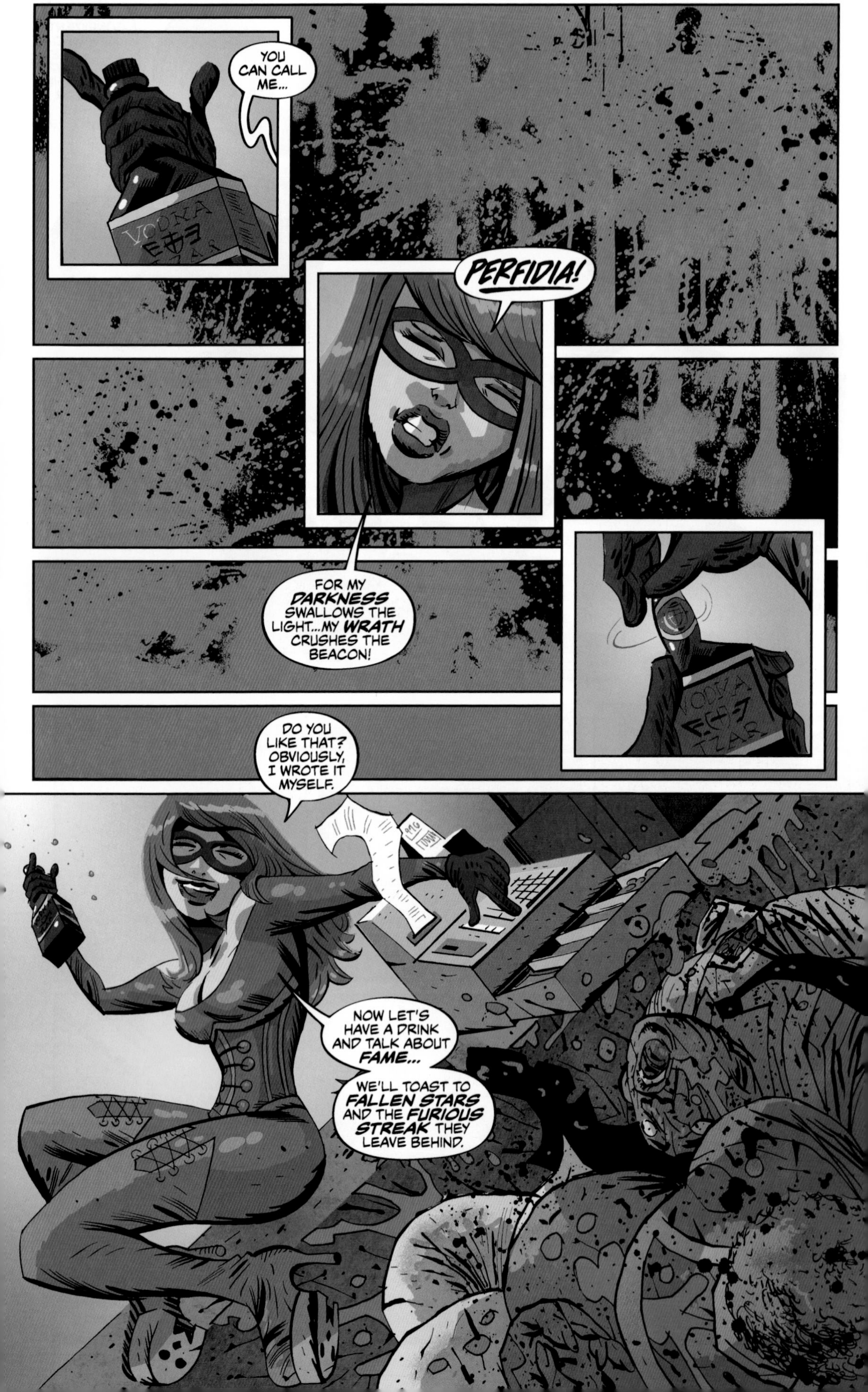
YOU CAN CALL ME...
VODKA TZAR
PERFIDIA!
FOR MY DARKNESS SWALLOWS THE LIGHT...MY WRATH CRUSHES THE BEACON!
VODKA TZAR
DO YOU LIKE THAT? OBVIOUSLY, I WROTE IT MYSELF.
NOW LET'S HAVE A DRINK AND TALK ABOUT FAME...
WE'LL TOAST TO FALLEN STARS AND THE FURIOUS STREAK THEY LEAVE BEHIND.

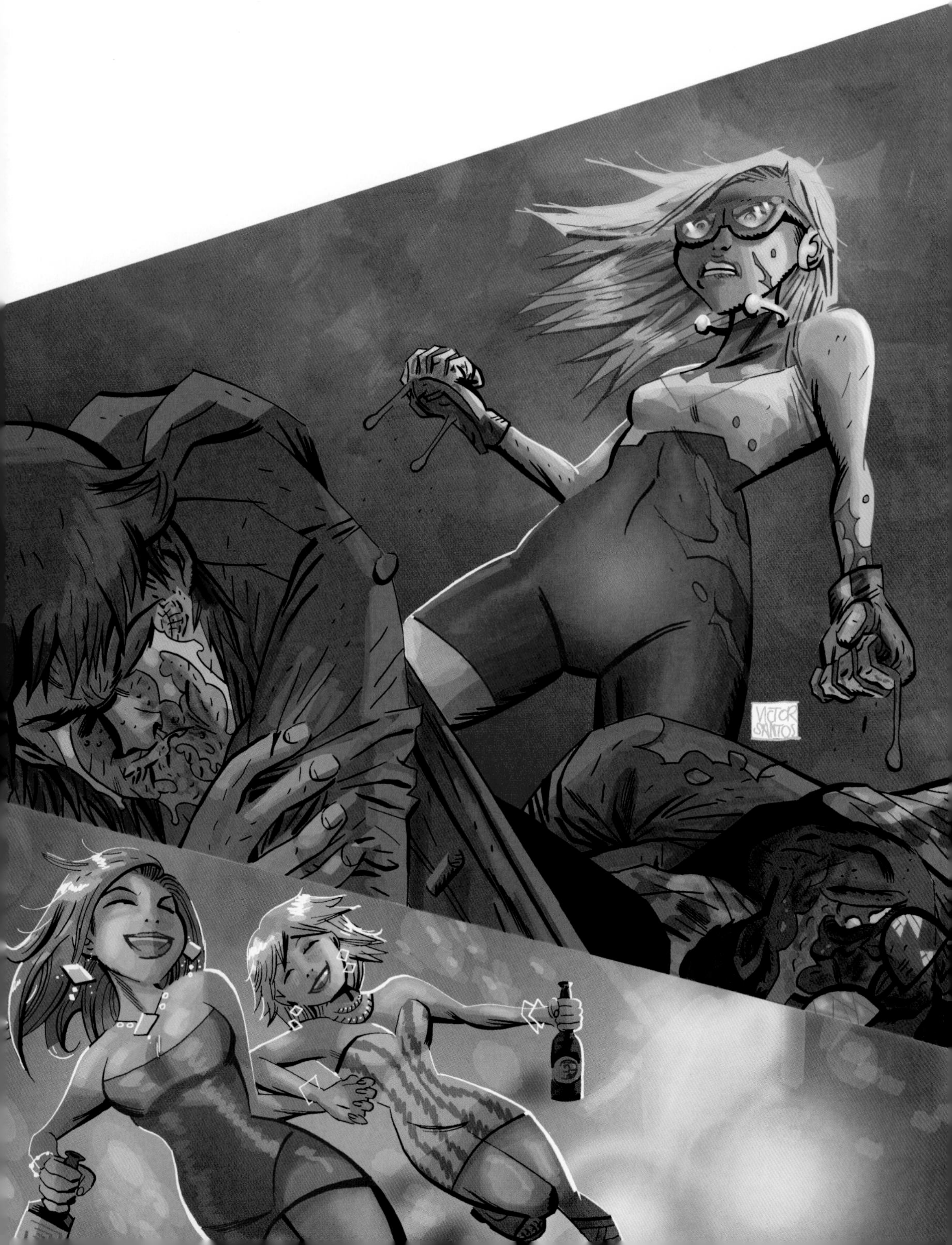
VICTOR SANTOS

CHAPTER FOUR: FAME IS A FICKLE MISTRESS

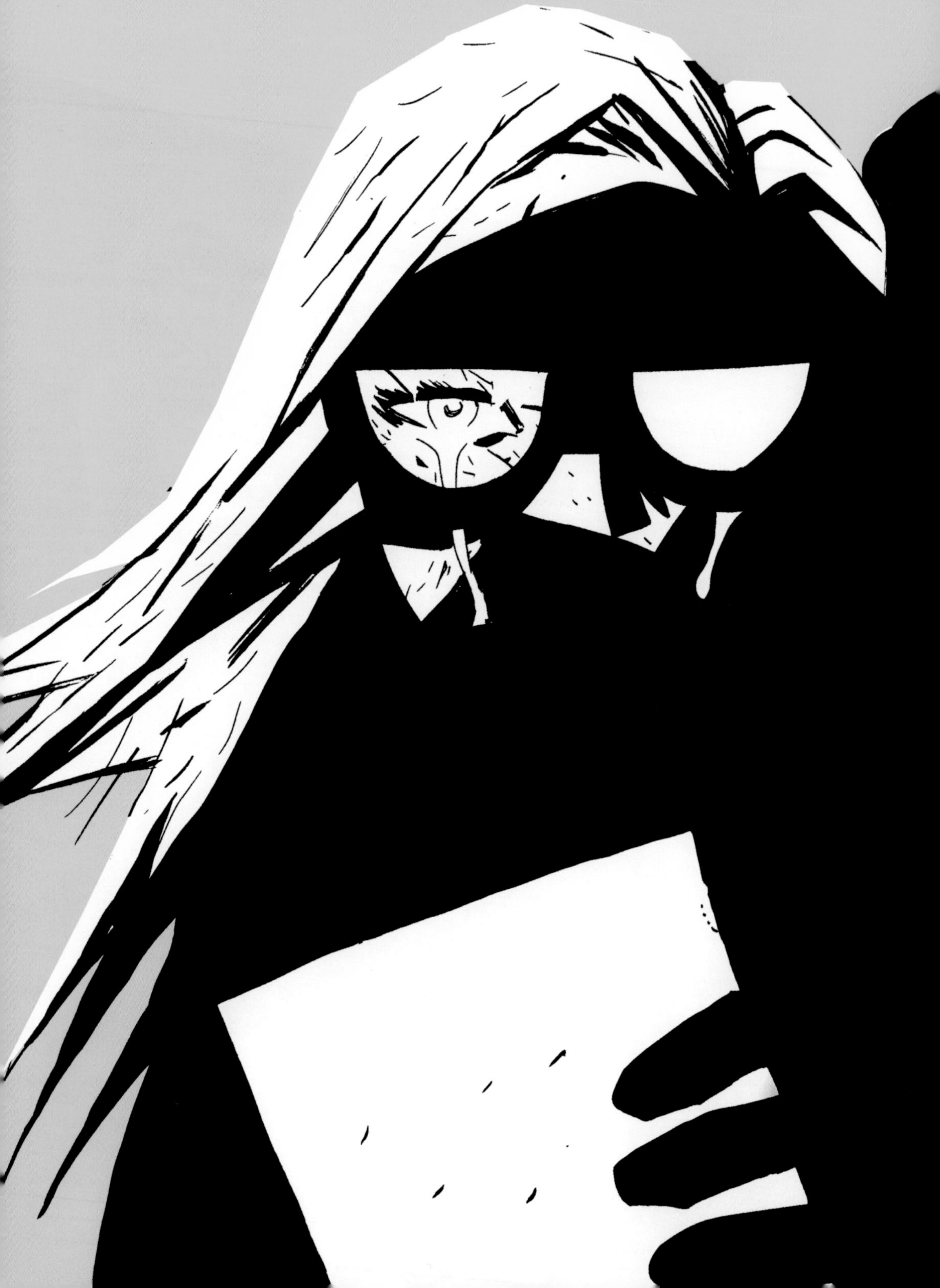

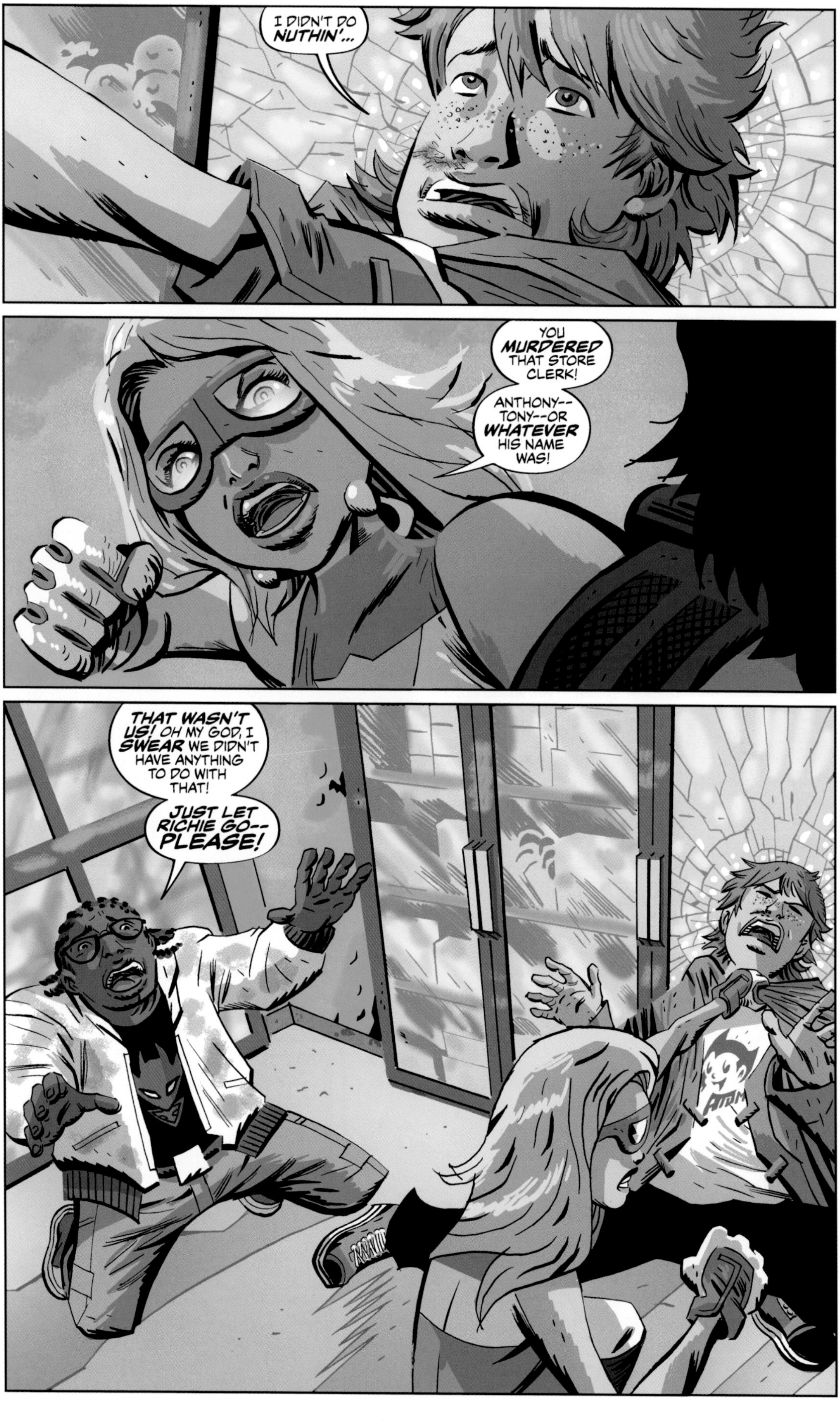
I DIDN'T DO NUTHIN'...
YOU MURDERED THAT STORE CLERK!
ANTHONY-- TONY--OR WHATEVER HIS NAME WAS!
THAT WASN'T US! OH MY GOD, I SWEAR WE DIDN'T HAVE ANYTHING TO DO WITH THAT!
JUST LET RICHIE GO-- PLEASE!

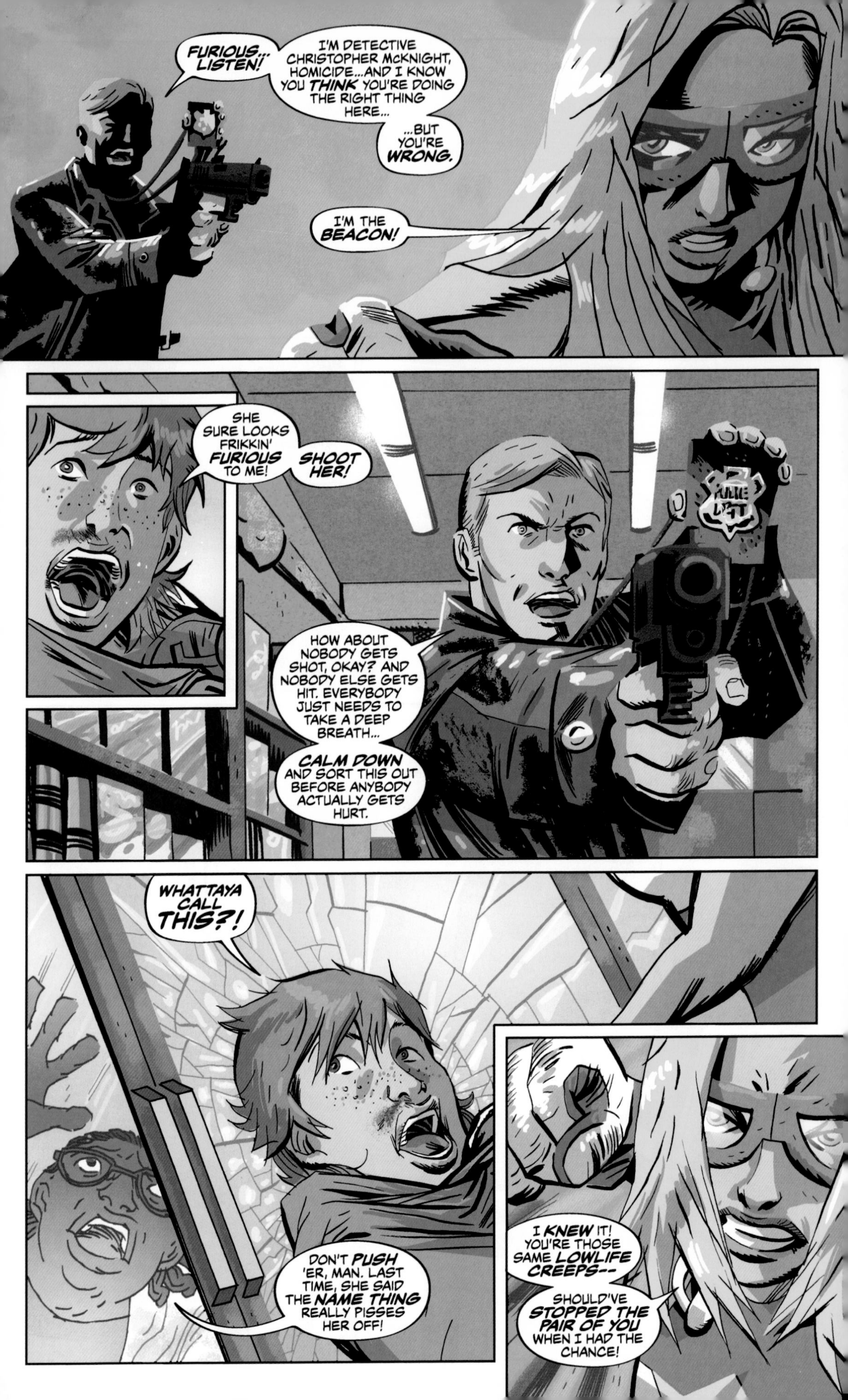
FURIOUS... LISTEN!
I'M DETECTIVE CHRISTOPHER McKNIGHT, HOMICIDE...AND I KNOW YOU THINK YOU'RE DOING THE RIGHT THING HERE...
...BUT YOU'RE WRONG.
I'M THE BEACON!
SHE SURE LOOKS FRIKKIN' FURIOUS TO ME!
SHOOT HER!
HOW ABOUT NOBODY GETS SHOT, OKAY? AND NOBODY ELSE GETS HIT. EVERYBODY JUST NEEDS TO TAKE A DEEP BREATH...
CALM DOWN AND SORT THIS OUT BEFORE ANYBODY ACTUALLY GETS HURT.
WHATTAYA CALL THIS?!
DON'T PUSH 'ER, MAN. LAST TIME, SHE SAID THE NAME THING REALLY PISSES HER OFF!
I KNEW IT! YOU'RE THOSE SAME LOWLIFE CREEPS--
SHOULD'VE STOPPED THE PAIR OF YOU WHEN I HAD THE CHANCE!

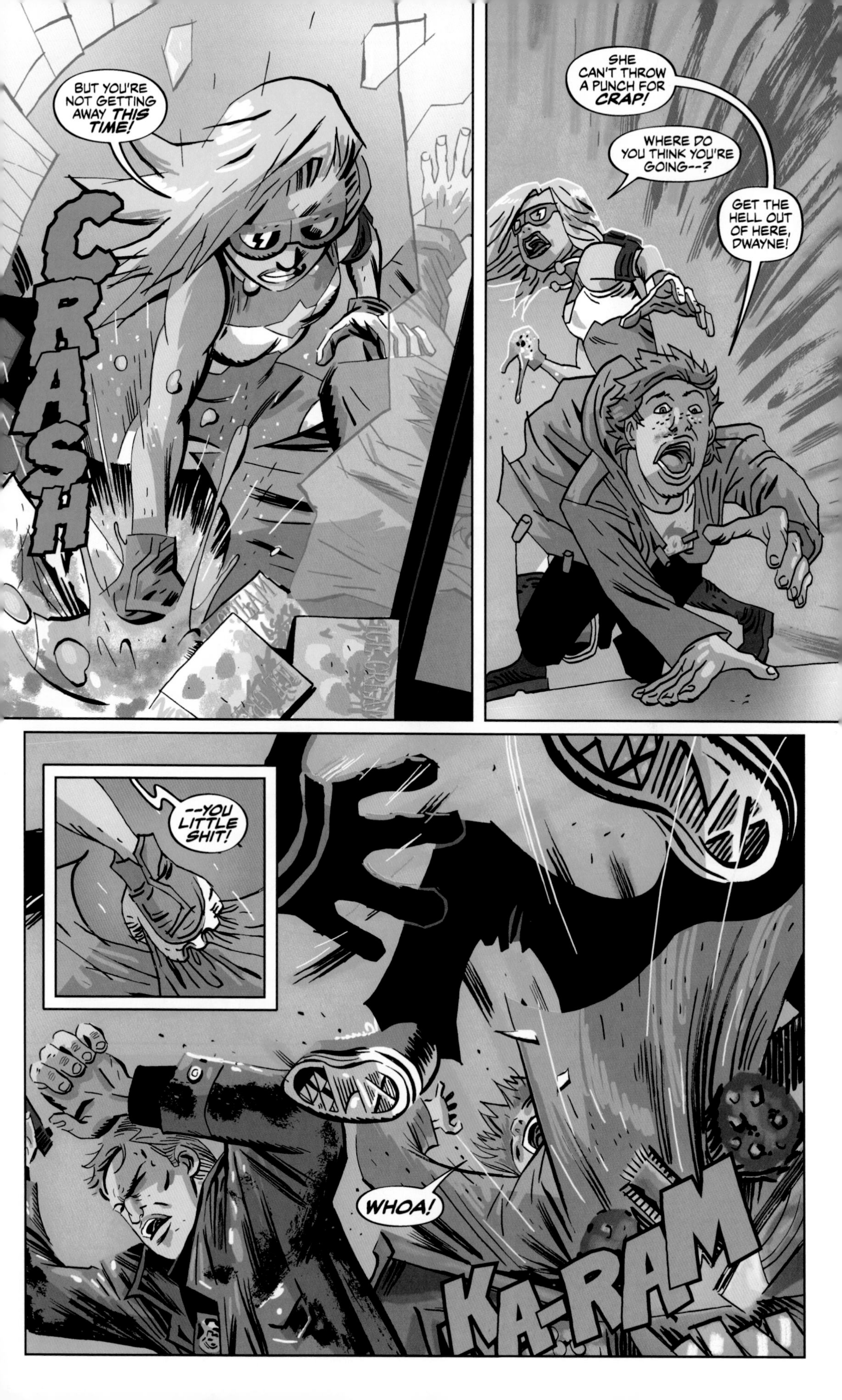

BUT YOU'RE NOT GETTING AWAY *THIS TIME!*
CRASH
SHE CAN'T THROW A PUNCH FOR *CRAP!*
WHERE DO YOU THINK YOU'RE GOING--?
GET THE HELL OUT OF HERE, DWAYNE!
--YOU LITTLE SHIT!
WHOA!
KA-RAM

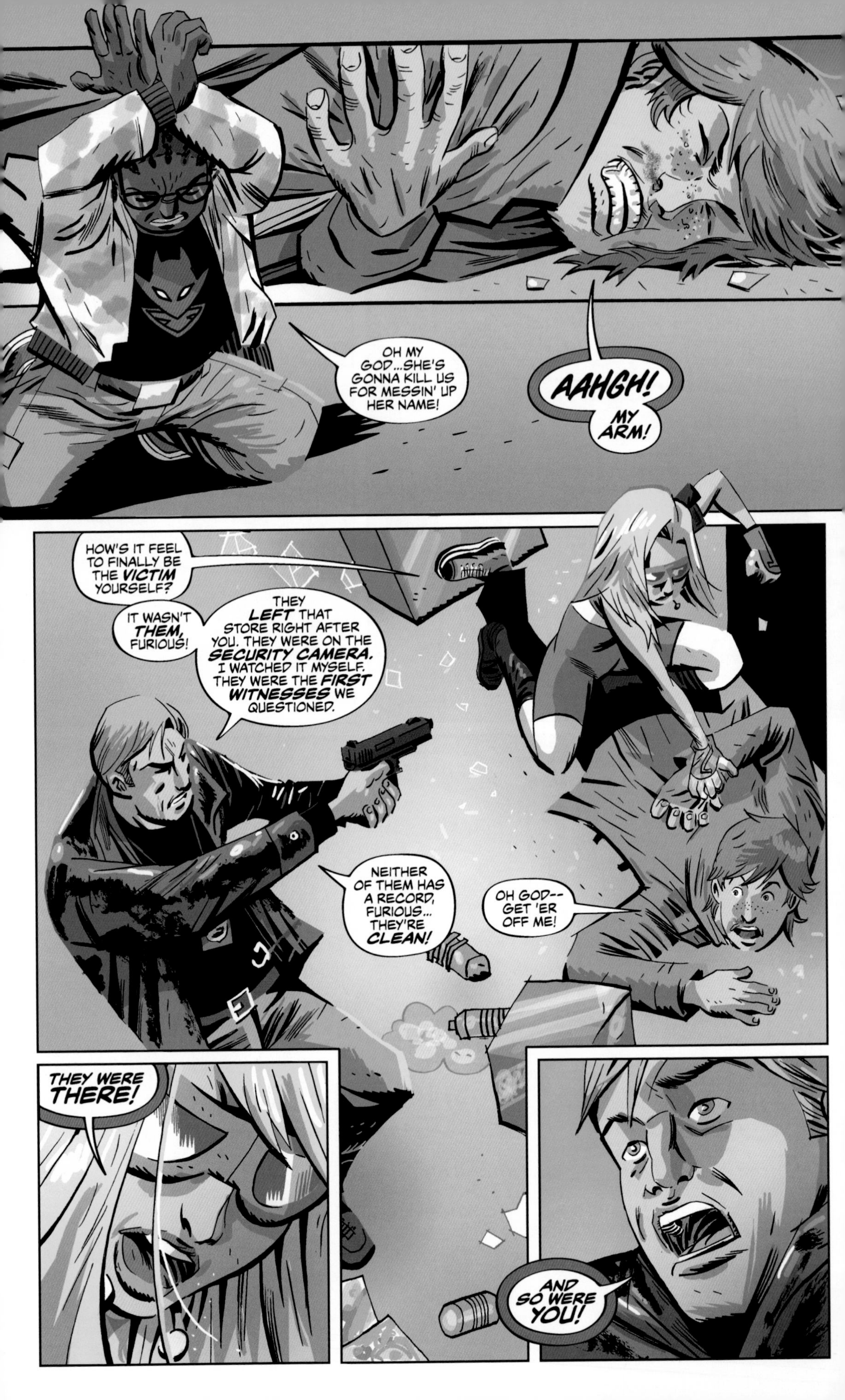
OH MY GOD...SHE'S GONNA KILL US FOR MESSIN' UP HER NAME!
AAHGH! MY ARM!
HOW'S IT FEEL TO FINALLY BE THE VICTIM YOURSELF?
IT WASN'T THEM, FURIOUS!
THEY LEFT THAT STORE RIGHT AFTER YOU. THEY WERE ON THE SECURITY CAMERA. I WATCHED IT MYSELF. THEY WERE THE FIRST WITNESSES WE QUESTIONED.
NEITHER OF THEM HAS A RECORD, FURIOUS... THEY'RE CLEAN!
OH GOD-- GET 'ER OFF ME!
THEY WERE THERE!
AND SO WERE YOU!

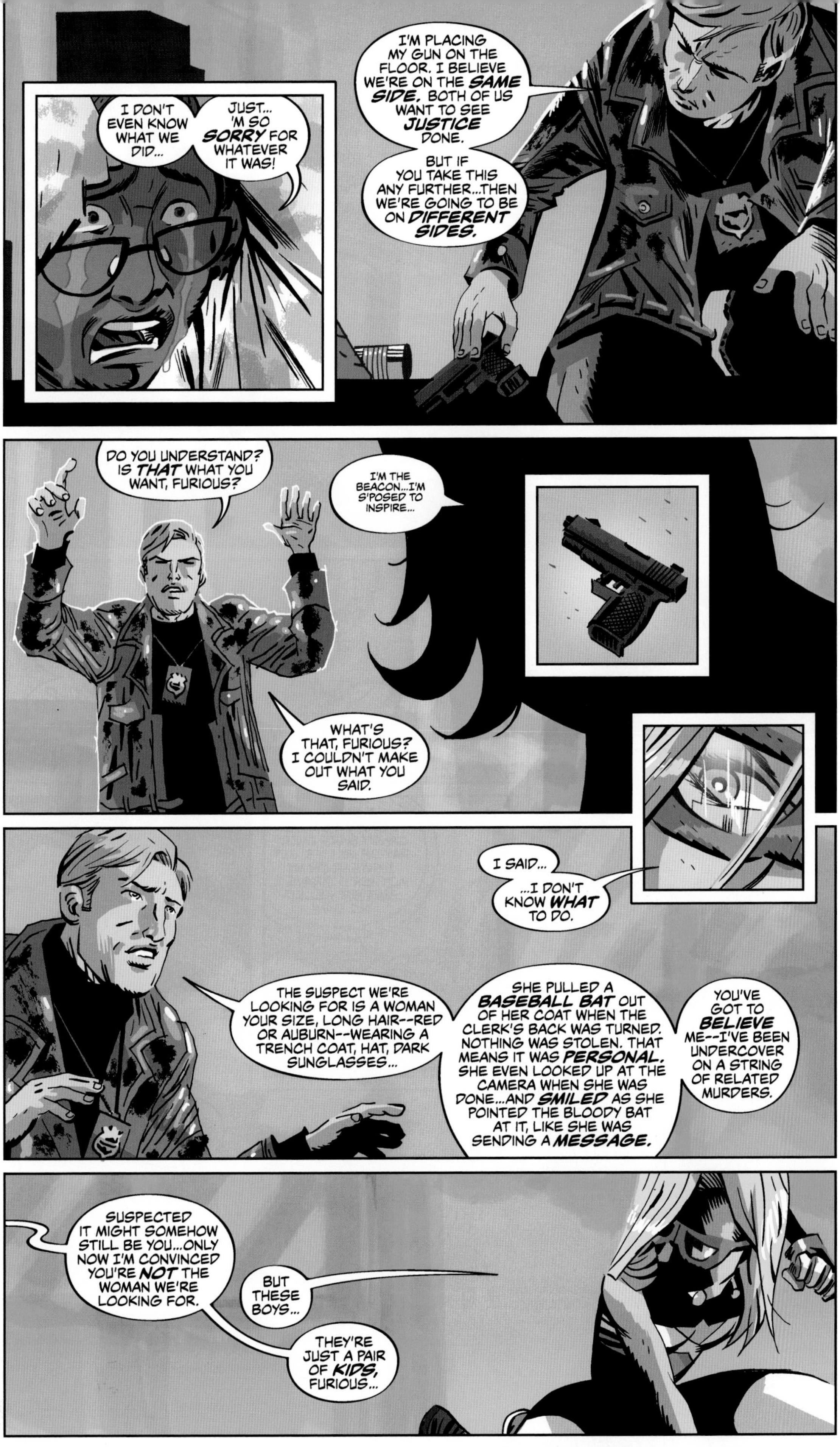

I'M PLACING MY GUN ON THE FLOOR. I BELIEVE WE'RE ON THE SAME SIDE. BOTH OF US WANT TO SEE JUSTICE DONE.
BUT IF YOU TAKE THIS ANY FURTHER...THEN WE'RE GOING TO BE ON DIFFERENT SIDES.
I DON'T EVEN KNOW WHAT WE DID...
JUST... 'M SO SORRY FOR WHATEVER IT WAS!
DO YOU UNDERSTAND? IS THAT WHAT YOU WANT, FURIOUS?
I'M THE BEACON...I'M S'POSED TO INSPIRE...
WHAT'S THAT, FURIOUS? I COULDN'T MAKE OUT WHAT YOU SAID.
I SAID...
...I DON'T KNOW WHAT TO DO.
THE SUSPECT WE'RE LOOKING FOR IS A WOMAN YOUR SIZE, LONG HAIR--RED OR AUBURN--WEARING A TRENCH COAT, HAT, DARK SUNGLASSES...
SHE PULLED A BASEBALL BAT OUT OF HER COAT WHEN THE CLERK'S BACK WAS TURNED. NOTHING WAS STOLEN. THAT MEANS IT WAS PERSONAL. SHE EVEN LOOKED UP AT THE CAMERA WHEN SHE WAS DONE...AND SMILED AS SHE POINTED THE BLOODY BAT AT IT, LIKE SHE WAS SENDING A MESSAGE.
YOU'VE GOT TO BELIEVE ME--I'VE BEEN UNDERCOVER ON A STRING OF RELATED MURDERS.
SUSPECTED IT MIGHT SOMEHOW STILL BE YOU...ONLY NOW I'M CONVINCED YOU'RE NOT THE WOMAN WE'RE LOOKING FOR.
BUT THESE BOYS...
THEY'RE JUST A PAIR OF KIDS, FURIOUS...

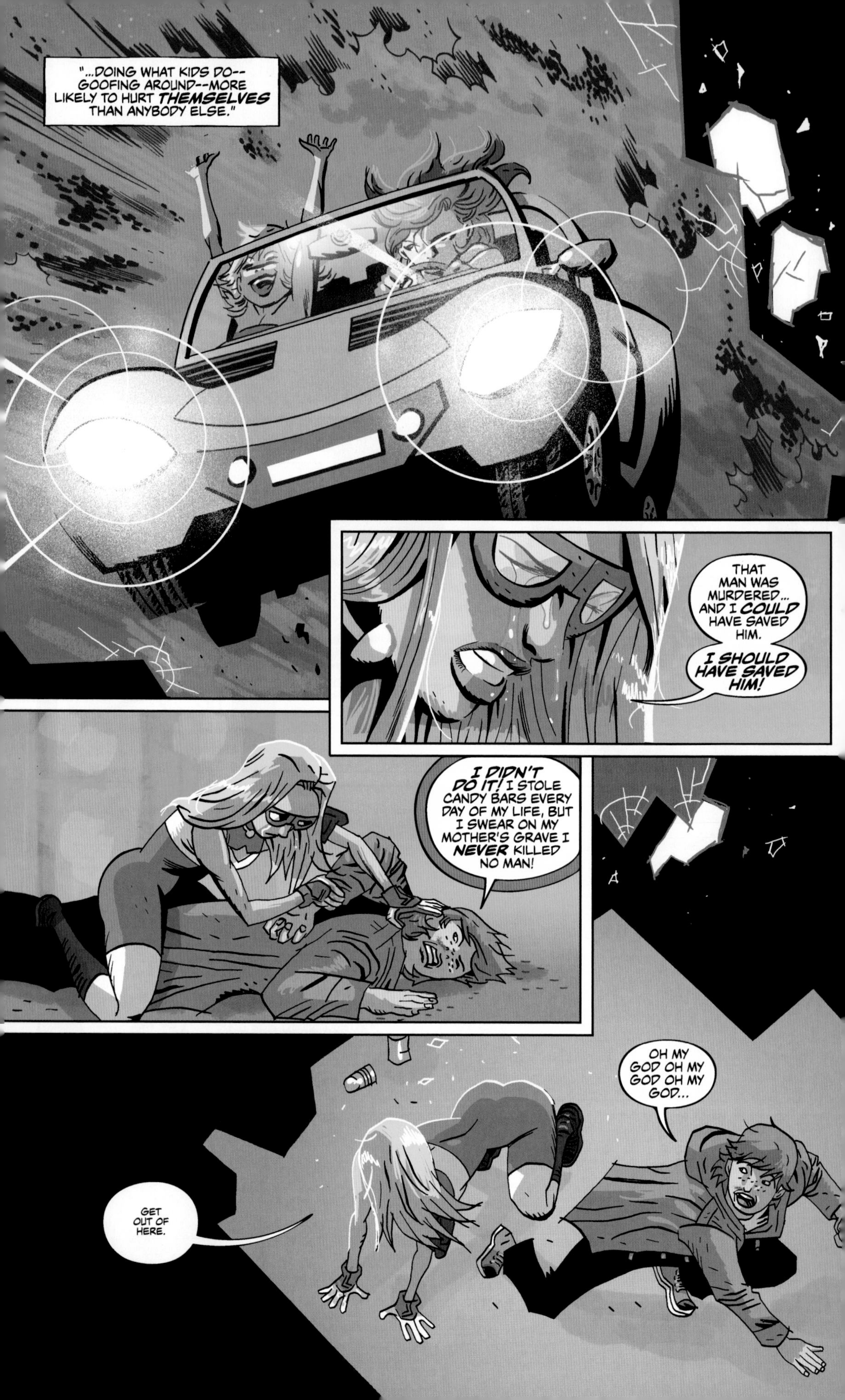
"...DOING WHAT KIDS DO--GOOFING AROUND--MORE LIKELY TO HURT THEMSELVES THAN ANYBODY ELSE."
THAT MAN WAS MURDERED... AND I COULD HAVE SAVED HIM.
I SHOULD HAVE SAVED HIM!
I DIDN'T DO IT! I STOLE CANDY BARS EVERY DAY OF MY LIFE, BUT I SWEAR ON MY MOTHER'S GRAVE I NEVER KILLED NO MAN!
OH MY GOD OH MY GOD OH MY GOD...
GET OUT OF HERE.

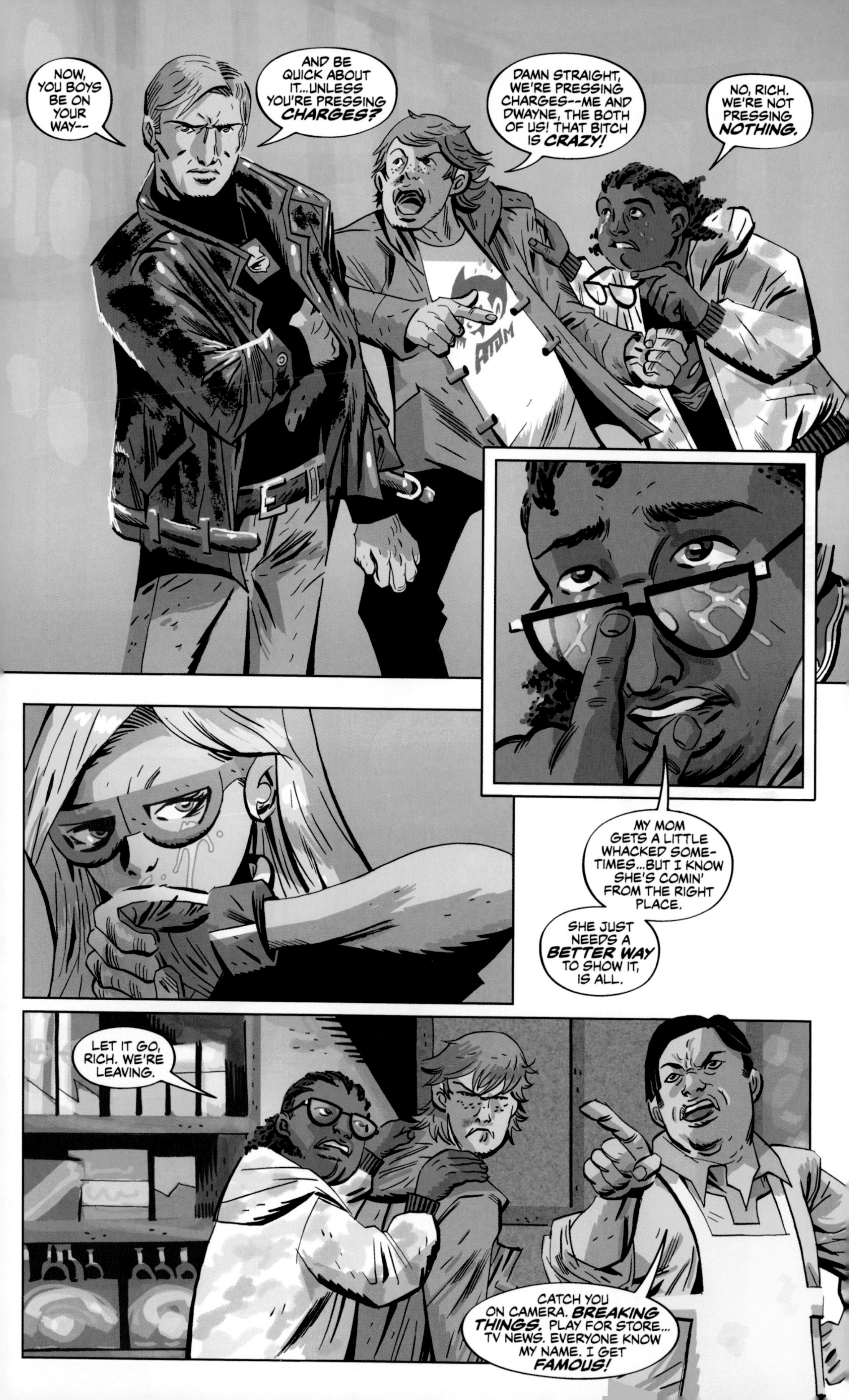
NOW, YOU BOYS BE ON YOUR WAY--
AND BE QUICK ABOUT IT...UNLESS YOU'RE PRESSING CHARGES?
DAMN STRAIGHT, WE'RE PRESSING CHARGES--ME AND DWAYNE, THE BOTH OF US! THAT BITCH IS CRAZY!
NO, RICH. WE'RE NOT PRESSING NOTHING.
MY MOM GETS A LITTLE WHACKED SOME-TIMES...BUT I KNOW SHE'S COMIN' FROM THE RIGHT PLACE.
SHE JUST NEEDS A BETTER WAY TO SHOW IT, IS ALL.
LET IT GO, RICH. WE'RE LEAVING.
CATCH YOU ON CAMERA. BREAKING THINGS. PLAY FOR STORE... TV NEWS. EVERYONE KNOW MY NAME. I GET FAMOUS!

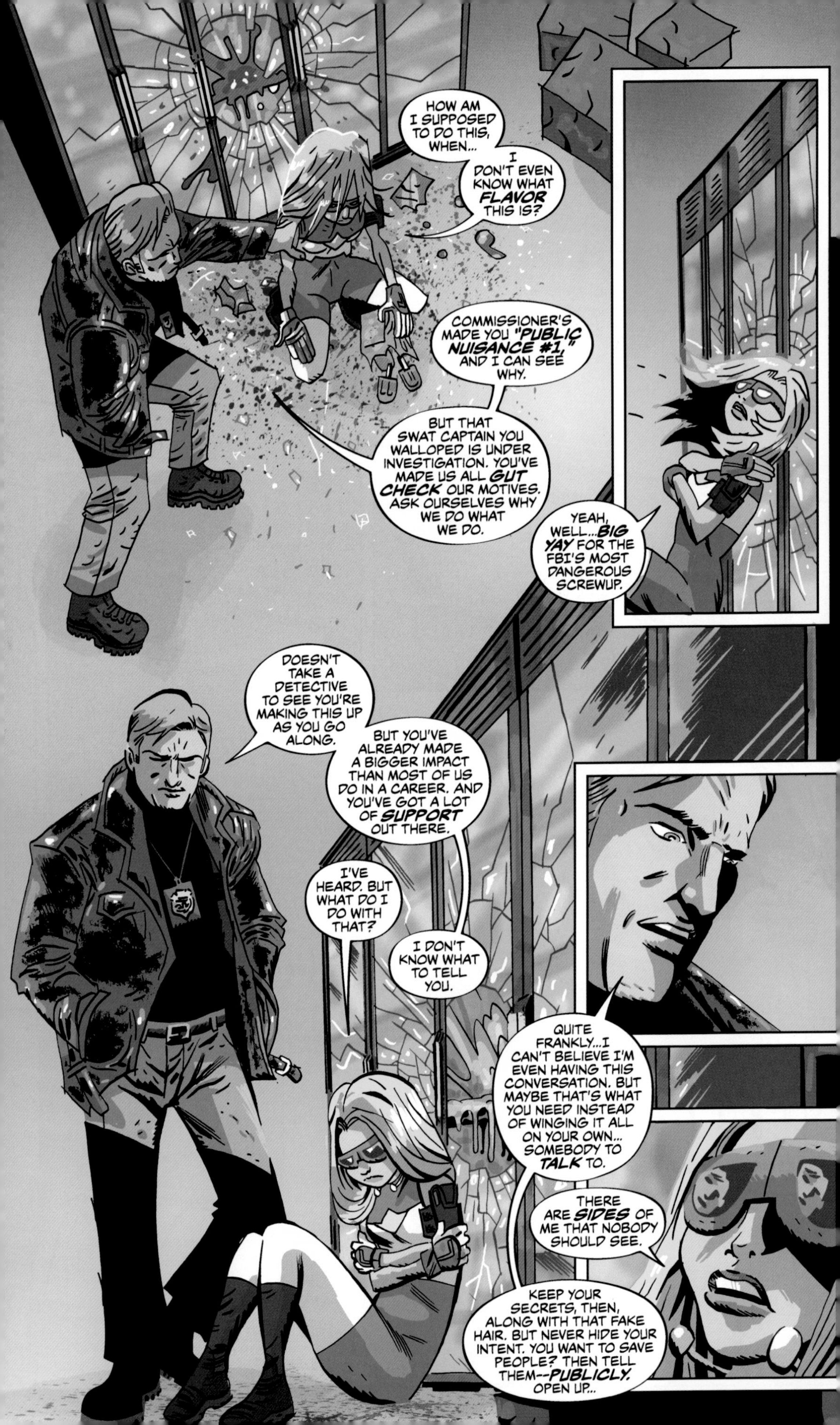
HOW AM I SUPPOSED TO DO THIS, WHEN...
I DON'T EVEN KNOW WHAT FLAVOR THIS IS?
COMMISSIONER'S MADE YOU "PUBLIC NUISANCE #1," AND I CAN SEE WHY.
BUT THAT SWAT CAPTAIN YOU WALLOPED IS UNDER INVESTIGATION. YOU'VE MADE US ALL GUT CHECK OUR MOTIVES. ASK OURSELVES WHY WE DO WHAT WE DO.
YEAH, WELL...BIG YAY FOR THE FBI'S MOST DANGEROUS SCREWUP.
DOESN'T TAKE A DETECTIVE TO SEE YOU'RE MAKING THIS UP AS YOU GO ALONG.
BUT YOU'VE ALREADY MADE A BIGGER IMPACT THAN MOST OF US DO IN A CAREER. AND YOU'VE GOT A LOT OF SUPPORT OUT THERE.
I'VE HEARD. BUT WHAT DO I DO WITH THAT?
I DON'T KNOW WHAT TO TELL YOU.
QUITE FRANKLY...I CAN'T BELIEVE I'M EVEN HAVING THIS CONVERSATION. BUT MAYBE THAT'S WHAT YOU NEED INSTEAD OF WINGING IT ALL ON YOUR OWN... SOMEBODY TO TALK TO.
THERE ARE SIDES OF ME THAT NOBODY SHOULD SEE.
KEEP YOUR SECRETS, THEN, ALONG WITH THAT FAKE HAIR. BUT NEVER HIDE YOUR INTENT. YOU WANT TO SAVE PEOPLE? THEN TELL THEM--PUBLICLY. OPEN UP...

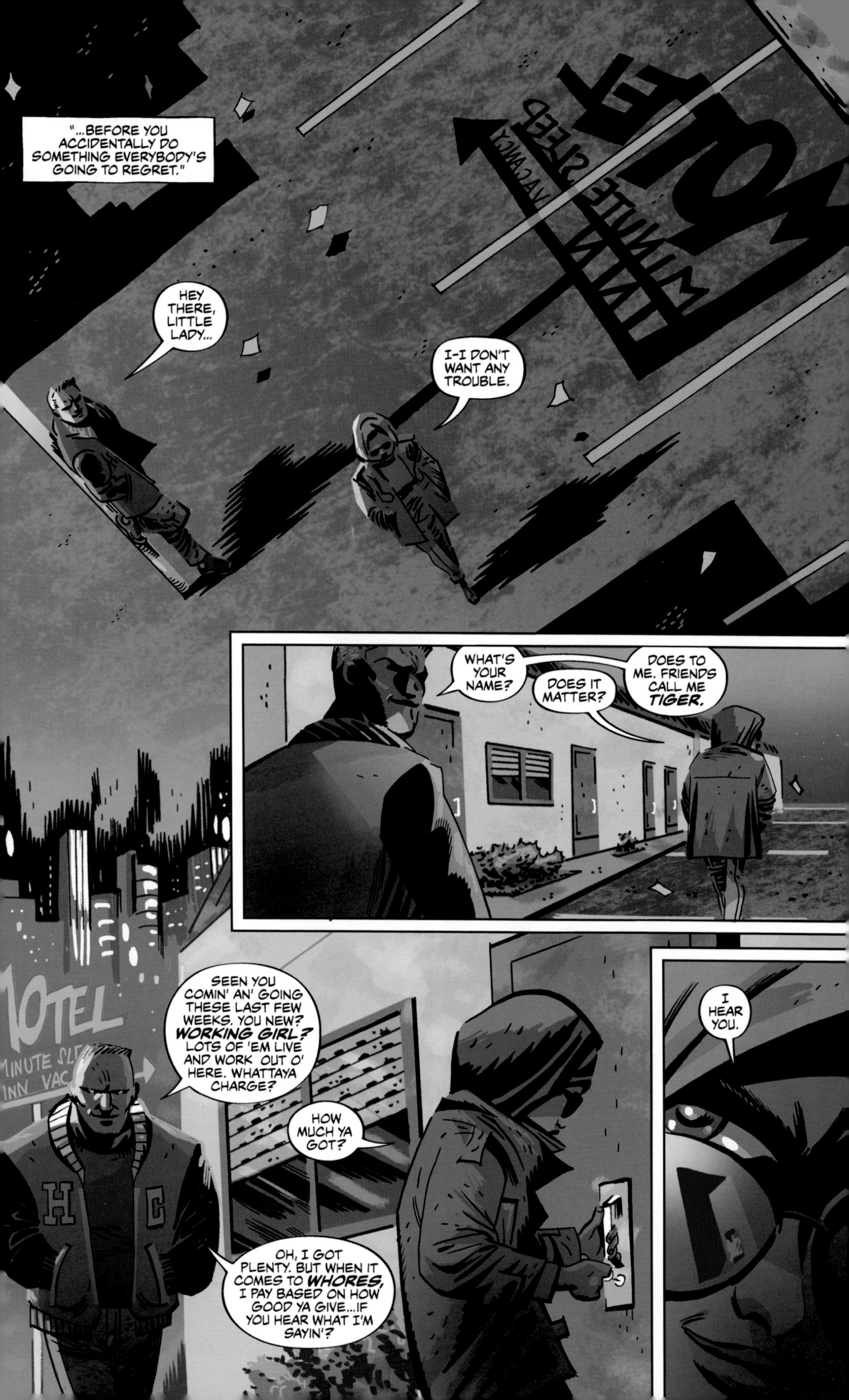
"...BEFORE YOU ACCIDENTALLY DO SOMETHING EVERYBODY'S GOING TO REGRET."
HEY THERE, LITTLE LADY...
I-I DON'T WANT ANY TROUBLE.
WHAT'S YOUR NAME?
DOES IT MATTER?
DOES TO ME. FRIENDS CALL ME *TIGER.*
SEEN YOU COMIN' AN' GOING THESE LAST FEW WEEKS. YOU NEW? *WORKING GIRL?* LOTS OF 'EM LIVE AND WORK OUT O' HERE. WHATTAYA CHARGE?
HOW MUCH YA GOT?
OH, I GOT PLENTY. BUT WHEN IT COMES TO *WHORES,* I PAY BASED ON HOW GOOD YA GIVE...IF YOU HEAR WHAT I'M SAYIN'?
I HEAR YOU.

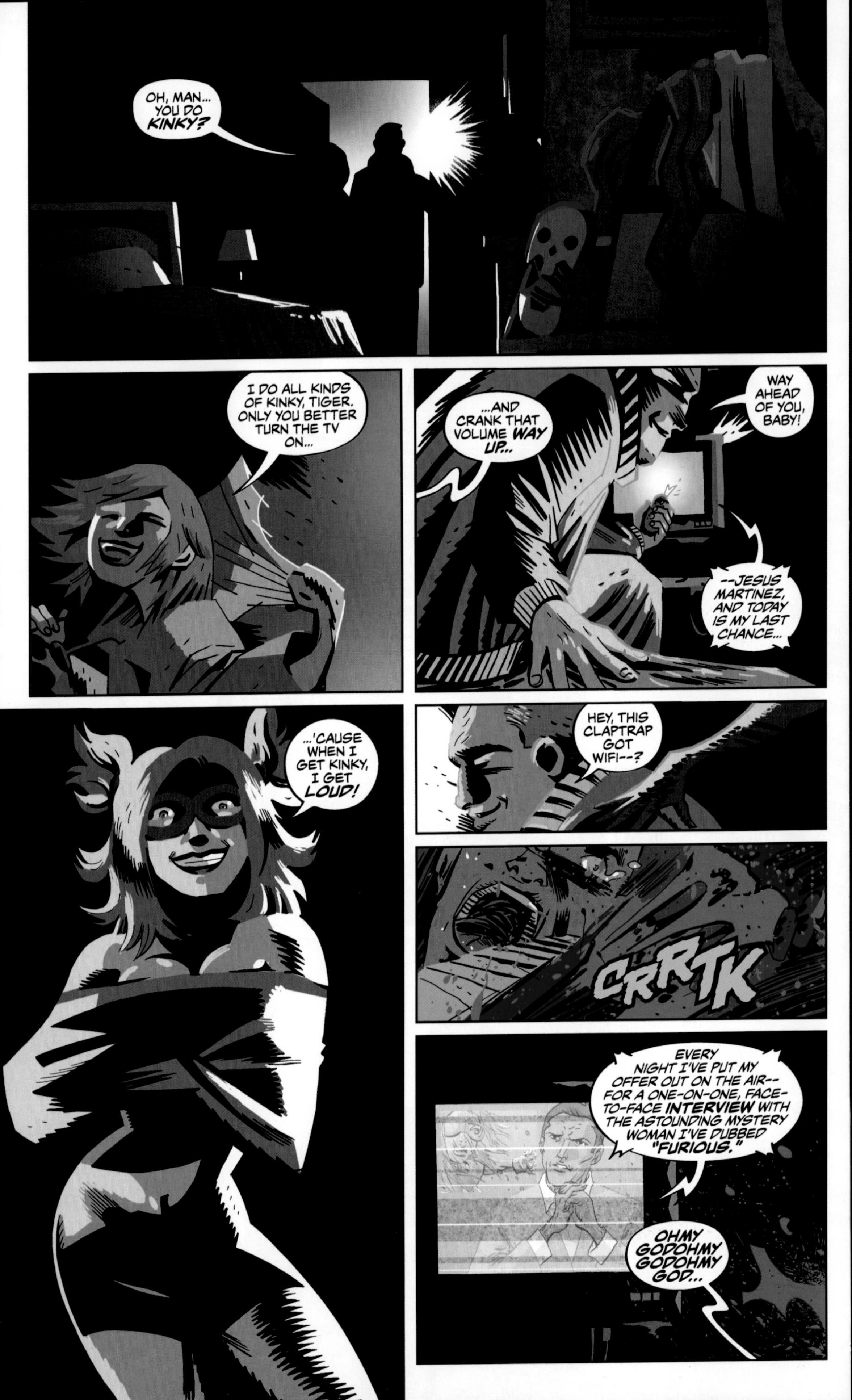
OH, MAN... YOU DO KINKY?
I DO ALL KINDS OF KINKY, TIGER. ONLY YOU BETTER TURN THE TV ON...
...AND CRANK THAT VOLUME WAY UP...
WAY AHEAD OF YOU, BABY!
--JESUS MARTINEZ, AND TODAY IS MY LAST CHANCE...
...'CAUSE WHEN I GET KINKY, I GET LOUD!
HEY, THIS CLAPTRAP GOT WIFI--?
CRRTK
EVERY NIGHT I'VE PUT MY OFFER OUT ON THE AIR-- FOR A ONE-ON-ONE, FACE-TO-FACE INTERVIEW WITH THE ASTOUNDING MYSTERY WOMAN I'VE DUBBED "FURIOUS."
OHMY GODOHMY GODOHMY GOD...

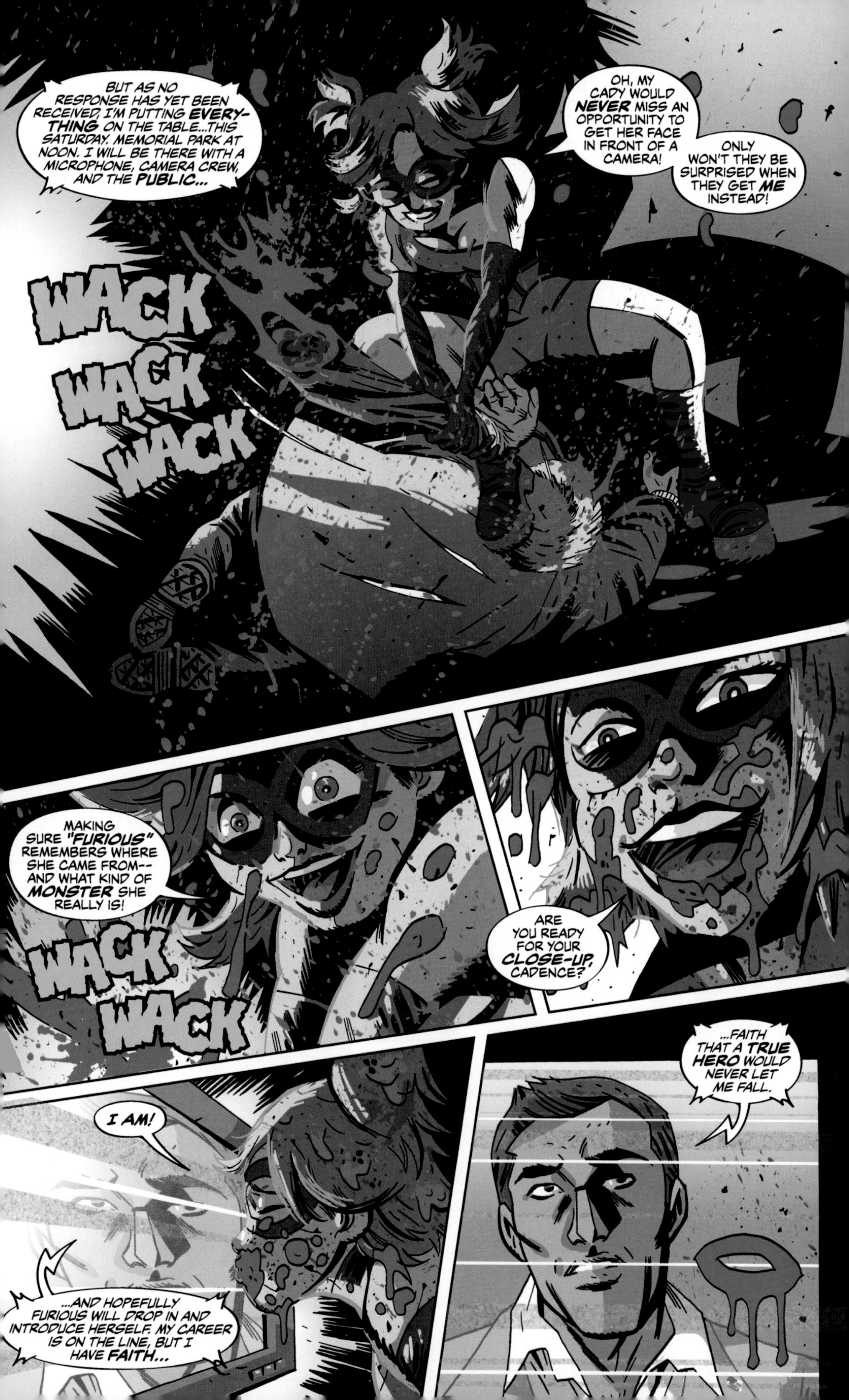
BUT AS NO RESPONSE HAS YET BEEN RECEIVED, I'M PUTTING EVERY-THING ON THE TABLE...THIS SATURDAY. MEMORIAL PARK AT NOON. I WILL BE THERE WITH A MICROPHONE, CAMERA CREW, AND THE PUBLIC...
OH, MY CADY WOULD NEVER MISS AN OPPORTUNITY TO GET HER FACE IN FRONT OF A CAMERA!
ONLY WON'T THEY BE SURPRISED WHEN THEY GET ME INSTEAD!
WACK
WACK
WACK
MAKING SURE "FURIOUS" REMEMBERS WHERE SHE CAME FROM--AND WHAT KIND OF MONSTER SHE REALLY IS!
WACK
WACK
ARE YOU READY FOR YOUR CLOSE-UP, CADENCE?
I AM!
...AND HOPEFULLY FURIOUS WILL DROP IN AND INTRODUCE HERSELF. MY CAREER IS ON THE LINE, BUT I HAVE FAITH...
...FAITH THAT A TRUE HERO WOULD NEVER LET ME FALL.

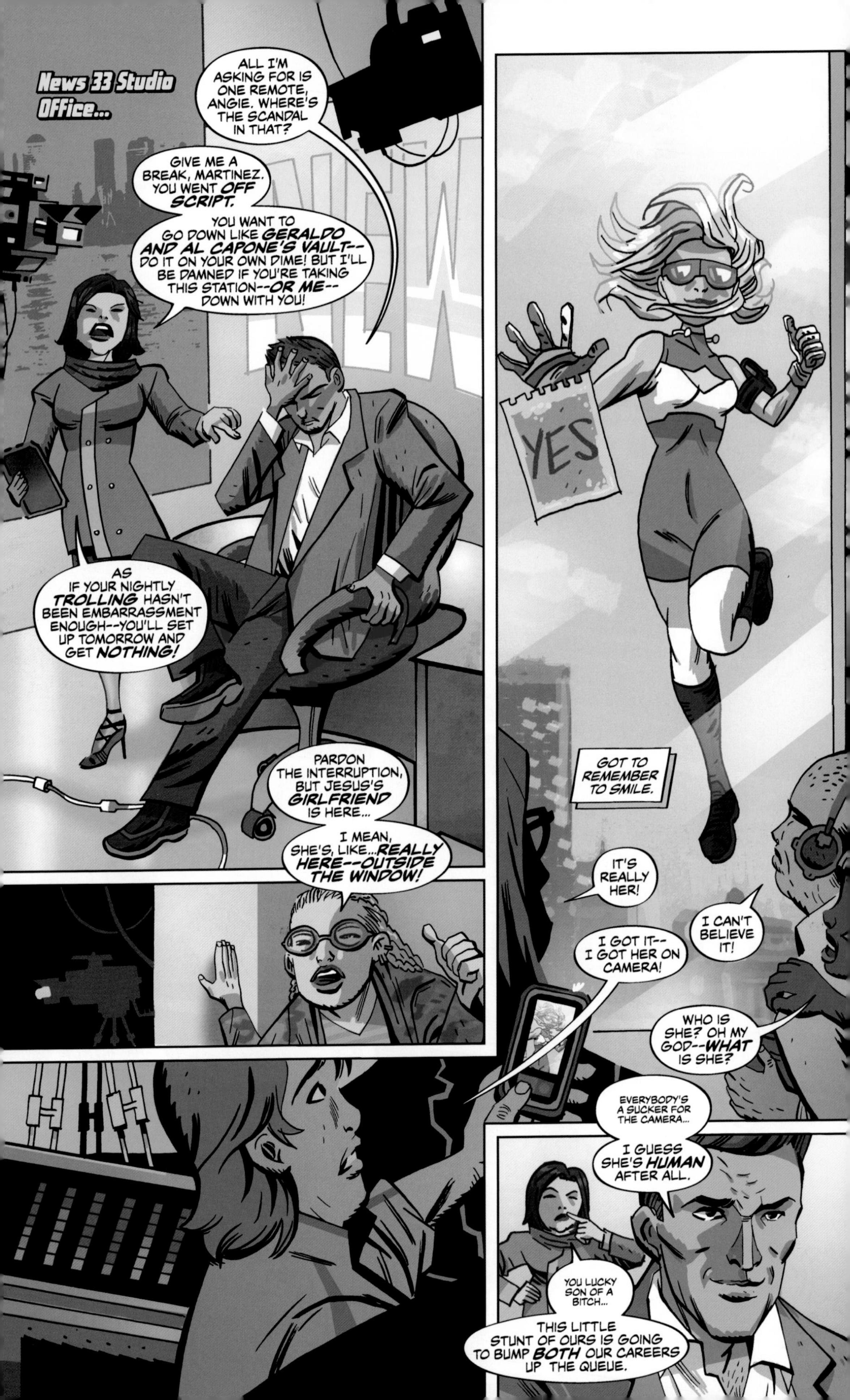
News 33 Studio Office...
ALL I'M ASKING FOR IS ONE REMOTE, ANGIE. WHERE'S THE SCANDAL IN THAT?
GIVE ME A BREAK, MARTINEZ. YOU WENT OFF SCRIPT.
YOU WANT TO GO DOWN LIKE GERALDO AND AL CAPONE'S VAULT-- DO IT ON YOUR OWN DIME! BUT I'LL BE DAMNED IF YOU'RE TAKING THIS STATION--OR ME-- DOWN WITH YOU!
AS IF YOUR NIGHTLY TROLLING HASN'T BEEN EMBARRASSMENT ENOUGH--YOU'LL SET UP TOMORROW AND GET NOTHING!
PARDON THE INTERRUPTION, BUT JESUS'S GIRLFRIEND IS HERE...
I MEAN, SHE'S, LIKE...REALLY HERE--OUTSIDE THE WINDOW!
YES
GOT TO REMEMBER TO SMILE.
IT'S REALLY HER!
I CAN'T BELIEVE IT!
I GOT IT-- I GOT HER ON CAMERA!
WHO IS SHE? OH MY GOD--WHAT IS SHE?
EVERYBODY'S A SUCKER FOR THE CAMERA...
I GUESS SHE'S HUMAN AFTER ALL.
YOU LUCKY SON OF A BITCH...
THIS LITTLE STUNT OF OURS IS GOING TO BUMP BOTH OUR CAREERS UP THE QUEUE.

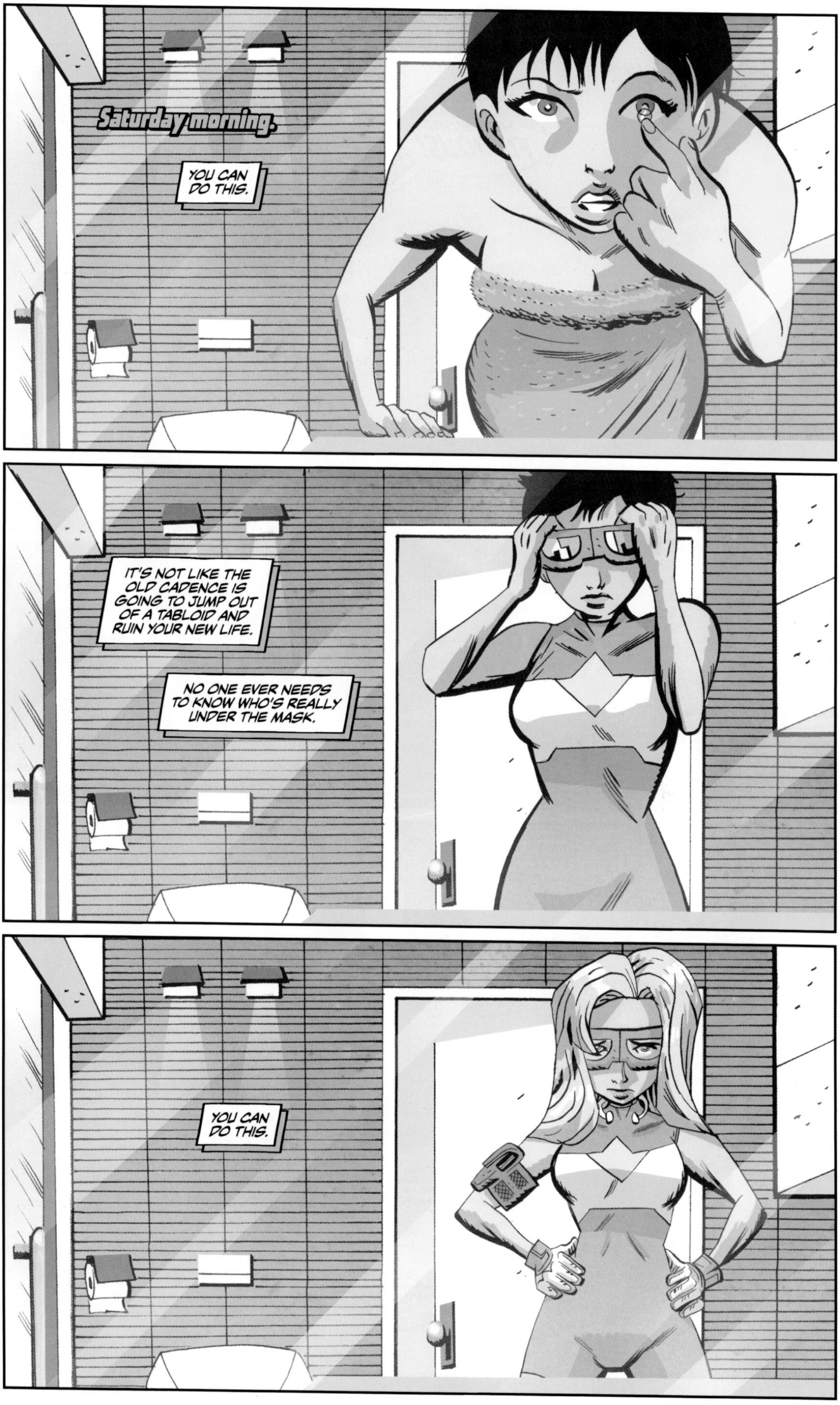
Saturday morning.
YOU CAN DO THIS.
IT'S NOT LIKE THE OLD CADENCE IS GOING TO JUMP OUT OF A TABLOID AND RUIN YOUR NEW LIFE.
NO ONE EVER NEEDS TO KNOW WHO'S REALLY UNDER THE MASK.
YOU CAN DO THIS.

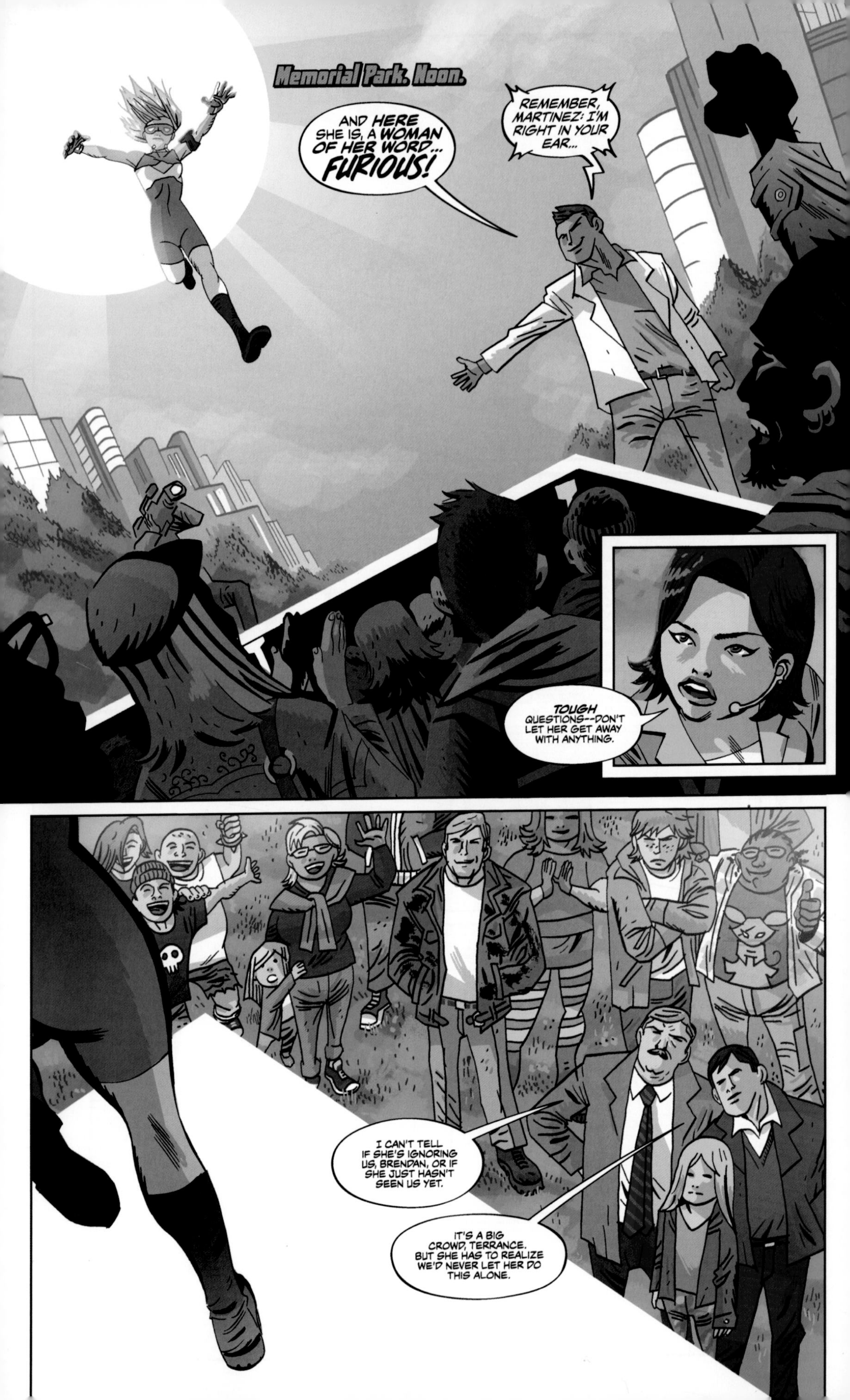
Memorial Park. Noon.
AND HERE SHE IS, A WOMAN OF HER WORD... FURIOUS!
REMEMBER, MARTINEZ: I'M RIGHT IN YOUR EAR...
TOUGH QUESTIONS--DON'T LET HER GET AWAY WITH ANYTHING.
I CAN'T TELL IF SHE'S IGNORING US, BRENDAN, OR IF SHE JUST HASN'T SEEN US YET.
IT'S A BIG CROWD, TERRANCE. BUT SHE HAS TO REALIZE WE'D NEVER LET HER DO THIS ALONE.

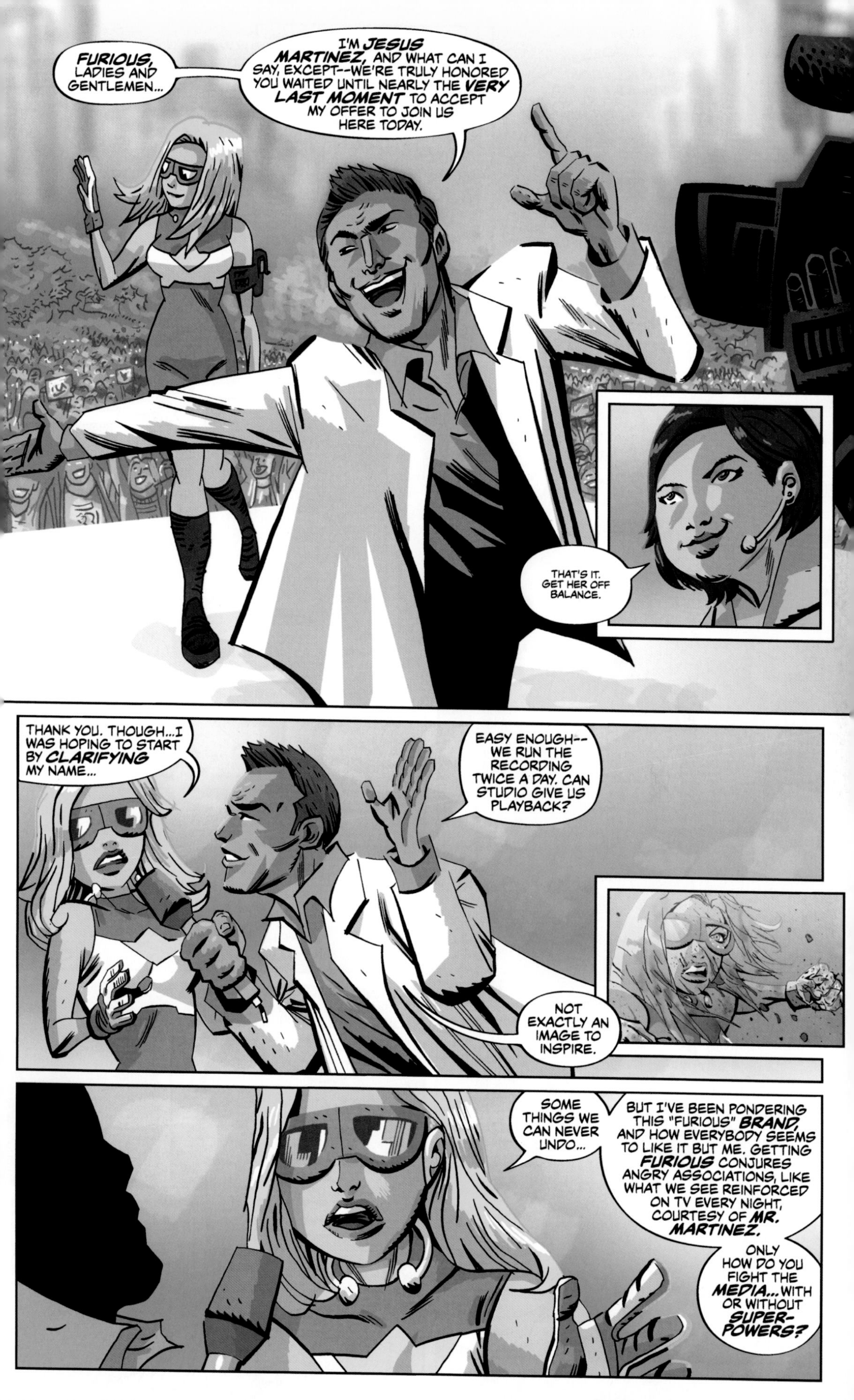
FURIOUS, LADIES AND GENTLEMEN...
I'M JESUS MARTINEZ, AND WHAT CAN I SAY, EXCEPT--WE'RE TRULY HONORED YOU WAITED UNTIL NEARLY THE VERY LAST MOMENT TO ACCEPT MY OFFER TO JOIN US HERE TODAY.
THAT'S IT. GET HER OFF BALANCE.
THANK YOU. THOUGH...I WAS HOPING TO START BY CLARIFYING MY NAME...
EASY ENOUGH--WE RUN THE RECORDING TWICE A DAY. CAN STUDIO GIVE US PLAYBACK?
NOT EXACTLY AN IMAGE TO INSPIRE.
SOME THINGS WE CAN NEVER UNDO...
BUT I'VE BEEN PONDERING THIS "FURIOUS" BRAND, AND HOW EVERYBODY SEEMS TO LIKE IT BUT ME. GETTING FURIOUS CONJURES ANGRY ASSOCIATIONS, LIKE WHAT WE SEE REINFORCED ON TV EVERY NIGHT, COURTESY OF MR. MARTINEZ.
ONLY HOW DO YOU FIGHT THE MEDIA... WITH OR WITHOUT SUPER-POWERS?

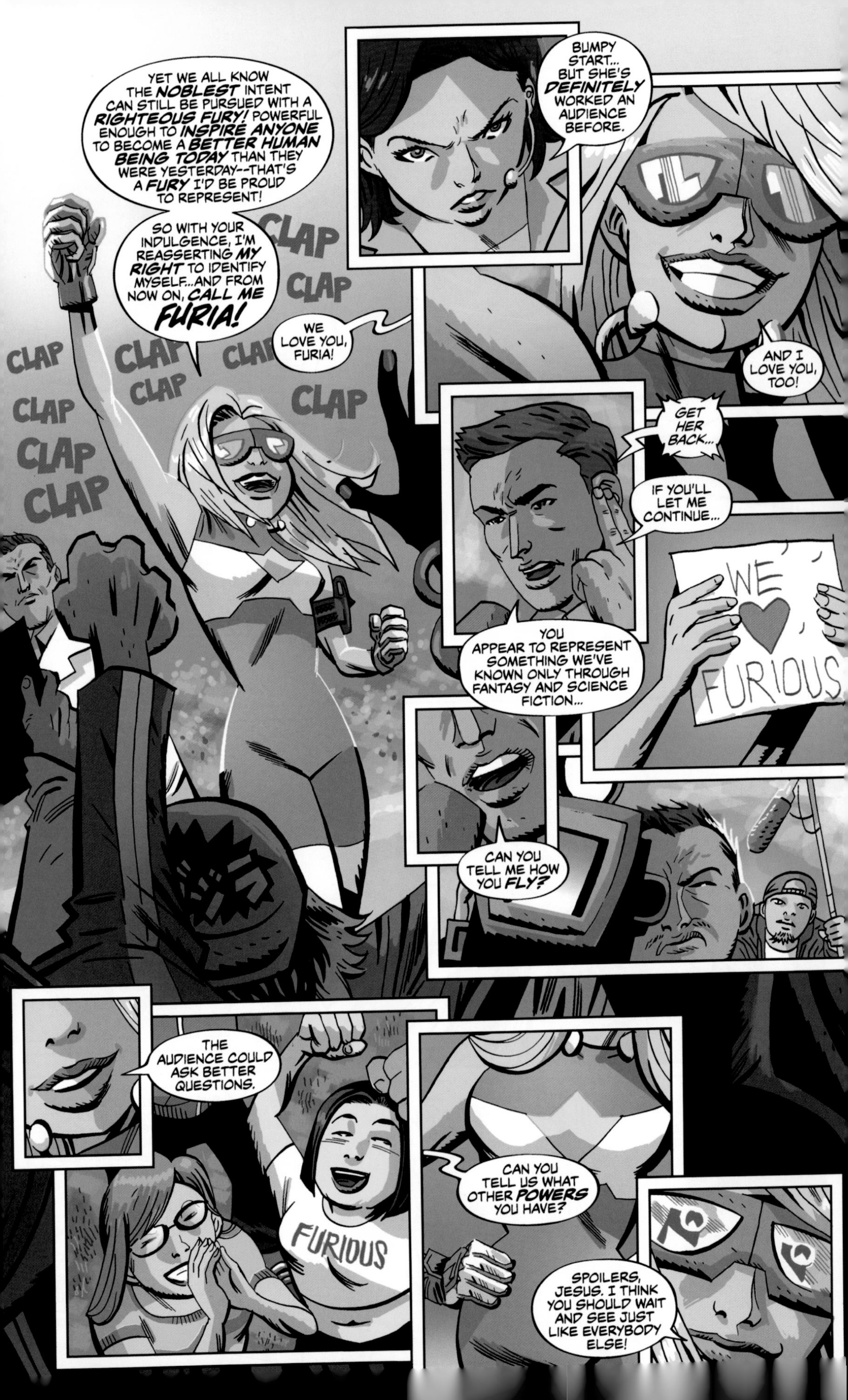
YET WE ALL KNOW THE NOBLEST INTENT CAN STILL BE PURSUED WITH A RIGHTEOUS FURY! POWERFUL ENOUGH TO INSPIRE ANYONE TO BECOME A BETTER HUMAN BEING TODAY THAN THEY WERE YESTERDAY--THAT'S A FURY I'D BE PROUD TO REPRESENT!
SO WITH YOUR INDULGENCE, I'M REASSERTING MY RIGHT TO IDENTIFY MYSELF...AND FROM NOW ON, CALL ME FURIA!
CLAP CLAP CLAP CLAP CLAP CLAP CLAP CLAP CLAP CLAP
WE LOVE YOU, FURIA!
BUMPY START... BUT SHE'S DEFINITELY WORKED AN AUDIENCE BEFORE.
AND I LOVE YOU, TOO!
GET HER BACK...
IF YOU'LL LET ME CONTINUE...
WE ♥ FURIOUS
YOU APPEAR TO REPRESENT SOMETHING WE'VE KNOWN ONLY THROUGH FANTASY AND SCIENCE FICTION...
CAN YOU TELL ME HOW YOU FLY?
THE AUDIENCE COULD ASK BETTER QUESTIONS.
FURIOUS
CAN YOU TELL US WHAT OTHER POWERS YOU HAVE?
SPOILERS, JESUS. I THINK YOU SHOULD WAIT AND SEE JUST LIKE EVERYBODY ELSE!

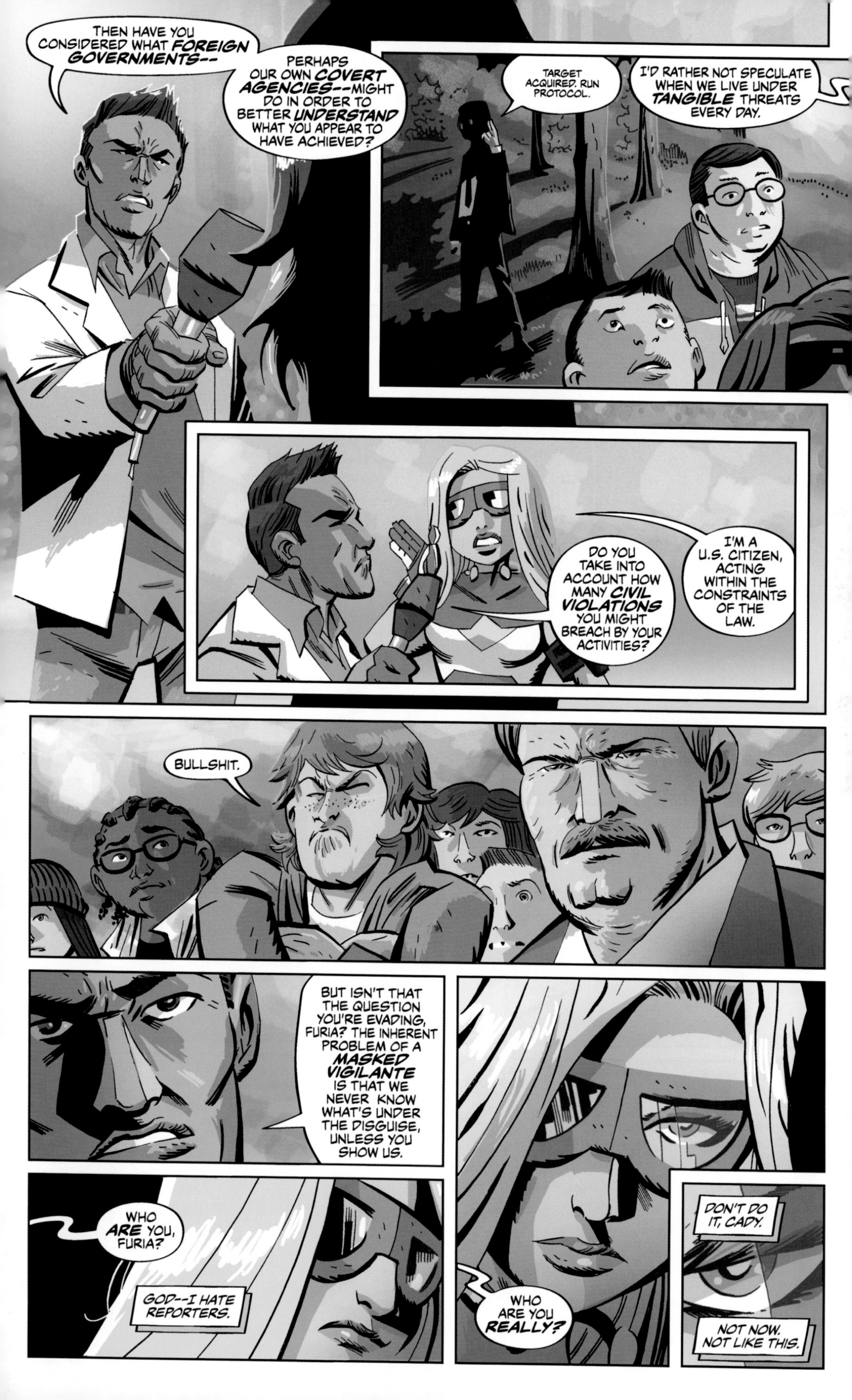
THEN HAVE YOU CONSIDERED WHAT FOREIGN GOVERNMENTS--
PERHAPS OUR OWN COVERT AGENCIES--MIGHT DO IN ORDER TO BETTER UNDERSTAND WHAT YOU APPEAR TO HAVE ACHIEVED?
TARGET ACQUIRED. RUN PROTOCOL.
I'D RATHER NOT SPECULATE WHEN WE LIVE UNDER TANGIBLE THREATS EVERY DAY.
DO YOU TAKE INTO ACCOUNT HOW MANY CIVIL VIOLATIONS YOU MIGHT BREACH BY YOUR ACTIVITIES?
I'M A U.S. CITIZEN, ACTING WITHIN THE CONSTRAINTS OF THE LAW.
BULLSHIT.
BUT ISN'T THAT THE QUESTION YOU'RE EVADING, FURIA? THE INHERENT PROBLEM OF A MASKED VIGILANTE IS THAT WE NEVER KNOW WHAT'S UNDER THE DISGUISE, UNLESS YOU SHOW US.
WHO ARE YOU, FURIA?
GOD--I HATE REPORTERS.
WHO ARE YOU REALLY?
DON'T DO IT, CADY.
NOT NOW. NOT LIKE THIS.

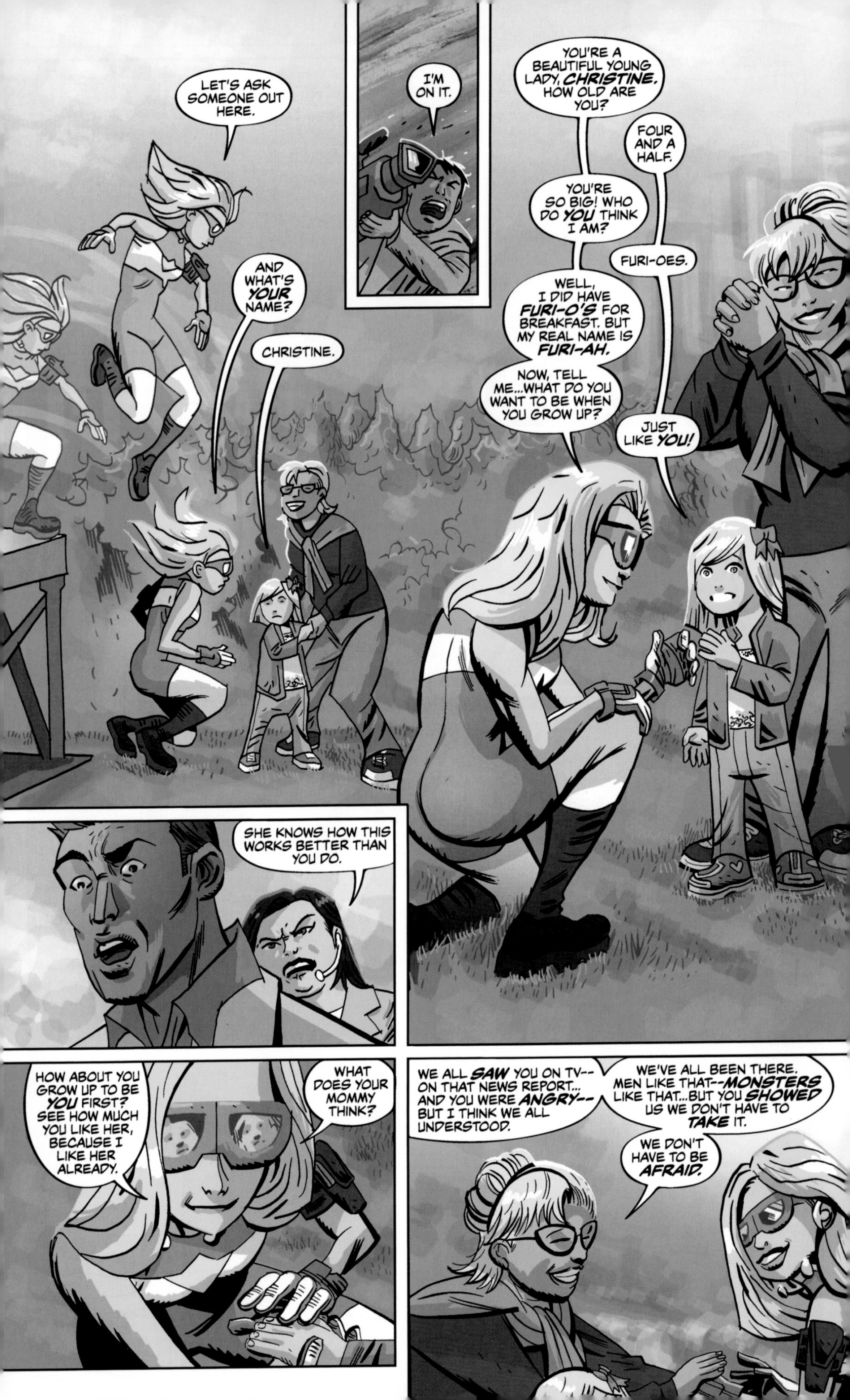
LET'S ASK SOMEONE OUT HERE.
I'M ON IT.
AND WHAT'S YOUR NAME?
CHRISTINE.
YOU'RE A BEAUTIFUL YOUNG LADY, CHRISTINE. HOW OLD ARE YOU?
FOUR AND A HALF.
YOU'RE SO BIG! WHO DO YOU THINK I AM?
FURI-OES.
WELL, I DID HAVE FURI-O'S FOR BREAKFAST. BUT MY REAL NAME IS FURI-AH.
NOW, TELL ME...WHAT DO YOU WANT TO BE WHEN YOU GROW UP?
JUST LIKE YOU!
SHE KNOWS HOW THIS WORKS BETTER THAN YOU DO.
HOW ABOUT YOU GROW UP TO BE YOU FIRST? SEE HOW MUCH YOU LIKE HER, BECAUSE I LIKE HER ALREADY.
WHAT DOES YOUR MOMMY THINK?
WE ALL SAW YOU ON TV-- ON THAT NEWS REPORT... AND YOU WERE ANGRY-- BUT I THINK WE ALL UNDERSTOOD.
WE'VE ALL BEEN THERE. MEN LIKE THAT--MONSTERS LIKE THAT...BUT YOU SHOWED US WE DON'T HAVE TO TAKE IT.
WE DON'T HAVE TO BE AFRAID.

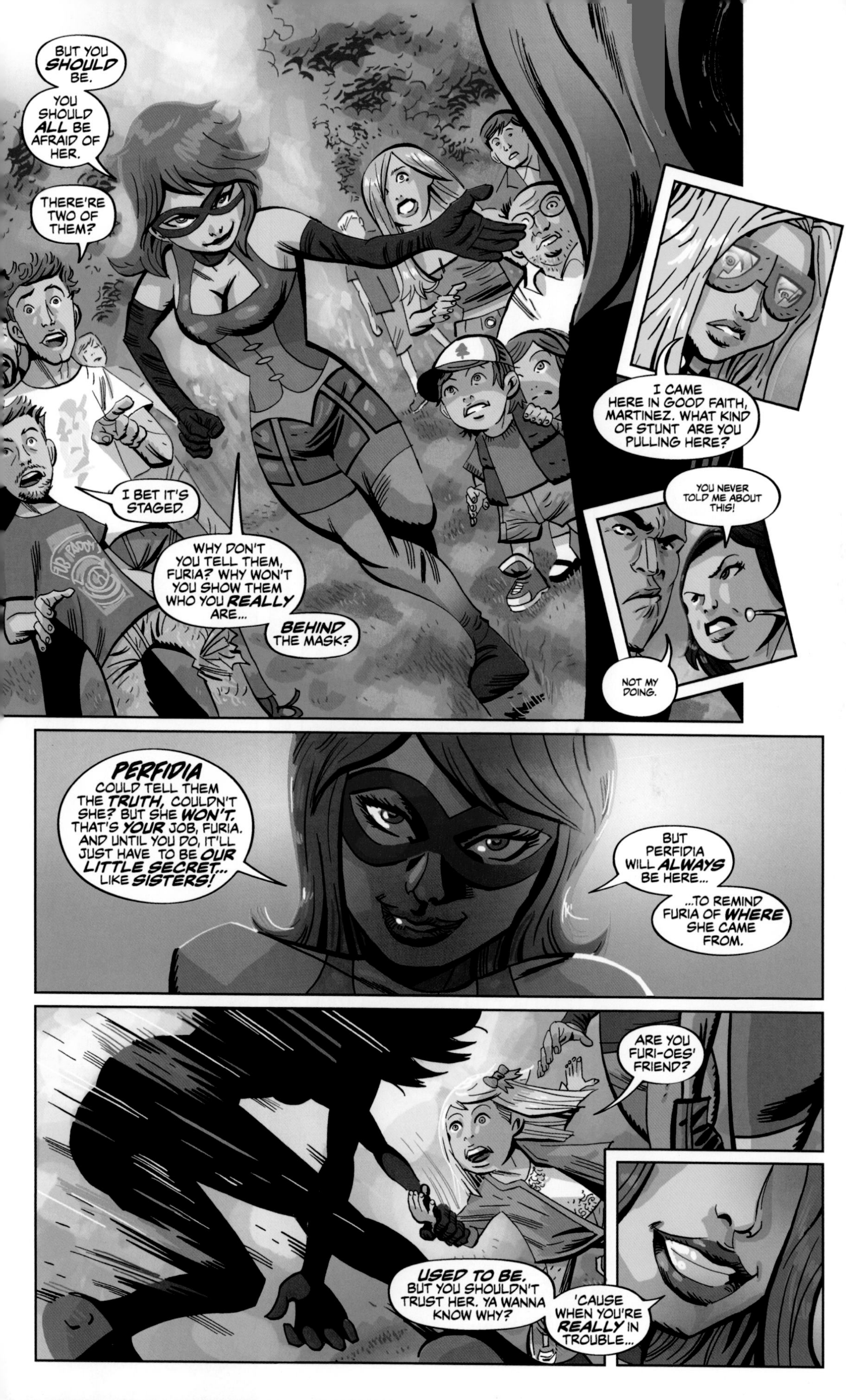
BUT YOU SHOULD BE.
YOU SHOULD ALL BE AFRAID OF HER.
THERE'RE TWO OF THEM?
I BET IT'S STAGED.
WHY DON'T YOU TELL THEM, FURIA? WHY WON'T YOU SHOW THEM WHO YOU REALLY ARE... BEHIND THE MASK?
I CAME HERE IN GOOD FAITH, MARTINEZ. WHAT KIND OF STUNT ARE YOU PULLING HERE?
YOU NEVER TOLD ME ABOUT THIS!
NOT MY DOING.
PERFIDIA COULD TELL THEM THE TRUTH, COULDN'T SHE? BUT SHE WON'T. THAT'S YOUR JOB, FURIA. AND UNTIL YOU DO, IT'LL JUST HAVE TO BE OUR LITTLE SECRET... LIKE SISTERS!
BUT PERFIDIA WILL ALWAYS BE HERE...
...TO REMIND FURIA OF WHERE SHE CAME FROM.
ARE YOU FURI-OES' FRIEND?
USED TO BE. BUT YOU SHOULDN'T TRUST HER. YA WANNA KNOW WHY?
'CAUSE WHEN YOU'RE REALLY IN TROUBLE...

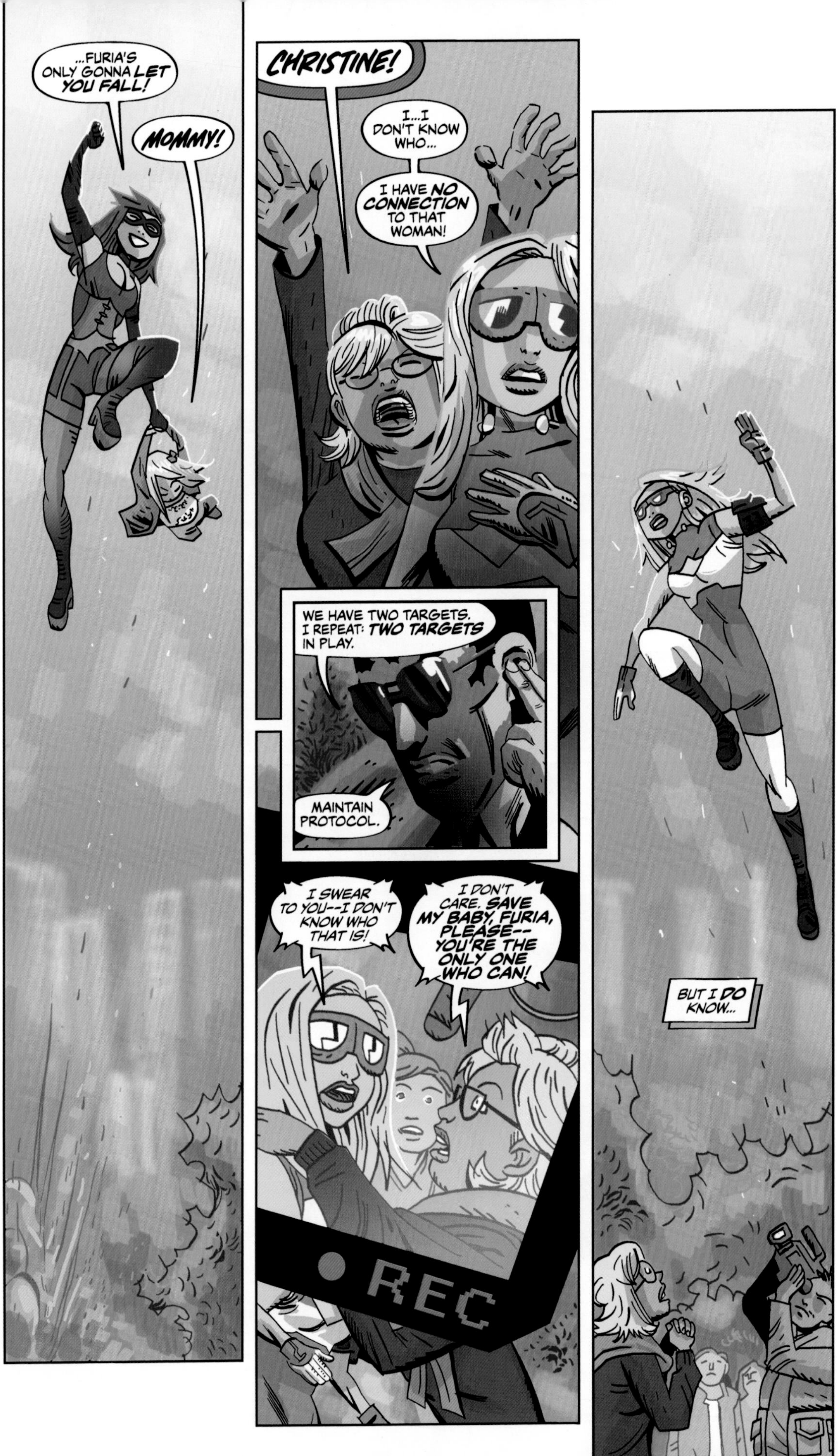
...FURIA'S ONLY GONNA LET YOU FALL!
MOMMY!
CHRISTINE!
I...I DON'T KNOW WHO...
I HAVE NO CONNECTION TO THAT WOMAN!
WE HAVE TWO TARGETS. I REPEAT: TWO TARGETS IN PLAY.
MAINTAIN PROTOCOL.
I SWEAR TO YOU--I DON'T KNOW WHO THAT IS!
I DON'T CARE. SAVE MY BABY, FURIA, PLEASE--YOU'RE THE ONLY ONE WHO CAN!
REC
BUT I DO KNOW...

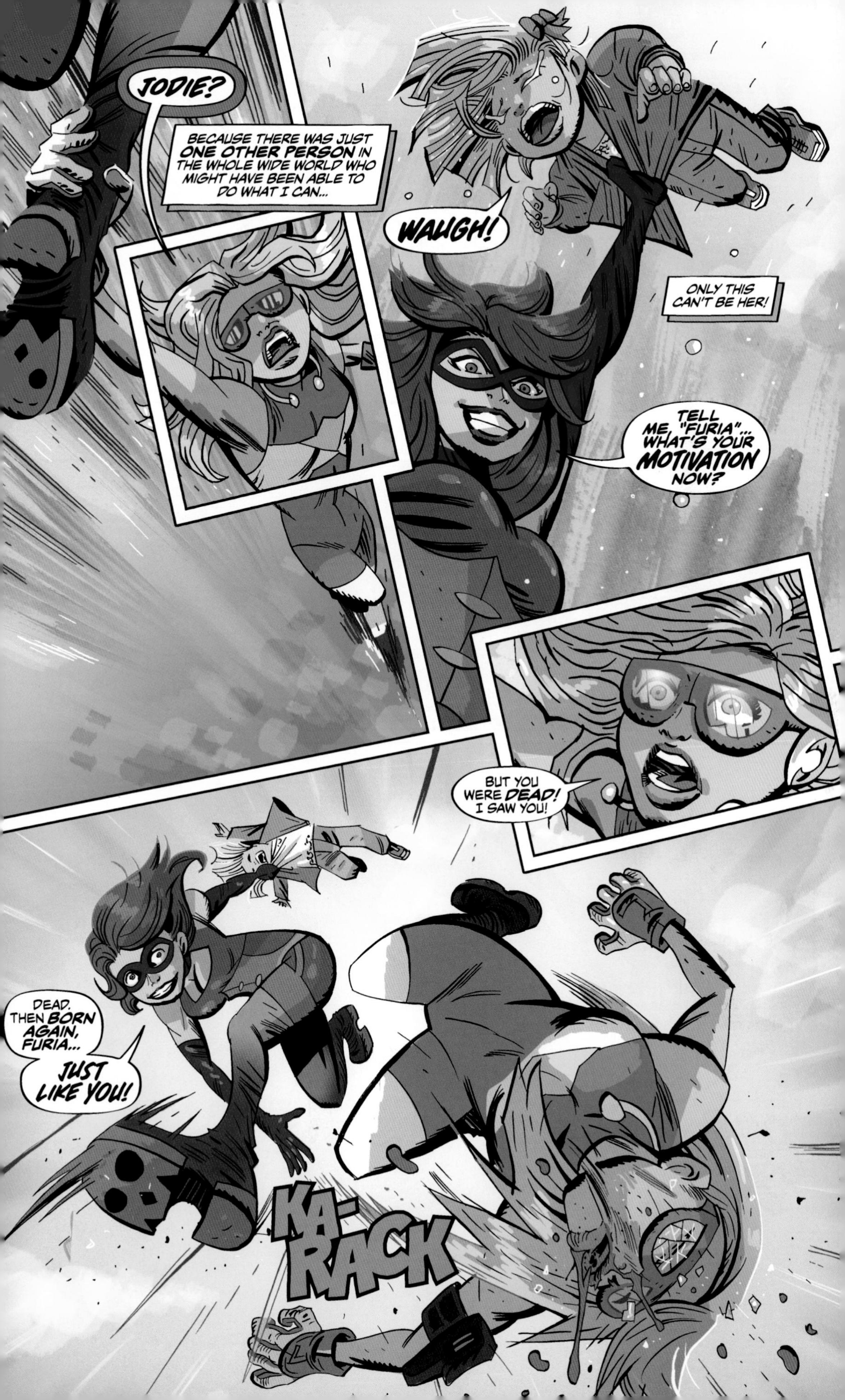

JODIE?
BECAUSE THERE WAS JUST ONE OTHER PERSON IN THE WHOLE WIDE WORLD WHO MIGHT HAVE BEEN ABLE TO DO WHAT I CAN...
WAUGH!
ONLY THIS CAN'T BE HER!
TELL ME, "FURIA"... WHAT'S YOUR MOTIVATION NOW?
BUT YOU WERE DEAD! I SAW YOU!
DEAD. THEN BORN AGAIN, FURIA...
JUST LIKE YOU!
KA-RACK

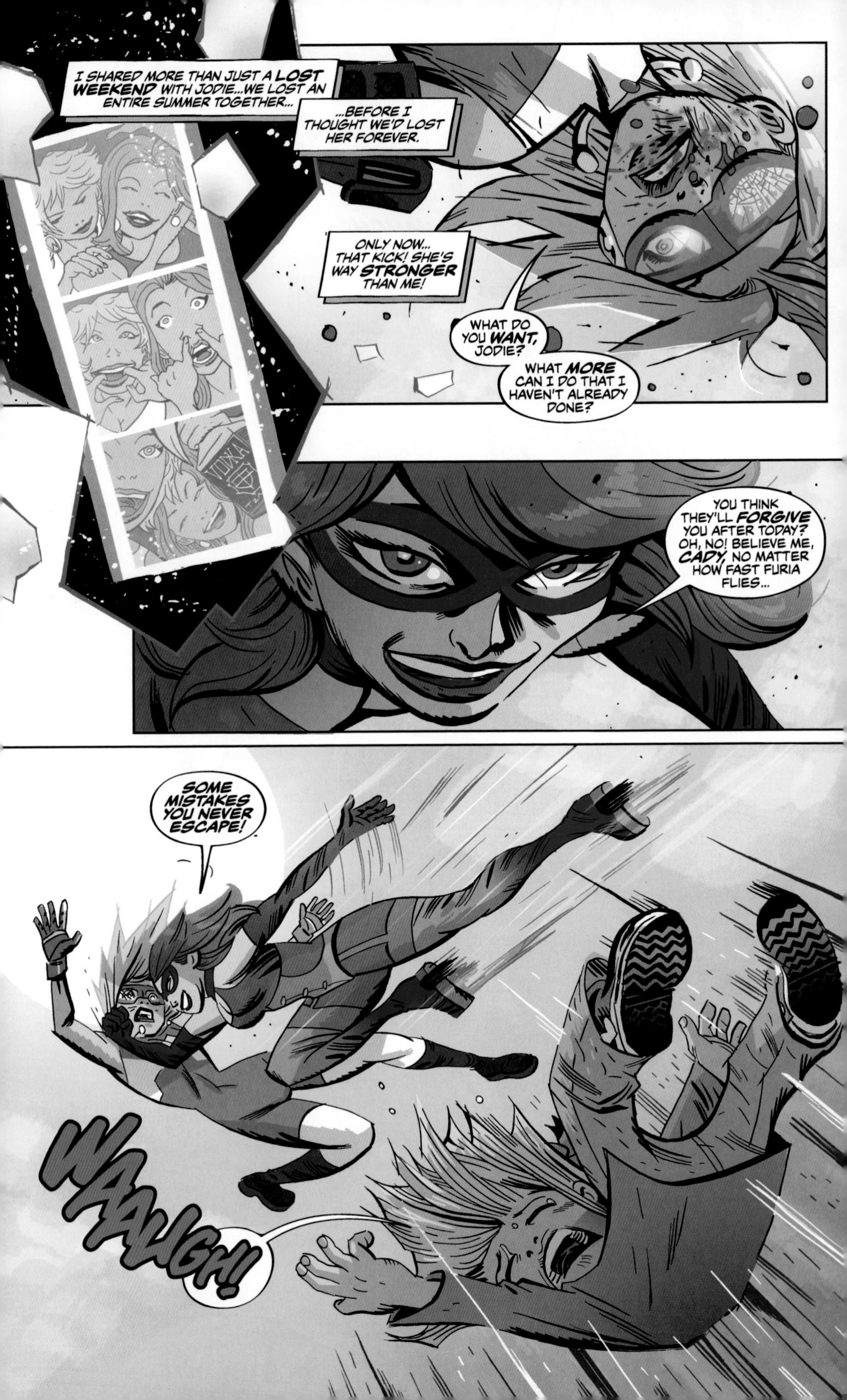
I SHARED MORE THAN JUST A LOST WEEKEND WITH JODIE...WE LOST AN ENTIRE SUMMER TOGETHER...
...BEFORE I THOUGHT WE'D LOST HER FOREVER.
ONLY NOW... THAT KICK! SHE'S WAY STRONGER THAN ME!
WHAT DO YOU WANT, JODIE?
WHAT MORE CAN I DO THAT I HAVEN'T ALREADY DONE?
YOU THINK THEY'LL FORGIVE YOU AFTER TODAY? OH, NO! BELIEVE ME, CADY, NO MATTER HOW FAST FURIA FLIES...
SOME MISTAKES YOU NEVER ESCAPE!
WAUGH!

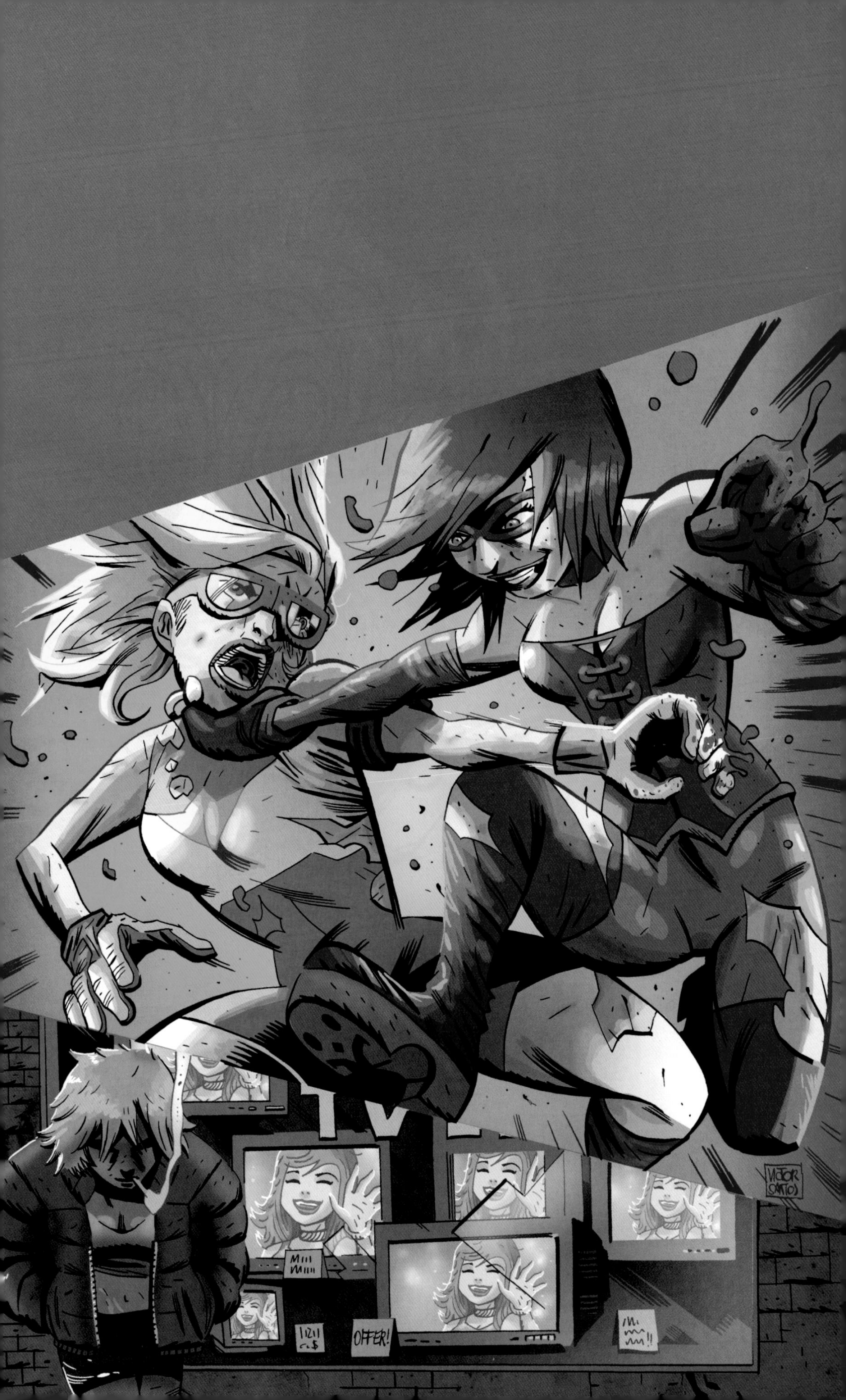
VICTOR SANTOS
OFFER!

CHAPTER FIVE: CATCH A FALLING STAR

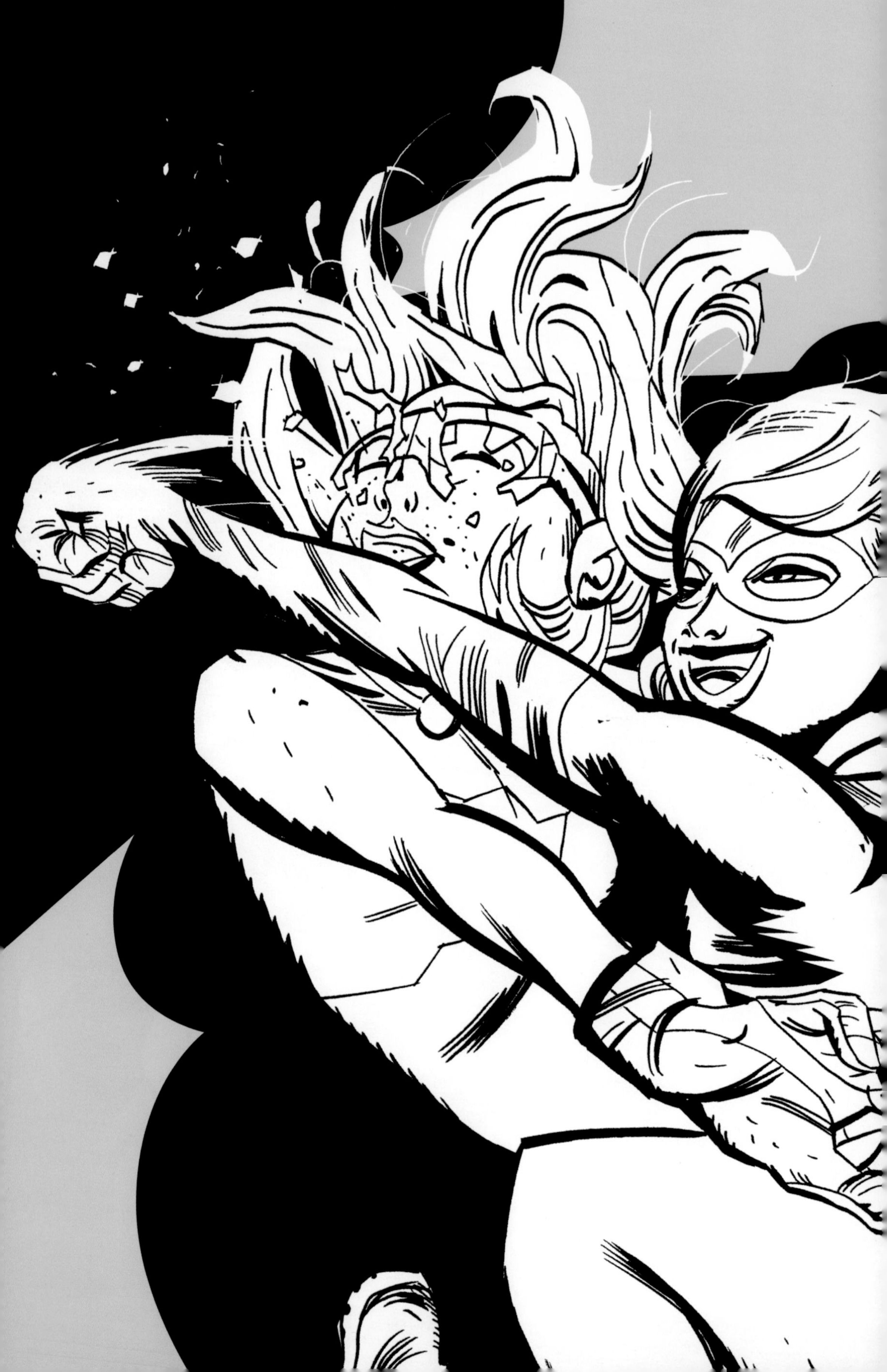

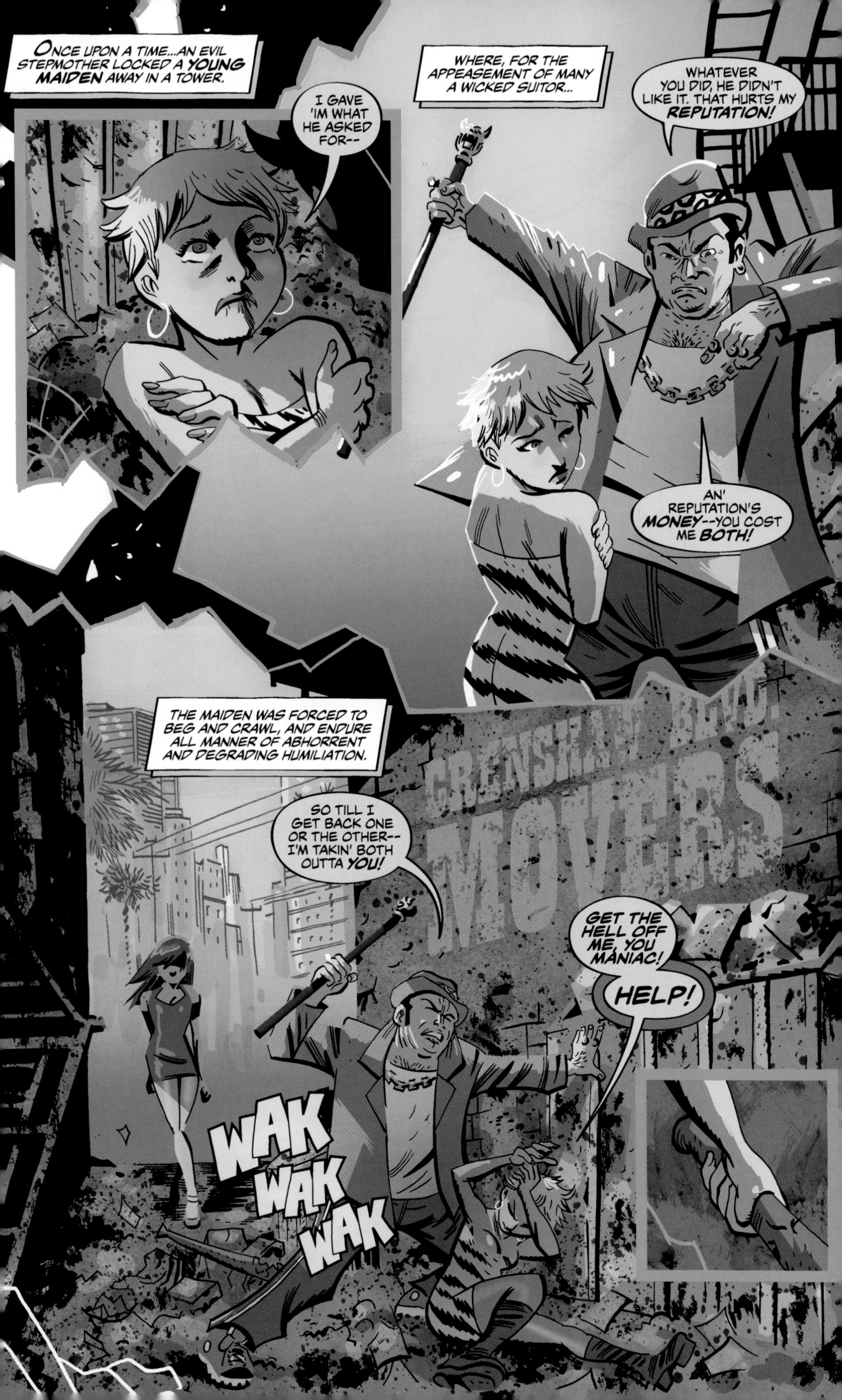
ONCE UPON A TIME...AN EVIL STEPMOTHER LOCKED A YOUNG MAIDEN AWAY IN A TOWER.
I GAVE 'IM WHAT HE ASKED FOR--
WHERE, FOR THE APPEASEMENT OF MANY A WICKED SUITOR...
WHATEVER YOU DID, HE DIDN'T LIKE IT. THAT HURTS MY REPUTATION!
AN' REPUTATION'S MONEY--YOU COST ME BOTH!
THE MAIDEN WAS FORCED TO BEG AND CRAWL, AND ENDURE ALL MANNER OF ABHORRENT AND DEGRADING HUMILIATION.
MOVERS
SO TILL I GET BACK ONE OR THE OTHER-- I'M TAKIN' BOTH OUTTA YOU!
GET THE HELL OFF ME, YOU MANIAC!
HELP!
WAK
WAK
WAK

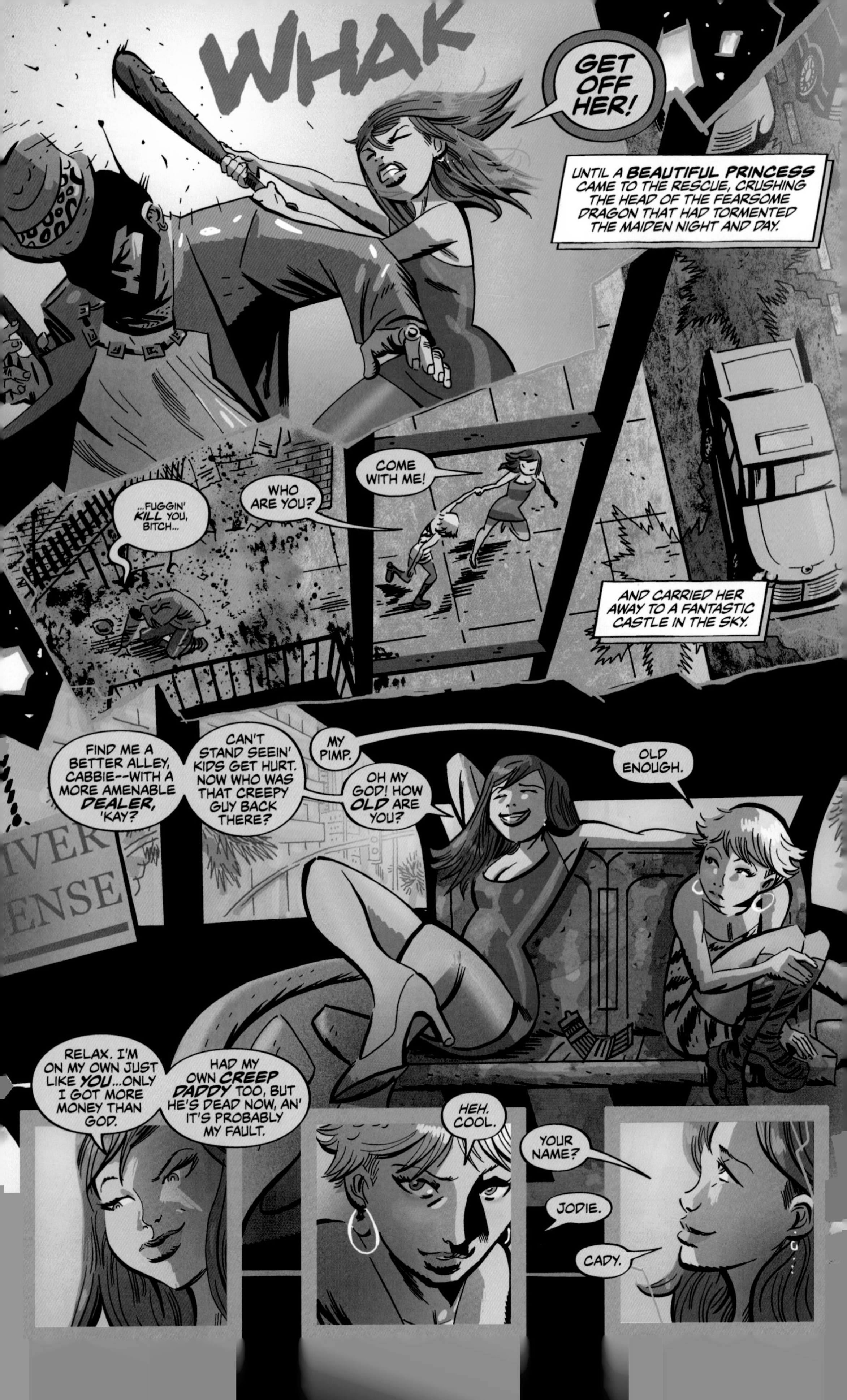

WHAK
GET OFF HER!
UNTIL A BEAUTIFUL PRINCESS CAME TO THE RESCUE, CRUSHING THE HEAD OF THE FEARSOME DRAGON THAT HAD TORMENTED THE MAIDEN NIGHT AND DAY.
...FUGGIN' KILL YOU, BITCH...
WHO ARE YOU?
COME WITH ME!
AND CARRIED HER AWAY TO A FANTASTIC CASTLE IN THE SKY.
FIND ME A BETTER ALLEY, CABBIE--WITH A MORE AMENABLE DEALER, 'KAY?
CAN'T STAND SEEIN' KIDS GET HURT. NOW WHO WAS THAT CREEPY GUY BACK THERE?
MY PIMP.
OH MY GOD! HOW OLD ARE YOU?
OLD ENOUGH.
IVER
ENSE
RELAX. I'M ON MY OWN JUST LIKE YOU...ONLY I GOT MORE MONEY THAN GOD.
HAD MY OWN CREEP DADDY TOO, BUT HE'S DEAD NOW, AN' IT'S PROBABLY MY FAULT.
HEH. COOL.
YOUR NAME?
JODIE.
CADY.

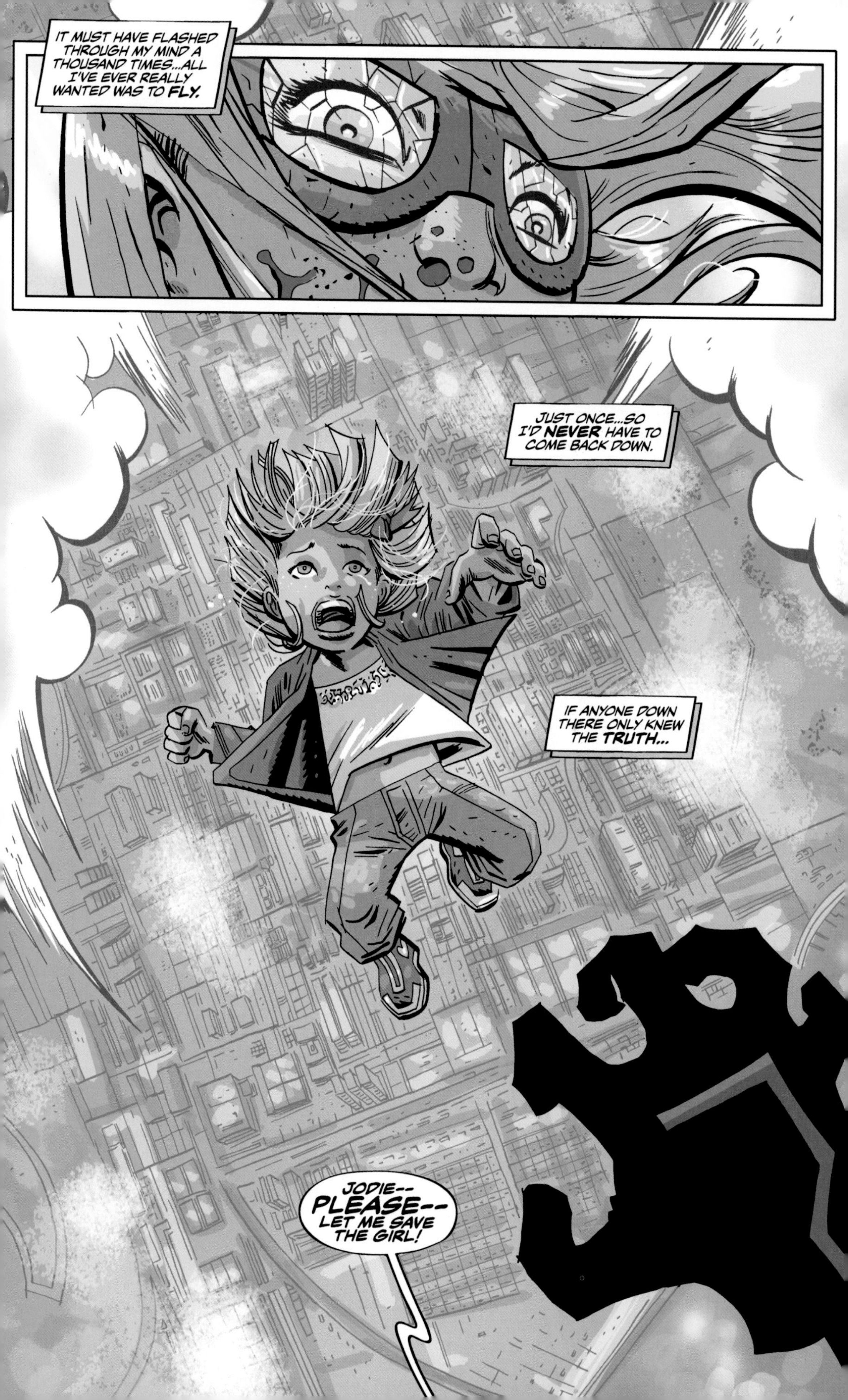
IT MUST HAVE FLASHED THROUGH MY MIND A THOUSAND TIMES...ALL I'VE EVER REALLY WANTED WAS TO **FLY.**
JUST ONCE...SO I'D **NEVER** HAVE TO COME BACK DOWN.
IF ANYONE DOWN THERE ONLY KNEW THE **TRUTH...**
JODIE-- **PLEASE--** LET ME SAVE THE GIRL!

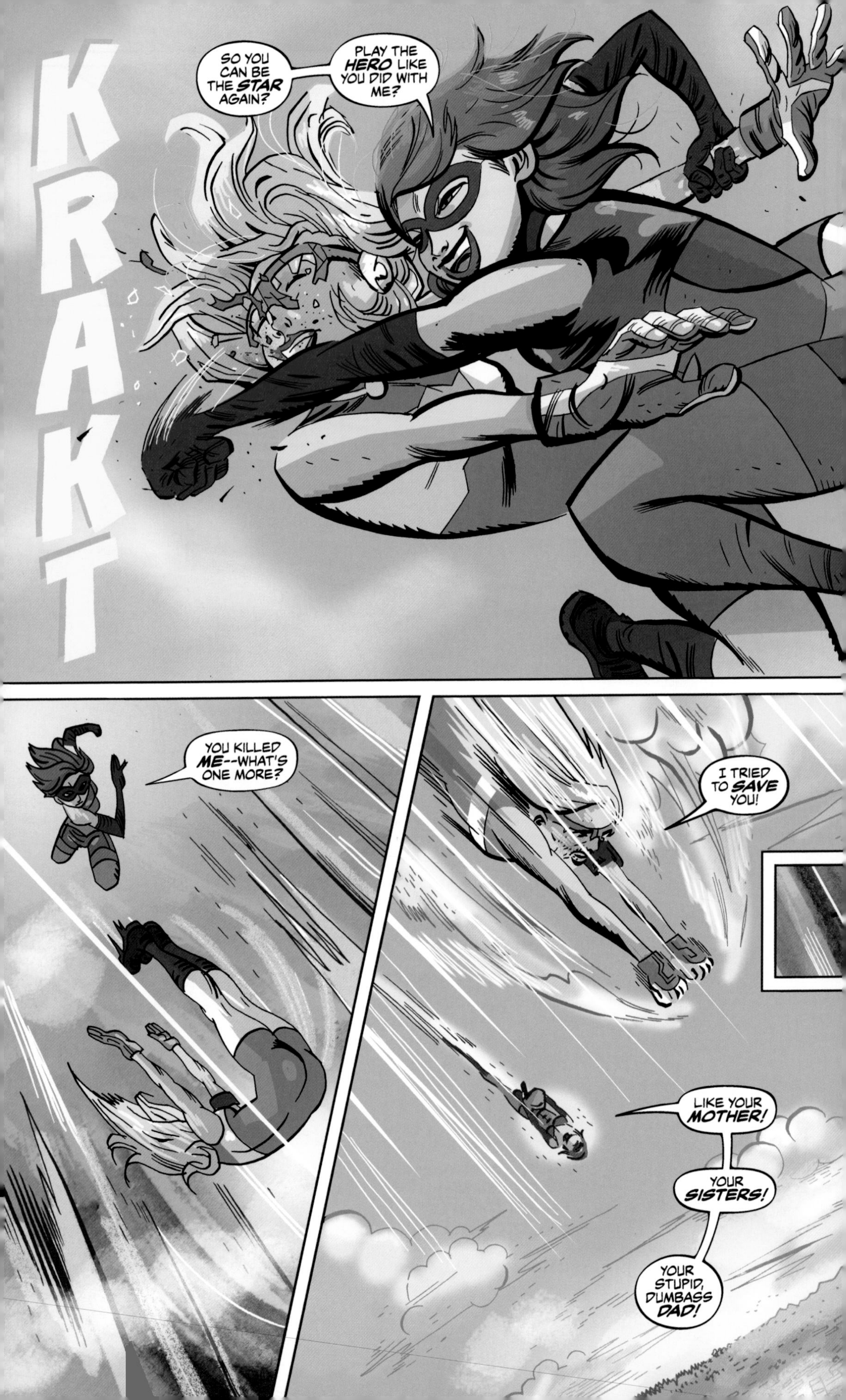
KRAKT
SO YOU CAN BE THE STAR AGAIN?
PLAY THE HERO LIKE YOU DID WITH ME?
YOU KILLED ME--WHAT'S ONE MORE?
I TRIED TO SAVE YOU!
LIKE YOUR MOTHER!
YOUR SISTERS!
YOUR STUPID, DUMBASS DAD!

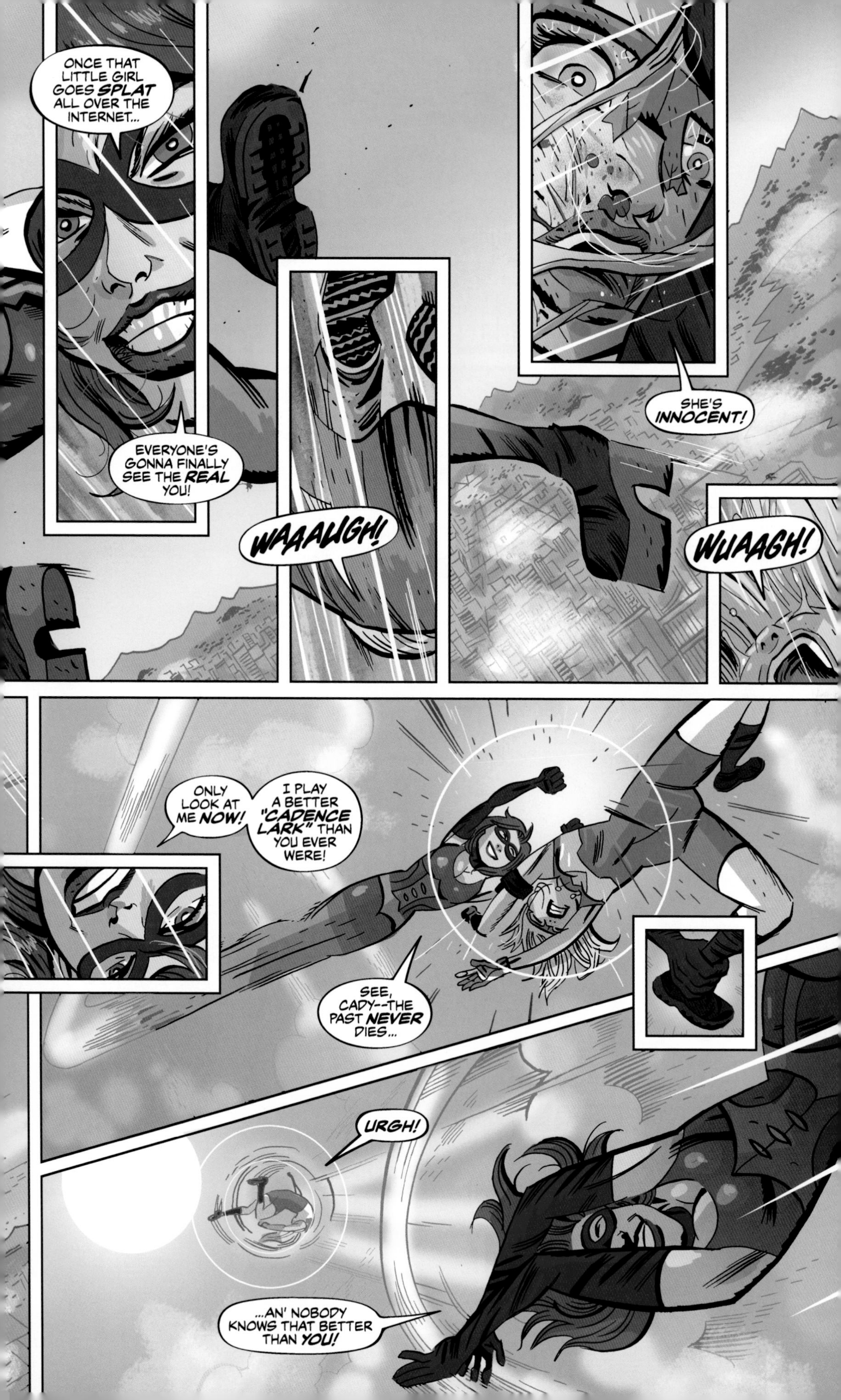
ONCE THAT LITTLE GIRL GOES SPLAT ALL OVER THE INTERNET...
EVERYONE'S GONNA FINALLY SEE THE REAL YOU!
WAAAUGH!
SHE'S INNOCENT!
WUAAGH!
ONLY LOOK AT ME NOW!
I PLAY A BETTER "CADENCE LARK" THAN YOU EVER WERE!
SEE, CADY--THE PAST NEVER DIES...
URGH!
...AN' NOBODY KNOWS THAT BETTER THAN YOU!

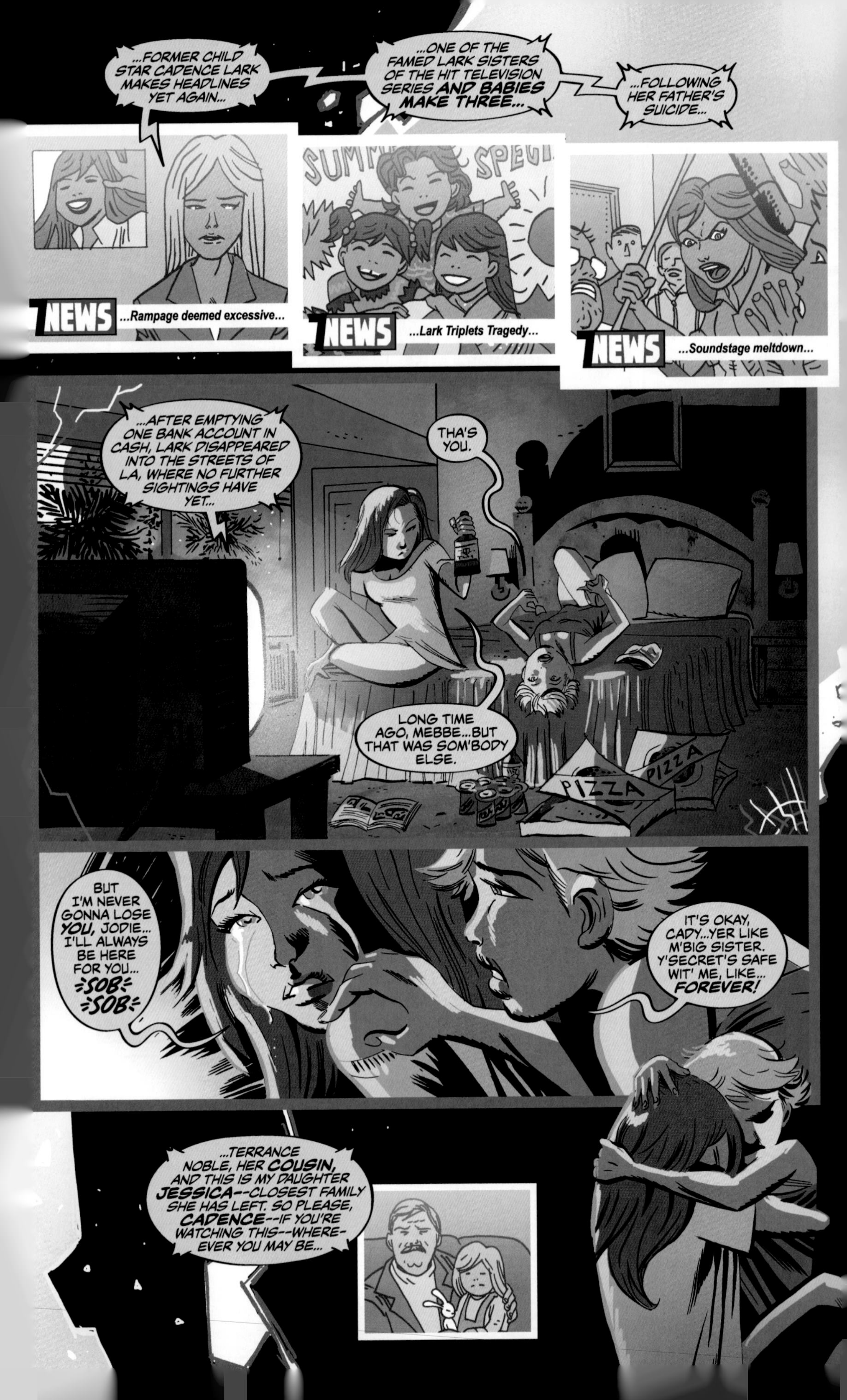
...FORMER CHILD STAR CADENCE LARK MAKES HEADLINES YET AGAIN...
...ONE OF THE FAMED LARK SISTERS OF THE HIT TELEVISION SERIES AND BABIES MAKE THREE...
...FOLLOWING HER FATHER'S SUICIDE...
NEWS ...Rampage deemed excessive...
SUMM... SPECI...
NEWS ...Lark Triplets Tragedy...
NEWS ...Soundstage meltdown...
...AFTER EMPTYING ONE BANK ACCOUNT IN CASH, LARK DISAPPEARED INTO THE STREETS OF LA, WHERE NO FURTHER SIGHTINGS HAVE YET...
THA'S YOU.
LONG TIME AGO, MEBBE...BUT THAT WAS SOM'BODY ELSE.
PIZZA
PIZZA
BUT I'M NEVER GONNA LOSE YOU, JODIE... I'LL ALWAYS BE HERE FOR YOU... SOB SOB
IT'S OKAY, CADY...YER LIKE M'BIG SISTER. Y'SECRET'S SAFE WIT' ME, LIKE... FOREVER!
...TERRANCE NOBLE, HER COUSIN, AND THIS IS MY DAUGHTER JESSICA--CLOSEST FAMILY SHE HAS LEFT. SO PLEASE, CADENCE--IF YOU'RE WATCHING THIS--WHEREEVER YOU MAY BE...

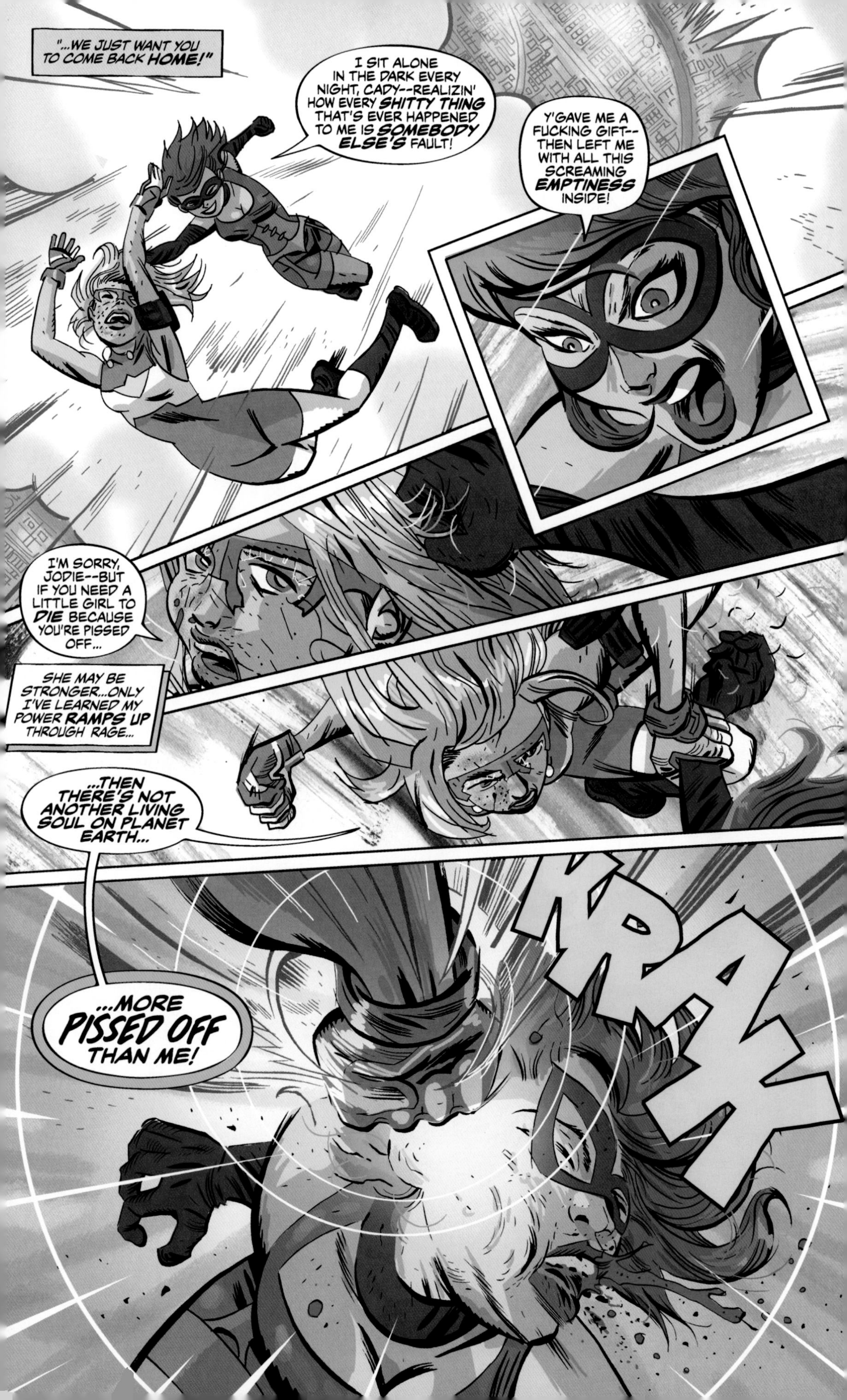
"...WE JUST WANT YOU TO COME BACK HOME!"
I SIT ALONE IN THE DARK EVERY NIGHT, CADY--REALIZIN' HOW EVERY SHITTY THING THAT'S EVER HAPPENED TO ME IS SOMEBODY ELSE'S FAULT!
Y'GAVE ME A FUCKING GIFT-- THEN LEFT ME WITH ALL THIS SCREAMING EMPTINESS INSIDE!
I'M SORRY, JODIE--BUT IF YOU NEED A LITTLE GIRL TO DIE BECAUSE YOU'RE PISSED OFF...
SHE MAY BE STRONGER...ONLY I'VE LEARNED MY POWER RAMPS UP THROUGH RAGE...
...THEN THERE'S NOT ANOTHER LIVING SOUL ON PLANET EARTH...
...MORE PISSED OFF THAN ME!
KRAK

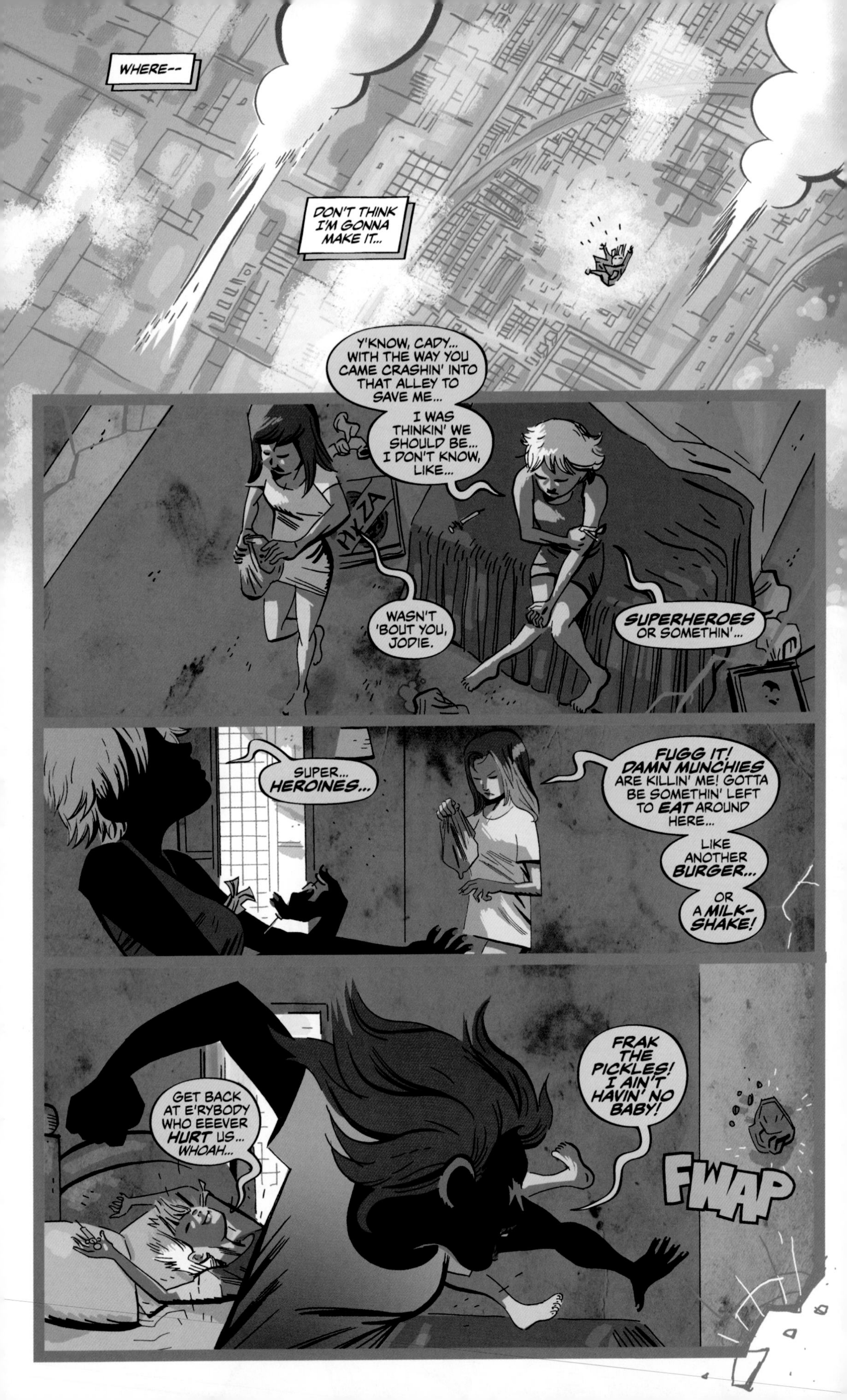
WHERE--
DON'T THINK I'M GONNA MAKE IT...
Y'KNOW, CADY... WITH THE WAY YOU CAME CRASHIN' INTO THAT ALLEY TO SAVE ME...
I WAS THINKIN' WE SHOULD BE... I DON'T KNOW, LIKE...
PIZZA
WASN'T 'BOUT YOU, JODIE.
SUPERHEROES OR SOMETHIN'...
SUPER... HEROINES...
FUGG IT! DAMN MUNCHIES ARE KILLIN' ME! GOTTA BE SOMETHIN' LEFT TO EAT AROUND HERE...
LIKE ANOTHER BURGER...
OR A MILK-SHAKE!
GET BACK AT E'RYBODY WHO EEEVER HURT US... WHOAH...
FRAK THE PICKLES! I AIN'T HAVIN' NO BABY!
FWAP

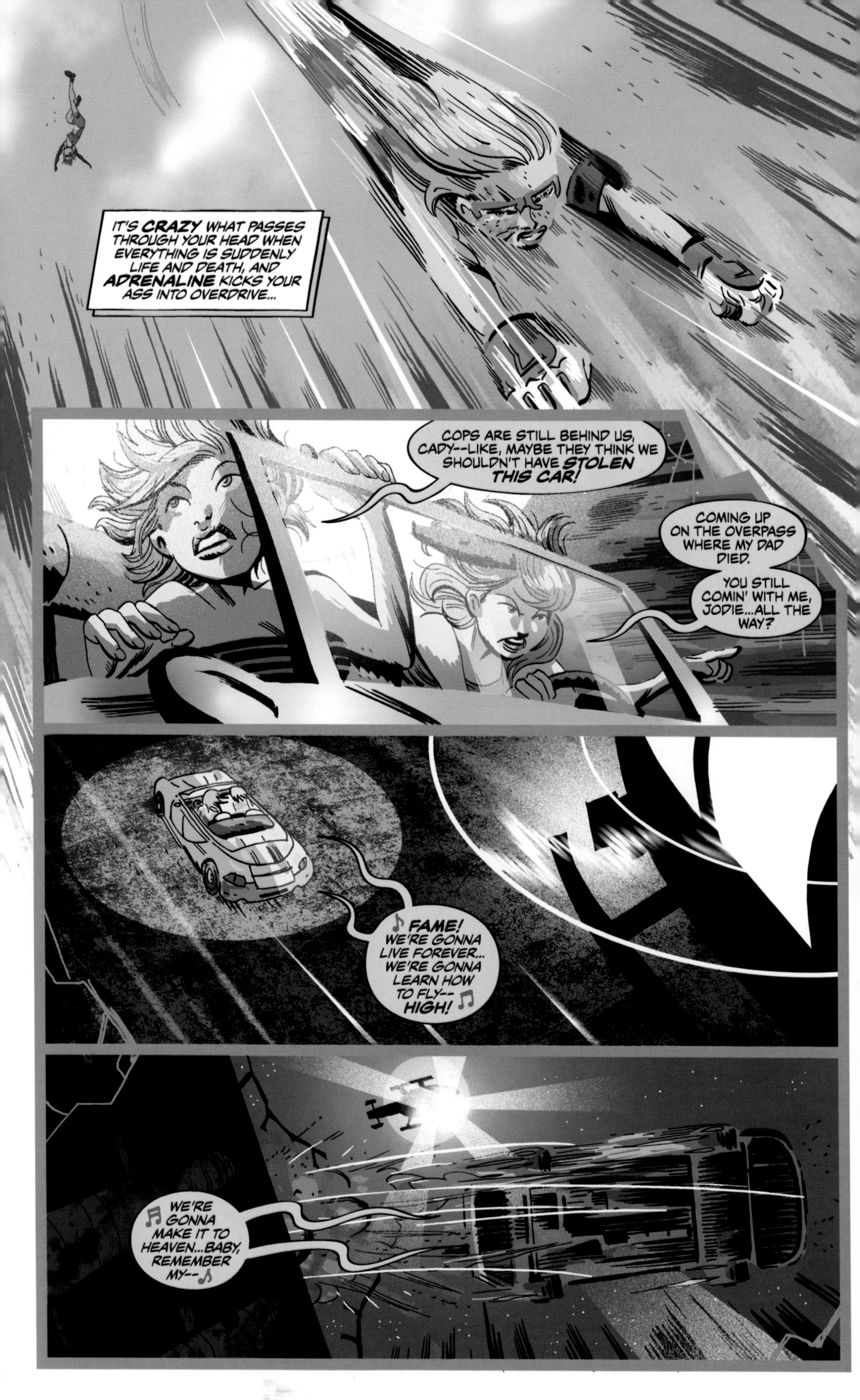
IT'S CRAZY WHAT PASSES THROUGH YOUR HEAD WHEN EVERYTHING IS SUDDENLY LIFE AND DEATH, AND ADRENALINE KICKS YOUR ASS INTO OVERDRIVE...
COPS ARE STILL BEHIND US, CADY--LIKE, MAYBE THEY THINK WE SHOULDN'T HAVE STOLEN THIS CAR!
COMING UP ON THE OVERPASS WHERE MY DAD DIED.
YOU STILL COMIN' WITH ME, JODIE...ALL THE WAY?
♪ FAME! WE'RE GONNA LIVE FOREVER... WE'RE GONNA LEARN HOW TO FLY-- HIGH! ♫
♫ WE'RE GONNA MAKE IT TO HEAVEN...BABY, REMEMBER MY-- ♪

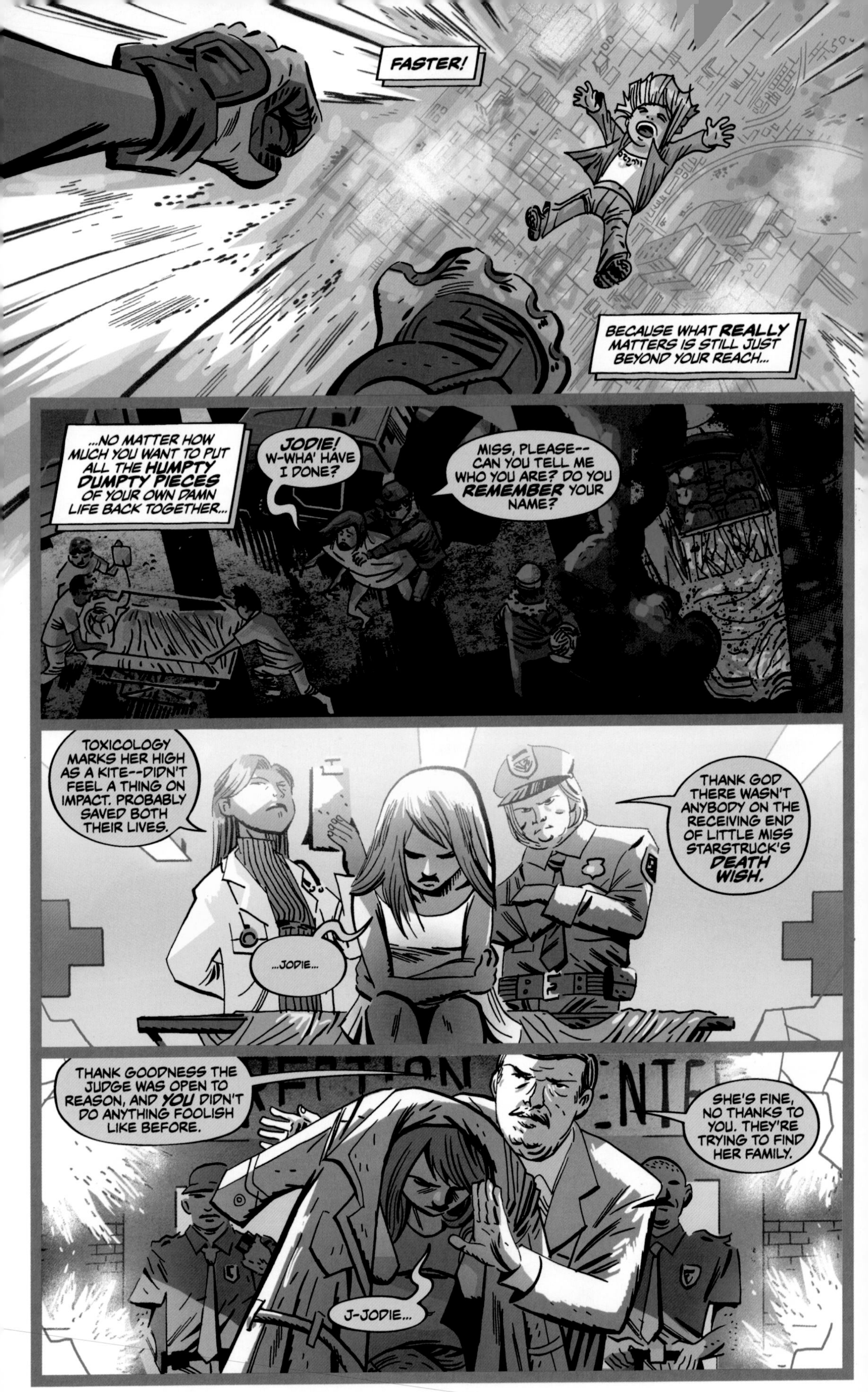
FASTER!
BECAUSE WHAT REALLY MATTERS IS STILL JUST BEYOND YOUR REACH...
...NO MATTER HOW MUCH YOU WANT TO PUT ALL THE HUMPTY DUMPTY PIECES OF YOUR OWN DAMN LIFE BACK TOGETHER...
JODIE! W-WHA' HAVE I DONE?
MISS, PLEASE-- CAN YOU TELL ME WHO YOU ARE? DO YOU REMEMBER YOUR NAME?
TOXICOLOGY MARKS HER HIGH AS A KITE--DIDN'T FEEL A THING ON IMPACT. PROBABLY SAVED BOTH THEIR LIVES.
THANK GOD THERE WASN'T ANYBODY ON THE RECEIVING END OF LITTLE MISS STARSTRUCK'S DEATH WISH.
...JODIE...
THANK GOODNESS THE JUDGE WAS OPEN TO REASON, AND YOU DIDN'T DO ANYTHING FOOLISH LIKE BEFORE.
SHE'S FINE, NO THANKS TO YOU. THEY'RE TRYING TO FIND HER FAMILY.
J-JODIE...

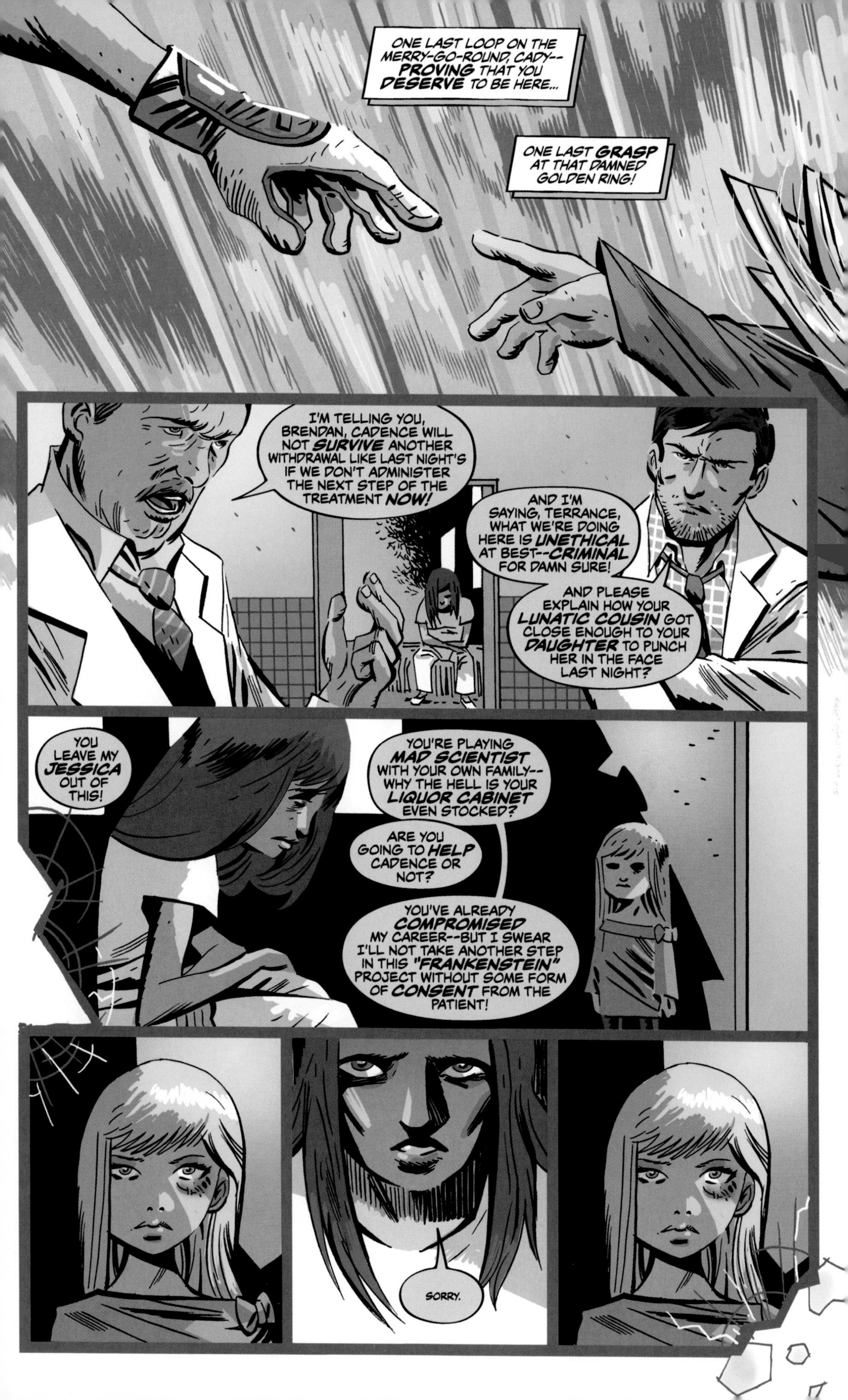

ONE LAST LOOP ON THE MERRY-GO-ROUND, CADY--PROVING THAT YOU DESERVE TO BE HERE...
ONE LAST GRASP AT THAT DAMNED GOLDEN RING!
I'M TELLING YOU, BRENDAN, CADENCE WILL NOT SURVIVE ANOTHER WITHDRAWAL LIKE LAST NIGHT'S IF WE DON'T ADMINISTER THE NEXT STEP OF THE TREATMENT NOW!
AND I'M SAYING, TERRANCE, WHAT WE'RE DOING HERE IS UNETHICAL AT BEST--CRIMINAL FOR DAMN SURE!
AND PLEASE EXPLAIN HOW YOUR LUNATIC COUSIN GOT CLOSE ENOUGH TO YOUR DAUGHTER TO PUNCH HER IN THE FACE LAST NIGHT?
YOU LEAVE MY JESSICA OUT OF THIS!
YOU'RE PLAYING MAD SCIENTIST WITH YOUR OWN FAMILY--WHY THE HELL IS YOUR LIQUOR CABINET EVEN STOCKED?
ARE YOU GOING TO HELP CADENCE OR NOT?
YOU'VE ALREADY COMPROMISED MY CAREER--BUT I SWEAR I'LL NOT TAKE ANOTHER STEP IN THIS "FRANKENSTEIN" PROJECT WITHOUT SOME FORM OF CONSENT FROM THE PATIENT!
SORRY.

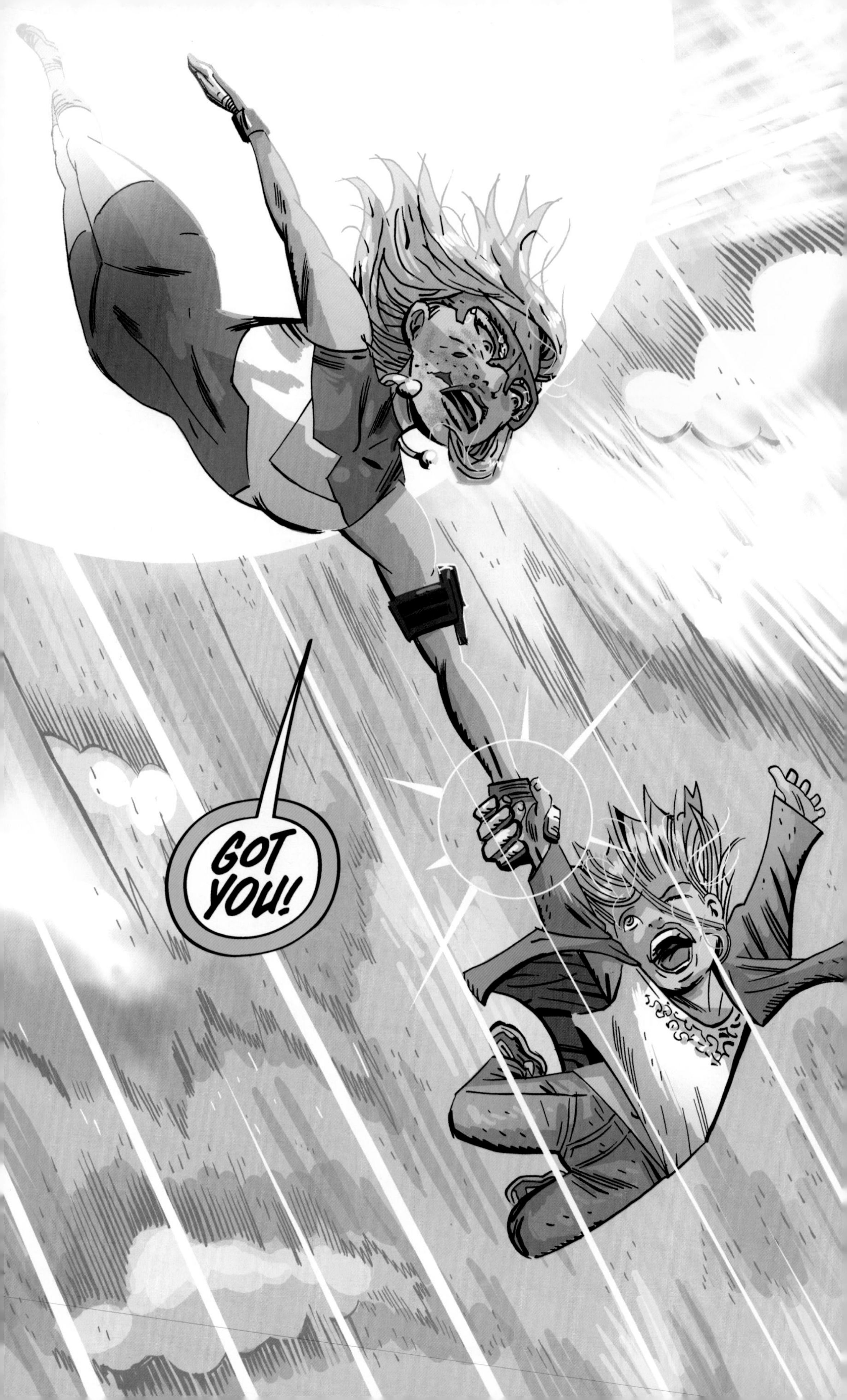
GOT YOU!

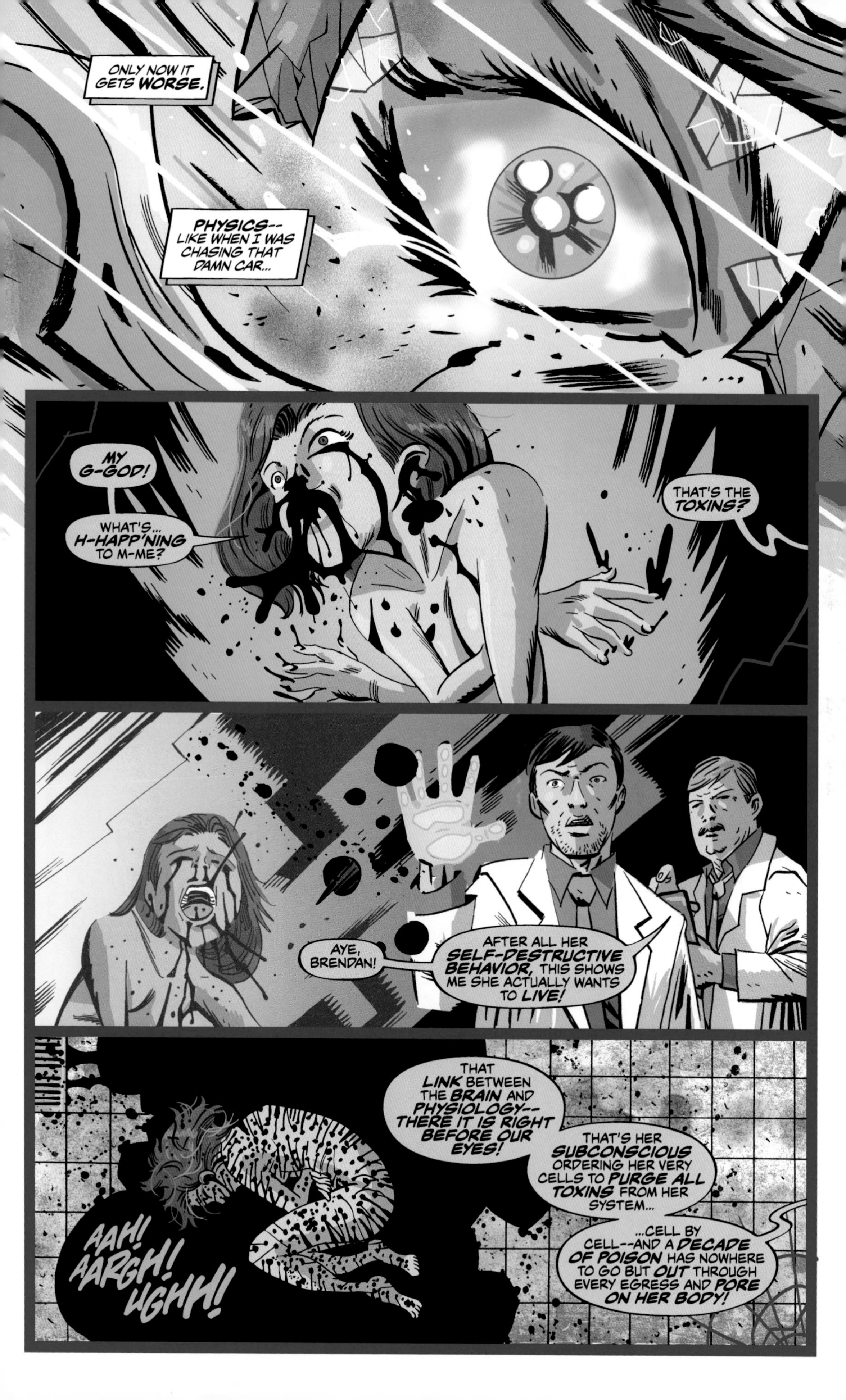

ONLY NOW IT GETS WORSE.
PHYSICS-- LIKE WHEN I WAS CHASING THAT DAMN CAR...
MY G-GOD!
WHAT'S... H-HAPP'NING TO M-ME?
THAT'S THE TOXINS?
AYE, BRENDAN!
AFTER ALL HER SELF-DESTRUCTIVE BEHAVIOR, THIS SHOWS ME SHE ACTUALLY WANTS TO LIVE!
THAT LINK BETWEEN THE BRAIN AND PHYSIOLOGY-- THERE IT IS RIGHT BEFORE OUR EYES!
THAT'S HER SUBCONSCIOUS ORDERING HER VERY CELLS TO PURGE ALL TOXINS FROM HER SYSTEM...
...CELL BY CELL--AND A DECADE OF POISON HAS NOWHERE TO GO BUT OUT THROUGH EVERY EGRESS AND PORE ON HER BODY!
AAH! AARGH! UGHH!

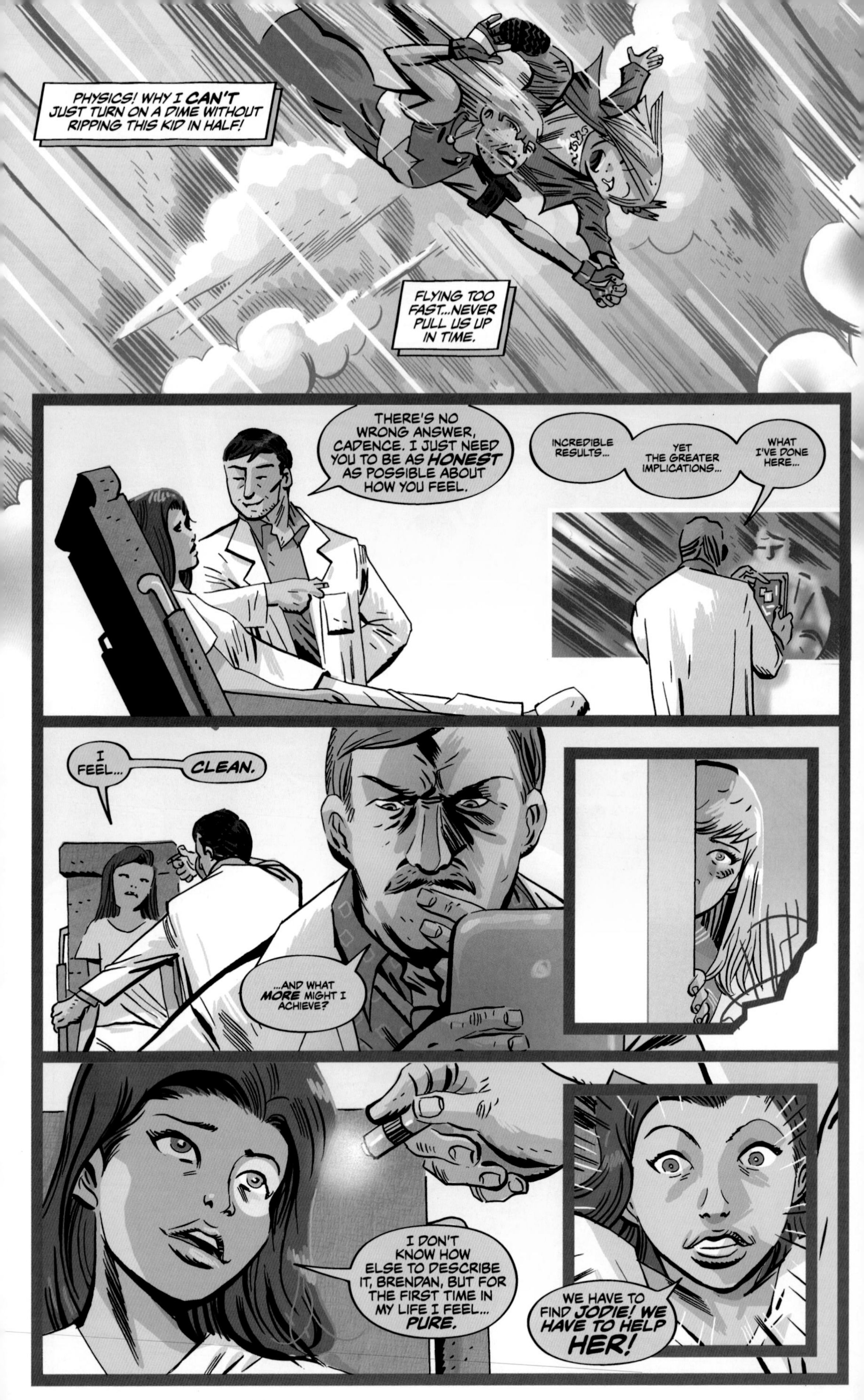
PHYSICS! WHY I CAN'T JUST TURN ON A DIME WITHOUT RIPPING THIS KID IN HALF!
FLYING TOO FAST...NEVER PULL US UP IN TIME.
THERE'S NO WRONG ANSWER, CADENCE. I JUST NEED YOU TO BE AS HONEST AS POSSIBLE ABOUT HOW YOU FEEL.
INCREDIBLE RESULTS...
YET THE GREATER IMPLICATIONS...
WHAT I'VE DONE HERE...
I FEEL... CLEAN.
...AND WHAT MORE MIGHT I ACHIEVE?
I DON'T KNOW HOW ELSE TO DESCRIBE IT, BRENDAN, BUT FOR THE FIRST TIME IN MY LIFE I FEEL... PURE.
WE HAVE TO FIND JODIE! WE HAVE TO HELP HER!

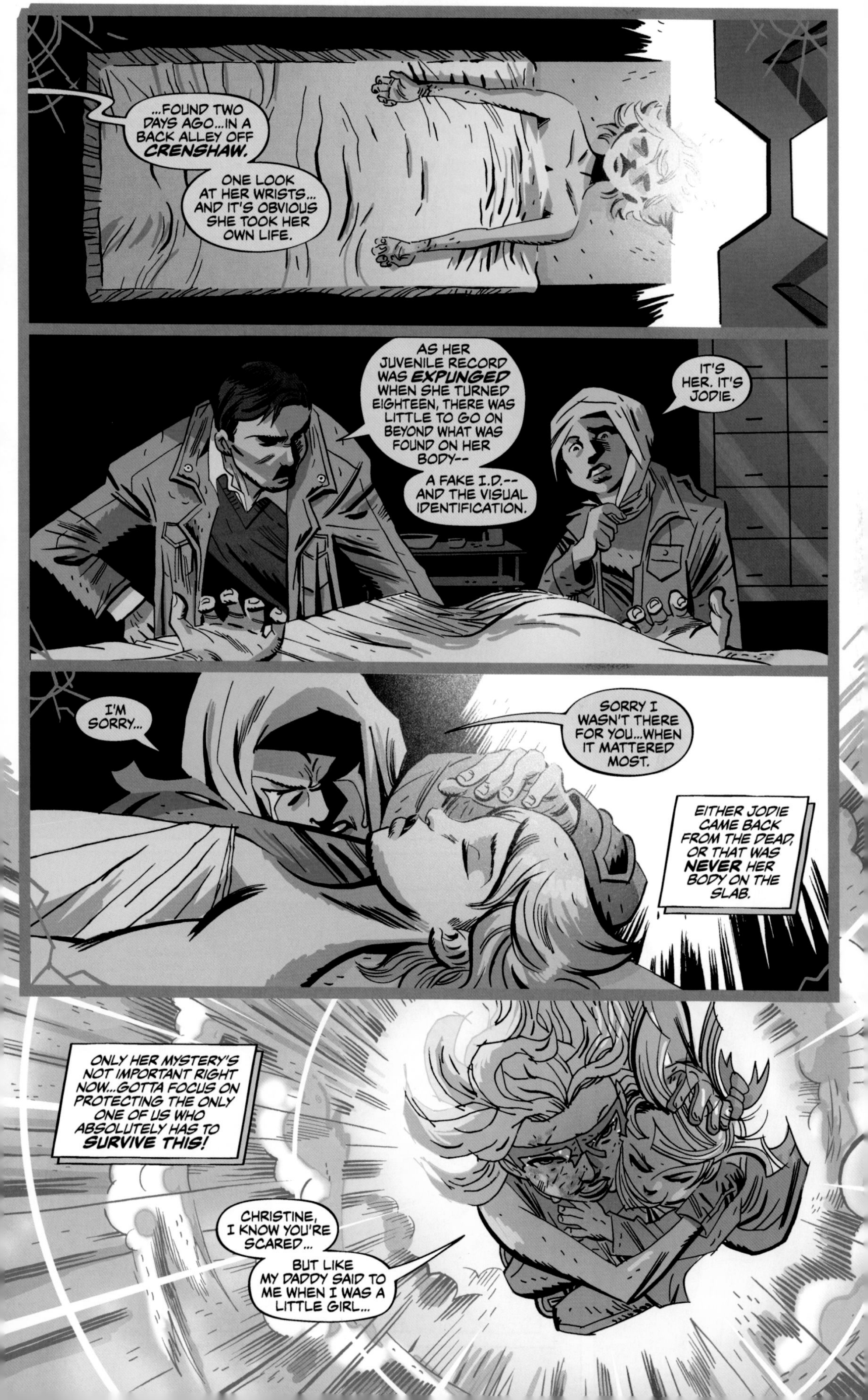
...FOUND TWO DAYS AGO...IN A BACK ALLEY OFF **CRENSHAW.**
ONE LOOK AT HER WRISTS... AND IT'S OBVIOUS SHE TOOK HER OWN LIFE.
AS HER JUVENILE RECORD WAS **EXPUNGED** WHEN SHE TURNED EIGHTEEN, THERE WAS LITTLE TO GO ON BEYOND WHAT WAS FOUND ON HER BODY--
A FAKE I.D.-- AND THE VISUAL IDENTIFICATION.
IT'S HER. IT'S JODIE.
I'M SORRY...
SORRY I WASN'T THERE FOR YOU...WHEN IT MATTERED MOST.
EITHER JODIE CAME BACK FROM THE DEAD, OR THAT WAS **NEVER** HER BODY ON THE SLAB.
ONLY HER MYSTERY'S NOT IMPORTANT RIGHT NOW...GOTTA FOCUS ON PROTECTING THE ONLY ONE OF US WHO ABSOLUTELY HAS TO **SURVIVE THIS!**
CHRISTINE, I KNOW YOU'RE SCARED...
BUT LIKE MY DADDY SAID TO ME WHEN I WAS A LITTLE GIRL...

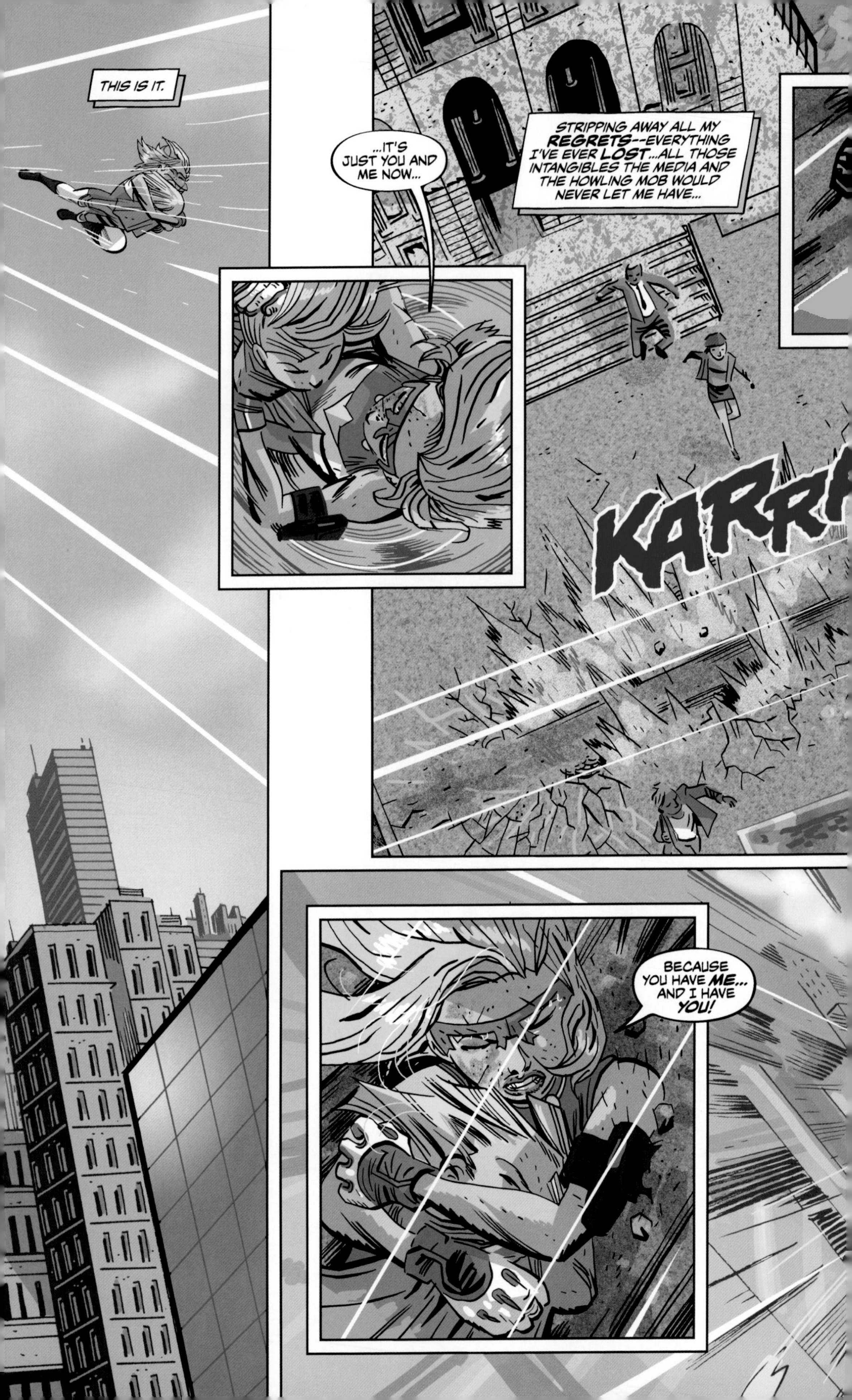
THIS IS IT.
...IT'S JUST YOU AND ME NOW...
STRIPPING AWAY ALL MY REGRETS--EVERYTHING I'VE EVER LOST...ALL THOSE INTANGIBLES THE MEDIA AND THE HOWLING MOB WOULD NEVER LET ME HAVE...
KARR
BECAUSE YOU HAVE ME... AND I HAVE YOU!

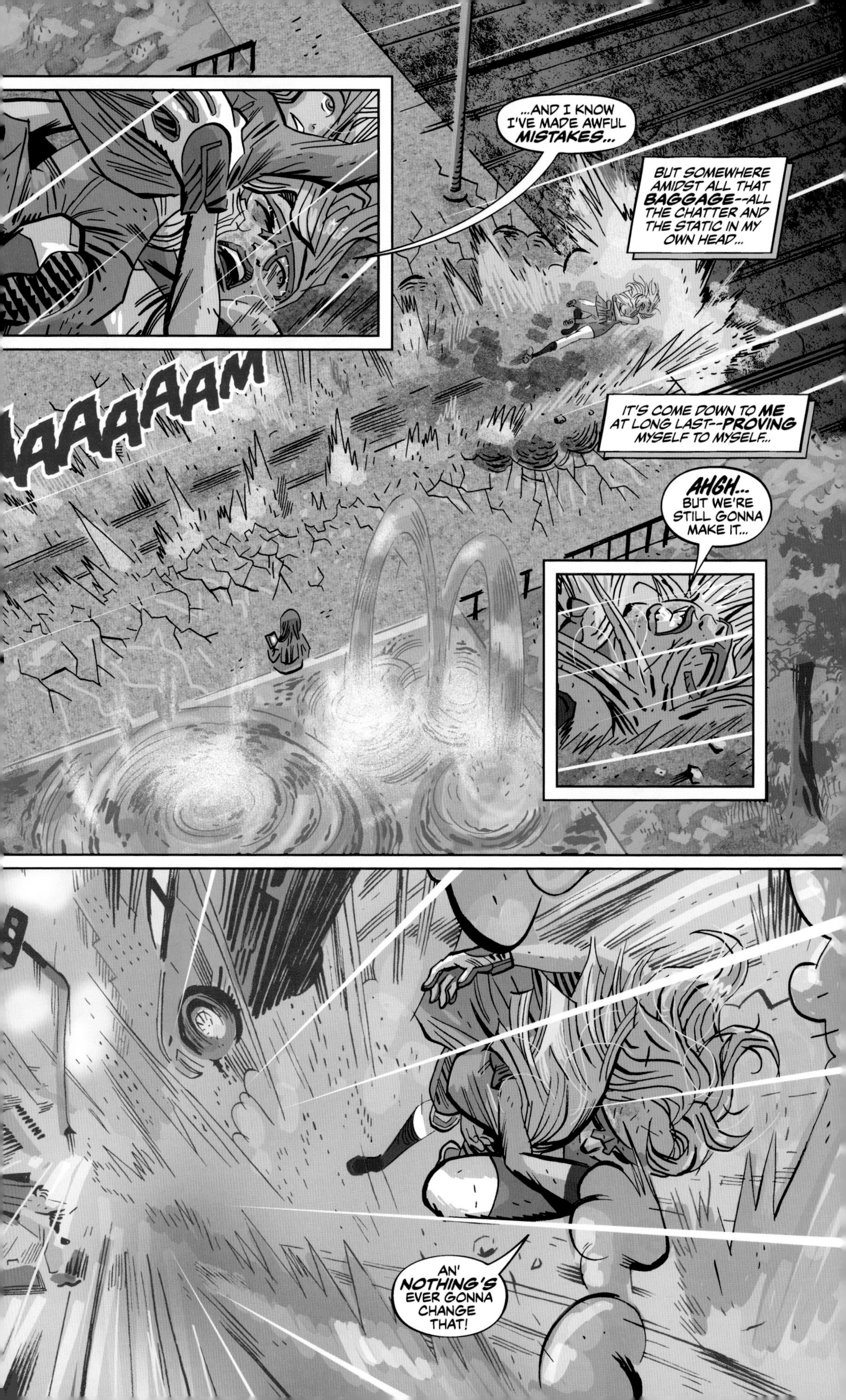

...AND I KNOW I'VE MADE AWFUL MISTAKES...
BUT SOMEWHERE AMIDST ALL THAT BAGGAGE--ALL THE CHATTER AND THE STATIC IN MY OWN HEAD...
AAAAAAM
IT'S COME DOWN TO ME AT LONG LAST--PROVING MYSELF TO MYSELF...
AHGH... BUT WE'RE STILL GONNA MAKE IT...
AN' NOTHING'S EVER GONNA CHANGE THAT!

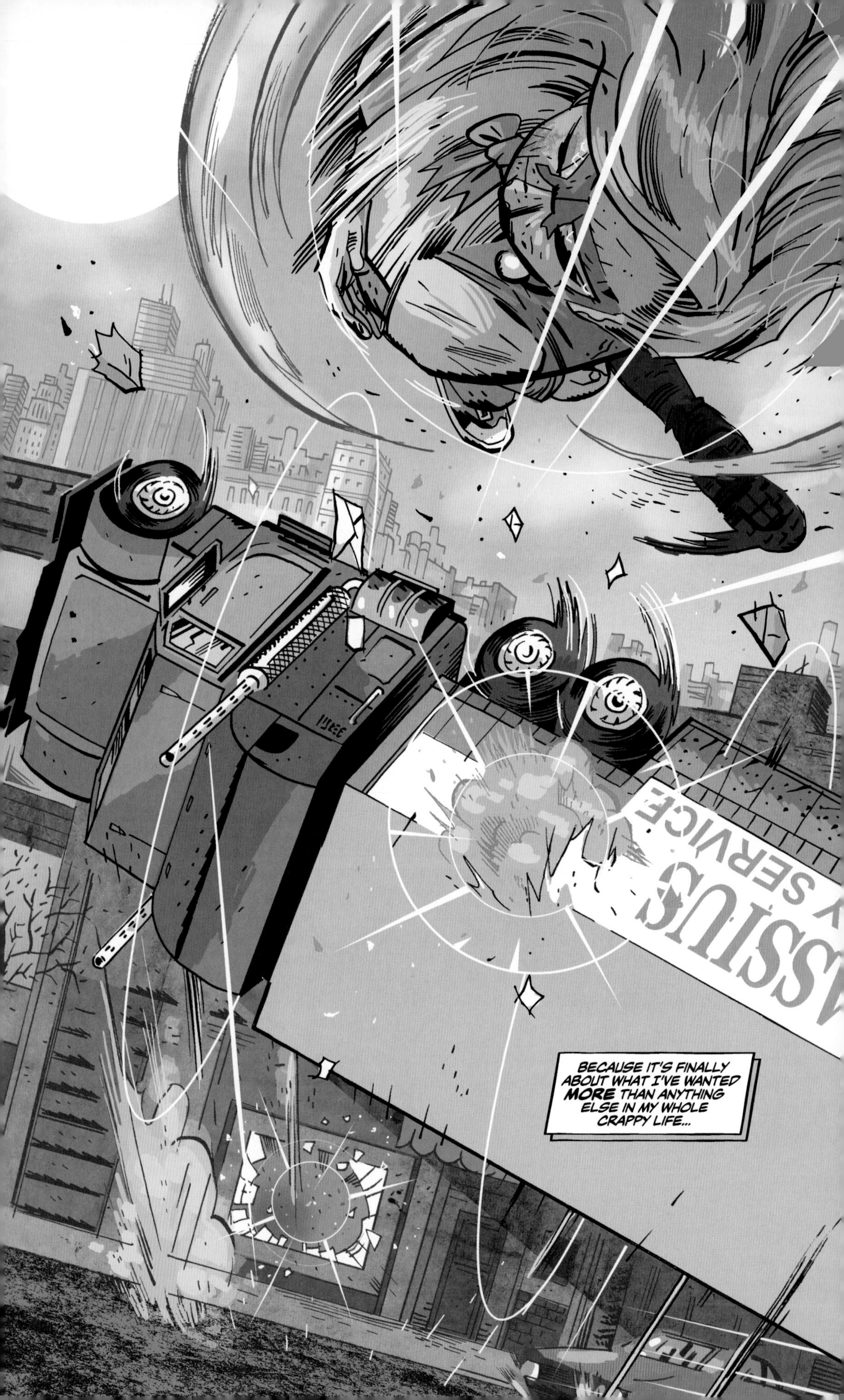
BECAUSE IT'S FINALLY ABOUT WHAT I'VE WANTED **MORE** THAN ANYTHING ELSE IN MY WHOLE CRAPPY LIFE...

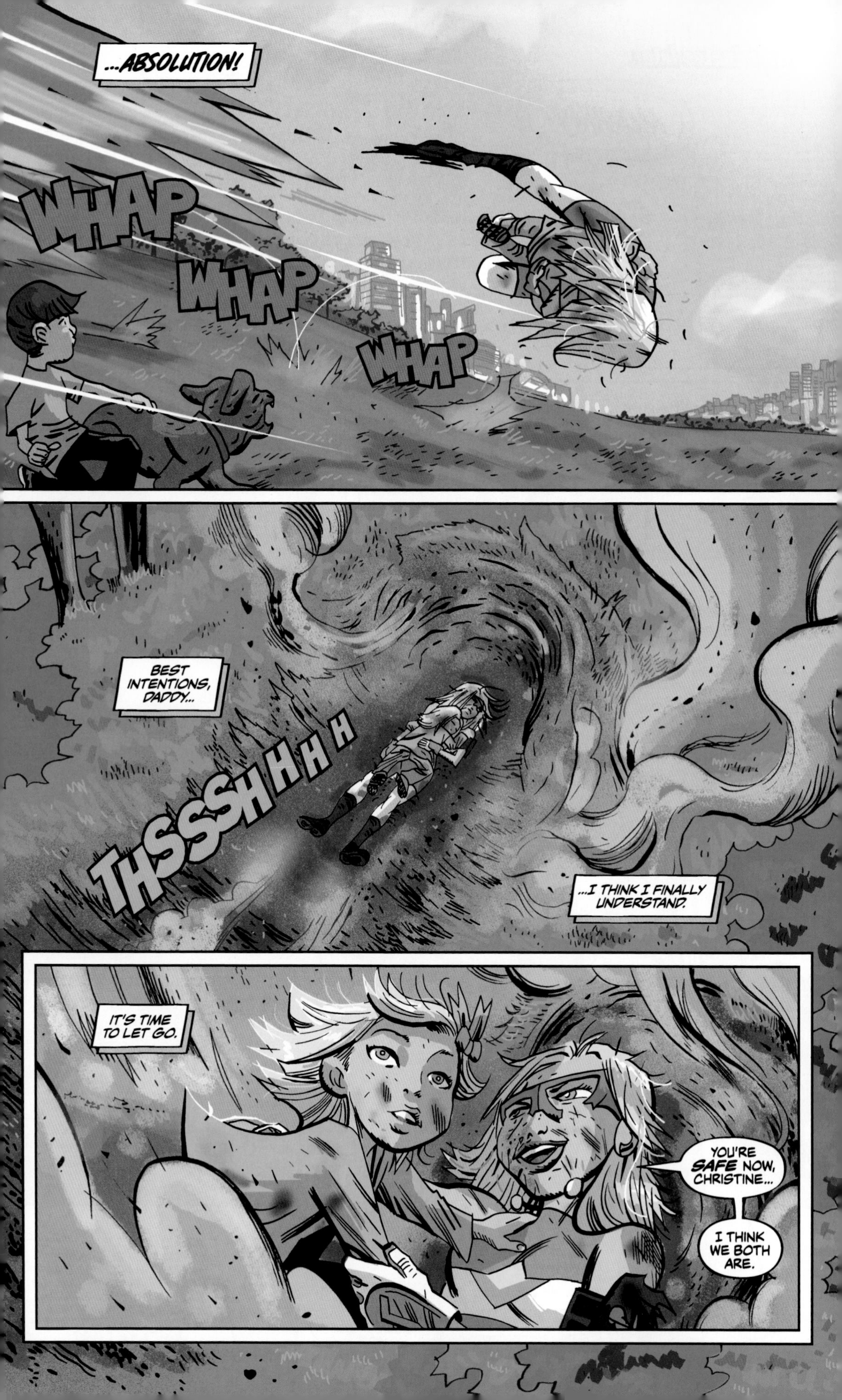
...ABSOLUTION!
WHAP
WHAP
WHAP
BEST INTENTIONS, DADDY...
THSSSHHHH
...I THINK I FINALLY UNDERSTAND.
IT'S TIME TO LET GO.
YOU'RE SAFE NOW, CHRISTINE...
I THINK WE BOTH ARE.

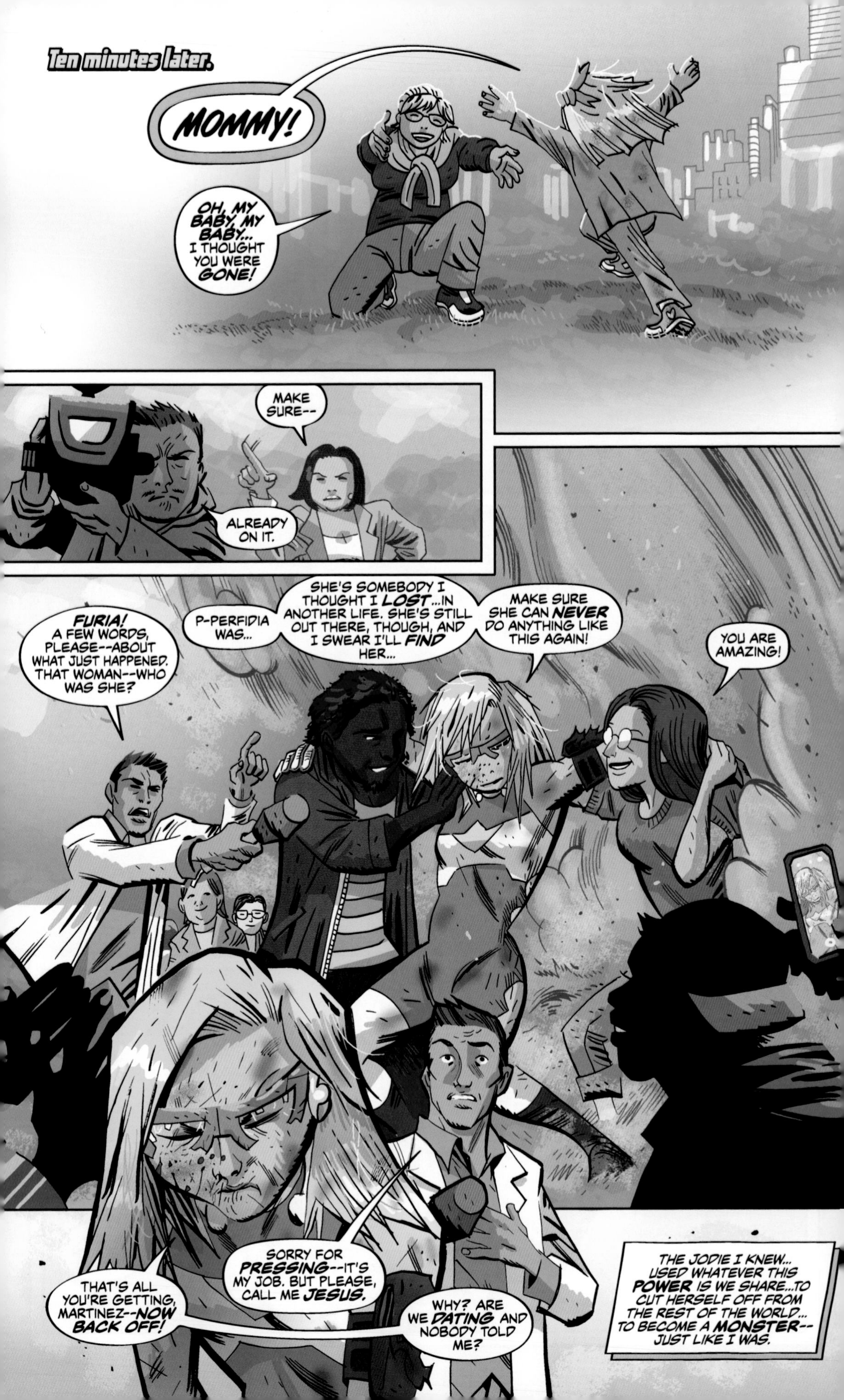
Ten minutes later.
MOMMY!
OH, MY BABY, MY BABY... I THOUGHT YOU WERE GONE!
MAKE SURE--
ALREADY ON IT.
FURIA! A FEW WORDS, PLEASE--ABOUT WHAT JUST HAPPENED. THAT WOMAN--WHO WAS SHE?
P-PERFIDIA WAS...
SHE'S SOMEBODY I THOUGHT I LOST...IN ANOTHER LIFE. SHE'S STILL OUT THERE, THOUGH, AND I SWEAR I'LL FIND HER...
MAKE SURE SHE CAN NEVER DO ANYTHING LIKE THIS AGAIN!
YOU ARE AMAZING!
THAT'S ALL YOU'RE GETTING, MARTINEZ--NOW BACK OFF!
SORRY FOR PRESSING--IT'S MY JOB. BUT PLEASE, CALL ME JESUS.
WHY? ARE WE DATING AND NOBODY TOLD ME?
THE JODIE I KNEW... USED WHATEVER THIS POWER IS WE SHARE...TO CUT HERSELF OFF FROM THE REST OF THE WORLD... TO BECOME A MONSTER-- JUST LIKE I WAS.

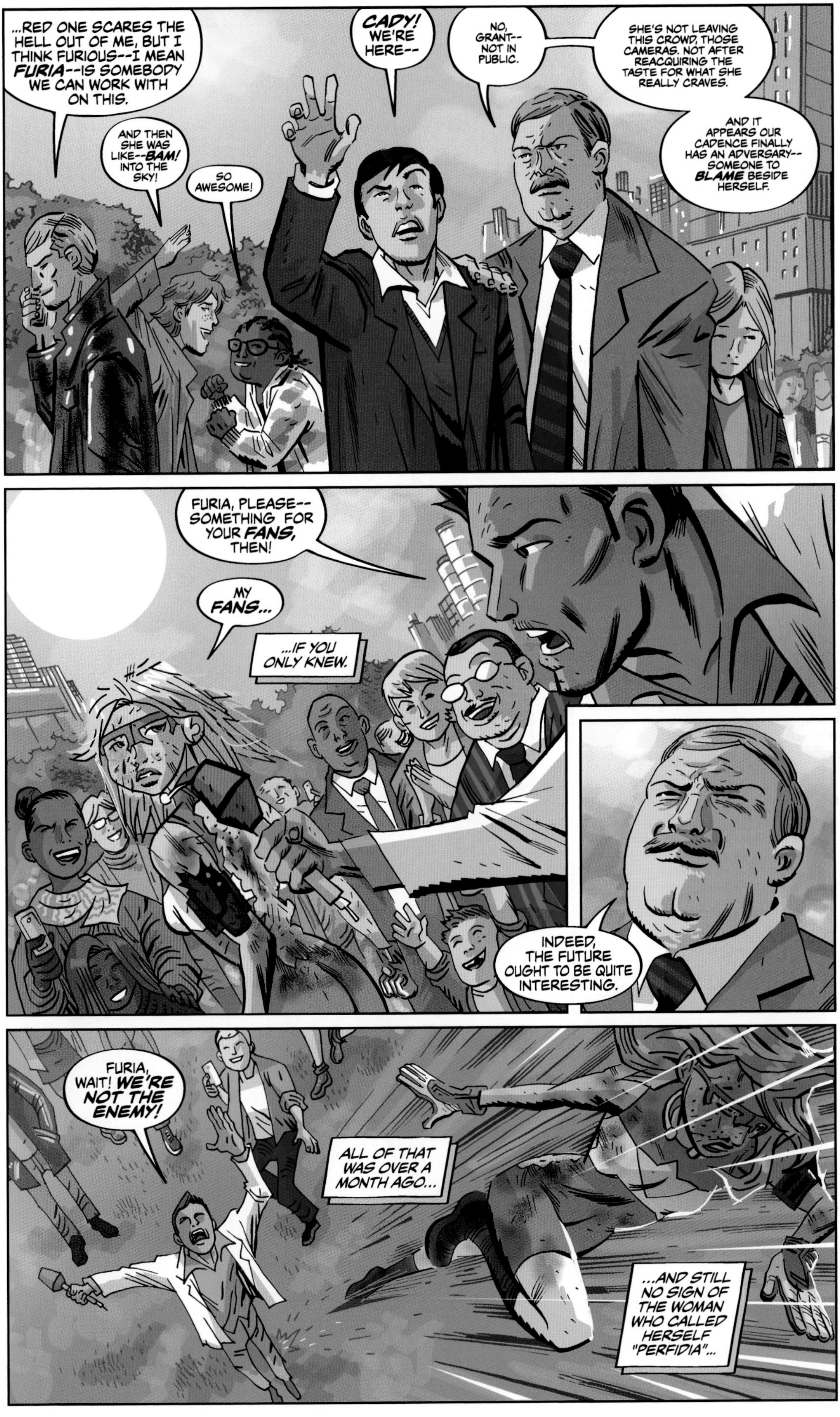

...RED ONE SCARES THE HELL OUT OF ME, BUT I THINK FURIOUS--I MEAN FURIA--IS SOMEBODY WE CAN WORK WITH ON THIS.
AND THEN SHE WAS LIKE--BAM! INTO THE SKY!
SO AWESOME!
CADY! WE'RE HERE--
NO, GRANT--NOT IN PUBLIC.
SHE'S NOT LEAVING THIS CROWD, THOSE CAMERAS. NOT AFTER REACQUIRING THE TASTE FOR WHAT SHE REALLY CRAVES.
AND IT APPEARS OUR CADENCE FINALLY HAS AN ADVERSARY--SOMEONE TO BLAME BESIDE HERSELF.
FURIA, PLEASE--SOMETHING FOR YOUR FANS, THEN!
MY FANS...
...IF YOU ONLY KNEW.
INDEED, THE FUTURE OUGHT TO BE QUITE INTERESTING.
FURIA, WAIT! WE'RE NOT THE ENEMY!
ALL OF THAT WAS OVER A MONTH AGO...
...AND STILL NO SIGN OF THE WOMAN WHO CALLED HERSELF "PERFIDIA"...

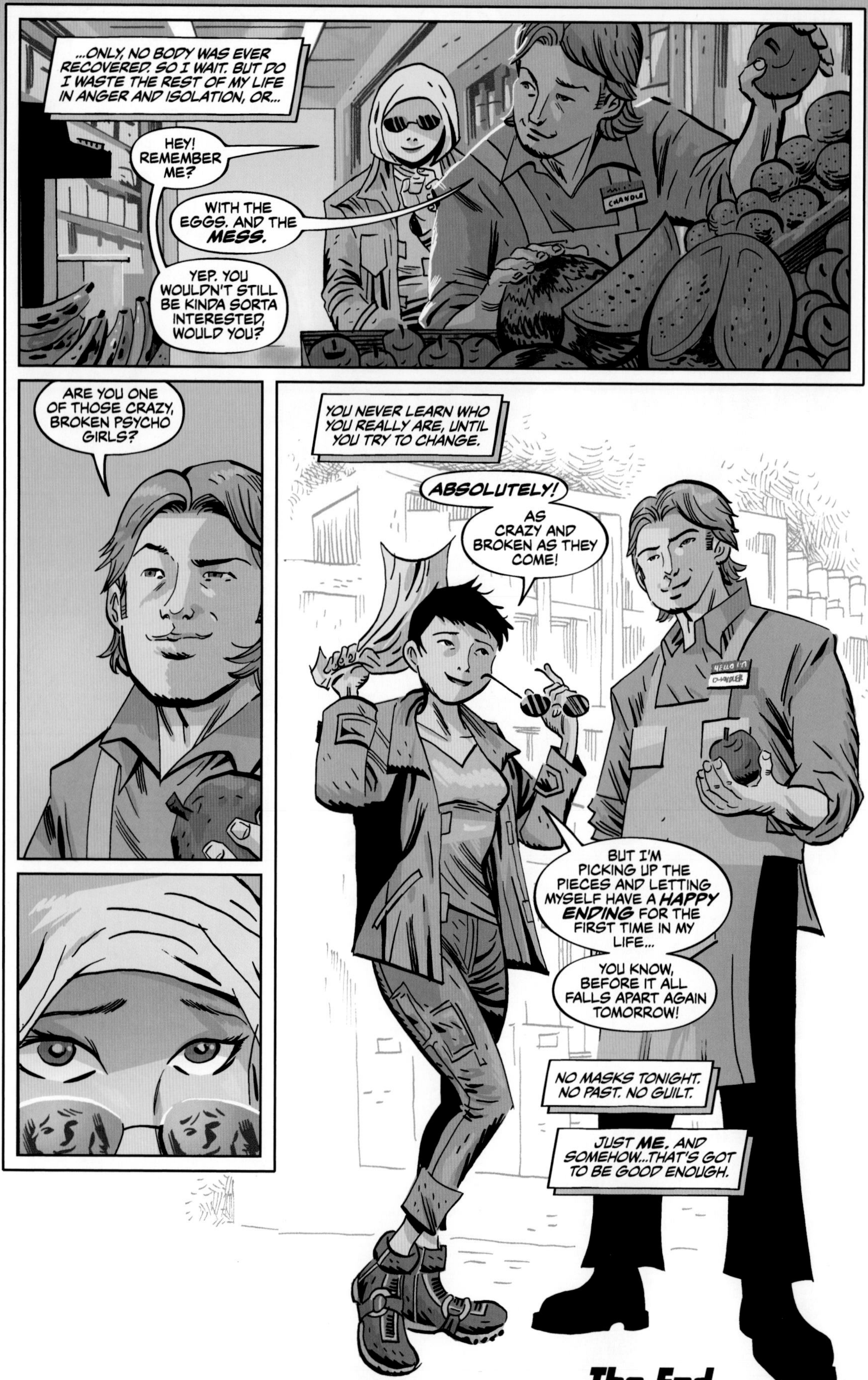
...ONLY, NO BODY WAS EVER RECOVERED. SO I WAIT. BUT DO I WASTE THE REST OF MY LIFE IN ANGER AND ISOLATION, OR...
HEY! REMEMBER ME?
WITH THE EGGS. AND THE MESS.
YEP. YOU WOULDN'T STILL BE KINDA SORTA INTERESTED, WOULD YOU?
ARE YOU ONE OF THOSE CRAZY, BROKEN PSYCHO GIRLS?
YOU NEVER LEARN WHO YOU REALLY ARE, UNTIL YOU TRY TO CHANGE.
ABSOLUTELY!
AS CRAZY AND BROKEN AS THEY COME!
BUT I'M PICKING UP THE PIECES AND LETTING MYSELF HAVE A HAPPY ENDING FOR THE FIRST TIME IN MY LIFE...
YOU KNOW, BEFORE IT ALL FALLS APART AGAIN TOMORROW!
NO MASKS TONIGHT. NO PAST. NO GUILT.
JUST ME. AND SOMEHOW...THAT'S GOT TO BE GOOD ENOUGH.
The End.

COSTUME DESIGN

Bryan J. L. Glass: One of the most fascinating aspects of a creative collaboration in comics is when a writer with a vision surrenders visual control to an artist's inspiration. From the beginning I wanted Victor's design imprint upon the series and gave him creative freedom in the designs, within the parameters of the story's dramatic and thematic requirements.

2A

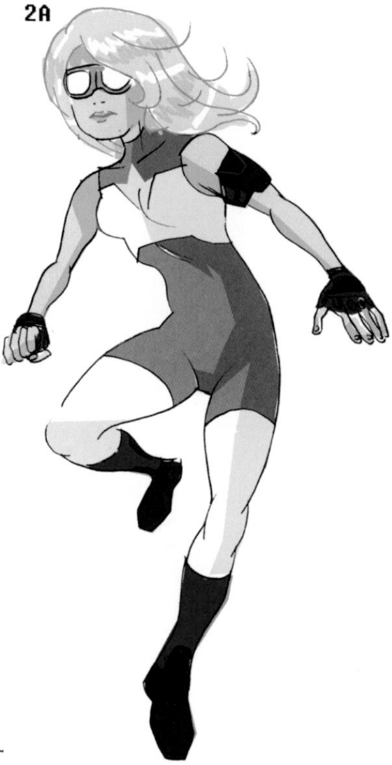

2B

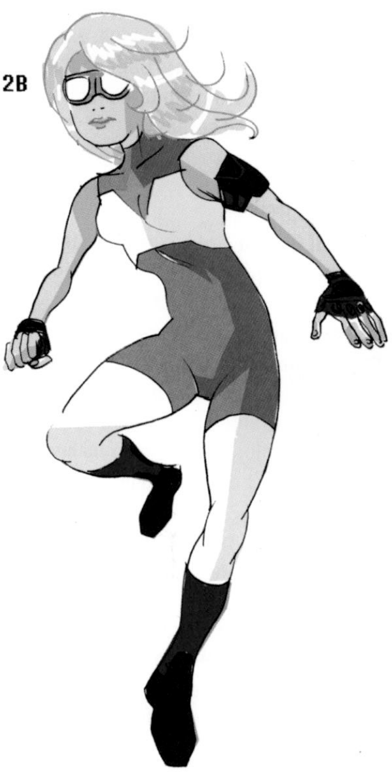

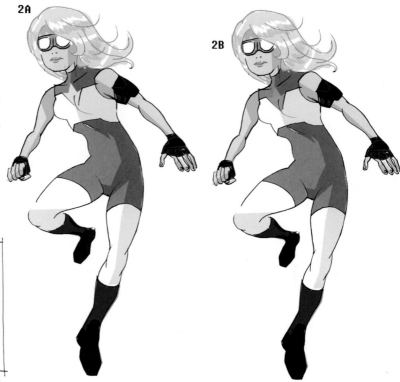

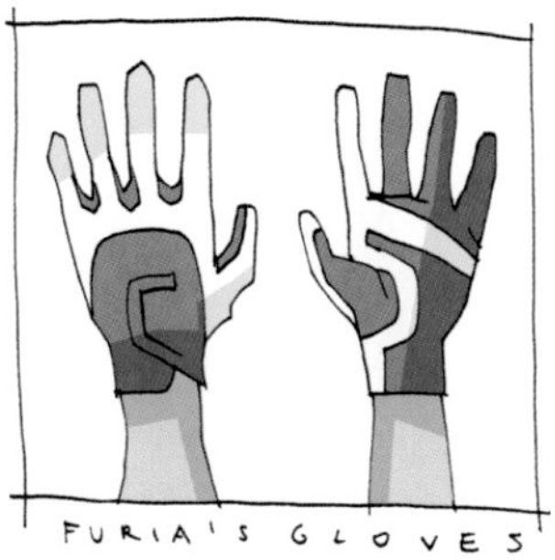
FURIA'S GLOVES

1

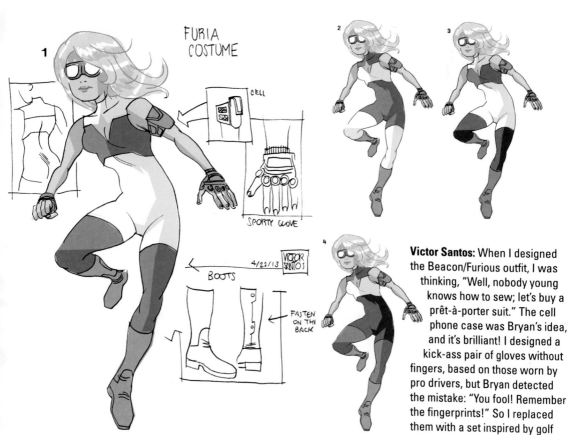

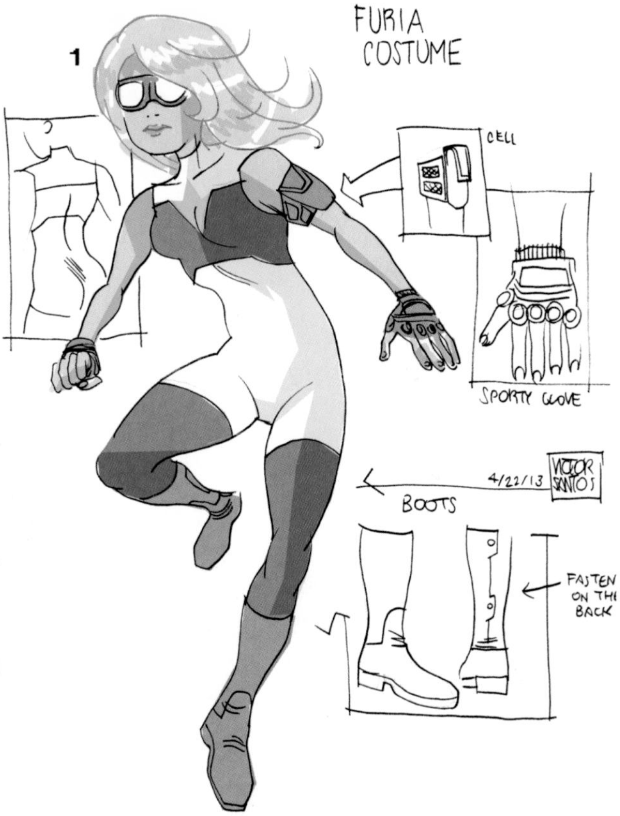
FURIA
COSTUME
CELL
SPORTY GLOVE
4/22/13
VICTOR SANTOS
BOOTS
FASTEN ON THE BACK

2

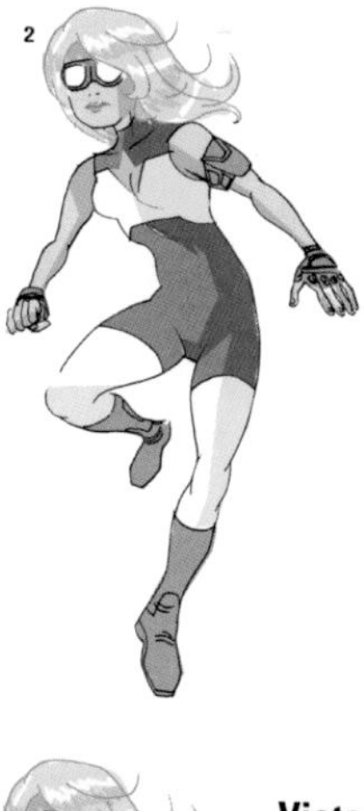

3

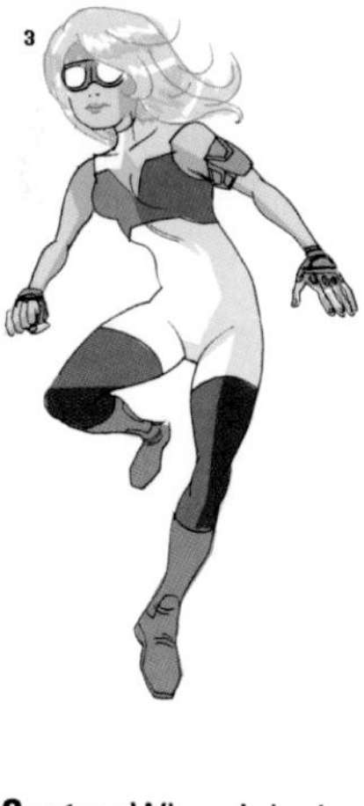

4

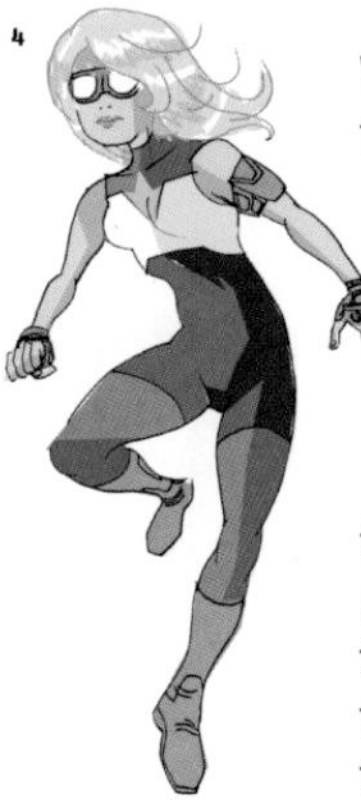

Victor Santos: When I designed the Beacon/Furious outfit, I was thinking, "Well, nobody young knows how to sew; let's buy a prêt-à-porter suit." The cell phone case was Bryan's idea, and it's brilliant! I designed a kick-ass pair of gloves without fingers, based on those worn by pro drivers, but Bryan detected the mistake: "You fool! Remember the fingerprints!" So I replaced them with a set inspired by golf gloves—tough but flexible.

COLOR PALETTE

VS: Following Bryan's guidelines, I used basic color values linked to light and sky for Cadence: blue, white, orange, and yellow. Cadence, as a beacon, wants to transmit hope, warmth, and serenity.

HAIRSTYLES

BJLG: As a story, *Furious* is about identity, promotion, and perception, chronicling Cadence Lark from age 7 to 25, with many hairstyles and hair colors to identify her at the various stages of her life. Once Victor created the design, I offered these color notes to help us keep Cadence's personal timeline straight.

VS: Sometimes the change in hair color was a headache, but if you follow the story line you'll see it's coherent and important, evolving with Cadence's mood. I love how, in anime and manga, the look of the character changes. It's a really useful visual tool.

2A

FURIA'S GLOVES

The Lark Triplets all have light brunette hair from ages 4-7

CADENCE CHILD STAR

TRIPLED CARE

Post-Tragedy Cadence has darker brown from ages 7-17

On her 18th birthday, Cadence fires her dad and colors her hair fiery red from ages 18-22

From 22-through experimental rehab fiery red fades back to

TEENAGE CADENCE

12

BRUNETTE

5'2"

17
PETITE/
RED

PUBERTY

SVELTE

21

RED DYED

REHABILITATIO

SHAPE OF
FACE
EVOLUTION

Natural Eye Color is Brown ages 4-17

Green contacts with dyed red hair ages 18-22

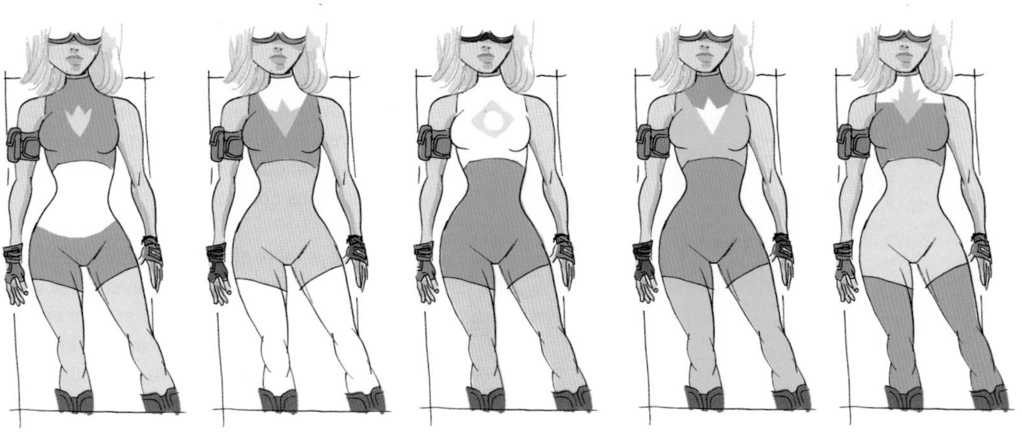

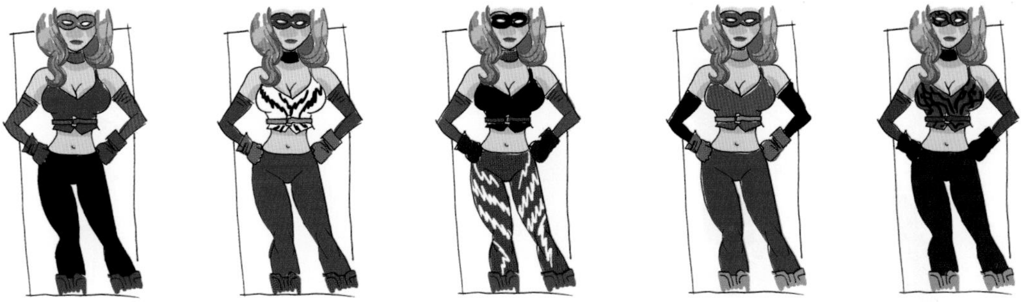

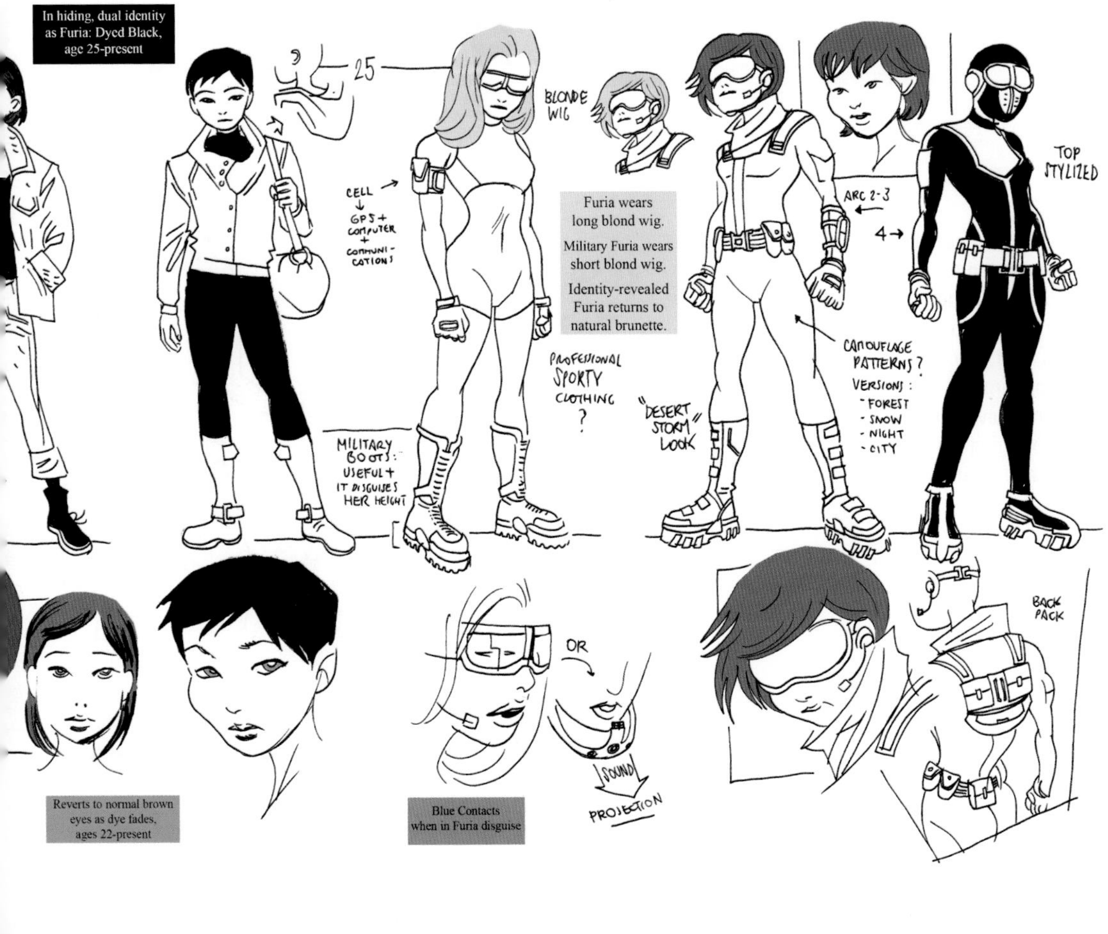
In hiding, dual identity as Furia: Dyed Black, age 25-present
25
CELL → GPS + COMPUTER + COMMUNI-CATIONS
BLONDE WIG
Furia wears long blond wig.
Military Furia wears short blond wig.
Identity-revealed Furia returns to natural brunette.
ARC 2-3
4
TOP STYLIZED
PROFESSIONAL SPORTY CLOTHING ?
MILITARY BOOTS: USEFUL + IT DISGUISES HER HEIGHT
"DESERT STORM" LOOK
CAMOUFLAGE PATTERNS? VERSIONS: - FOREST - SNOW - NIGHT - CITY
OR
SOUND PROJECTION
BACK PACK
Reverts to normal brown eyes as dye fades, ages 22-present
Blue Contacts when in Furia disguise

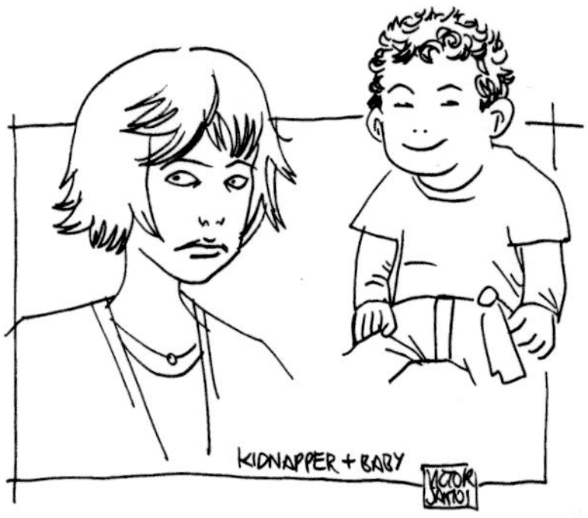
KIDNAPPER + BABY
VICTOR SANTOS

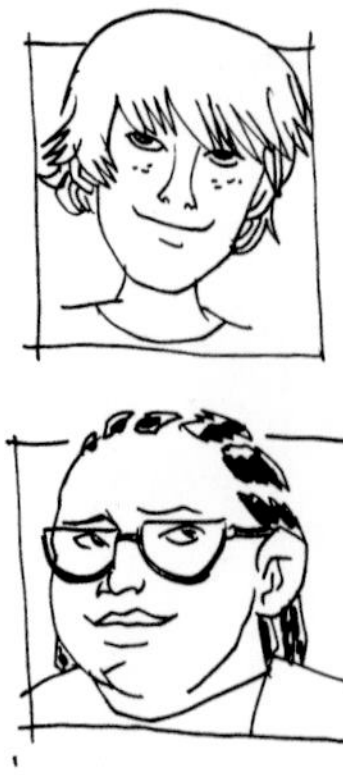

RICHARD AND DWAYNE

BJLG: While not designed after any specific people, these fanboys are representative of fan types I have experienced in comic shops and on the convention circuit. Bursting with knowledge about their fandom, I wanted to convey their enthusiasm as contagious.

VS: I always think about black and white areas, the light and the dark spaces, even if I'm working on a color book. These characters are physically different, but share the black-and-white-shaded parts of their wardrobe. I love this couple! I love the fanboy point of view in the series.

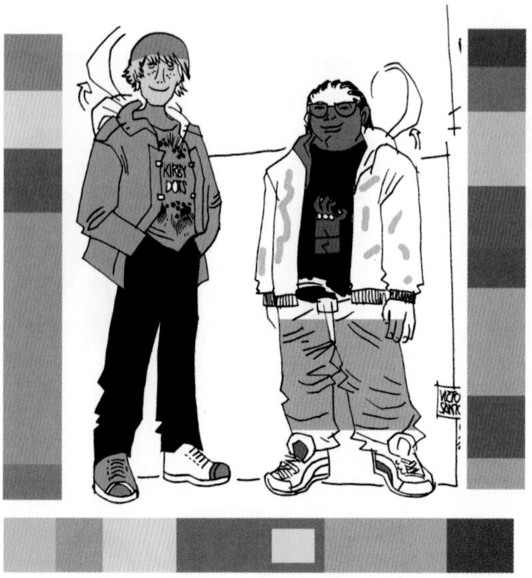
KIRBY DOTS
VICTOR SANTOS

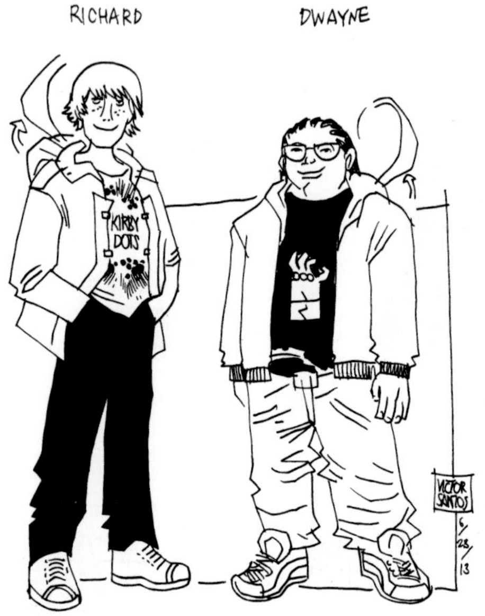
RICHARD
DWAYNE
KIRBY DOTS
VICTOR SANTOS
6/28/13

BALES

BJLG: For our serial killer, I wanted a type that might be easily ignored in a crowd, and yet could transform into a monstrous evil without ever changing his actual appearance.

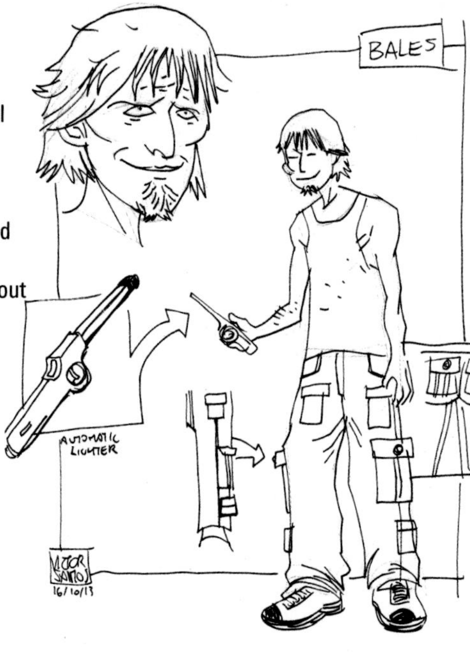
BALES
AUTOMATIC LIGHTER
VICTOR SANTOS
16/10/13

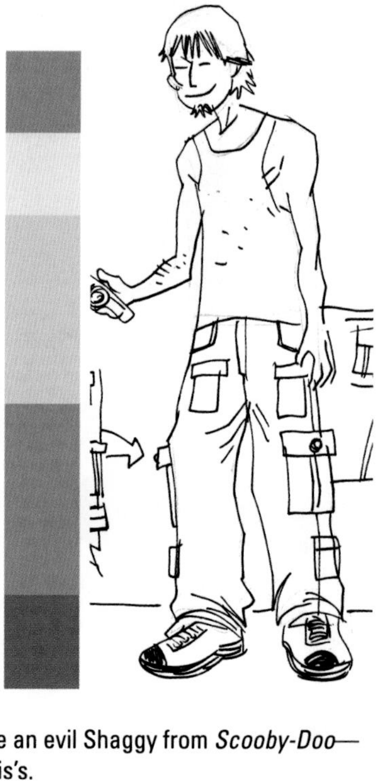

VS: This guy is obviously insane. We designed him like an evil Shaggy from *Scooby-Doo*—clumsy and unpredictable, with long arms like a mantis's.

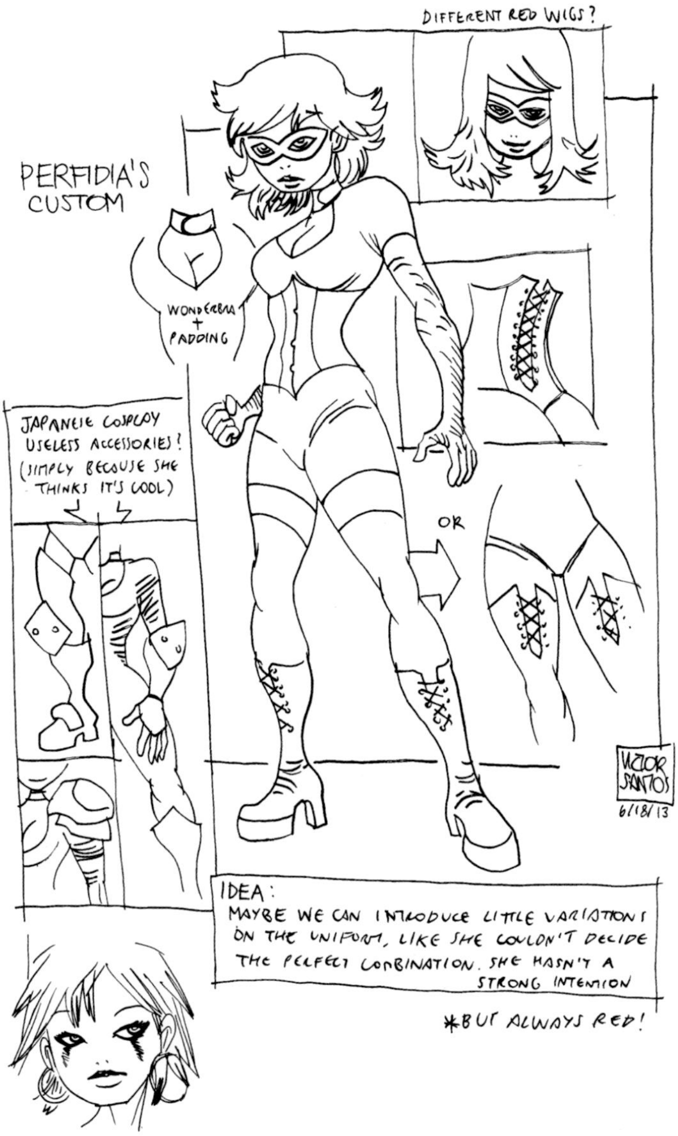
DIFFERENT RED WIGS?
PERFIDIA'S CUSTOM
WONDERBRA + PADDING
JAPANESE COSPLAY USELESS ACCESSORIES? (SIMPLY BECAUSE SHE THINKS IT'S COOL)
OR
VICTOR SANTOS
6/18/13
IDEA:
MAYBE WE CAN INTRODUCE LITTLE VARIATIONS ON THE UNIFORM, LIKE SHE COULDN'T DECIDE THE PERFECT COMBINATION. SHE HASN'T A STRONG INTENTION
*BUT ALWAYS RED!

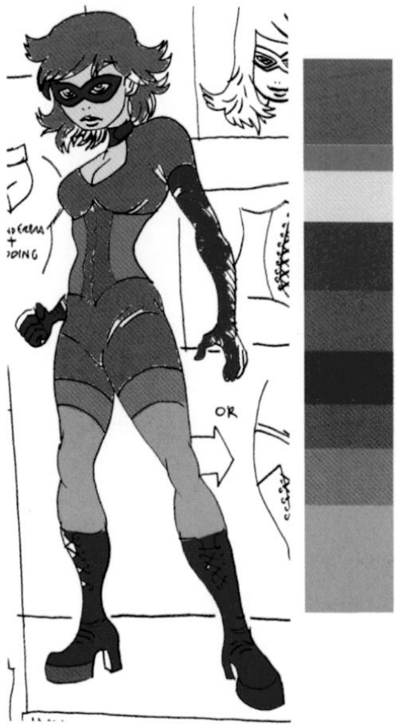

PERFIDIA

BJLG: *Perfidy* means *betrayal*, thus Jodie needed to make herself a distorted reflection of Cadence Lark from her darkest years: a living, breathing reminder of who Furia was, as conveyed by a woman who cannot comprehend redemption and forgiveness.

VS: The dark side, red and purple fury. I designed her costume by thinking about a *Jersey Shore* girl doing cosplay. In every appearance, her outfit and wig are subtly different. I wanted to show that she's not stable.

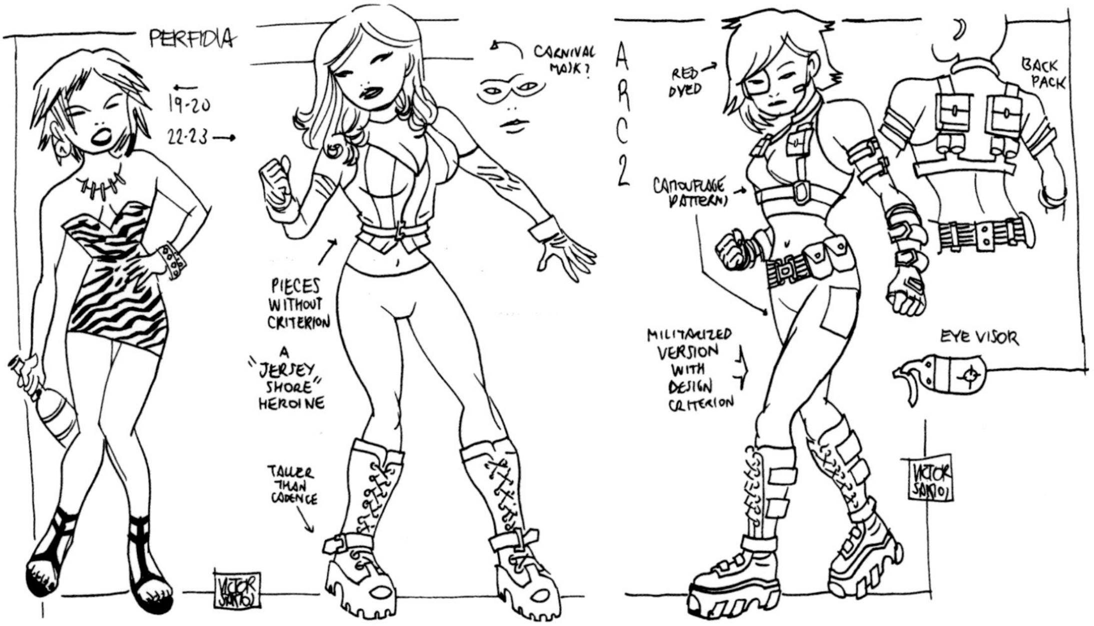
PERFIDIA
19-20
22-23
CARNIVAL MASK?
ARC 2
PIECES WITHOUT CRITERION
A "JERSEY SHORE" HEROINE
TALLER THAN CADENCE
RED DYED
CAMOUFLAGE PATTERN)
MILITARIZED VERSION WITH DESIGN CRITERION
BACK PACK
EYE VISOR
VICTOR SANTOS

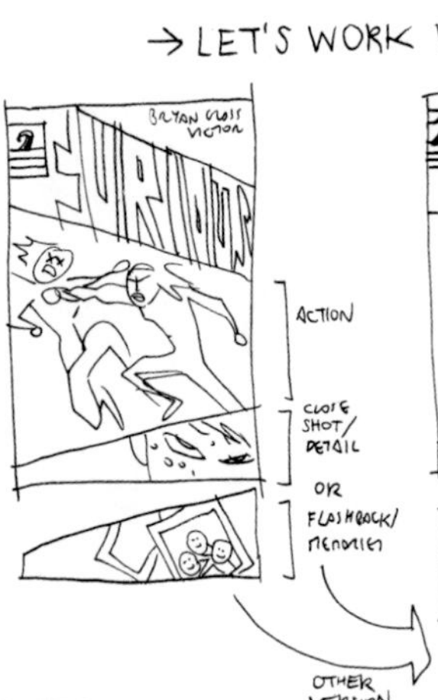
→ LET'S WORK WITH A TITLE ON THE TOP
BRYAN GLASS VICTOR
FURIOUS
ACTION
CLOSE SHOT/ DETAIL
OR FLASHBACK/ MEMORIES
OTHER VERSION

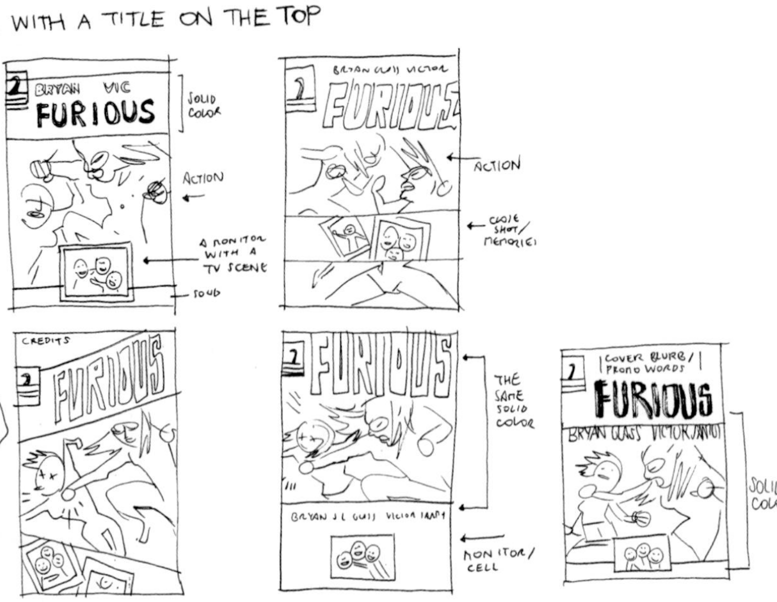
BRYAN VIC
FURIOUS
SOLID COLOR
ACTION
A MONITOR WITH A TV SCENE
SOLID
BRYAN GLASS VICTOR
ACTION
CLOSE SHOT/ MEMORIES
CREDITS
THE SAME SOLID COLOR
MONITOR/ CELL
COVER BLURB/ PROMO WORDS
BRYAN GLASS VICTOR SANTOS
SOLID COLOR

COVERS

VS: I think every book needs a unique look. It's a constant struggle and debate, because I want to do crazy designs, but we can't forget commercial aspects like legibility or the visibility of a cover in the stores.

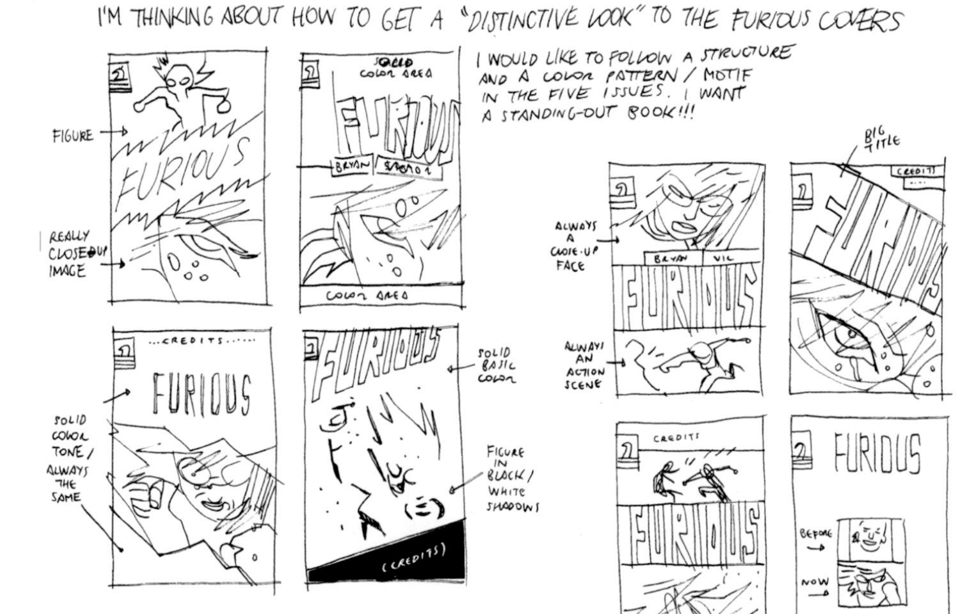
I'M THINKING ABOUT HOW TO GET A "DISTINCTIVE LOOK" TO THE FURIOUS COVERS
I WOULD LIKE TO FOLLOW A STRUCTURE AND A COLOR PATTERN / MOTIF IN THE FIVE ISSUES. I WANT A STANDING-OUT BOOK!!!
FIGURE
FURIOUS
REALLY CLOSE-UP IMAGE
SOLID COLOR AREA
BRYAN
COLOR AREA
CREDITS
SOLID COLOR TONE / ALWAYS THE SAME
SOLID BASIC COLOR
FIGURE IN BLACK / WHITE SHADOWS
(CREDITS)
BIG TITLE
ALWAYS A CLOSE-UP FACE
BRYAN VIC
ALWAYS AN ACTION SCENE
BEFORE
NOW

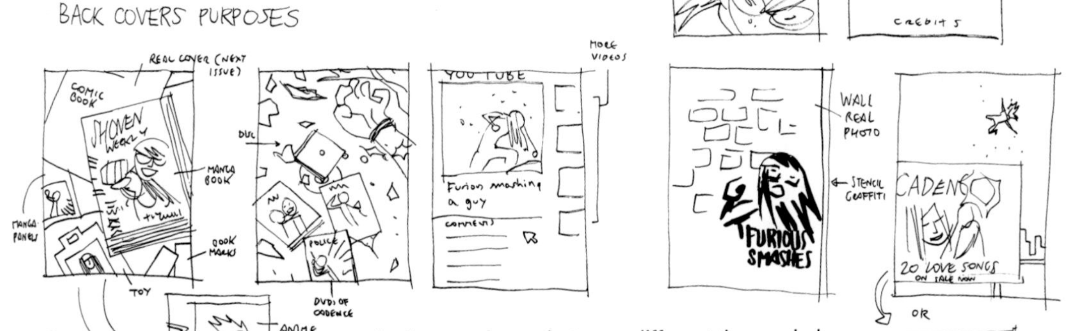
BACK COVERS PURPOSES
REAL COVER (NEXT ISSUE)
COMIC BOOK
SHONEN WEEKLY
MANGA BOOK
MANGA PANELS
BOOK MARKS
TOY
DVDS OF CADENCE
YOU TUBE
MORE VIDEOS
Furious smashing a guy
comments
WALL REAL PHOTO
STENCIL GRAFFITI
FURIOUS SMASHES
CADENCE
20 LOVE SONGS
OR

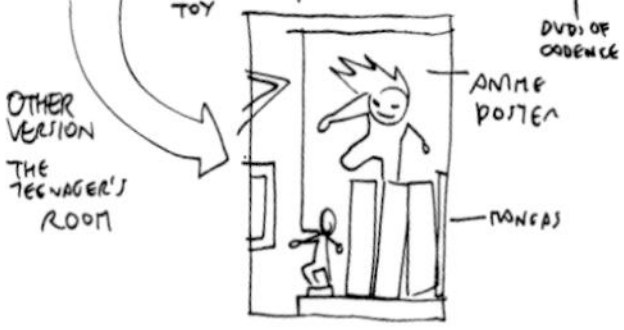
OTHER VERSION
THE TEENAGER'S ROOM
ANIME POSTER
MANGAS

As the story jumps between different time periods, I proposed we split the cover into past and present, because the weight of her memories is always a factor in Cadence's story.

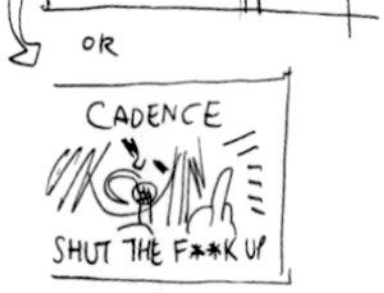
CADENCE
SHUT THE F**K UP

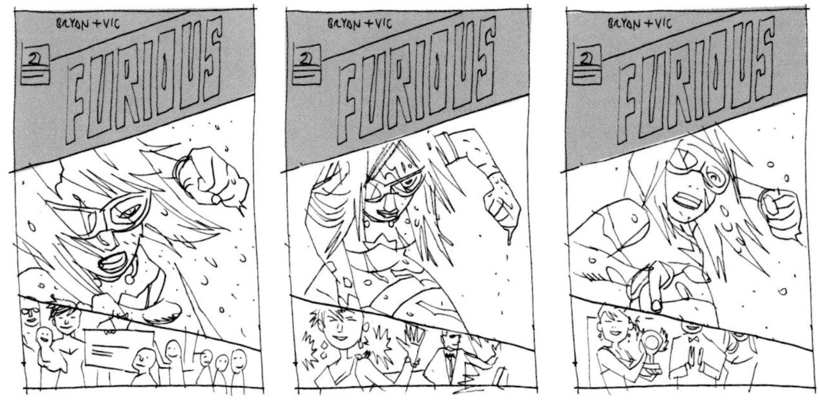
BRYON + VIC
FURIOUS
BRYON + VIC
FURIOUS
BRYON + VIC
FURIOUS

CHOOSE
YOUR FAVOURITE
COMBINATION

The flat colors on the top third of the cover act as a contrast.

FURIOUS #4 COVER OPTIONS

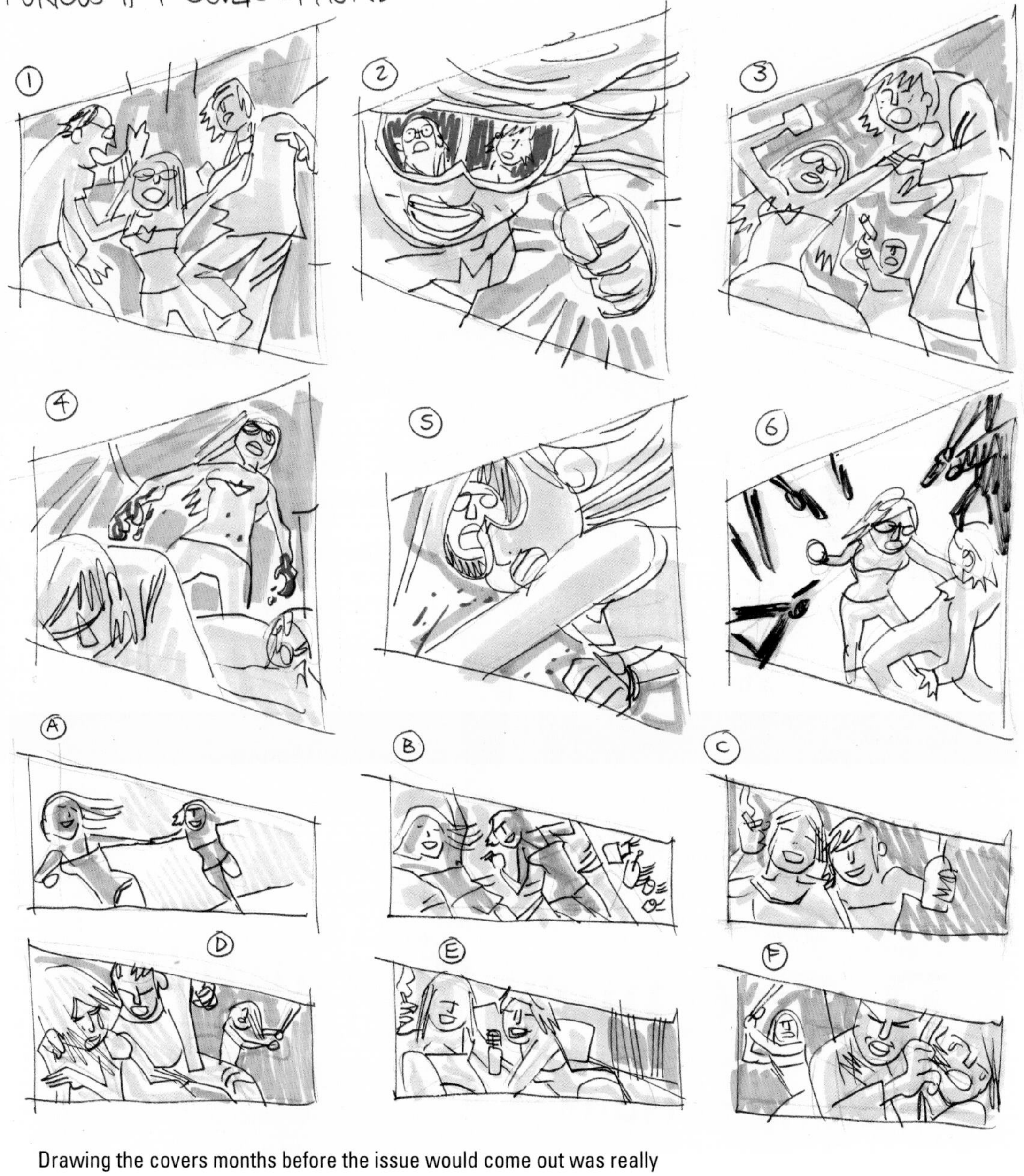
1
2
3
4
5
6
A
B
C
D
E
F

Drawing the covers months before the issue would come out was really strange for me. I'd detect inconsistencies after we'd finished. Remember, we artists love our work for a time, but later the images stab our eyes with fury!

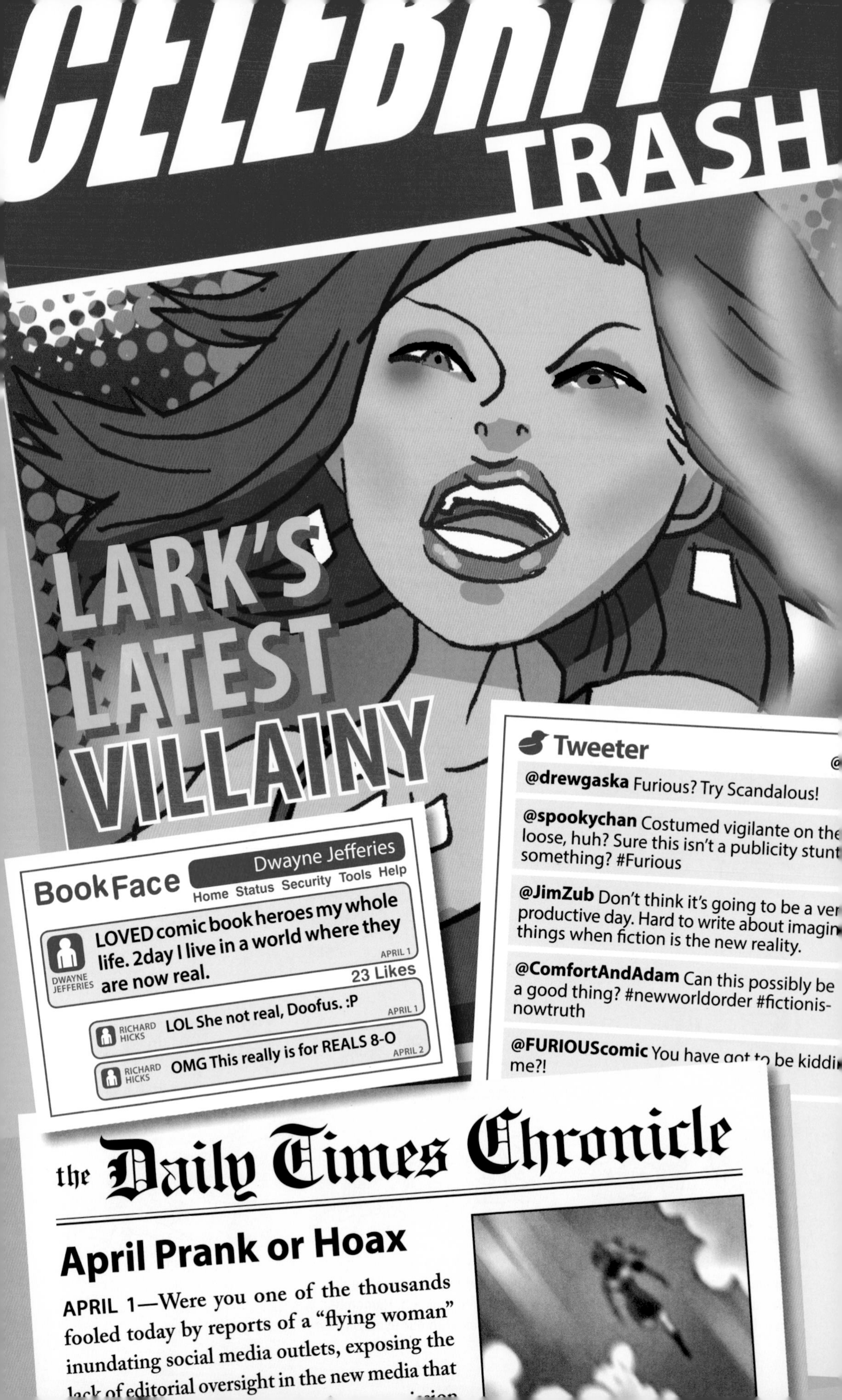

CELEBRITY TRASH
LARK'S LATEST VILLAINY
BookFace
Dwayne Jefferies
Home Status Security Tools Help
DWAYNE JEFFERIES
LOVED comic book heroes my whole life. 2day I live in a world where they are now real.
APRIL 1
23 Likes
RICHARD HICKS
LOL She not real, Doofus. :P
APRIL 1
RICHARD HICKS
OMG This really is for REALS 8-O
APRIL 2
Tweeter
@drewgaska Furious? Try Scandalous!
@spookychan Costumed vigilante on the loose, huh? Sure this isn't a publicity stunt something? #Furious
@JimZub Don't think it's going to be a ver productive day. Hard to write about imagin things when fiction is the new reality.
@ComfortAndAdam Can this possibly be a good thing? #newworldorder #fictionis-nowtruth
@FURIOUScomic You have got to be kiddi me?!
the Daily Times Chronicle
April Prank or Hoax
APRIL 1—Were you one of the thousands fooled today by reports of a "flying woman" inundating social media outlets, exposing the lack of editorial oversight in the new media that

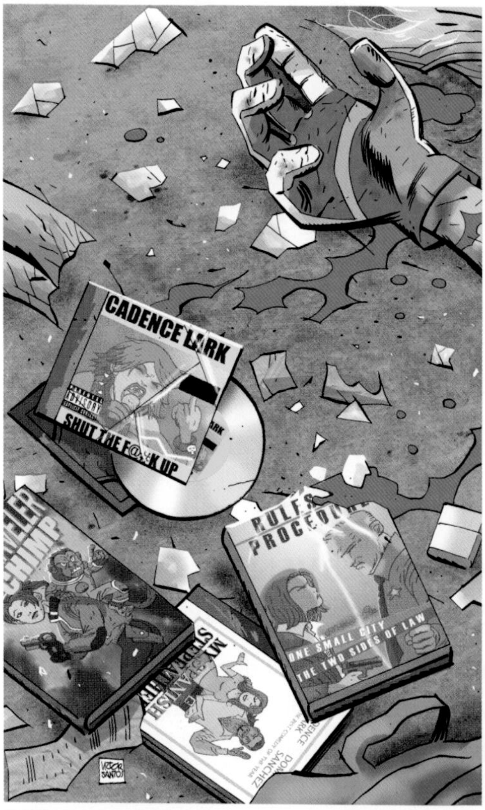
CADENCE LARK
SHUT THE F@%K UP
ONE SMALL CITY
THE TWO SIDES OF LAW

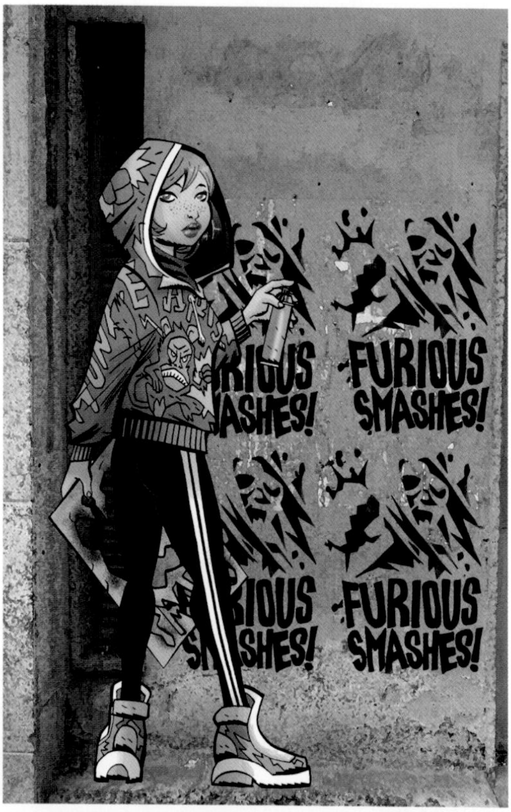
FURIOUS SMASHES!
FURIOUS SMASHES!

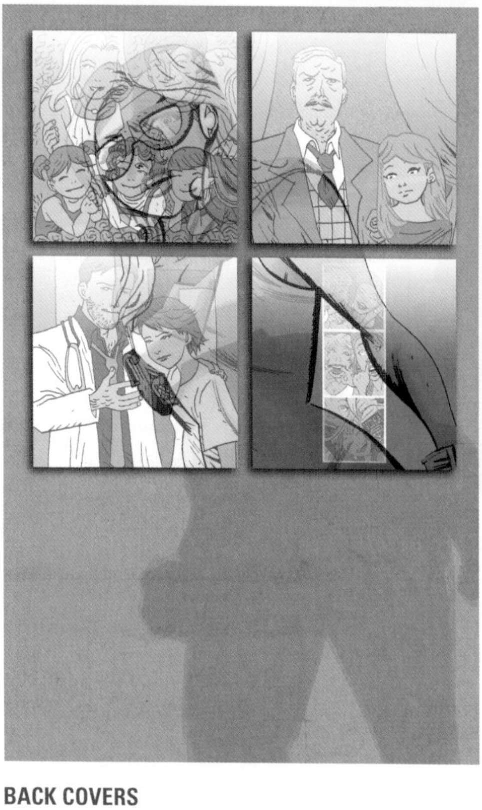

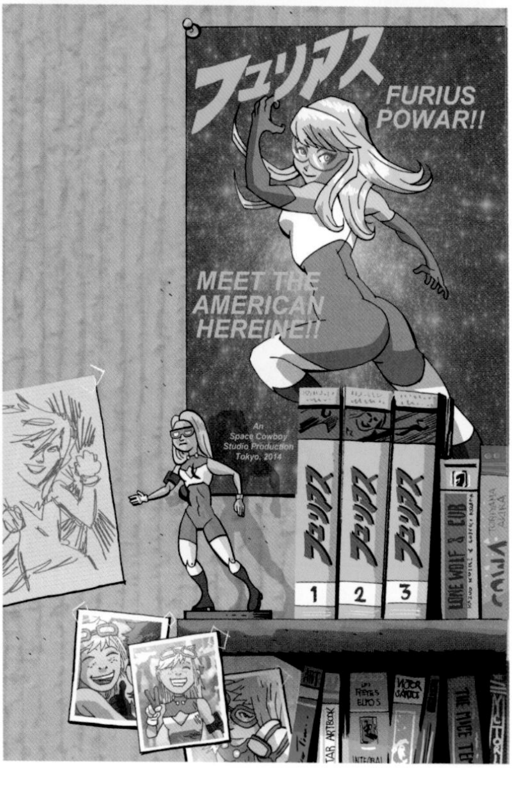
フュリアス
FURIUS POWAR!!
MEET THE AMERICAN HEREINE!!
An Space Cowboy Studio Production Tokyo, 2014
1
2
3
LONE WOLF & CUB

BACK COVERS

BJLG: These are designed to elaborate on the world we've created, to showcase the impact of Cadence Lark, as well as the inspiration of Furia.

VS: Okay, they stopped me on the covers, but those crazy things I wanted to do became the back covers! It was a lot of extra work, but I had fun designing fake movies, discs, and pop media art featuring our heroine.

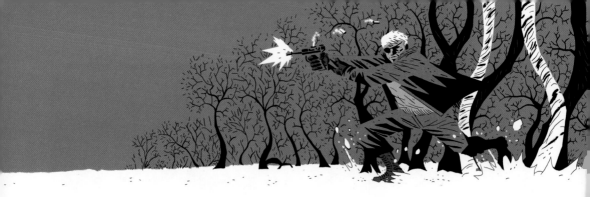

ALSO AVAILABLE FROM VICTOR SANTOS

POLAR: CAME FROM THE COLD

A GUNS-BLAZING ESPIONAGE ACTION-ADVENTURE IN THE GRAND TRADITION OF JIM STERANKO AND FRANK MILLER.

Ripped out of retirement by an assassination attempt, the world's most deadly spy—Black Kaiser—is on a collision course with a stab-happy torture expert and a seductive but deadly redhead. His mission only ends if he dies or kills everyone out to get him, and he's not in the habit of dying. This webcomic hit has been rescripted for print!

POLAR
CAME FROM THE COLD
VICTOR SANTOS

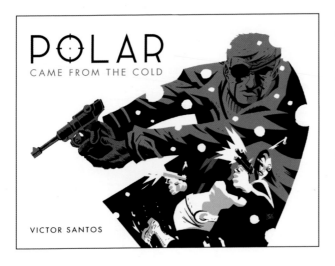

"A visual tour de force. With *Polar*, Victor Santos takes his seat at the table of the great graphic storytellers. A book to read again and again."

—Brian Azzarello
100 Bullets, Wonder Woman

"A beautiful, if bloody, webcomic . . . an engaging experiment in color, style, and wordless storytelling."

—Comic Book Resources'
Robot 6

Be on the lookout for
POLAR
EYE FOR AN EYE
in April 2015!

Price: $17.99 • ISBN 978-1-61655-232-9